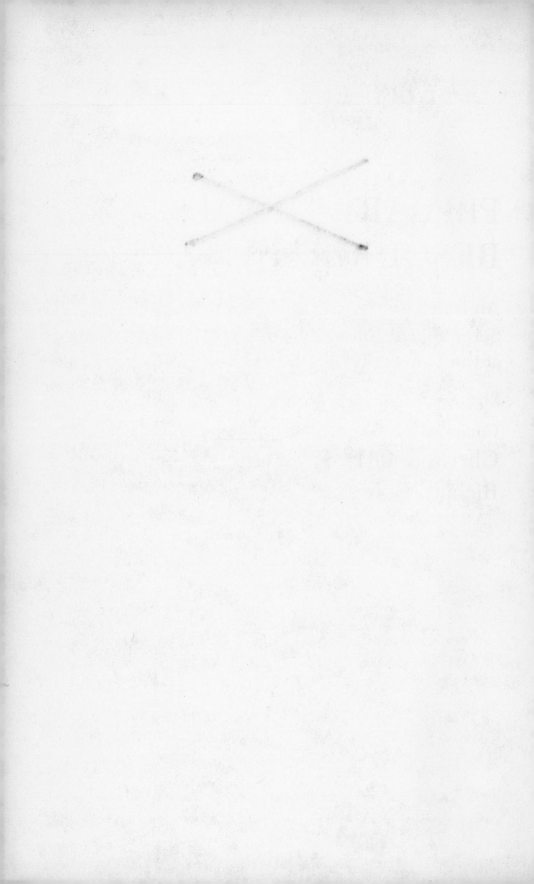

PRIMARY CINEMA RESOURCES:

An Index to
Screenplays, Interviews and Special Collections
at the University of Southern California

Compiled by
Christopher D. Wheaton
Richard B. Jewell

G. K. HALL & CO., 70 LINCOLN STREET, BOSTON, MASS.

Library of Congress Cataloging in Publication Data

Wheaton, Christopher D
 Primary cinema resources.

 Index to materials in the Dept. of Special Collections,
University of Southern California Library.
 1. Library resources on moving-pictures--California--
Los Angeles. 2. Los Angeles. University of Southern
California. Library. Dept. of Special Collections.
I. Jewell, Richard B., joint author. II. Los Angeles.
University of Southern California. Library. Dept. of
Special Collections. III. Title.
Z5784.M9W5   016.79143   75-5571
 ISBN 0-8161-1198-7

This publication is printed on permanent/durable acid-free paper.

MANUFACTURED IN THE UNITED STATES OF AMERICA

Foreword

The importance of archival material in film has only recently
been recognized. Recently, it must be admitted, may be a relative
term, but the motion picture industry like so many others has had no
historical sense. There has been so much material lost and strayed,
so many scripts which no longer exist that it is not at all surpris-
ing that the papers of entire film companies have been lost to history in more instances than one would easily believe.

Several years ago the Division of Cinema staff learned of a
building that was being bull-dozed down at one of the studios. It
contained only papers: accounts of pictures, scripts, budgets, correspondence, etc. Given permission by the studio, we moved those
papers directly into storage, knowing that we would have to pay for
the storage space until such time as we could afford the kind of library space that would allow us to properly make these materials
available to our own and other students. Three years later the
exact same thing happened at another studio. The then owners of MGM
were about to tear down a building and dispose of the scripts produced by that company. Part of what is contained in this book is
the record of that salvage job.

The original salvage job is yet to be cataloged, but we hope to
get this project underway within the next year.

What are the values of such materials? In the first place, they
are the only records that we actually have other than the films themselves and the newspaper accounts of the making of the films that
can give us any understanding of this most complex of all arts which
is almost always part of a large industry. If we had the original
manuscript of Hamlet would we trade it for the papers of the Globe
Theater? The answer is that we would. We already have copies of
the play, but we know very little about how the theater company for
which it was written functioned. In our understanding of that, we
may learn more about the play and how it was originally produced.
Who knows? We may even find the earlier drafts of the play or the
correspondence which brought it into being.

FOREWORD

In a sense that is what the archives described here actually are: materials for a greater understanding of the films which we already have in most instances. The Division of Cinema is placing no holds on this material as far as its use by scholars from other institutions. There is nothing that is held in the collection that will not be made available to scholars who are interested in using these archives.

It must be remembered that what is cataloged here is -- to use the obvious cliche -- only the tip of the iceberg. There is a vast amount of material in our archive that is not yet cataloged. We will attempt to answer any questions concerning any of this material, and should it be necessary for any scholar to look into the uncataloged material prior to our sorting it out, we shall attempt to assist. It is hoped that a catalog of the Division of Cinema's collection of printed books will be available within the next year or two. This appears to be the largest collection in the world, and the organization of a bibliography is complicated by the fact that it includes the largest collection of printed materials in foreign languages. Until this catalog is available, inquiries can be made, and we will try to assist scholars on an inter-library loan basis.

This catalog is the first step toward making our materials available to other institutions and individual scholars. The way in which it is used is really up to them and the future. This is the raw material for future histories and critical studies. Our faculty and students will be working with this material, and others are invited to do the same.

BERNARD R. KANTOR
Chairman, Division of Cinema

Preface

The following work is a series of descriptions of various parts of the Cinema Library, Department of Special Collections, University of Southern California. The contents of this volume is limited to primary research material in the Cinema Library. A second volume is planned which will deal with secondary research materials, especially those which originate in Europe or Asia.

The primary materials in the Library come under the following categories: screenplays and related materials, interviews on tape, and special collections of items contributed to the Library by individuals. A more detailed description of each category is given at the beginning of the section. Because each group contains wholly different types of items, the organization within each category differs. In each case, however, the intent has been to present the material to facilitate research. It is important to note that the Titles Index and the Individuals Index are cross-referenced to all the items in this volume. If the reader seeks to discover whether the Cinema Library at the University of Southern California contains primary research material relating to a particular film or a particular individual, then he should look first at the Titles Index or Individuals Index respectively.

The diffuse nature of cinematic resources makes the precision customary in other scholarly fields a standard more to be aspired to than to be attained. Nevertheless, every effort has been expended to insure the accuracy of the descriptions of the various collections. Errors must, of course, remain the responsibility of the authors.

This work is not simply a distillation of the information set forth in the Library's card catalogue, because no complete card index of the cinema materials has yet been established. A systematic examination and itemization of the Library's primary resources has been conducted item by item when available. The result has been a description of the materials in the Cinema Library as it now exists. For example, scripts which are filed on the Library's shelves under alternate titles to their film release title are listed <u>under the</u>

PREFACE

<u>alternate title</u>, with an appropriate cross-reference to that title from the film release title, if known.

Inquiries concerning the use of the materials should be directed to the Head, Department of Special Collections, Doheny Library, University of Southern California, Los Angeles, California 90007.

This work would not have been possible without the co-operation of the Head of the Department of Special Collections, Dr. Robert L. Knutson, and his assistants, Mrs. Alvista Perkins and James C. Wagner. Most of all, we owe gratitude to the unstinting efforts of Professor Irwin R. Blacker, USC Department of Cinema, who saw the value of this work, encouraged its completion, and urged its publication. Without the support provided by his high estimation of our efforts, it is likely that they would never have reached this form.

Contents

Introduction

The screenplay is the blueprint for the construction of the motion picture. Many times the completed movie bears little resemblance to that beginning design, a dubious distinction to many minds, especially screenwriters'. Nevertheless, examination of the screenplay for a given movie often generates special insights into the workings of motion picture production.

But access to such screenplays is generally the privilege of a select few, those with the contacts or the luck to come across one of the relatively few mimeographed or Xeroxed copies of the screenplay. Those screenplays which do reach the public in published form are rarely screenplays as such, but rather are frequently no more than transcripts of a movie's dialogue passages. These transcripts are useful as records, but they are records primarily of the director's conception of the movie and not the screenwriter's. It is well established that, no matter how many drafts or revisions are made before a screenplay reaches a director's hands, he may still regard it with no more respect than a draft to be changed at will. In many cases, learning the director's changes in a screenplay can be more instructive about the director's working habits than an analysis of the resulting film. The Cinema Library at the University of Southern California contains screenplays, in various forms, for over 3,000 of Hollywood's movies.

In this the age of _auteur_ criticism, the search for American _auteurs_ is limited to the Hollywood directorial corps: Ford, Welles, Capra, _et al._, are compared to the likes of Bergman, Fellini, Renoir, and Kurosawa. However, most of those European and Asian directors recognized as being _auteurs_, those few who place their own unique personal stamp of value upon their works, not only direct their own movies, but also write them. This union of writing and directing talents does not guarantee good movies as many would-be _auteur_ writer/directors have proved through the years. Perhaps the hazard of this union lies in the loss of artistic distance when the primary creative functions in a movie are grasped in the hands of one man. The hazard, yes, but occasionally the glory, as the whole concept of the _auteur_ bespeaks.

In Hollywood-produced films, it is generally acknowledged that both screenplays and films are tampered with by forces beyond the control of either writer or director. Yet the case has been made by a number of critics that many times the Hollywood director can over-come the obstacles of the studio system and produce a movie of in-terest and of value. It may well be that a screenwriter--a Riskin, a Nichols, or a lesser-known talent--might aspire to the heights of critical acclaim hitherto awarded only American directors.

Screenwriters traditionally have been shackled to an anonymity which has hampered a proper evaluation of their creative contribu-tions to the art of the motion picture. Individually, and through united efforts led by the Screen Writers' Guild, writers for the movies have demanded attention both from the audience and from the critics. Though in many cases writers have deserved such attention, their demands have too often been ignored. Of the 95 screenplays which have received Academy Awards since 1927, only 21 are available in published form. Stranger still, of the scripts given annual awards by the Screen Writers' Guild beginning in 1948, only 7% have been published for public consumption. The scripts screenwriters themselves have recognized as being the year's best in their respec-tive genres are almost totally unavailable in published form.

Given the odd circumstance that approximately 99% of all the screenplays which have been made into movies and released in America have never been published, the collection of studio-produced, mimeo-graphed screenplays in the Cinema Library of the University of Southern California assumes a particular value to the film student. Access to screenplays is requisite for many facets of film study and is desirable in many others.

This list of scripts in the USC Screenplay Collection is provid-ed to make these items more generally available to the film student. Fortunately, the collection is still growing: an impressive number of scripts from the files of Twentieth Century-Fox Film Corporation was received too late to be included in this volume, and the M-G-M Collection (described below) is soon to be enlarged, thanks to the generosity of Metro-Goldwyn-Mayer.

The screenplays in this collection are included in a master list called the Titles Index. In addition to listing all screenplays in the collection alphabetically by title, the Titles Index includes cross references to other portions of the cinema collection: the Interviews on Tape and Special Collections.

The citations of screenplays include the title of the screenplay as it is filed on the Library's shelves, release title if different, alternate titles, number of copies in the collection and the col-

lection number, form of the screenplay (i.e. draft, treatment,
shooting script, and so forth), year of release, distributor, and
screenwriter(s). The year of release is determined by the relevant
data provided in the Film Daily Year Book (New York: Film and Television Daily, 1973), as is the name of the distributor. Writing
credits are derived from the official screenplay credits for the
film as reported by the Academy of Motion Picture Arts and Sciences
and the Writers' Guild of America, West in Who Wrote the Movie and
What Else Did He Write?: An Index of Screen Writers and Their Film
Works, 1936-1969 (Ed. by Leonard Spigelgass, Los Angeles, 1970).

If the dates, distributors, or screenwriters cited in this
Titles Index were not found in the above-named sources and they were
found elsewhere, in reviews or other such supplementary material,
the data is enclosed in brackets [ ]. Many times the source for
this information is the screenplay itself, especially if the screenplay was not made into a movie. Frequently a listing of authors in
brackets follows the official credits supplied by Who Wrote the
Movie? These authors are those listed in addition to, or instead
of, the credited authors on the copy of the screenplay in the collection. For instance, in the following listing, Philip Dunne is
credited with writing the screenplay for The Last of the Mohicans,
but the screenplay in the USC Collection has John L. Balderston's
name on it as writer. Therefore, Balderston's name is in brackets,
while Dunne's is not.

THE LAST OF THE MOHICANS. 1936, United Artists. No. 8. Philip
        Dunne and [John L. Balderston]

All scripts for movies produced prior to 1936 and after 1969 which
list one or more screenwriters have the writers' names enclosed in
brackets because Who Wrote the Movie? contains listings only for
films produced between 1936 and 1969. In some cases, identifying
information has not been found and the pertinent information areas
are left blank. For unproduced screenplays or treatments, the listed date and/or distributor are obtained directly from the material
itself and then enclosed in brackets showing that it was derived
from "unofficial" sources. If no date is found, the abbreviation
n. d. is noted.

The screenplays in this collection represent many of the different forms in which one might find a movie script: drafts of screenplays, treatments, finished screenplays of produced or unproduced
movies, shooting scripts complete with director's or script girl's
notes, cutting continuities listing dialogue, shots, and footage
lengths for completed films, scenarios of silent films, and in a few
cases, production department scripts together with budgeting files.
We have tried, insofar as possible, to indicate which version of the
screenplay is in the collection by placing that information following the title in the listing. If no notation is made, it is because
specific information was not available and the presumption should be

that the copy on hand is the "finished" screenplay. It should be noted, however, that we have discovered a number of exceptions to this generalization. For some of the titles, a variety of the above items is available, so that a movie can be followed almost from the moment of its conception, through production, to the final release print.

The screenplays housed within the Cinema Library are placed in three separate locations: in the Unified Collection in closed stacks, arranged alphabetically by title on shelves; in the Special Collections area of the Library stored in boxes and arranged by individual collection number; and in the M-G-M Collection which is arranged alphabetically by title in boxes in a third location. Screenplays for films in the Titles Index are to be found in the Unified Collection unless otherwise indicated. Screenplays found in one of the individual collections in the Special Collections area have the number of that collection indicated. In the example below, screenplays in various forms for <u>The Boston Strangler</u> are to be found in individual collections No. 27, Edward Anhalt and No. 31, Richard Fleischer. Special Collections are described in detail beginning on page 279.

THE BOSTON STRANGLER. · 2 step outlines, 4 drafts, and final scr.
      1968, Fox. No. 27. No. 31. Edward Anhalt.

Frequently, subsidiary or supporting materials relating to that title can be found in the Screenwriters and Film Personalities Index.

Items in the M-G-M Collection are of particular interest and value to the student of the movies. They have been donated by Metro-Goldwyn-Mayer and often include production correspondence, drafts of screenplays, stills, posters, budgeting files, and masses of additional materials too various to describe. The titles in this M-G-M Collection are marked with an asterisk to the left of the listing. If there are additional copies of the screenplay in one of the other locations in the library, the M-G-M Collection item is listed separately because of its extreme potential value to the researcher. The M-G-M Collection citations do not include information on the types of material, simply because the multiplicity of items forbids such treatment.

CAT ON A HOT TIN ROOF. Step outline. 1958, MGM. James Poe.

CAT ON A HOT TIN ROOF. 1958, MGM. Richard Brooks and James Poe.

*CAT ON A HOT TIN ROOF. 1958, MGM. Richard Brooks and James Poe.

The abbreviations used within the Titles Index have been used sparingly, but space considerations required this implementation. Following is a list of the abbreviations and symbols in this index.

Symbols and Abbreviations

*	part of the M-G-M Collection
aka	also known as
cc	cutting continuity and screenplay
(cc)	cutting continuity only
cont	continuity
edit.	editors
n. d.	film release date unavailable
No.	Special Collection number
orig.	originally
re-ed.	re-edited
rel.	release(d)
rev.	revised
scr.	screenplay/script
sht.	shooting
SWG	Screen Writers' Guild
vers.	version

INTERVIEWS AND MATERIALS ON TAPE

Abbreviations used to identify those interviewed.

a -- actor, actress
ag -- agent
c -- cameraman, cinematographer
co -- composer
cr -- critic
d -- director
e -- editor
ex -- executive
law -- lawyer
nov -- novelist
p -- producer
w -- writer, screenwriter

Key to Special Collections

0. Irving Wallace
1. George Cukor
2. Elizabeth Leslie Roos
3. Arthur Knight
4. George J. Hopkins
5. Leonard Spigelgass
6. William Farnum
7. Freeman Gosden and Charles Correll
8. William DeMille
9. Misha Bakaleinikoff
10. Hal Roach
11. John M. Stahl
12. Eleanor Peters
13. Dorr Historical
14. Constance Littlefield
15. Saul Chaplin
16. Pacific Pioneer Broadcasters
17. William Dieterle
18. Samuel Colt
19. Ernest Lehman
20. Maurice Jarre
21. Luther Davis
22. Gladys Cooper
23. Morton Fine
24. George Burns and Gracie Allen
25. King Vidor
26. Jim and Henny Backus
27. Edward Anhalt
28. Jay Burton
29. Louella Parsons
30. Irving Brecher
31. Richard Fleischer
32. Jack Oakie
33. Sally Eilers
34. Walter Doniger
35. Hal Goodman and Larry Klein
36. Jimmy McHugh
37. Mack David
38. Millard Kaufman
39. Harry Ruby
40. Fred Freiberger
41. Philip Dunne
42. Robert Hamner
43. Johnny Rivers
44. Albert Lewin
45. Ernie Kovacs
46. Joseph Schildkraut
47. Betty Harte
48. Greg Garrison
49. Robert Wise
50. David Weisbart
51. Dmitri Tiomkin
52. Jerry Lewis
53. Parker Advertising
54. Clarie Windsor
55. Nelson Eddy
56. Biltmore Theater
57. Roger Imhoff
58. Howard Rodman
59. Lawrence Weingarten
60. Abby Mann
61. Theodore Flicker
62. Arthur Freed
63. Fay Wray
64. Steve Allen
65. Tay Garnett
66. Robert Sisk
67. Eleanor Powell
68. Sol Lesser
69. Dan Duryea
70. Fred Astaire
71. Mrs. Otto Haebel
72. Y. Frank Freeman
73. Roger Edens

74. Alfred Newman
75. Don Defore
76. Hal Humphrey
77. Fay Bainter
78. Jimmy Durante
79. Jack Lord
80. Andy Devine
81. Joe Pasternak
82. Edward Small
83. Walter Grauman
84. Marvin and Mary Carlock
85. Ole Olsen
86. John J. Anthony
87. Ann Sothern
88. Benny Rubin
89. Richmond Shepard
90. Arthur P. Jacobs
91. Stanley K. Scheuer
92. John Brahm
93. Cesar Romero
94. Ernest Laszlo
95. Frances Marion
96. Adeline deWalt Reynolds
97. Walter Seltzer
98. Ed Wynn
99. Cecil B. DeMille
--. Paramount Research Department
--. Twentieth Century-Fox Set-Stills

TITLES INDEX

*ABBOTT AND COSTELLO IN HOLLYWOOD. 1945, Universal. Nat Perrin and
      Lou Breslow.

ABBOTT AND COSTELLO MEET THE KILLER. 1949, Universal. No. 32.
      Hugh Wedlock, Howard Snyder, John Grant and [Oscar Brodney].

ABOUT MRS. LESLIE. 1954, Paramount. No. 94. Ketti Frings and
      Hal Kanter.

*ABOVE AND BEYOND. 1952, MGM. Melvin Frank, Beirne Lay, Jr. and
      Norman Panama.

ABSENT WITHOUT LOVE. n. d., No. 50. [David Weisbart].

ACCORDING TO HOYLE. Treatment only. [1946]. No. 0. [Irving
      Wallace].

ACE ELI AND RODGER OF THE SKIES. Rev. 1st draft. 1971, Fox.
      [Claudia Salter].

ACROSS THE WIDE MISSOURI. 1951, MGM. No. 66. Talbot Jennings.

*ACROSS TO SINGAPORE. 1928, MGM. [Ted Shane and Richard Schayer].

*ACT OF VIOLENCE. 1948, MGM. Robert L. Richards.

*ACTION OF THE TIGER. 1957, MGM. Robert Carson.

*THE ACTRESS. 1928, MGM. [Albert Lewin and Richard Schayer].

THE ACTRESS. Budgeting files only. 1953, MGM.

ADAM AND ATHENA. See Athena.

ADAM HAD FOUR SONS. 1941, Columbia. William Hurlbut and Michael
      Blankfort.

1

ADAM'S RIB   TITLES INDEX

*ADAM'S RIB. 1949, MGM. Ruth Gordon and Garson Kanin. See also
     Interview with George Cukor.

THE ADDING MACHINE. n. d., Universal. [Jerome Epstein].

THE ADMIRAL HOSKINS STORY. n. d., [Republic]. [Allen Rivkin].

ADORABLE. 1933, Fox. [Frank Paul].

ADORABLE. Final sht. scr. 1933, Fox. No. 19.

*ADVENTURE. 1945, MGM. Frederick Hazlitt Brennan and Vincent Law-
     rence.

*THE ADVENTURES OF TARTU. Rel. as TARTU. 1943, MGM. John Lee Mahin
     and Howard Emmett Rogers.

AERIAL CINEMATOGRAPHY. Treatment. [1942]. No. 0. [Irving Wal-
     lace].

THE AFFAIR. n. d. No. 50. [David Weisbart].

THE AFFAIR IN ARCADY. 2 drafts. No. 27. [Edward Anhalt].

AFFAIR IN RENO. 1957, Republic. John K. Butler.

AFFAIRS OF JIMMY VALENTINE. 1942, Republic. Olive Cooper and Robert
     Tasker.

THE AFFAIRS OF MARTHA. See ONCE UPON A THURSDAY.

THE AFFAIRS OF SUSAN. 1945, Paramount. No. 75. Thomas Monroe,
     Lazlo Gorog and Richard Flournoy.

AFRICA--TEXAS STYLE! British title: COWBOY IN AFRICA. Also
     rev. scr. 1967, Paramount. No. 37. Andy White.

AFTER THE JAMES GANG. See WEST OF ABILINE.

THE AGONY AND THE ECSTACY. 1965, Fox. No. 41. Philip Dunne.

AL CAPONE. See Interview with Henry Greenberg.

ALEXANDER'S RAGTIME BAND. 2 copies. 1938, Fox. Kathryn Scola and
     Lamar Trotti.

*ALIAS A GENTLEMAN. 1948, MGM. William R. Lipman.

ALIAS BILLY THE KID. 1946, Republic. Earle Snell and Betty Bur-
     bridge.

2

*ALIAS JIMMY VALENTINE. 1920, MGM. [Finis Fox].

*ALIAS JIMMY VALENTINE. 1927, MGM. [A. P. Younger and Sarah Mason].

ALIAS MIKE FURY. [1949], [RKO]. [Warren Duff and Marvin Borowsky].

ALICE IN WONDERLAND. n. d., No. 66. [Joseph Mankiewicz].

ALICE'S ADVENTURES IN WONDERLAND. 1933, Paramount.

THE ALIEN. Orig. and rev. scr. [1971], [Universal]. [Douglas Heyes].

ALL ABOUT EVE. 1950, Fox. Joseph L. Mankiewicz.

*ALL AT SEA. 1929, MGM. [Byron Morgan].

*ALL AT SEA. 1958, MGM. Thomas E. B. Clarke.

*ALL THE BROTHERS WERE VALIENT. 1953, MGM. Harry Brown.

ALL THIS, AND HEAVEN TOO. 1940, Warner Bros. Casey Robinson.

ALL'S WELL THAT ENDS WELL. n. d., No. 94.

ALOMA OF THE SOUTH SEAS. 1941, Paramount. Frank Butler, Seena Owen and Lillie Hayward.

*ALTARS OF DESIRE. 1927, MGM. [Agnes Christine Johnston].

*THE AMAZING MR. NORDILL. [1947]. [John Nesbitt].

AMBASSADOR BILL. Rel. as DOLLAR BILL. 1931, Fox. No. 8. [Guy Bolton].

AMBUSH. 1949, MGM. Marguerite Roberts.

*AMBUSH. 1949, MGM. Marguerite Roberts.

THE AMBUSHERS. 1967, Columbia. Herbert Baker.

*AN AMERICAN IN PARIS. 1951, MGM. Alan Jay Lerner.

AMERICAN LEGION. Treatment only, 1943. n. d., No. 0. [Irving Wallace].

AMERICAN MADNESS. 1932, Columbia. No. 63. [Robert Riskin].

*AN AMERICAN ROMANCE. 1944, MGM. Herbert Dalmas and William Ludwig.

AN AMERICAN ROMANCE. 1944, MGM. No. 25. Herbert Dalmas, William Ludwig and [Gordon Kahn].

AN AMERICAN TRAGEDY. 1949, Paramount. [Michael Wilson].

AN AMERICAN TRAGEDY. 1931, Paramount. [Samuel Hoffenstein].

AMERICANIZATION OF EMILY. See Interview with Arthur Hiller.

AMGO. [1947]. No. 50. [David Weisbart].

*ANCHORS AWEIGH. 1945, MGM. Isobel Lennart.

ANDRASSY U+60. n. d., No. 66. [Sam Roella and Tom Hubbard].

ANDREW JACKSON. [1942], [MGM]. No. 8. [John L. Balderston].

ANDROCLES AND THE LION. 1952, RKO. No. 26. Chester Erskine and Ken Englund.

THE ANDROMEDA STRAIN. 1971, Universal. No. 49. [Nelson Gidding]. See also Interview with Ray Bradbury.

*ANDY HARDY COMES HOME. 1958, MGM. Edward E. Hutshing and Robert M. Donley.

*ANDY HARDY GROWS UP. Rel. as ANDY HARDY'S PRIVATE SECRETARY. 1941, MGM. Jane Murfin and Harry Ruskin.

*ANDY HARDY'S BLONDE TROUBLE. 1944, MGM. Harry Ruskin, William Ludwig and Agnes Christine Johnston.

*ANDY HARDY'S DOUBLE LIFE. 1942, MGM. Agnes Christine Johnston.

ANDY HARDY'S PRIVATE SECRETARY. See ANDY HARDY GROWS UP.

ANGEL, ANGEL, DOWN WE GO. 1969, American International. Robert Thom.

AN ANGEL COMES TO BROOKLYN. 2 copies. 1945, Republic. June Carroll and Stanley Paley.

ANGEL ON THE AMAZON. (cc). 1948, Republic. Lawrence Kimble.

THE ANGEL RUM. n. d., No. 41. [Philip Dunne].

ANGEL'S FLIGHT. See Interview with Gene Fowler.

*ANGELS IN THE OUTFIELD. 1951, MGM. Dorothy Kingsley and George
     Wells.

*ANGRY HILLS. 1959, MGM. A. I. Bezzerides.

ANN CARVER'S PROFESSION. 1933, Columbia. No. 63. [Robert Riskin].

ANNA CHRISTIE. 1929, MGM. [E. G. O'Neill].

ANNE OF THE INDIES. 1951, Fox. No. 41. Philip Dunne and Arthur
     Caeser.

*ANNIE GET YOUR GUN. 1950, MGM. Sidney Sheldon.

*ANNIE LAURIE. 1927, MGM. [Josephine Lovett].

*ANOTHER LANGUAGE. 1933, MGM. [Herman Mankiewicz and Donald Ogden
     Stewart].

ANTON THE TERRIBLE. 2 copies of scenario. 1916, Paramount. No. 8.

ANY NUMBER CAN PLAY. 1949, MGM. Richard Brooks.

*ANY NUMBER CAN PLAY. 1949, MGM. Richard Brooks.

ANYTHING FOR A LAUGH. 1943, No. 0. [Irving Wallace].

*APACHE TRAIL. 1942, MGM. Maurice Geraghty.

*APACHE WAR SMOKE. 1952, MGM. Jerome L. Davis.

THE APE. 1940, Monogram. Richard Carroll and Curt Siodmak.

THE APPOINTMENT. 1969, MGM. [James Salter].

APPOINTMENT ON "A" DECK. [1955]. No. 75. [Sidney Biddell and
     Fredric Frank].

THE APRIL FOOLS. 1969, National General. Hal Dresner.

APRIL LOVE. Final sht. scr. 1957, Fox. No. 19. Winston Miller.
     See also materials in the David Weisbart Collection.
     No. 50.

THE ARAB. 1924, Metro-Goldwyn.

*ARCH OF TRIUMPH. 1948, United Artists. Harry Brown and Lewis
     Milestone.

ARE ALL MEN ALIKE   TITLES INDEX

*ARE ALL MEN ALIKE. Also THE WAFFLE IRON. 1920, Metro. [Florence
        Hein?].

ARE HUSBANDS NECESSARY? 1942, Paramount. Tess Slesinger and Frank
        Davis.

ARE YOU THERE? Story, dialogue, and cont. [1930]. No. 19.
        [Ernest Lehman].

ARENA. 1953, MGM. No. 31. Harold Jack Bloom.

ARIZONA BUSHWACKERS. 1968, Paramount. Steve Fisher.

ARIZONA LEGION. Final scr. 1939, RKO. Oliver Drake.

THE ARK OF DR. HOLLISTER. Treatment and rev. treatment. n. d. No.
        27. [Edward Anhalt].

ARMORED CAR. 1937, Universal. Lewis R. Foster and Robert N. Lee.

ARMOURED CAR ROBBERY. 1950, RKO. No. 31. Earl Felton and Gerald
        Drayson Adams.

*THE ARNELO AFFAIR. 1947, MGM. Arch Oboler.

AROUND THE WORLD IN EIGHTY DAYS. 1956, United Artists. No. 32.
        James Poe, John Farrow and S. J. Perelman.

*ARSENE LUPIN. 1932, MGM. [Carey Wilson, Bayard Veiller and
        Lenore Coffee].

ARSENIC AND OLD LACE. 1944, Warner Bros. Julius and Philip G. Ep-
        stein.

*AS YOU DESIRE ME. 1932, MGM. [Gene Markey].

AS YOU DESIRE ME. 1932, MGM. [Gene Markey].

*ASK ANY GIRL. 1959, MGM. George Wells.

*THE ASPHALT JUNGLE. 1950, MGM. Ben Maddow and John Huston.

THE ASSASSIN. 1953, United Artists. [Victor Canning].

THE ASSASSINATION BUREAU. 1969, Paramount. Michael Relph.

ASSIGNMENT K. 1st sht. scr. 1968, Columbia. Val Guest,
        Bill Strutton and Maurice Foster.

ASSIGNMENT TO KILL. Estimating scr. 1968, Warner Bros. Sheldon
       Reynolds.

*ATHENA. Also ADAM AND ATHENA. And budgeting files. 1954, MGM.
       William Ludwig and Leonard Spigelgass.

ATLANTIC CITY HONEYMOON. Re-ed from ATLANTIC CITY. cc. n. d., Re-
       public. Doris Gilbert, Frank J. Gill, Jr. and George
       Carleton Brown.

THE ATOMIC KID. 1954, Republic. Benedict Freemen and John Fenton
       Murray.

*THE AUCTION BLOCK. 1926, MGM. [Frederick Hatton and Fanny Hatton].

THE AUDUBON EYRIE. Rough draft. n. d. No. 41. [Philip Dunne].

AVALANCHE. See Interview with Richard Bach.

THE AVENGER OF THE DESERT. 1st draft. [1959]. [Paddy Manning
       O'Brine].

THE AVENGERS. (cc). 1950, Republic. Lawrence Kimble and Aeneas
       MacKenzie.

THE AWAKENING OF JOHN SLATER. n. d. [Charles F. Harrison].

*B. F.'S DAUGHTER. 1948, MGM. Luther Davis.

BABY DOLL. 1956, Warner Bros. Tennessee Williams.

BABY FACE HARRINGTON. Orig. PUBLIC ENEMY NO. 2. 1935, MGM.
       [Nunnally Johnson].

THE BABY MAKER. See Interview with James Bridges.

*BABY MINE. 1928, MGM. [F. Hugh Herbert and Lew Lipton].

BABY TAKE A BOW. Rev. final draft. 1934, Fox. No. 19. [Ernest
       Lehman].

*BACHELOR FATHER. 1931, MGM. [Lawrence Johnson].

BACHELOR OF ARTS. 1934, Fox. [John Erskine].

BACK IN THE SADDLE. cc. 3 copies. 1941, Republic. Richard Murphy
       and Jesse Lasky, Jr.

BACK STREET   TITLES INDEX

BACK STREET. 1932, Universal. No. 11.

*BACK TO NATURE. Treatment. [1942]. [Jack Pollexfen].

*THE BAD AND THE BEAUTIFUL. 1952, MGM. Charles Schnee.

*BAD BASCOMB. 1946, MGM. William Lipman and Grant Garrett.

BAD BLOOD. See Interview with Ken Handler.

BAD BOY. 1935, Fox. [Vina Delmar].

*BAD DAY AT BLACK ROCK. 1954, MGM. Millard Kaufman.

BAD DAY AT BLACK ROCK. 1954, MGM. Millard Kaufman.

BAD GIRL. 1931, Fox. [Edwin Burke].

*THE BADLANDERS. 1958, MGM. Richard Collins.

BAL TABARIN. 1952, Republic. Houston Branch.

THE BALLAD OF CAT BALLOU. 1st estimating draft-final draft. 1965,
     Columbia. No. 37. Walter Newman and Frank R. Pierson.

BALLAD OF JOSIE. 1967, Universal. Harold Swanton.

BALLIN. rel. as COOL BREEZE. 1972, MGM. [Barry Pollack].

BANCO. rel. as LOST-A WIFE. 1925, Paramount. [Alfred Savoir].

BAND OF GOLD. Rev. final scr. [1966]. [Stanley Shapiro and
     Nate Monaster].

THE BAND WAGON. Rev. sht. final scr. 1953, MGM. No. 19. Betty
     Comden and Adolph Green.

*BAND WAGON. 1953, MGM. Betty Comden and Adolph Green.

BANDERAS. n. d. [William George].

BANDIDO. 2 copies. 1956, United Artists. No. 31. No. 94. Earl
     Felton.

BANDOLERO! 2 copies. 1968, Fox. No. 50. James Lee Barrett.

BANJO. 1947, RKO. No. 31. Lillie Hayward.

BANJO ON MY KNEE. 1936, Fox. No. 8. Nunnally Johnson.

*BANNERLINE. 1951, MGM. Charles Schnee.

THE BAR SINISTER. Bound with THE WORLD'S APPLAUSE. [1927], [MGM].
    [Clara Beranger].

*THE BAR SINISTER. Rel. as IT'S A DOG'S LIFE. 1955, MGM. John
    Michael Hayes.

BARABBAS. 1962, Columbia. No. 31. Christopher Fry.

*THE BARBARIAN. 1933, MGM. [Anita Loos and Elmer Harris].

THE BARBER OF SEVILLE. Dubbing script. 1947, Excelsior.

*BARDELYS THE MAGNIFICENT. 1926, MGM. [Dorothy Farnum].

*THE BARKLEYS OF BROADWAY. 1949, MGM. Betty Comden and Adolph
    Green.

BARQUERO. 1970, United Artists. [George Schenck and William Marks].

*BARRETTS OF WIMPOLE STREET. 1934, MGM. [Ernest Vajda, Claudine
    West and Donald Ogden Stewart].

*BATAAN. 1943, MGM. Robert D. Andrews.

BATAAN. 1943, MGM. No. 65. Robert D. Andrews.

BATTLE! n. d. No. 49. [Nelson Gidding].

BATTLE BENEATH THE EARTH. 1968, MGM. L. Z. Hargreaves.

BATTLE BEYOND THE STARS. [1967].

*BATTLE CIRCUS. 1953, MGM. Richard Brooks.

THE BATTLE HORNS. See COUNTERPOINT.

*BATTLE HYMN. [1942], [MGM]. [MacKinlay Kantor].

BATTLE HYMN. 1956, Universal. No. 75. Charles Grayson and Vincent
    V. Evans.

*BATTLEGROUND. 1949, MGM. Robert Pirosh.

THE BEACHCOMBER. [1932]. [1938], [Paramount]. No. 8.

BEACHHEAD. 1954, United Artists. Richard Alan Simmons.

THE BEAT GENERATION   TITLES INDEX

*THE BEAT GENERATION. 1959, MGM. Richard Matheson and Lewis
      Meltzer.

*BEAU BRUMMELL. 1954, MGM. Karl Tunberg.

BEAU GESTE. 1939, Paramount. Robert Carson.

BEAU GESTE. 2nd draft. 1966, Universal. [Frank D. Gilroy] 1963
      and Douglas Heyes.

BEAU GESTE. 1966, Universal. No. 97. Douglas Heyes.

*BEAUTY FOR SALE. 1933, MGM. [Zelda Sears and Eve Greene].

*BECAUSE YOU'RE MINE. 1952, MGM. [Karl Tunberg and Leonard Spigel-
      gass].

BECKET. Final scr. 1964, Paramount. No. 27. Edward Anhalt.

*BECKY. 1927, MGM. [Marian Constance Blackton].

THE BED SITTING ROOM. 1969, United Artists. [John Antrobus].

BEDAZZLED. 1967, Fox. Peter Cook.

*BEDEVILLED. 1955, MGM. Jo Eisinger.

THE BEDROOM WINDOW. Bound with LOCKED DOORS. 1924, Paramount.
      [Clara Beranger].

BEDTIME STORY. 1964, Universal. Stanley Shapiro and Paul Henning.

BEFORE I HANG. 1940, Columbia. Robert D. Andrews.

THE BEGINNERS. [n. d.]. No. 94.

*THE BEGINNING OR THE END. 1947, MGM. Frank Wead.

THE BEGUILED. See Interview with Don Siegel.

BEHIND CITY LIGHTS. cc. 1945, Republic. [Richard Weil].

BEHOLD THE BRIDEGROOM. [1942]. No. 66. [Maurine Watkins].

BELIEVE IN ME. Orig. Title: SPEED IS OF THE ESSENCE. 1970, MGM.
      [Israel Horovitz].

10

A BELL FOR ADANO. 1944, A-F Films. Lamar Trotti and Norman Reilly Raine.

*BELLE OF NEW YORK. 1952, MGM. Robert O'Brien and Irving Elinson.

BELLS OF ROSARITA. cc. 1945, Republic. Jack Townley.

THE BELOVED ADVENTURESS. 1917, Pearless-World. [Frances Marion].

BEN-HUR. 1959, MGM. Karl Tunberg.

*BEN-HUR. 1926, MGM. [Carey Wilson and Bess Meredyth].

*BEN-HUR. cc. 1933, MGM.

BERKELY SQUARE. 1933, Fox. [J. L. Balderston].

BERLIN EXPRESS. 1948, RKO. Harold Medford.

BERNADINE. 2 copies. .1957, Fox. No. 19. Theodore Reeves.

BERSERK! 1968, Columbia. Herman Cohen and Aben Kandel.

*BEST FOOT FORWARD. 1943, MGM. Irving Brecher and Fred F. Finkel-hoffe.

THE BEST HOUSE IN LONDON. 1969, MGM. Denis Norden.

THE BEST MAN. See Interview with Lawrence Turman.

*BEST OF LUCK. [1926]. [1920], [MGM]. [Henry Hamilton, Cecil Raleigh and Arthur Collins].

THE BEST THINGS IN LIFE ARE FREE. Rev. final scr. 1956, Fox. No. 19. William Bowers and Phoebe Ephron.

THE BEST YEARS OF OUR LIVES. 2 copies. 1946, RKO. Robert E. Sherwood.

BETWEEN HEAVEN AND HELL. See materials in the David Weisbart Collection. No. 50.

*BETWEEN TWO NIGHTS. Prologue. [1941], [MGM]. [Lili Hatvany].

*BETWEEN TWO WOMEN. 1944, MGM. Harry Ruskin.

BEYOND THE BORDER. 1945, Republic. [Frank Gill, Jr.].

*BEYOND THE SIERRAS. 1928, MGM. [Robert Lord].

*BHOWANI JUNCTION. 1956, MGM. Sonya Levien and Ivan Moffat.

THE BIG BAM BOO. 2 copies and revised. [1971], [MGM]. [Roger
     Lewis].

THE BIG BONANZA. 1945, Republic. Dorrell McGowan, Stuart McGowan
     and Paul Gangelin.

THE BIG BRASS. [1971], [Universal]. [Peter Stone].

*THE BIG CITY. 1948, MGM. Whitfield Cook and Anne Morrison Chapin.

THE BIG CLEAN-UP. Final scr. [1948].

THE BIG GAMBLE. 2 copies. Re-ed from 1948 THE INSIDE STORY. cc.
     1954, Republic. Mary Loos and Richard Sale.

THE BIG GAMBLE. 1961, Fox. No. 31. Irwin Shaw.

*BIG GAME. 1921, Metro. [Edward T. Lowe, Jr.].

*THE BIG HANGOVER. 1950, MGM. Norman Krasna.

*BIG HOUSE. 1930, MGM. [Frances Marion].

THE BIG KILL. 4 drafts and outline. n. d. No. 27. [Edward
     Anhalt].

THE BIG KNIFE. 2 copies. 1955, United Artists. No. 94. James
     Poe.

*THE BIG LEAGUER. 1953, MGM. Herbert Baker.

THE BIG MOUTH. 1st draft. 1967, Columbia. Jerry Lewis and Bill
     Richmond.

*THE BIG OPERATOR. 1959, MGM. Robert Smith and Allen Rivkin.

THE BIG PARADE. See Interview with King Vidor. See also materials
     in the King Vidor Collection, No. 25.

THE BIG SHOW-OFF. 1945, Republic. Leslie Vadnay and Richard Weil.

THE BIG SLEEP. 1946, Warner Bros. William Faulkner, Leigh Brackett
     and Jules Furthman.

THE BIG STEP. [1961].

THE BIG TIMER. 1932 ,Columbia. No. 63. [Robert Riskin and Dorothy Howell].

THE BIG WAR. See IN LOVE AND WAR. No. 32.

THE BIG WHEEL. 1949, United Artists. No. 94. Robert Smith.

THE BIGGEST BUNDLE OF THEM ALL. 1968, MGM. Sy Salkowitz.

BILLIE. 1965, United Artists. No. 26. Ronald Alexander.

*BILLIONS. [1920?], [MGM]. [A. Hanks].

BILLY BRIGHT. Rel. as THE COMIC. 1969, Columbia. Carl Reiner.

BILLY BUDD. See Interview with A. Ronald Lubin.

BILLY ROSE'S DIAMOND HORSESHOE. See DIAMOND HORSESHOE.

*BIOGRAPHY OF A BACHELOR GIRL. 1935, MGM. [Anita Loos].

THE BIRTHDAY PARTY. 1968, Continental Dist. Harold Pinter. See also Interview with William Friedkin.

THE BISHOP'S WIFE. 2 copies. 1947, RKO. Robert E. Sherwood and Leonardo Bercovici.

THE BLACK CAT. 1941, Universal. Robert Lees, Fred Rinaldo, Eric Taylor and Robert Neville.

BLACK FRIDAY. 1940, Universal. Curt Siodmak and Eric Taylor.

*BLACK HAND. 1950, MGM. Luther Davis.

BLACK HILLS AMBUSH. 1952, Republic. Ronald Davidson and M. Coates Webster.

THE BLACK KNIGHT. 1954, Columbia. No. 65. Alec Coppel.

BLACK ORCHID. 1959, Paramount. Joseph Stefano.

BLACKBIRDS. Rel. as SLIGHTLY SCARLET. 1930, Paramount. [Harry James Smith].

THE BLACKBOARD JUNGLE. 1955, MGM. Richard Brooks.

THE BLACKBOARD JUNGLE   TITLES INDEX

*THE BLACKBOARD JUNGLE. 1955, MGM. Richard Brooks.

*BLACKMAIL. 1939, MGM. David Hertz and William Ludwig.

BLAST OF SILENCE. See Interview with Allan Barrett.

THE BLEMISH. Bound with WHITE YOUTH. [1918], [MGM]. [Clara
        Beranger].

BLESS THE BEASTS AND THE CHILDREN. See Interview with Stanley
        Kramer.

BLIND ALLEY. 1939, Columbia. Philip MacDonald, Michael Blackfort
        and Albert Duffy.

BLINDFOLD. 1966, Universal. No. 41. Philip Dunne and W. H. Menger.

THE BLISS OF MRS. BLOSSOM. 1968, Paramount. Alec Coppel and Denis
        Norden.

*BLONDIE OF THE FOLLIES. 1932, MGM. [Frances Marion and Anita
        Loos].

BLOOD ARROW. 1958, Fox. No. 40. Fred Freiberger.

BLOOD ON THE MOON. 1948, RKO. No. 49. Lillie Hayward.

THE BLOODHOUNDS OF BROADWAY. 1952, Fox. No. 19. Sy Gomberg.

BLOODY MAMA. 1970, American International. [Robert Thom].

BLOSSOMS IN THE DUST. 1941, MGM. Anita Loos.

BLUE. Final scr. 1968, Paramount. Meade Roberts and Ronald M.
        Cohen.

BLUE DENIM. 1959, Fox. No. 41. Edith Sommer and Philip Dunne.

BLUE MONTANA SKIES. cc. 1939, Republic. Gerald Geraghty.

THE BLUE VEIL. 1951, RKO. Norman Corwin.

BLUEPRINT FOR CRIME. Treatment. n. d. Larry Jackson, Art Estrada
        and Steve Masino.

*BODY AND SOUL. 1927, MGM. [Elliot Clawson].

THE BODY SNATCHER. 2 copies. 1945, RKO. No. 49. Philip Mac-
     Donald and Carlos Keith.

BODYGUARD. 1948, RKO. No. 31. Fred Niblo, Jr. and Harry Essex.

BOEING-BOEING. 3 drafts and final scr. 1965, Paramount. No. 27.
     Edward Anhalt.

THE BOFORS GUN. 1968, Regional Film Dist. John McGrath.

BONNIE AND CLYDE. 1967, Warner Bros. David Newman and Robert
     Benton.

BOOM. 1968, Universal. Tennessee Williams.

BOOMERANG! 1947, Fox. Richard Murphy.

BOOTS AND SADDLES. 1937, Republic. Jack Natteford and Oliver
     Drake.

THE BORDER PATROLMAN. 1936, Fox. No. 68. Dan Jarrett and Ben
     Cohen.

BORDERTOWN TRAIL. cc. 1944, Republic. Bob Williams and Jesse
     Duffy.

BORN TO BE WILD. cc. 1938, Republic. Nathanael West.

BORN TO KILL. 1947, RKO. No. 49. Eve Greene and Richard Macaulay.

BORN WILD. See YOUNG ANIMALS.

THE BOSS. 1956, United Artists. No. 97. Ben Perry.

THE BOSTON STRANGLER. 2 step outlines, 4 drafts and final scr.
     1968, Fox. No. 27. No. 31. Edward Anhalt. See also
     Interview with Tony Curtis.

BOTTOMS UP. Final sht. scr. 1934, Fox. No. 19. G. B.
     DeSylva, David Butler and Sid Silvers.

BOUGHT AND PAID FOR. 1922, Paramount. [G. H. Broadhurst].

BOY MEETS GIRL. 1938, Warner Bros. Bella Spewack and Samuel
     Spewack.

THE BOY WHO GREW OLDER. Treatment only. n. d. No. 11. [Heywood
     Broun].

THE BOYFRIEND   TITLES INDEX

THE BOYFRIEND. 1971, MGM. [Ken Russell].

BOYS NIGHT OUT. 1962, MGM. No. 26. Ira Wallach.

BOYS' RANCH. 1946, MGM. No. 66. William Ludwig.

*BOYS' RANCH. 1946, MGM. William Ludwig.

THE BRAIN. [1968], Paramount. [Gerard Oury].

THE BRAT. 1931, Fox. [Maud Fulton].

BREAKAWAY. n. d.

BREAKING THE ICE. 1931, RKO. No. 68.

*THE BRIDE GOES WILD. 1948, MGM. Albert Beich.

BRIDE OF FRANKENSTEIN. 1934, Universal. [John L. Balderston].

*BRIGADOON. 1954, MGM. Alan J. Lerner.

BRIGHT EYES. 1934, Fox. [David Butler].

*BRIGHT ROAD. 1953, MGM. Emmet G. Lavery.

BROADWAY. 2 copies. 1929, Universal. [Edward T. Lowe, Jr.].

BROADWAY BILL. 1934, Columbia. No. 63. [Robert Riskin] and Mark
        Hellinger.

BROADWAY BILL. 1934, Columbia. Mark Hellinger.

*BROADWAY MELODY. 1929, MGM. Jack McGowan.

*BROADWAY RHYTHM. 1944, MGM. Dorothy Kingsley and Harry Clark.

*BROADWAY TO HOLLYWOOD. 1933, MGM. [Willard Mack and Edgar Allan
        Woolf].

BROKEN SOIL. [1934]. No. 25. [Ben Hecht and Charles Lederer].

BRONCHO APACHE. n. d. No. 94.

BROTHER JOHN. Orig. title KANE. 2 drafts of scr. 1971, Columbia.
        [Ernest Kinoy].

THE BROTHERHOOD. 1968, Paramount. Lewis John Carlino.

THE BROTHERS KARAMAZOV. 2 copies. 1958, MGM. No. 66. Richard Brooks, [Julius and Philip Epstein].

*THE BROTHERS KARAMZOV. 1958, MGM. Richard Brooks.

*BROWN OF HARVARD. 1926, MGM. [A. P. Younger].

THE BUCCANEER. 1938, Paramount. No. 8. Edwin Justus Mayer, Harold Lamb and C. Gardner Sullivan.

BUCK AND THE PREACHER. 1972, Columbia. Ernest Kinoy.

BUCKSKIN. Orig. title THE FRONTIERSMAN. 1968, Paramount. Michael Fisher.

*THE BUGLE BLOWS AT MIDNIGHT. [1942], MGM. [Vincent Lawrence and William R. Lipman].

BUGSY SIEGAL. 2 drafts and final scr. n. d. No. 27. [Edward Anhalt].

BULLFIGHTER AND THE LADY. Foreign vers. 1951, Republic. James Edward Grant.

BULLITT. See Interview with Phil D'Antoni.

BUONA SERA, MRS. CAMPBELL. 1968, United Artists. Melvin Frank, Denis Norden and Sheldon Keller.

BURLESQUE. Rel. as WHEN MY BABY SMILES AT ME. Final and rev. final scr. 1948, Fox. Lamar Trotti.

*BURNING DAYLIGHT. [1919], [1929?], Metro. [A. S. LeVino].

THE BURNING HILLS. 1956, Warner Bros. No. 0. Irving Wallace.

BURNT FINGERS. [1936], MGM. [Anita Loos].

BUS RILEY'S BACK IN TOWN. 1965, Universal. William Inge.

THE BUSH BABIES. Rel. as THE BUSHBABY. 1969, MGM. [Robert Max-- well and William H. Stevenson].

THE BUSHBABY. See THE BUSH BABIES.

BUSINESS AND PLEASURE. 1932, Fox. [William Conselman].

BUSMAN'S HOLIDAY. n. d. No. 26. [Bernard Kahn and Arthur Wein-
    garten].

*BUT THE FLESH IS WEAK. 1932, MGM. [Ivor Novello].

BUTTERFLIES ARE FREE. See Interview with Charles Lang.

C. C. AND CO. See Interview with Alan Carr.

CAFE METROPOLE. 1937, Fox. Jacques Deval.

*CAIRO. 1942, MGM. John McClain.

*CALIFORNIA. 1927, MGM. [Elliot Clawson and W. S. Van Dyke].

CALIFORNIA OUTPOST. cc. Re-edited from OLD LOS ANGELES. 1948,
    Republic. Gerald Adams and Clements Ripley.

THE CALIFORNIAN. 1937, Fox. No. 68. Gilbert Wright.

CALL A MESSENGER. 1939, Universal. Arthur T. Horman.

CALL ME MADAM. Final sht. scr. 1953, Fox. No. 19. Arthur
    Sheekman.

CALL ME MISTER. Final sht. scr. 1951, Fox. No. 19. Albert E.
    Lewin and Burt Styler.

*CALL OF THE FLESH. 1930, MGM. [Dorothy Farnum and John Colton].

CALL OUT THE MARINES. Estimating scr. 1942, RKO. Frank Ryan and
    Williams Hamilton.

*CALLAWAY WENT THATAWAY. 1951, MGM. Norman Panama and Melvin
    Frank.

CALLING ALL MARINES. 1939, Republic. Earl Felton.

*CALLING BULLDOG DRUMMOND. 1951, MGM. Howard Emmett Rogers, Gerard
    Farlie and Arthur Wimperis.

*CALLING DR. GILLESPIE. 1942, MGM. Willis Goldbeck and Harry
    Ruskin.

THE CALLING OF DAN MATTHEWS. 1936, Columbia. No. 68. [Karl Brown,
    Don Swift and Dan Jarrett].

*THE CAMERAMAN. 1928, MGM. [Clyde Brackman and Lew Lipton?].

CAN HEIRONYMOUS MERKIN EVER FORGET MERCY HUMPE AND FIND TRUE HAPPI-
     NESS? 1969, Universal. Herman Raucher and Anthony Newley.

CAN-CAN. 5 drafts and final. 1960, Fox. No. 15. No. 19.
     Dorothy Kingsley and Charles Lederer.

THE CANDIDATE. 1972, Warner Bros. [Jeremy Larner].

CAPE FEAR. 1962, Universal. James R. Webb.

CAPRICE. 1st draft. 1967, Fox. Jay Jason and Frank Tashlin.

CAPTAIN AND THE JOLLY ROGER. n. d. [Walter Newman].

CAPTAIN BLOOD. 1935, First National. [Casey Robinson].

CAPTAIN FURY. 1939, United Artists. No. 8. Grover Jones.

CAPTAIN NEWMAN, M.D. Rev. final scr. 1963, Universal. Richard L.
     Breen, Phoebe and Henry Ephron.

CAPTAIN O'FLYNN. Treatment. n. d. No. 32.

*CAPTAIN SALVATION. 1927, MGM. [Jack Cunningham].

THE CAPTIVE CITY. 1952, United Artists. No. 49. Karl Kamb and
     Alvin M. Josephy, Jr.

CAPTIVE OF BILLY THE KID. 1952, Republic. M. Coates Webster and
     Richard Wormser.

CARAVAN. French vers. 1934, Fox. [Bernard Zimmer].

CARAVANS. [1967], [MGM]. No. 31. [Steven Karpf].

*CARBINE WILLIAMS. 1952, MGM. Art Cohn.

THE CARETAKERS. See Interview with Hall Bartlett.

CAREER. 1939, RKO. No. 66. Dalton Trumbo and [Bert Granet].

*CARGO OF INNOCENTS. [1941], MGM. [R. C. Sherriff and H. S.
     Haislip].

CARGO OF INNOCENTS. [1942], [MGM]. No. 8. [John L. Balderston].

CARMEN   TITLES INDEX

CARMEN. [1934], [MGM]. [William DeMille and Clara Beranger].

CARMEN. Scenario. [1915]. No. 8. [William DeMille].

CARMEN JONES. 1954, Fox. Harry Kleiner.

CARNIVAL. 1935, Colubmia. No. 63. [Robert Riskin].

CARNIVAL IN COSTA RICA. Rev. sht. final. 1947, Fox. No. 19. John
     Larkin, Samuel Hoffenstein and Elizabeth Reinhardt.

CAROLINA CANNONBALL. 1955, Republic. Barry Shipman.

CAROUSEL. Sht. final scr. 1956, Fox. No. 19. Phoebe and Henry
     Ephron.

CARRIE. Treatment. [1949], 1952, Paramount. Ruth and Augustus
     Goetz.

CASANOVA IN BURLESQUE. cc. 1944, Republic. Frank Gill.

THE CASE OF THE MOONLIGHTERS. n. d.

A CASE OF NEED. [1971], [MGM]. [Irving Ravetch and Harriet Frank,
     Jr.].

*CASINO MURDER CASE. 1935, MGM. [Florence Ryerson and Edgar Allan
     Woolf].

*CASS TIMBERLANE. 1947, MGM. Donald Ogden Stewart.

CASS TIMBERLANE. 1947, MGM. Donald Ogden Stewart.

CAST A GIANT SHADOW. See Interview with Mel Shavelson.

THE CASTAWAY. Rev. from THE CHEATERS. cc. 1945, Republic.
     Frances Hyland.

CASTLE KEEP. 1969, Columbia. Daniel Taradash and David Rayfiel.

CAT BALLOU. See THE BALLAD OF CAT BALLOU.

CAT ON A HOT TIN ROOF. Step outline. 1958, MGM. James Poe.

CAT ON A HOT TIN ROOF. 1958, MGM. Richard Brooks and James Poe.

*CAT ON A HOT TIN ROOF. 1958, MGM. Richard Brooks and James Poe.

CATCH-22. Final rev. scr., rel. dialogue scr., and scr. outline. 1970, Paramount. [Buck Henry].

*THE CATERED AFFAIR. 1956, MGM. Gore Vidal.

CATLOW. 1971, MGM. [Scot Finch and J. J. Griffith].

CATTLE KING. 1963, MGM. No. 65. Thomas Thompson.

*CAUGHT SHORT. 1930, MGM. [Willard Mack and Robert E. Hopkins].

*CAUSE FOR ALARM. [1940], MGM. [Charles Bennett, Len Hammond and Herman Mankiewicz].

*CAUSE FOR ALARM. 1951, MGM. Mel Dinelli and Tom Lewis.

CAUSE FOR ALARM. 1951, MGM. No. 65. Mel Dinelli and Tom Lewis.

CAVALCADE. 1933, Fox. [N. P. Coward].

CELEBRATION AT BIG SUR. See Interview with Baird Bryant.

CELEBRITY. [1928], [Pathe]. No. 65. [Tay Garnett and George Drumgold].

THE CHAIRMAN. 1969, Fox. No. 90. Ben Maddow.

THE CHALK GARDEN. 3 copies. 1964, Universal. No. 22. No. 37. John Michael Hayes.

A CHALLENGE FOR ROBIN HOOD. See THE LEGEND OF ROBIN HOOD.

CHAMBER OF HORRORS. 1945, RKO. [Norman Lee and Gilbert Gunn].

THE CHAMP. See materials in the King Vidor Collection, No. 25.

THE CHAMPAGNE MURDERS. 1968, Universal. [Claude Binyon and Derek Prouse].

CHAMPION. 1949, United Artists. Carl Foreman.

CHANGE OF HABIT. 1969, Universal. James Lee, S. S. Schweitzer and Eric Bercovici.

CHANGE OF HEART. Rev. from HIT PARADE OF 1943. 1949, Republic. Frank Gill, Jr.

CHANGES. See Interview with Hall Bartlett.

CHARLIE BUBBLES   TITLES INDEX

CHARLIE BUBBLES. 1968, Regional Film Dist. Shelagh Delaney.

CHARLIE CHAN AT THE OLYMPICS. 1937, Fox. Robert Ellis and Helen
    Logan.

CHARLIE CHAN AT THE OPERA. 1936, Fox. Scott Darling and Charles S.
    Belden.

CHARLIE CHAN AT THE RACE TRACK. 1936, Fox. Robert Ellis, Helen
    Logan and Edward T. Lowe.

CHARLIE CHAN'S COURAGE. 1934, Fox. [Seton I. Miller].

CHARLIE CHAN'S GREATEST CASE. 1933, Fox. [Lester Cole].

CHARLY. See Interview with Ralph Nelson.

*CHASING RAINBOWS. 1930, MGM. [Bess Meredyth].

THE CHAUTAUQUA. [1968], [MGM]. [Arnold and Lois Peyser].

CHE! 2 copies. 1969, Fox. No. 31. Michael Wilson and Sy
    Bartlett.

*THE CHEATER. Titles only. 1920, Metro.

*THE CHEATER. [1931], MGM. [Henry Arthur Jones?].

THE CHEATERS. 1945, Republic. Frances Hyland.

CHECKERS. 1937, Fox. Lynn Root, Frank Fenton, Robert Chapin and
    Karen DeWolf.

CHEERS FOR MISS BISHOP. 1941, United Artists. No. 65. Adelaide
    Heilbron and Sheridan Gibney.

THE CHICAGO KID. cc. 1945, Republic. Jack Townley.

*THE CHICAGO METHOD. [1942], MGM. [Cyril Hume and Robert Thoeren].

A CHILD IS WAITING. See Interview with Gene Fowler.

CHILD OF DIVORCE. 1946, RKO. No. 31. Lillie Hayward.

*CHILDREN OF PLEASURE. [1929], MGM. [Richard Schayer].

THE CHILDREN'S HOUR. See Interview with William Wyler.

22

*CHINA CARAVAN. Rel. as A YANK ON THE BURMA ROAD. 1942, MGM.
    Gordon Kahn, Hugo Butler and David Lang.

CHINA SEAS. 1935, MGM. No. 65. [Crosbie Garstin].

CHOICE. See Interview with Gene Fowler.

*THE CHORUS GIRL'S ROMANCE. 1920, Metro.

CHRISTIAN OF THE BOUNTY. Treatment and scr. 1943. No. 8. [John
    Balderston].

CHUKA. Rev. final sht. scr. 1966, Paramount. Richard Jessup.

*CIMARRON. [1942], MGM. [Vincent Lawrence].

CINCINNATI KID. See Interview with Martin Ransohoff.

CIRCUS GIRL. cc. 1955, Republic.

CIRCUS GIRL. cc. 2 copies. 1937, Republic. Adele Buffington and
    Bradford Ropes.

THE CISCO KID. 2 copies. 1931, Fox. [A. A. Cohn].

THE CITADEL. See materials in the King Vidor Collection, No. 25.

CITIZEN KANE. See Interview with Richard Wilson.

CITY OF SHADOWS. cc and trailer cc. 2 copies. 1955, Republic.
    [Houston Branch].

CLAMBAKE. 1967, United Artists. Arthur Browne, Jr.

CLARENCE. 1937, Paramount. Seena Owen and Grant Garrett.

THE CLAY PIGEON. 2 copies. 1949, RKO. No. 31. Carl Foreman.

*CLEAR ALL WIRES. 1933, MGM. [Delmer Daves, Bella and Sam Spewack].

CLEO DE 5 A 7. (CLEO FROM 5 TO 7). 1962, Zenith Int. [Agnes
    Varda].

CLEOPATRA. 1963, Fox. No. 91. Joseph L. Mankiewicz, Ranald Mac-
    Dougall and Sidney Buchman.

THE CLIMBERS. 1927, Warner Bros. [Tom Gibson].

THE CLOCK   TITLES INDEX

*THE CLOCK. 1945, MGM. Robert Nathan and Joseph Schrank.

THE CLOWN. Scenario. [1916].

*THE CLOWN. 1953, MGM. Martin Rackin.

CLUNY BROWN. 1946, Fox. Elizabeth Reinhardt and Samuel Hoffen-
     stein.

*THE COBWEB. 1955, MGM. John Paxton.

*THE COCKEYED MIRACLE. 1946, MGM. Karen DeWolf.

CODE OF THE PRAIRIE. 1944, Republic. Albert DeMond and Anthony
     Coldeway.

*CODE TWO. 1953, MGM. Marcel Klauber.

THE COLOR OF LOVE. n. d. Frank De Felitta.

COLOSSUS: THE FORBIN PROJECT. 1969, Universal. James Bridges.

COMANCHE CROSSING. n. d.

COME BACK CHARLESTON BLUE. 1972, Warner Bros. [Bontche Schweig and
     Peggy Elliott].

COME BLOW YOUR HORN. See Interview with Norman Lear.

COME NEXT SPRING. cc. 1956, Republic. Montgomery Pittman.

COME ON RANGERS. cc. 1938, Republic. Gerald Geraghty and John
     Natteford.

COME SHARE MY LOVE. Outline, 2nd draft cont. and final scr. [1944].
     [Charles E. Roberts].

THE COMEDIANS. Final scr. 1967, MGM. Graham Greene.

THE COMIC. See BILLY BRIGHT.

*COMING AT YOU. Rough scr. [1942], MGM. [Borden Chase].

*COMMAND DECISION. 1948, MGM. William R. Laidlaw and George
     Froeschel.

THE COMMANDOPES. Outline. [1942].

24

COMPULSION. See Interview with William Reynolds.

THE COMPUTER WORE TENNIS SHOES. 2 copies. 1969, Buena Vista.
     [Joseph L. McEveety].

COMRADE X. 1940, MGM. No. 25. Ben Hecht and Charles Lederer.

CONDEMNED WOMAN. 1938, RKO. No. 66. Lionel Houser.

CONEY ISLAND. Rev. sht. final scr. 1943, Fox. No. 19. George
     Seaton.

*CONFIDENTIALLY CONNIE. 1953, MGM. Max Shulman.

THE CONGRESS DANCES. cc. 3 copies. 1957, Republic. [Kurt
     Nachmann].

THE CONNECTICUT YANKEE. 1931, Fox. [William Conselman].

A CONNECTICUT YANKEE IN KING ARTHUR'S COURT. 1949, Paramount.
     No. 65. Edmund Beloin.

CONNECTION. See Interview with Arthur Mayer.

CONRAD IN QUEST OF HIS YOUTH. Scenario. 1920, Paramount. No. 8.
     [Olga Printzlau].

CONSPIRATOR. 1950, MGM. Sally Benson and Gerard Fairlie.

COOGAN'S BLUFF. 1968, Universal. Herman Miller, Dean Riesner and
     Howard Rodman.

COOL BREEZE. See BALLIN.

COP. n. d. [Frank R. Pierson].

CORNERED. See WAR LORD.

CORPORAL DOLAN GOES AWOL. Re-issue of RENDEZVOUS WITH ANNIE.
     [1946]. 1951, Republic. Mary Loos and Richard Sale.

CORPUS CHRISTI BANDITS. 2 copies. 1945, Republic. Norman S. Hall.

THE COUNT OF MONTE CRISTO. 1934, United Artists. No. 41.

*COUNT YOUR BLESSINGS. 1959, MGM. Karl Tunberg.

COUNTDOWN. Final scr. 1968, Warner Bros. Loring Mandel.

COUNTER FORCE   TITLES INDEX

COUNTER FORCE. n. d. No. 66. [Tony Lazzarino].

COUNTERFEIT. [1950]. No. 75. [Milton Raison, Bert Brown and Leo
    Townsend].

COUNTERPOINT. Final scr. Formerly THE BATTLE HORNS. [1968],
    [Universal]. James Lee and Joel Oliansky.

THE COUNTRY DOCTOR. 1936, Fox. Sonya Levien.

THE COUNTRY GIRL. 1954, Paramount. No. 91. George Seaton.

*COURAGE OF LASSIE. 1946, MGM. Lionel Houser.

COWBOY IN AFRICA. See AFRICA--TEXAS STYLE.

THE COWBOY MILLIONAIRE. 1935, Fox. No. 68.

THE COWBOYS. 1972, Warner Bros. [Irving Ravetch, Harriet Frank, Jr.
    and William Dale Jennings]. See also Interview with Mark
    Rydell.

CRACK IN THE MIRROR. 1960, Fox. No. 31. Mark Canfield and
    [Michael Bern].

CRAIG'S WIFE. 1928, Pathe. No. 8. [Clara Beranger].

CRANES ARE FLYING. Loop dialogue only. 1966, Artkino. [Victor
    Rozov].

CREATURES THE WORLD FORGOT. 1971, Columbia. [Michael Carreras].

THE CRIME OF SYLVESTRE BONNARD. [1935]. No. 66. [Francis Edwards
    Faragoh].

CRIMINAL COURT. 1946, RKO. No. 49. Lawrence Kimble.

THE CROOKED CIRCLE. 2 copies. 1957, Republic. Jack Townley.

CROSS CHANNEL. cc. 2 copies. 1955, Republic. [Rex Rienits].

THE CROSS OF LORAINE. 2 copies. 1943, MGM. No. 65. Michael
    Kanin, Ring Lardner, Jr., Alexander Esway and Robert D.
    Andrews.

CROSSPLOT. [1969], United Artists. Leigh Vance.

*CROSSROADS. 1942, MGM. Guy Trosper.

*THE CROWD. 1928, MGM. [King Vidor].

THE CRUSADES. 1935, Paramount. [Harold Lamb].

*CRY HAVOC. 1943, MGM. Paul Osborn.

*CRY OF THE HUNTED. 1953, MGM. Jack Leonard.

*CRY TERROR. 1958, MGM. Andrew L. Stone.

CUBAN FIREBALL. 3 copies and estimating scr. 1951, Republic.
    Charles E. Roberts and Jack Townley.

*THE CUBAN LOVE SONG. 1931, MGM. [C. Gardner Sullivan and Bess
    Meredyth].

CULPEPPER CATTLE CO. 1972, Fox. [Eric Bercovici and Gregory
    Prentiss].

THE CURSE OF THE CAT PEOPLE. 1944, RKO. No. 49. Dewitt Bodeen.

CUSTER OF THE WEST. 1968, Cinerama. Bernard Gordon and Julian
    Halevy.

*CYNTHIA. 1947, MGM. Harold Buchman and Charles A. Kaufman.

DADDY LONG LEGS. 1931, Fox. [Sonya Levien].

DADDY LONG LEGS. 2 copies. 1954, Fox. No. 8. No. 19. Phoebe
    and Henry Ephron.

*DADDY'S GONE A-HUNTING. 1925, Metro Goldwyn. [Kenneth B. Clark].

DADDY'S GONE A-HUNTING. 1969, National General. No. 94. Larry
    Cohen and Lorenzo Semple, Jr.

DAKOTA INCIDENT. 1956, Republic. Frederick Louis Fox.

THE DAKOTA KID. 1951, Republic. William Lively.

THE DAMNED. n. d. No. 66. [Mort Briskin].

*DANCE FOOLS DANCE. 1931, MGM. [Ausania Rouverol and Richard
    Schayer].

DANCING FEET. 1936, Republic. Jerry Chodorov, Olive Cooper and
    Wellyn Totman.

27

*DANCING LADY. 1933, MGM. [Allan Rivkin and P. J. Wolfson].

A DANDY IN ASPIC. 1968, Columbia. Derek Marlowe.

DANGER: DIABOLIK. 1968, Paramount. [Dino Maiuri, Brian Degas, Tudor Gates and Mario Bava].

DANGER ROUTE. 1968, United Artists. Meade Roberts.

*DANGEROUS PARTNERS. 1945, MGM. Marion Parsonnet.

*DANGEROUS TO MEN. [1920], MGM. [June Mathis?].

DANIEL BOONE, TRAIL BLAZER. cc and trailer cc and dialogue. 1956, Republic. Tom Hubbard and Jack Patrick.

DANTE'S INFERNO. 2 copies. 1935, Fox. [Philip Klein].

THE DARING AND THE DAMNED. No. 40. [Fred Freiberger].

DARK CITY. 2 copies. 1950, Paramount. No. 75. John Meredyth Lucas and Lawrence B. Marcus.

DARK COMMAND. cc. 1940, Republic. Grover Jones, Lionel Houser, and F. Hugh Herbert.

A DARK LANTERN. Bound with WHITE YOUTH. 1920, Realart. [Burus Mantle].

DARK OF THE SUN. 1968, MGM. Quentin Werty and Adrian Spies.

THE DARK PASSAGE. 1947, Warner Bros. Delmer Daves.

DARK PAST. 1949, Columbia. Philip MacDonald, Michael Blankfort and Albert Duffy.

DARK VIOLENCE. cc. Re-issue of ANGEL IN EXILE. 1949. 1954, Republic. Charles Larson.

DARKER THAN AMBER. n. d. No. 97.

*A DATE WITH JUDY. And radio scr. 1948, MGM. Dorothy Cooper and Dorothy Kingsley.

DAUGHTER OF THE JUNGLE. 1949, Republic. William Lively.

*DAUGHTER OF THE REGIMENT. [1941], MGM. [Frederick Faust and Frank Partos].

DAVID AND BATHSHEBA. 1951, Fox. No. 41. Philip Dunne.

DAVID HARUM. 1934, Fox. [E. N. Westcott].

*DAVY. 1960, MGM. William Rose.

*DAWNS EARLY LIGHT. [1940], MGM. [Marion Parsonnet, Howard Esta-
     brook, Jane Murfin and Elizabeth Page].

A DAY AT THE RACES. See materials in the Lawrence Weingarten Col-
     lection, No. 59.

THE DAY CUSTER FELL. n. d. No. 50.

DAY OF THE CHAMPION. Treatment, outline and final scr. n. d.
     No. 27. [Edward Anhalt].

DAY OF THE GUN. n. d. No. 94.

THE DAY OF THE LANDGRABBERS. Formerly THE GRINGOS. [1968]. [Ken
     Pettus].

THE DAY THE BOOKIES WEPT. 1939, RKO. No. 66. Bert Granet and
     George Jeske.

THE DAY THE EARTH STOOD STILL. 1951, Fox. No. 49. Edmund H. North.

DAYBREAK. 1918, Metro. [Niven Busch].

*DAYBREAK. 1931, MGM. [Cyril Hume, Zelda Sears and Ruth Cummings].

DAYS OF JESSE JAMES. cc. 1939, Republic. Earle Snell.

DAYS OF WINE AND ROSES. See Interview with Jack Lemmon.

DEAD ON ARRIVAL. D.O.A.? n. d. No. 94.

DEADFALL. 1968, Fox. Bryan Forbes.

DEADHEAD MILES. See Interview with Tony Bill.

DEADLINE FOR DEVLON. n. d. No. 75. [Jerry Lauren, Bernard
     Ederer and Robert A. White].

DEALING, OR THE BERKELEY-TO-BOSTON FORTY BRICK LOST-BAG BLUES.
     1972, Warner Bros. [David Odell Williams].

DEAR RUTH. 1947, Paramount. No. 94. Arthur Sheekman.

DEATH OF A SALESMAN   TITLES INDEX

DEATH OF A SALESMAN. 1951, Columbia. Stanley Roberts.

DEATH VALLEY MANHUNT. 1943, Republic. Norman S. Hall and Anthony
     Coldeway.

DECEPTION. 1946, Warner Bros. John Collier and Joseph Than.

*DECISION AGAINST TIME. 1957, MGM. William Rose and John Eldridge.

DECISION AT DELPHI. Draft and final scr. n. d. No. 27. [Edward
     Anhalt].

*THE DECKS RAN RED. 1958, MGM. Andrew Stone.

*DEEP IN MY HEART. And budgeting files. 1954, MGM. Leonard
     Spigelgass.

THE DEERSLAYER. 1957, Fox. Carroll Young and Kurt Neumann.

THE DEFIANT ONES. 1958, United Artists. Harold J. Smith and Nathan
     Douglas.

DELICIOUS. 3 copies. 1931, Fox. [G. R. Bolton].

*DELILAH. [1941], MGM. [Patricia Coleman].

DELIVERANCE. 2nd draft. 1972, Warner Bros. [James Dickey].

THE DELTA FACTOR. 1969. No. 65. [Tay Garnett].

DEMETRIUS. n. d. [Francis York].

DEMETRIUS AND THE GLADIATORS. 1954, Fox. No. 41. Philip Dunne.

*DEMI-BRIDE. 1927, MGM. [Agnes Christine Johnston].

THE DENVER KID. 1948, Republic. Robert Creighton Williams.

DERBY. See Interview with Michael Hamilburg.

DE SADE. 2 copies. 1969, American International. Richard
     Matheson.

DESERT OF LOST MEN. 1951, Republic. [M. Coates Webster].

DESIGN FOR DEATH. Documentary. 1948, RKO. No. 31. Theodor S.
     Geisel and Helen Geisel.

*DESIGNING WOMAN. 1957, MGM. George Wells.

*DESIRE ME. 1947, MGM. Marguerite Roberts and Zoe Akins.

THE DESPERADOES. See THE MARAUDERS.

DESPERADOES OF DODGE CITY. cc. 1948, Republic. Robert Creighton
    Williams.

A DESPERATE ADVENTURE. 1938, Republic. Barry Trivers and Hans
    Kraly.

*THE DESPERATE SEARCH. 1952, MGM. Walter Doniger.

*DETECTIVES. 1928, MGM. [Robert Lord and Chester Franklin].

THE DEVIL IS DEAD. See Interview with Carl Linder.

*THE DEVIL MAKES THREE. 1952, MGM. Jerry Davis.

THE DEVIL'S ADVOCATE. 2 drafts and final. n. d. No. 27. [Edward
    Anhalt].

THE DEVIL'S BRIDE. 1968, Fox. [Richard Matheson].

*THE DEVIL'S BROTHER. 1933, MGM. [Jeannie Macpherson].

*DEVIL'S DOORWAY. 1950, MGM. Guy Trosper.

DEVIL'S DOORWAY. 1950, MGM. Guy Trosper.

DEVIL'S ISLAND. 1940, Warner Bros. Kenneth Gamet and Don Ryan.

THE DEVILS. 1971, Warner Bros. [Ken Russell].

*DIAL 1119. 1950, MGM. John Monks, Jr.

DIAL 1119. Formerly THE VIOLENT HOUR. 1950, MGM. John Monks, Jr.

*DIAMOND HANDCUFFS. 1928, MGM. [Willis Goldbeck and Bradley King].

DIAMOND HORSESHOE. Rel. as BILLY ROSE'S DIAMOND HORSESHOE. 1945,
    Fox. No. 19. George Seaton.

DIAMONDS FOR BREAKFAST. 1968, Paramount. [N. F. Simpson and Rouve
    and Ronald Harwood].

DIANA AT MIDNIGHT. n. d. No. 44. [Albert Lewin].

*DIANE. 1955, MGM. Christopher Isherwood.

DIARY OF A BRIDE   TITLES INDEX

DIARY OF A BRIDE. [1948], Republic. [Lawrence Kimble].

DIARY OF ANNE FRANK. 1959, Fox. Frances Goodrich and Albert
    Hackett.

DID YOU HEAR THE ONE ABOUT THE TRAVELING SALESLADY? Final scr.
    1968, Universal. John Fenton Murray.

THE DIEHARDS. n. d., [Universal]. No. 41. [Philip Dunne].

DIMPLES. 1936, Fox. Arthur Sheekman and Nat Perrin.

*DINNER AT EIGHT. 1933, MGM. [Frances Marion].

DIRTY HARRY. 1971, Warner Bros. [Harry Julian Fink, R. M. Fink and
    Dean Riesner].

A DISPATCH FROM REUTERS. See also THIS MAN REUTERS. 1940, Warner
    Bros. No. 17. Milton Krims and [Tom Taylor].

DISRAELI. 1929, Warner Bros. [Julian Josephson].

THE DIVIDED HEART. cc. 2 copies. 1955, Republic. [Jack Whitting-
    ham].

*THE DIVINE WOMAN. 1928, MGM. [Dorothy Farnum].

*DIVORCE IN THE FAMILY. 1932, MGM. [Delmer Daves].

*THE DIVORCEE. 1930, MGM. [John Meehan].

DO YOU LOVE ME? 2nd rev. sht. final. 1946, Fox. No. 19. Robert
    Ellis and Helen Logan. [Aka KITTEN ON THE KEYS].

*THE DOCTOR AND THE GIRL. 1949, MGM. Theodore Reeves.

DOCTOR AT SEA. (cc). 1956, Republic. [Richard Gordon].

DOCTOR BULL. Orig. title THE LAST ADAM. 1933, Fox. [Paul Green
    and Jane Storm].

DR. DOLITTLE. 1967, Fox. No. 31. Leslie Bricusse.

DOCTOR EHRLICH'S MAGIC BULLET. See THE STORY OF DOCTOR EHRLICH'S
    MAGIC BULLET. See also TEST 606.

DOCTOR FAUSTUS. 1968, Columbia. Nevill Coghill.

DR. JOSEPH GOEBBELS, HIS LIFE AND LOVES. n. d. [Alfred Zeisler and
Herbert Philips].

*DOCTOR KILDARE'S TRIPLE X. [1942], MGM. [Harry Ruskin and Willis
Goldbeck].

DR. STRANGELOVE. See Interview with Louis Blaugh(2).

*DOCTOR'S DILEMMA. 1958, MGM. [Anatole de Grunwald].

DOCTOR'S SECRET. [HALF AN HOUR]. Script and notes. 1929, Paramount. No. 8. [James M. Barrie].

A DOG OF FLANDERS. See Interview with Robert Radnitz.

DOLL FACE. Rev. final scr. 1946, Fox. No. 19. Leonard Praskins.

DOLLAR BILL. See AMBASSADOR BILL.

THE DOLLY SISTERS. 6th rev. sht. final. 1945, Fox. No. 19. John
Larkin and Marian Spitzer.

DON JUAN'S NIGHT OF LOVE. cc and trailer cc. 1955, Republic.
[Mario Soldati, Vittorio Nino Novarese, Giorgio Bassani and
Augusto Frassineti].

DON'T CALL IT LOVE. See RITA COVENTRY.

DON'T GET PERSONAL. 1942, Universal. Hugh Wedlock, Jr. and Howard
Snyder.

DON'T FORGET TO REMEMBER. See THERE GOES THE GROOM.

*DON'T GO NEAR THE WATER. And budgeting files. 1957, MGM. Dorothy
Kingsley and George Wells. See also materials in the
Lawrence Weingarten Collection, No. 59.

DON'T JUST STAND THERE! Final scr. 1968, Universal. Charles
Williams.

DON'T MAKE WAVES. 1967, MGM. No. 26. Ira Wallach and George Kirgo.

DON'T RAISE THE BRIDGE, LOWER THE RIVER. 1968, Columbia. Max Wilk.

DON'T TURN 'EM LOOSE. 1936, RKO. No. 66. Harry Segall and
Ferdinand Reyher.

DOOMED TO DIE. 1940, Monogram. Michael Jacoby.

DOPPEL GANGER   TITLES INDEX

DOPPEL GANGER. [1968]. [Gerry and Sylvia Anderson and Donald
        James].

THE DOUBLE CROSS. 3 copies. 1941, Prod. Distrib. Corp. Milton
        Raison and Ron Ferguson.

DOUBLE JEOPARDY. 2 copies. 1955, Republic. [Don Martin].

THE DOUBLE MAN. Final scr. 1968, Warner Bros. Frank Tarloff
        and Alfred Hayes.

DOUBLE TROUBLE. 2 copies. n. d. Leslie Goodwins, Charles E.
        Roberts and Arthur Ross.

DOWN ABOUT THE SHELTERING PALMS. Final scr. 1953, Fox. No. 19.
        Claude Binyon, Albert Lewin and Burt Styler.

DOWN ARGENTINE WAY. Sht. final. 1940, Fox. No. 19. Darrell Ware
        and Karl Tunberg.

DOWN DAKOTA WAY. cc. 1949, Republic. John K. Butler and A. Sloan
        Nibley.

DOWN LAREDO WAY. 1953, Republic. Gerald Geraghty.

DOWN MEXICO WAY. 1941, Republic. Olive Cooper and Albert Duffy.

DOWNHILL RACER. 1969, Paramount. James Salter.

DRACULA HAS RISEN FROM THE GRAVE. 1968, Warner Bros. [John Elder].

DRAGNET. 1947, Screen Guild. No. 75. Barbara Worth, Harry Essex
        and [Richard Macauley].

DREAM GIRL. 1948, Paramount. No writer credit.

A DREAM OF KINGS. 1969, National General. Ian Hunter and Harry
        Mark Petrakis.

*DREAM OF LOVE. 1928, MGM. [Dorothy Farnum].

*DREAM WIFE. 1953, MGM. Sidney Sheldon, Herbert Baker and Alfred
        Lewis Levitt.

DRUMBEATS OVER WYOMING. Re-issue of THE PLAINSMAN AND THE LADY.
        [1946]. cc. 1954, Republic. Richard Wormser.

*DU BARRY WAS A LADY. 1943, MGM. Irving Breecher.

34

THE DUCHESS OF IDAHO. 1950, MGM. Dorothy Cooper and Jerome L. Davis.

THE DUDE RANGER. 1934, Fox. No. 68. [M. Roberts and Bernard Schubert].

DUEL AT APACHE WELLS. cc. 1957, Republic. Robert Creighton Williams.

DUEL IN THE SUN. 1946, Selznick. No. 25. David O. Selznick and [Oliver H. P. Garrett].

DUKE OF CHICAGO. 1949, Republic. Albert DeMond.

*DUNKIRK. 1958, MGM.

THE DUNWICH HORROR. 1970, American International. Curtis Lee Hanson, Henry Rosenbaum and Ronald Silkosky.

EACH DAWN I DIE. 1939, Warner Bros. Norman Reilly Raine and Warren Duff.

EADIE WAS A LADY. 1944, Columbia. Monte Brice.

EARL CARROLL SKETCHBOOK. cc. 2 copies. 1946, Republic. Frank J. Gill, Jr. and Parke Levy.

EARL CARROLL VANITIES. cc. 1945, Republic. Frank J. Gill, Jr.

*EARLY TO BED. [1928], MGM. Titles by H. M. Walker].

*THE EASIEST WAY. 1931, MGM. [Edith Ellis].

*EAST SIDE, WEST SIDE. 1949, MGM. Isobel Lennart.

*EASTER PARADE. 1948, MGM. Sidney Sheldon, Frances Goodrich and Albert Hackett.

EASY COME, EASY GO. 1947, Paramount. Francis Edwards Faragoh, John McNulty and Anne Froelich.

EASY TO LOVE. Budgeting files only. 1953, MGM.

*EASY TO WED. 1946, MGM. Dorothy Kingsley.

THE EDGE OF RUNNING WATER. 1940, Columbia. [Robert D. Andrews and Milton Gunzburg].

EDWARD, MY SON   TITLES INDEX

*EDWARD, MY SON. 1949, MGM. Donald Ogden Stewart.

THE EGYPTIAN. 1954, Fox. No. 41. Philip Dunne and Casey Robinson.

*8 LITTLE BLACK BOYS. [1942], MGM. [Lili Hatvany].

EIGHT ON THE LAM. 1967, United Artists. Albert E. Lewin, Burt
    Styler, Bob Fisher and Arthur Marx.

EIGHTEEN AND ANXIOUS. 1957, Republic. No. 40. Dale and Katherine
    Eunson and [Fred Freiberger].

EIGHTY STEPS TO JONAH. [1969]. [Frederick Louis Fox].

ELDORADO. Draft. [1952]. No. 66. [Seeleg Lester and Merwin
    Gerard].

THE EL PASO KID. cc. 2 copies. 1946, Republic. Norman Sheldon.

EL PASO STAMPEDE. cc. 3 copies. And trailer cc. 1953, Republic.
    Arthur E. Orloff.

ELIZABETH BLACKWELL. [1946]. No. 11. [Florence Ryerson and Colin
    Clements].

ELOPEMENT. 1951, Fox. Bess Taffel.

EMBEZZLED HEAVEN. Loop dialogue only. 1959, Louis de Rochemont.
    [Ernst Marischka].

*EMMA. 1932, MGM. [Leonard Praskins].

EMPEROR CONCERTO. 1st draft. [1944]. Ellen Lowe.

THE ENCHANTED COTTAGE. Treatment and final scr. by Bodeen. 1945,
    RKO. DeWitt Bodeen and Herman J. Mankiewicz.

END OF THE ROAD. cc. 3 copies. 1944, Republic. Dennison Clift
    and Gertrude Walker.

*THE ENEMY. 1928, MGM. [Agnes Johnston and Willis Goldbeck].

THE ENEMY GENERAL. 1960, Columbia. Dan Pepper and Burt Picard.

ENEMY OF MAN. See STORY OF LOUIS PASTEUR.

ENTER LAUGHING. 1967, Columbia. Joseph Stein and Carl Reiner.

THE ENTERTAINER. Rev. release scr. 1960, Continental Dist. John
     Osborne and Nigel Kneale.

ESCAPE. 1948, Fox. No. 41. Philip Dunne.

*ESCAPE FROM FORT BRAVO. 1953, MGM. Frank Fenton.

ESCAPE TO PARADISE. 1939, RKO. No. 68. Weldon Melick.

THE ETERNAL SEA. cc and trailer cc. 1955, Republic. Allen Rivkin.

ETERNALLY YOURS. 1939, United Artists. No. 65. Gene Towne and
     Graham Baker.

THE EVE OF ST. MARK. 1st draft cont. 1944, Fox. George
     Seaton.

EVERY LITTLE CROOK AND NANNY. 1972, MGM. [Cy Howard, Jonathan
     Axelrod and Robert Klane].

EVERYBODY DOES IT. Final scr. 1949, Fox. No. 19. Nunnally
     Johnson.

EVERYBODY SING. 1938, MGM. Florence Ryerson and Edgar Allan Woolf.

*EVERYTHING I HAVE IS YOURS. And budgeting files. 1952, MGM.
     George Wells.

EVERYTHING'S ON ICE. 1939, RKO. No. 68. Adrian Landis and
     Sherman Lowe.

THE EVIL GUN. [1967], [MGM]. Eric Bercovici and Charles W. Warren.

*EXCUSE MY DUST. 1951, MGM. George Wells.

THE EXECUTIONERS. Treatment. n. d. John MacDonald.

*EXECUTIVE SUITE. 1954, MGM. Ernest Lehman.

EXECUTIVE SUITE. 1954, MGM. No. 49. Ernest Lehman.

*EXIT LEADING LADY. Treatment. [1941], MGM. [Jan Fortune].

*EXIT SMILING. 1926, MGM.

EXPLOSION. [1969]. [Samuel Fuller].

EXPOSED. cc. 1947, Republic. Royal K. Cole and Charles Moran.

THE EXTRAORDINARY SEAMAN   TITLES INDEX

THE EXTRAORDINARY SEAMAN. 1969, MGM. Phillip Rock and Hal Dresner.

*EYES IN THE NIGHT. 1942, MGM. Guy Trosper and Howard Emmett Rogers.

EYES OF TEXAS. cc. 1948, Republic. A. Sloan Nibley.

THE FABULOUS SENORITA. 1952, Republic. Charles E. Roberts and Jack Townley.

THE FABULOUS SUZANNE. cc. 2 copies. 1946, Republic. Tedwell Chapman and Randall Faye.

THE FABULOUS TEXAN. 1947, Republic. Lawrence Hazard and Horace McCoy.

FACES IN THE FOG. cc. 1944, Republic. Jack Townley.

FACULTY ROW. Assorted pages and retakes. [1943]. No. 66. [Bill Noble].

FADE IN. Final scr. [1967], [Paramount]. [Jerry Ludwig].

*FAIR AND WARMER. 1919, Metro. [Avery Hopgood].

*THE FAIR CO-ED. 1927, MGM. [Byron Morgan].

*FAITHFUL IN MY FASHION. 1946, MGM. Lionel Houser.

*FAITHLESS. 1932, MGM. [Carey Wilson].

*FALL GUY. [1944], MGM. [Martin Berkeley].

FALLING STARS: THE CAVALCADE OF HOLLYWOOD. Revised final scr. [1939], Fox. No. 19. [Ernest Pascal].

FALSE FACES. 1943, Republic. Curt Siodmak.

FANNY. 2 copies. 1961, Warner Bros. Julius J. Epstein.

A FAN'S NOTES. [1970]. [William Lee Kinsolving].

THE FANTASTIC PUPPET PEOPLE. n. d. No. 94.

FANTASTIC VOYAGE. 1966, Fox. No. 31. Harry Kleiner.

THE FAR FRONTIER. (cc). 1949, Republic. A. Sloan Nibley.

FAREWELL FRIEND. [1968]. [Jean Herman and Sebastien Japrisot].

FAREWELL MY LOVELY. See MURDER, MY SWEET.

A FAREWELL TO ARMS. [1932], Paramount. [Benjamin Glazer and Oliver
     H. P. Garrett].

THE FARMER TAKES A WIFE. 1953, Fox. No. 19. Walter Bullock,
     Sally Benson and Joseph Fields.

*FAST COMPANY. 1953, MGM. William Roberts.

*FAST LIFE. 1932, MGM. [Byron Morgan and Ralph Spence].

THE FAST SET. 1924, Paramount. [Frederick Lonsdale].

*FAST WORKERS. 1933, MGM. [Karl Brown, Ralph Wheelwright and
     Laurence Stallings].

THE FASTEST GUITAR ALIVE. 1967, MGM. Robert E. Kent.

FATAL HOUR. 1940, Monogram. Scott Darling.

FATAL WITNESS. (cc). 1945, Republic. Jerry Sackheim.

*FATHER OF THE BRIDE. 1950, MGM. Frances Goodrich and Albert
     Hackett.

*FATHER'S LITTLE DIVIDEND. 1951, MGM. Frances Goodrich and Albert
     Hackett.

FATHOM. 1967, Fox. Lorenzo Semple, Jr.

THE FAUN. Prod. title MARRIAGE MAKER. 1923, Paramount. [Edward
     Knoblock].

*A FAVOR TO A FRIEND. 1919, Metro.

THE FEAR MARKET. Bound with WHITE YOUTH. 1920, Realart. [Clara
     Beranger].

THE FEARLESS VAMPIRE KILLERS, OR PARDON ME, BUT YOUR TEETH ARE IN MY
     NECK. 1967, MGM. Gerard Branch and Roman Polanski.

*FEAST OF REASON. [1942], MGM. [Elmer Harris].

FEDERAL AGENT AT LARGE. cc. 1950, Republic. Albert DeMond.

FEDERAL MANHUNT. 1939, Republic. Maxwell Shane.

FEVER HEAT. 1968, Paramount. Henry Gregor Felsen.

FEVER PITCH. n. d. No. 40. [Fred Freiberger and Richard Landau].

*FIEND WITHOUT A FACE. 1958, MGM. [Herbert J. Leder].

*FIESTA. 1947, MGM. George Bruce and Lester Cole.

15 MAIDEN LANE. 1936, Fox. David Silverstein, Lou Breslow and John
     Patrick.

THE FIFTH ESTATE. n. d. No. 27. [Edward Anhalt].

FIFTY-TWO MILES TO TERROR. [1966], [MGM]. [Robert E. Kent].

FIGHTING CHANCE. (cc) and trailer cc. 1955, Republic. Houston
     Branch.

THE FIGHTING COAST GUARD. cc. 1951, Republic. Kenneth Gamet.

THE FIGHTING DEVIL DOGS. (cc). 1943, Republic. Barry Shipman,
     Franklyn Adreon, Ronald Davidson and Sol Shor.

THE FIGHTING SEABEES. cc. 1944, Republic. Borden Chase and Aeneas
     MacKenzie.

THE FILE OF THE GOLDEN GOOSE. 1969, United Artists. [James B.
     Gordon and John C. Higgins].

FINDERS KEEPERS. 2nd draft. 1967, United Artists. Michael
     Pertwee.

FINIAN'S RAINBOW. 1968, Warner Bros. E. Y. Harburg and Fred Saidy.

*FINISHING SCHOOL. [1941], MGM. [William Thiele and Al Mannheimer].

THE FIREBALL. 1950, Fox. No. 65. Tay Garnett and Horace McCoy.

*THE FIRST MAN IN SPACE. 1959, MGM. John C. Cooper and Lance Z.
     Hargreaves.

FISHERMAN'S WHARF. 1939, RKO. No. 68. Bernard Schubert, Ian
     McLellan Hunter and H. Clyde Lewis.

*FIVE AND TEN. 1931, MGM. [Edith Fitzgerald].

FIVE CAME BACK. 1939, RKO. No. 66. Jerry Cady, Dalton Trumbo and
      Nathanael West.

5 CARD STUD. 1968, Paramount. Marguerite Roberts.

FIVE MAN ARMY. 1970, MGM. Dario Argento and Marc Richards.

FIVE MILLION YEARS TO EARTH. 1968, Fox. Nigel Kneale.

THE FIXER. 1968, MGM. Dalton Trumbo.

THE FLAME. cc. 1947, Republic. Lawrence Kimble.

*FLAME AND THE FLESH. 1954, MGM. Helen Deutsch.

FLAME OF SACRAMENTO. cc. Re-issue of IN OLD SACRAMENTO. 1951,
      Republic. Frances Hyland.

FLAME OF THE ISLANDS. (cc). 2 copies. 1955, Republic. Bruce
      Manning.

FLAME OF YOUTH. cc. 3 copies. 1949, Republic. Robert Yale
      Libott, Frank Burt and Bradford Ropes.

FLAME OVER INDIA. See Interview with J. Lee Thompson.

FLAMING STAR. 1960, Fox. No. 50. Clair Huffaker and Nunnally
      Johnson.

FLAP. See Interview with Clair Huffaker.

A FLEA IN HER EAR. Final scr. 1968, Fox. John Mortimer.

*FLESH AND THE DEVIL. 1927, MGM. [Frederica Sagor and Benjamin
      Glazer].

THE FLESH IS STRONG. n. d. No. 27. [Edward Anhalt].

FLIGHT FROM GLORY. 1937, RKO. No. 66. David Silverstein and John
      Twist.

FLIGHT OF THE DOVES. 1971, Columbia. [Frank Gabrielson and Ralph
      Nelson].

*THE FLORODORA GIRL. 1930, MGM. [Gene Markey].

FLOWER DRUM SONG. 1961, Universal. Joseph Fields.

FLUFFY. 1965, Universal. No. 26. Samuel Roeca.

*THE FLYING FLEET. [1928], MGM. [Richard Schayer].

THE FLYING FOOL. 1929, Pathe. No. 65. [Tay Garnett].

*FLYING HIGH. 1931, MGM. [A. P. Younger].

THE FLYING SQUADRON. (cc). n. d., Republic. ["A Robert L. Peters
    Film"].

FOLIES BERGERE DE PARIS. [1934]. 1935, Fox. No. 19. [Bess
    Meredyth and Hal Long].

FOLLOW ME QUIETLY. 1949, RKO. No. 31. Lillie Hayward.

FOLLOW YOUR HEART. cc. 1936, Republic. Lester Cole, Nathanael
    West and Sam Ornitz.

FOOLS. See Interview with Henri Bollinger.

FOOLS' PARADE. 1971, Columbia. [James Lee Barrett].

FOOTLIGHT SERENADE. Rev. final scr. 1942, Fox. No. 19.
    Robert Ellis, Helen Logan and Lynn Starling.

FOOTLOOSE HEIRESS. Orig. title THE HOBO AND THE HEIRESS?. 1937,
    Warner Bros. Robertson White.

*FOR ME AND MY GAL. 1942, MGM. Richard Sherman, Fred F. Finkel-
    hoffe and Sid Silvers.

*FOR OUR VINES HAVE TENDER GRAPES. Rel. as OUR VINES HAVE TENDER
    GRAPES. 1945, MGM. Dalton Trumbo.

FOR SINGLES ONLY. 1968, Columbia. Hal Collins and Arthur
    Dreifuss.

*FOR THE FIRST TIME. 1959, MGM. Andrew P. Solt.

FOR THE LOVE OF MIKE. 1960, Fox. Daniel D. Beauchamp.

FOR THOSE IN PERIL. 1943, Ealing. [Harry Watt, et al.].

FOR WHOM THE BELL TOLLS. 2 copies. 1943, Paramount. Dudley
    Nichols.

FOR YOUR EYES ONLY. Outline. n. d., Republic. Philip Yordan.

*FORBIDDEN PLANET. 1956, MGM. Cyril Hume.

THE FORBIDDEN WOMAN. 1927, Elmer Harris. [Clara Beranger].

A FOREIGN AFFAIR. 1948, Paramount. Charles Brackett, Billy Wilder
    and Richard L. Breen.

*FOREIGN DEVILS. 1928, MGM. [Marion Ainslee].

THE FOREST RANGERS. 1942, Paramount. No. 66. Harold Shumate.

FOREVER AMBER. 2 copies. 1947, Fox. No. 41. Philip Dunne and
    Ring Lardner, Jr.

*FOREVER DARLING. 1956, MGM. Helen Deutsch.

FORGED PASSPORT. 1939, Republic. Franklin Coen and Lee Loeb.

FORT DODGE STAMPEDE. cc. 2 copies. 1951, Republic. Richard
    Wormser.

FORTUNE AND MEN'S EYES. 1971, MGM. [John Herbert].

FORTY POUNDS OF TROUBLE. See Interview with Norman Jewison.

THE FOUNTAINHEAD. 1949, Warner Bros. No. 25. Ayn Rand.

*THE FOUR FLUSHER. 1919, Metro. [Izola Forrester and Mann Page].

*THE FOUR FLUSHER. Scenario. [1931]. [A. S. Le Vino].

4 FOR TEXAS. 1963, Warner Bros. No. 94. Teddi Sherman and Robert
    Aldrich.

FOUR JILLS IN A JEEP. Rev. final scr. 1944, Fox. No. 19. Robert
    Ellis, Helen Logan and Snag Harris.

FOUR WALLS. [1934], MGM. [Bernard Schubert].

FOX FOLLIES. Final scr. 1929, Fox. No. 19.

*THE FOXIEST GIRL IN PARIS. 1958, Times Film Corp. Jean Ferry,
    Jacques Emmanuel and Christian-Jacque.

FRANKENSTEIN MUST BE DESTROYED. 1969, Warner Bros. [Bert Batt].

*FREAKS. Spanish language vers. 1932, MGM.

FREE SOULS   TITLES INDEX

*FREE SOULS. 1931, MGM. [John Meehan].

THE FRENCH CONNECTION. 1971, Fox. [Ernest Tidyman]. See also
        Interview with Phil D'Antoni.

THE FRENCH KEY. cc. 1946, Republic. Frank Gruber.

FRENCHMAN'S CREEK. 1944, Paramount. Talbot Jennings.

*FRIENDLY PERSUASION. 1956, Allied Artists. Michael Wilson.

FRISCO TORNADO. cc and trailer cc. 1950, Republic. M. Coates
        Webster.

FRISCO WATERFRONT. cc. 1936, Republic. [Norman Houston].

FROM RAGS TO RICHES. [1941], Republic.

FROM RUSSIA WITH LOVE. See Interview with Steve Shagan.

FRONTIER INVESTIGATION. cc and trailer cc. 2 copies. 1949, Repub-
        lic. Robert Creighton Williams.

*FRONTIER RANGERS. [1958], MGM. [Gerald Drayson Adams].

FROZEN RIVER. 1929, Warner Bros. [Harry Behn].

FUGITIVE FROM SONORA. cc. 1943, Republic. Norman S. Hall.

FUGITIVE LADY. cc. 2 copies. 1951, Republic. John O'Dea.

*FUGITIVE LOVERS. 1934, MGM. [Frances Goodrich, Albert Hackett and
        George B. Seitz].

FULL CONFESSION. Estimating scr. 1939, RKO. No. 66. Jerry Cady.

FUNNY GIRL. See Interview with Walter Scharf.

G. I. WAR BRIDES. cc. 1946, Republic. John K. Butler.

THE GABRIEL HORN. n. d. No. 94.

*GABY. And budgeting files. 1956, MGM. Frances Goodrich, Albert
        Hackett and Charles Lederer.

GAILY, GAILY. See Interview with Norman Jewison.

*GALLANT BESS. 1946, MGM. Jeanne Bartlett.

THE GALLANT LEGION. cc and trailer cc. 1948, Republic. Gerald Drayson Adams.

GALLANT THOROUGHBRED. cc. Re-ed. from SOMEONE TO REMEMBER. [1943], Republic. Frances Hyland.

THE GAMBLING TERROR. 1937, Republic. George H. Plympton.

GAMES. See Interview with George Edwards.

THE GANG'S ALL HERE. 1943, Fox. No. 19. Walter Bullock.

GANGS OF CHICAGO. cc. 1940, Republic. Karl Brown.

GANGS OF NEW YORK. cc. 1938, Republic. Wellyn Totman, Samuel Fuller and Charles Francis Royal.

GANGS OF SONORA. cc. 1941, Republic. Albert DeMond and Doris Schroeder.

GANGS OF THE WATERFRONT. cc. 1945, Republic. Albert Beich.

GARDEN OF EVIL. Final scr. 1954, Fox. Frank Fenton.

*GASLIGHT. 1944, MGM. John Van Druten, Walter Reisch and John L. Balderston.

GASLIGHT. 2 copies. 1944, MGM. No. 8. John Van Druten, Walter Reisch and John L. Balderston.

GAUCHOS OF EL DORADO. cc. 1941, Republic. Albert DeMond.

GAY BLADES. cc. 2 copies. 1946, Republic. Albert Beich.

*THE GAY DECEIVER. 1926, MGM. [Benjamin F. Glazer].

GAY ILLITERATE. 1946, Fox. [Wanda Tuchoch].

THE GAY RETREAT. Treatment. n. d. No. 19. Ernest Lehman.

THE GAZEBO. 1959, MGM. George Wells.

GENERATION. 1969, Avco Embassy. [William Goodhart].

*GENTLE ANNIE. 1944, MGM. Lawrence Hazard.

A GENTLE GANGSTER. cc. 1943, Republic. Jefferson Parker and Al Martin.

GENTLE GIANT   TITLES INDEX

GENTLE GIANT. Rev. scr. 1967, Paramount. Edward Lakso, Jr. and
     Andy White.

GENTLEMAN FROM LOUISIANA. cc. 1936, Republic. Gordon Rigby and
     Joseph Fields.

A GENTLEMAN OF LEISURE. Scenario. 1923, Paramount. No. 8. [Jack
     Cunningham and Anthony Coldeway].

GENTLEMAN'S AGREEMENT. Rev. final. 1947, Fox. Moss Hart.

*GENTLEMAN'S FATE. 1931, MGM. [Ursula Parrott and Leonard Pras-
     kins].

GENTLEMEN PREFER BLONDES. Rev. final. 1953, Fox. No. 19. Charles
     Lederer.

GEORGE WHITE'S SCANDALS OF 1935. 2 copies. 1935, Fox. No. 19.
     [Patterson McNutt].

GERALDINE. 1953, Republic. Peter Milne and Frank Gill, Jr.

*GET RICH QUICK WALLINGFORD. [1931], [MGM]. [Charles MacArthur].

GET TO KNOW YOUR RABBIT. 1972, Warner Bros. [Jordan Crittenden].

*GETTYSBURG. Documentary. [1955], MGM. [Dr. J. Walter Coleman and
     Dore Schary].

THE GHOST AND MRS. MUIR. 1947, Fox. No. 41. Philip Dunne.

THE GHOST GOES WILD. cc and trailer cc. 1947, RKO. Randall Faye.

GHOST OF ZORRO. cc. 2 copies. Serial. 1959, Republic. Royal
     Cole, William Lively and Sol Shor.

GIANT. 1956, Warner Bros. Fred Guiol and Ivan Moffat. See also
     Interview with George Stevens.

THE GIFT HORSE. 1st draft treatment and final draft. 1952, Molton
     Films. [Clara Beranger].

*GIGI. 1958, MGM. Alan Jay Lerner.

THE GILDED LILY. 1935, Paramount.

*GIMME! 1923, Metro. [Adelaide and Rupert Hughes].

THE GIRL AND THE GENERAL. 1967, MGM. Luigi Malerba and Pasquale Festa Campanile.

THE GIRL CAN'T HELP IT. 1956, Fox. No. 19. Frank Tashlin and Herbert Baker.

*GIRL CRAZY. 1942, MGM. Fred F. Finkelhoffe.

THE GIRL FROM ALASKA. cc. 2 copies. 1942, Republic. Edward T. Lowe and Robert Ormond Case.

GIRL FROM GOD'S COUNTRY. cc. 1940, Republic. Elizabeth Meehan and Robert Lee Johnson.

THE GIRL FROM MEXICO. 1939, RKO. No. 66. Lionel Houser and Joseph Fields.

*THE GIRL FROM MISSOURI. 1934, MGM. [Anita Loos and John Emerson].

THE GIRL IN THE RED VELVET SWING. 1955, Fox. No. 31. Walter Reisch and Charles Brackett.

*THE GIRL IN WHITE. 1952, MGM. Irmgard Von Cube and Allen Vincent.

A GIRL NAMED TAMIKO. 1962, Paramount. No. 27. Edward Anhalt.

THE GIRL NEXT DOOR. 1953, Fox. No. 19. Isobel Lennart.

THE GIRL NOBODY KNEW. [1966]. No. 32.

*THE GIRL SAID NO. 1930, MGM. [Sarah Y. Mason].

THE GIRL WHO ALMOST GOT AWAY. See MAN'S FAVORITE SPORT.

THE GIRL WHO DARED. cc. 1944, Republic. John K. Butler.

*THE GIRL WHO HAD EVERYTHING. 1953, MGM. Art Cohn.

GIRLS' DORMITORY. 1936, Fox. Gene Markey.

GIRLS OF THE BIG HOUSE. cc. 1945, Republic. Houston Branch.

GIT ALONG LITTLE DOGIES. cc. 1937, Republic. Dorrell and Stuart McGowan.

*GIVE A GIRL A BREAK. 1953, MGM. Albert Hackett and Frances Goodrich.

GIVE MY REGARDS TO BROADWAY. 1948, Fox. No. 19. Samuel Hoffen-
     stein and Elizabeth Reinhardt.

GLAMOUR BOY #2. Rev. estimating scr. 1951, Paramount. [Bert
     Granet and Charles E. Robert]. SWG by Bradford Ropes and
     Val Burton.

THE GLASS KEY. 1935, Paramount. [Kathryn Scola and Kubec Glasmon].

*GLASS SLIPPER. And budgeting files. 1955, MGM. Helen Deutsch.

GLORY ALLEY. 1952, MGM. No. 37. Art Cohn.

*GLORY ALLEY. 1952, MGM. Art Cohn.

GLORY BOY. 1971, Cinerama. [Stanford Whitmore].

GO FOR BROKE. 1951, MGM. Robert Pirosh.

*GO FOR BROKE. 1951, MGM. Robert Pirosh.

GOBS AND GALS. 1952, Republic. Arthur T. Horman.

THE GO-BETWEEN. 1971, Columbia. Harold Pinter.

THE GODFATHER. 1972, Paramount. [Francis Ford Coppola and Mario
     Puzo].

GOING HOME. 1971, MGM. [Lawrence B. Marcus].

GOING MY WAY. 1944, Paramount. No. 75. Frank Butler and Frank
     Cavett.

GOIN' TO TOWN. [1944], [RKO]. [Charles E. Roberts and Charles R.
     Marion.

GOLDEN GIRL. Rev. final scr. 1951, Fox. No. 19. Walter Bullock,
     Charles O'Neal and Gladys Lehman.

THE GOLDEN HERD. Est. sht. scr. 1952, Republic. [Steve
     Fisher].

THE GOLDEN JOURNEY. 2 outlines, 2 treatments and 4 drafts. n. d.
     No. 27. [Edward Anhalt].

THE GOLDEN ONES. [1968], [Universal]. No. 41. [Franklin Coen and
     Charles Kaufman].

GONE WITH THE WIND. 2 copies. 1939, MGM. Sidney Howard.

*THE GOOD EARTH. 1937, MGM. Talbot Jennings, Tess Slesinger and
    Claudine West.

*GOOD NEWS. 1947, MGM. Betty Comden and Adolph Green.

*THE GOOD OLD SUMMERTIME. 1949, MGM. Albert Hackett, Frances
    Goodrich and Ivan Tors.

GOOD OLD SUMMERTIME. 1949, MGM. Frances Goodrich, Albert Hackett
    and Ivan Tors.

GOOD TIMES. 1967, Columbia. Tony Barrett.

GOODBYE CHARLIE. 1964, Fox. No. 50. Harry Kurnitz.

GOODBYE MY FANCY. Rev. final scr. 1951, Warner Bros. Ivan Goff
    and Ben Roberts.

GOODNIGHT, SWEETHEART. cc. 1944, Republic. Isabel Dawn and Jack
    Townley.

THE GOOSE GIRL. Scenario. [1914], Paramount. No. 8. [Harold
    McGrath].

GOOSE STEP. 1939, Prods. Pic. Corp. Shepard Traube.

THE GOVERNOR'S LADY. Synopsis. [1915]. No. 8.

THE GRADUATE. 1967, Avco Embassy. Calder Willingham and Buck
    Henry.

GRADUATION AT GETTYSBURG. Treatment. n. d. No. 41. [Philip
    Dunne and Sidney Harmon].

GRAND CANYON TRAIL. cc. 4 copies and trailer cc. 1948, Republic.
    Gerald Geraghty.

GRANDPA GOES TO TOWN. cc. 2 copies. 1940, Republic. Jack Townley.

THE GREAT ADVENTURES OF CAPTAIN KIDD. Serial. 1953, Columbia.
    George Plympton and Arthur Hoerl.

THE GREAT AMERICAN BROADCAST. 1941, Fox. No. 19. Don Ettlinger,
    Edwin Blum, Robert Ellis and Helen Logan.

*THE GREAT AMERICAN PASTIME. 1956, MGM. Nathaniel Benchley.

THE GREAT BANK ROBBERY   TITLES INDEX

THE GREAT BANK ROBBERY. 1969, Warner Bros. William Peter.

*THE GREAT CARUSO. 1951, MGM. Sonya Levien and William Ludwig.

*THE GREAT DIAMOND ROBBERY. 1953, MGM. Laslo Vadray and Martin
        Rackin.

THE GREAT ESCAPE. See Interview with John Sturges.

THE GREAT FLAMARION. cc and trailer cc. 1945, Republic. Anne
        Wigton, Heinz Herald and Richard Weil.

THE GREAT MAN. 1956, Universal. No. 26. Al Morgan and Jose
        Ferrar.

THE GREAT MAN'S LADY. 1942, Paramount. W. L. River.

*THE GREAT MEADOW. 1931, MGM. [Charles Brabin and Edith Ellis].

THE GREAT MOMENT. See GREAT WITHOUT GLORY.

THE GREAT NORTHFIELD MINNESOTA RAID. 1972, Universal. Philip
        Kaufman.

*THE GREAT SINNER. 1949, MGM. Ladislas Fodor and Christopher
        Isherwood.

GREAT STAGECOACH ROBBERY. cc. 1945, Republic. Randall Faye.

THE GREAT TRAIN ROBBERY. cc. 1941, Republic. Olive Cooper, Gar-
        nett Weston and Robert T. Shannon.

THE GREAT WALTZ. 1972, MGM. [Andrew Stone].

GREAT WITHOUT GLORY. 1 copy-1939; 1 copy-1942. Rel. as THE GREAT
        MOMENT. See also TRIUMPH OVER PAIN. 1944, Paramount.
        [Preston Sturges].

THE GREATEST SHOW ON EARTH. 1952, Paramount. No. 8. Frederic M.
        Frank, Barre Lyndon and Theodore St. John.

*GREED. 1924, Metro Goldwyn. [Erich von Stroheim and June Mathis].

THE GREEN BERETS. 1968, Warner Bros. James Lee Barrett.

THE GREEN BUDDHA. cc and trailer cc. 1955, Republic. [Paul
        Erickson].

GREEN DOLPHIN STREET. 3 copies. 1947, MGM. Samson Raphaelson.

*GREEN DOLPHIN STREET. 1947, MGM. Samson Raphaelson.

*GREEN FIRE. And budgeting files. 1954, MGM. Ivan Goff and Ben
     Roberts.

GREEN MANSIONS. Estimating scr. [1934], [RKO]. No. 8. [John L.
     Balderston].

*GREEN MANSIONS. 1959, MGM. Dorothy Kingsley.

GREEN PASTURES. 1936, Warner Bros. Marc Connelly.

*THE GREEN YEARS. 1946, MGM. Robert Ardrey and Sonya Levien.

GREENWICH VILLAGE. 1944, Fox. No. 19. Earl Baldwin and Walter
     Bullock.

THE GRINGOS. See THE DAY OF THE LANDGRABBERS.

GRISSLY'S MILLIONS. 1945, Republic. Muriel Roy Bolton.

THE GRISSOM GANG. 1971, Cinerama. Leon Griffiths.

A GROSS OF PINK TELEPHONES. n. d. No. 41. [Philip Dunne and W. H.
     Menger].

GROUND CREW. Estimating scr. [1938]. No. 66. [Lionel Houser],

*GROUNDS FOR MARRIAGE. 1950, MGM. Allen Rivkin and Laura Kerr.

GRUMPY. Scenario. 1923, Paramount. No. 8. [Clara Beranger].

GRUMPY. 1923, Paramount. [Horace Hodges].

GUESS WHO'S COMING TO DINNER. 2 copies. 1967, Columbia. No. 37.
     William Rose.

*GUN GLORY. And budgeting files. 1957, MGM. William Ludwig.

GUN LORDS OF STIRRUP BASIN. cc. 1937, Republic. George Plympton
     and Fred Myton.

A GUN FIGHT. See Interview with Lamont Johnson.

GUNFIGHT AT O.K. CORRAL. 1957, Paramount. Leon Uris.

GUNFIRE AT INDIAN GAP. cc. 1958, Republic. Barry Shipman.

THE GURU. 1969. [James Ivory and R. Prawer Jhabvala].

A GUY NAMED JOE. 1943, MGM. No. 75. Dalton Trumbo.

*A GUY NAMED JOE. 1943, MGM. Dalton Trumbo.

THE GUY WHO SANK THE NAVY. [1950]. No. 75. [Allan Scott].

*GUYS AND DOLLS. 1955, MGM. Joseph Mankiewicz. See also Interview
     with David Golding.

GWANGI THE GREAT. William Bast.

*GYPSY COLT. 1954, MGM. Martin Berkeley.

THE GYPSY MOTHS. 1969, MGM. William Hanley.

H. M. PULHAM, ESQ. 1941, MGM. No. 25. Elizabeth Hill and King
     Vidor.

HAIL HERO. 1969, National General. David Manber.

*HALF A HERO. 1953, MGM. Max Shulman.

HALF A SIXPENCE. 1968, Paramount. Beverly Cross.

THE HALF-WAY HOUSE. Draft sht. scr. 1945, AFE Corp. [Thomas E. B.
     Clarke].

A HALL OF MIRRORS. [1969], [Paramount]. [Robert Stone].

*HALLELUJAH. 1929, MGM. See also materials in the King Vidor Col-
     lection, No. 25.

HALLS OF ANGER. 1970, United Artists. [John Shaner and Al Ramrus].

HAMMERHEAD. 1968, Columbia. William Bast and Herbert Baker.

HANG 'EM HIGH. 1968, United Artists. Leonard Freeman and Mel
     Goldberg.

THE HANGING TREE. 2 copies. 1959, Warner Bros. Wendell Mayes and
     Halsted Welles.

HANNIBAL BROOKS. 1969, United Artists. Dick Clement and Ian
     LeFrenais.

THE HAPPENING. See Interviews with Elliot Silverstein.

THE HAPPIEST MILLIONAIRE. Sht. scr. 1967, Buena Vista. A. J.
     Carothers.

HAPPY GO LUCKY. cc. 1936, Republic. Raymond Schrock, Norman
     Panama and Melvin Frank.

*THE HAPPY ROAD. 1957, MGM. Arthur Julian, Joseph Morhaim and
     Harry Kurnitz.

THE HAPPY TIME. 1952, Columbia. No. 31. Earl Felton.

*THE HAPPY YEARS. 1950, MGM. Harry Ruskin.

HARD BARGAIN. 3 copies. [1948]. No. 32.

HARD CONTRACT. 1969, Fox. [S. Lee Pogostin]. See Interview with
     S. Lee Pogostin.

HARD ROCK HARRIGAN. 1935, Fox. No. 68. C. Furthman, R. L. Schrock
     and Dan Jarrett.

THE HARP THAT ONCE. Rel. as THE RECKONING. 1971, Columbia. [John
     McGrath].

HARVEY. 1950, Universal. No. 32. Mary Chase and Oscar Brodney.

*THE HARVEY GIRLS. 1946, MGM. Edmund Beloin, Nathaniel Curtis,
     Harry Crane, James O'Hanlon and Samson Raphaelson.

THE HASTY HEART. 1949, Warner Bros. Ranald MacDougall.

*THE HAUNTED STRANGLER. 1958, MGM. [Jan Read and John C. Cooper].

THE HAUNTING. 1963, MGM. No. 49. Nelson Gidding. See also
     Interview with Robert Wise.

HAVANA ROSE. Estimating and sht. scr. and cc. 1951, Republic.
     Charles E. Roberts and Jack Townley.

HAWAII. 1966, United Artists. No. 37. Dalton Trumbo and Daniel
     Taradash.

HAWAII CALLS. 1938, RKO. No. 68. Wanda Tuchoch.

HAWAIIAN BUCKAROO. 1938, Fox. No. 68. Dan Jarrett.

HE WHO GETS SLAPPED. [1937], [MGM]. No. 8. [John L. Balderston].

HEAD. 1968, Columbia. Bob Rapelson and Jack Nicholson.

HEADLINE HUNTERS. 2 copies and cc. Remake of BEHIND THE NEWS
        [1940]. 1955, Republic. Frederic Louis Fox and John K.
        Butler.

THE HEARING. n. d. No. 50. [David Weisbart].

*THE HEART OF A CHILD. 1920, Metro. [Ross Wills].

HEART OF THE GOLDEN WEST. cc. 1942, Republic. Earl Felton.

HEART OF THE RIO GRANDE. cc. 1942, Republic. Lillie Hayward and
        Winston Miller.

HEART OF THE ROCKIES. 1937, Republic. Jack Natteford and Oliver
        Drake.

HEART OF VIRGINIA. cc. Also PRIDE OF VIRGINIA. 1948, Republic.
        Jerry Sackheim.

*HEARTS ARE TRUMPS. 1920, MGM. [June Mathis].

HEARTS IN BONDAGE. cc. 1936, Republic. Bernard Schubert and
        Olive Cooper.

*HEAVEN ON EARTH. 1927, MGM. [Harvey Gates].

HEAVEN WITH A GUN. [1969], MGM. Richard Carr.

*THE HEAVENLY BODY. 1943, MGM. Michael Arlen and Walter Reisch.

HEIDI. 1937, Fox. Walter Ferris and Julien Josephson.

THE HEIR TO THE HOORAH. Scenario and photoplay. 1916, Paramount.
        No. 8.

THE HEIRESS. 1949, Paramount. Ruth and Augustus Goetz.

*HELD IN TRUST. 1920, Metro. [Sarah Y. Mason].

HELEN OF TROY. 1955, Warner Bros. No. 49. John Twist and Hugh
        Gray.

HELL AND HIGH WATER. 1954, Fox. No. 50. Jesse L. Lasky and
        Samuel Fuller.

*HELL BELOW. 1933, MGM. [Laird Doyle and Ray Schrock].

*HELL DIVERS. 1931, MGM. [Harvey Gates and Malcolm Stuart Boylan].

HELL IN THE PACIFIC. See Interview with Booker McClay.

HELL SHIP MUTINY. 1958, Republic. De Vallon Scott and Wells Root.

THE HELL WITH HEROES. 1968, Universal. Halsted Welles and Harold
    Livingston.

HELLFIGHTERS. (cc). 1968, Universal. Clair Huffaker.

HELLFIRE. And 2 copies of cc. 1949, Republic. Dorrell and Stuart
    McGowan.

HELLO, DOLLY. See materials in Ernest Lehman Collection, No. 19.

HELLO DOWN THERE. 1968, Paramount. John McGreevey and Frank
    Telford.

HELLO, FRISCO, HELLO. Final sht. scr. 1948, Fox. No. 19. Robert
    Ellis, Helen Logan and Richard Macaulay.

HELL'S CROSSROADS. cc. 1957, Republic. John K. Butler and Barry
    Shipman.

HELL'S HALF ACRE. cc. 1954, Republic. Steve Fisher.

HELL'S OUTPOST. 2 copies and cc. 1955, Republic. Kenneth Gamet.

HENRY ALDRICH, EDITOR. 1942, Paramount. Val Burton and Muriel Roy
    Bolton.

HENRY V. 1958, Rank. Lawrence Olivier.

*HER CARDBOARD LOVER. 1942, MGM. Jacques Deval, Anthony Veiller
    and William H. Wright.

HER CONSCIENCE. 1946, Warner Bros. [Joseph Than and John Collier].

*HER HIGHNESS AND THE BELLBOY. 1945, MGM. Richard Connell and
    Gladys Lehman.

HER MAJESTY'S CANNIBALS. n. d. No. 41. [Philip Dunne and Marvin
    Schwartz].

*HER 12 MEN. 1954, MGM. William S. Roberts and Laura Z. Hobson.

HERE WE GO   TITLES INDEX

HERE WE GO ROUND THE MULBERRY BUSH. 1968, Lopert. Hunter Davies.

HERE'S TO ROMANCE. Final sht. scr. 1935, Fox. No. 19.

HEROES OF THE HILLS. 1938, Republic. Betty Burbridge and Stanley
        Roberts.

HI NEIGHBOR. cc. 1942, Republic. Dorrell and Stuart McGowan.

HIDDEN GUNS. 2 copies. 1956, Republic. Sam Roeca and Al Gannaway.

*HIDE-OUT. 1934, MGM. [Albert Hackett and Frances Goodrich].

*THE HIGH COST OF LOVING. 1958, MGM. Rip Van Ronkel and Milo O.
        Frank, Jr.

HIGH IRON. Treatment and cc; 2 copies. 1954, Republic.
        [Frederick Louis Fox].

HIGH NOON. 1952, United Artists. Carl Foreman.

HIGH PLAINS DRIFTER. 1973, Universal. [Ernest Tidyman].

*HIGH SCHOOL CONFIDENTIAL. 1958, MGM. Lewis Meltzer and Robert
        Blees.

*HIGH SOCIETY. 1956, MGM. John Patrick.

HIGH SOCIETY. 2 copies. 1956, MGM. No. 15. No. 11. John
        Patrick.

HIGH TIME. 1960, Fox. No. 19. Tom and Frank Waldman.

*THE HIGH WALL. 1947, MGM. Sydney Boehm and Lester Cole.

HIGHWAYS BY NIGHT. 1942, RKO. Lynn Root and Frank Fenton.

HILDA CRANE. 1956, Fox. No. 41. Philip Dunne.

*HILLS OF HOME. 1948, MGM. William Ludwig.

THE HILLS OF HOME. 1948, MGM. No. 66. William Ludwig.

*THE HIRED GUN. 1957, MGM. Buckley Angell and David Lang.

HIS BROTHER'S WIFE. 1936, MGM. Leon Gordon and John Meehan.

*HIS GLORIOUS NIGHT. 1929, MGM. [Willard Mack].

THE HIT PARADE. 1937, Republic. Bradford Ropes and Sam Ornitz.

*HIT THE DECK. 1955, MGM. William Ludwig and Sonya Levien.

HITCHHIKE TO HAPPINESS. cc. 1945, Republic. Jack Townley.

HITLER: BEAST OF BERLIN. n. d., [Paramount]. [Shepard Traube].

THE HITLER GANG. 1944, Paramount. No. 94. Frances Goodrich and
    Albert Hackett.

THE HOAX. 1972, All-Scope International. [Kevin Davis].

*THE HOAXTERS. Documentary. 1953, MGM. Herman Hoffman.

HOLD HIGH THE TORCH. [1944], No. 66. [Lionel Houser].

A HOLE IN THE HEAD. Cast and credits, synopsis and prod. notes.
    1959, United Artists. No. 32. Arnold Schulman.

HOLIDAY FOR LOVERS. 1959, Fox. No. 26. Luther Davis. See also
    materials in the David Weisbart Collection, No. 50.

*HOLIDAY IN MEXICO. 1946, MGM. Isobel Lennart.

HOLIDAY INN. 1942, Paramount. Claude Binyon.

HOLLYWOOD AND RETURN. [1937]. No. 8. [William C. DeMille].

*HOLLYWOOD PARTY. 1934, MGM. [Howard Dietz and Arthur Kober].

HOLLYWOOD STADIUM MYSTERY. 1938, Republic. Stuart Palmer, Darrell
    and Stuart McGowan.

HOME OF THE BRAVE. 1949, United Artists. Carl Foreman.

*HOME STUFF. 1921, Metro.

*HOMECOMING. 1948, MGM. Paul Osborn.

HOMESTEADERS OF PARADISE VALLEY. cc. 1947, Republic. Earle Snell.

*HOMETOWN STORY. 1951, MGM. Arthur Pierson.

HOMICIDE FOR THREE. cc. 1948, Republic. Bradbury Foote.

HONEYCHILE. cc and sht. scr. and story outline and estimating scr.
    1951, Republic. Jack Townley and Charles E. Roberts.

*HONEYMOON. 1929, MGM. [Richard Schayer and George O'Hara].

*HONKY TONK. 1941, MGM. Marguerite Roberts and John Sanford.

HONOLULU HOLIDAY. cc and rev. sht. scr. [1938], Republic.

HOODLUM EMPIRE. cc and trailer cc. 1952, Republic. Bob Considine
        and Bruce Manning.

*THE HOODLUM SAINT. 1946, MGM. Frank Wead and James Hill.

HOOK, LINE, AND SINKER. 1969, Columbia. Rod Amateau.

HOPALONG CASSIDY. 1935, Paramount. [Doris Shroeder].

*THE HOPE. 1920, Metro. [A. S. Le Vino].

THE HORRIBLE AND UNNATURAL REBELLION OF DANIEL SHAYS. n. d. No. 41.
        [Sidney Harmon and Philip Dunne].

HOSTILE GUNS. 1967, Paramount. Sloane Nibley and Steve Fisher.

HOT MILLIONS. 1968, MGM. Ira Wallach and Peter Ustinov.

THE HOT ROCK. 1972, Fox. [William Goldman].

HOT SATURDAY. 1932, Paramount. [Harvey Fergusson].

HOT SPELL. Orig. title NEXT OF KIN. 2nd draft and rev. final scr.
        1958, Paramount. James Poe.

*HOT SUMMER NIGHT. 1957, MGM. Morton Fine and David Friedkin.

HOTEL FOR TERROR. Treatment. [1943]. No. 0. Irving Wallace.

HOUDINI. 2 copies. 1953, Paramount. No. 94. Philip Yordan.

HOUR OF THE GUN. Outline, treatment and final. 1967, United
        Artists. No. 27. Edward Anhalt.

HOUSE OF A THOUSAND CANDLES. 1936, Republic. H. W. Hanemann and
        Endre Bohem.

*THE HOUSE OF NUMBERS. And budgeting files. 1957, MGM. Russell
        Rouse and Don Mankiewicz.

HOW DO I LOVE THEE. See Interview with Robert Enders.

HOW GREEN WAS MY VALLEY. 1941, Fox. No. 41. Philip Dunne.

HOW SWEET IT IS!. 1968, National General. Garry Marshall.

HOW TO BE A WOLF. Estimating scr. and final draft and 1st draft
    cont. [1946], [RKO]. [Charles E. Roberts].

HOW TO BE VERY, VERY POPULAR. 1955, Fox. No. 19. Nunnally
    Johnson.

*THE HUCKSTERS. 1947, MGM. Luther Davis.

*HUDDLE. 1932, MGM. [Walton Hall Smith and C. Gardner Sullivan].

HULLABALOO. 1940, MGM. Nat Perrin.

*THE HUMAN COMEDY. 1943, MGM. No. 75. Howard Estabrook.

THE HUMAN COMEDY. 1943, MGM. Howard Estabrook.

HUMPHREY TAKES A CHANCE. 1950, Monogram. No. 32. Henry Blankfort.

THE HUNCHBACK OF NOTRE DAME. 1939, RKO. No. 17. Sonya Levien.

*HUNGRY HEARTS. 1922, Goldwyn. [Julien Josephson].

HURRY, CHARLIE, HURRY. Final and estimating scr. 1941, RKO. Paul
    Gerard Smith.

HURRY SUNDOWN. 1967, Paramount. No. 26. Thomas C. Ryon and Horton
    Foote.

HUSH-A-BYE. [1969], [MGM].

*I ACCUSE. 1958, MGM. Gore Vidal.

I AM LEGEND. [1970], [Warner Bros.]. John William Corrington and
    William Peter Blatty.

I COVER THE UNDERWORLD. cc and trailer cc. Remake of GANGS OF NEW
    YORK. 1938. 1955, Republic. John K. Butler.

THE I DON'T CARE GIRL. Rev. final scr. 1953, Fox. No. 19.
    Walter Bullock.

*I DOOD IT. 1943, MGM. Fred Saidy and Sig Herzig.

I DREAM OF JEANNIE. 1952, Republic. Alan LeMay.

I HEAR YOU CALLING ME   TITLES INDEX

I HEAR YOU CALLING ME. [1930]. No. 19. [Sonya Levien].

*I LOVE MELVIN. 1953, MGM. George Wells.

I MET HIM IN PARIS. 1937, Paramount. Claude Binyon.

I WANT TO LIVE!. 2 copies. 1958, United Artists. No. 91. No. 49.
    Nelson Gidding and Don Mankiewicz.

*I WAS A TEENAGE FRANKENSTEIN. 1957, American International.
    Kenneth Langtry.

*I WAS KIDNAPPED. [1958], [MGM]. [Robert Smith].

I WONDER WHO'S KISSING HER NOW. Rev. shooting final. 1947, Fox.
    No. 19. Lewis R. Foster.

ICE CAPADES. 1941, Republic. Jack Townley, Robert Harari and
    Olive Cooper.

ICE CAPADES REVIEW. cc. 1942, Republic. Bradford Ropes and
    Gertrude Purcell.

ICEBOUND. 1924, Paramount. Play by Owen Davis and scr. Clara
    Beranger.

ICELAND. Sht. final scr. 1942, Fox. No. 19. Robert Ellis
    and Helen Logan.

IDAHO. 1943, Republic. Roy Chanslor and Olive Cooper.

*IDLE RICH. From play, White Collars. 1929, MGM. [Clara
    Beranger].

IF. 1969, Paramount. David Sherwin.

IF HE HOLLERS, LET HIM GO. 1968, Cinerama. Charles Martin.

IF I'M LUCKY. Final scr. 1946, Fox. No. 19. Snag Werris, Robert
    Ellis, Helen Logan and George Bricker.

*IF WINTER COMES. 1947, MGM. Marguerite Roberts and Arthur
    Wimperis.

ILLEGAL ENTRY. 1949, Universal. Joel Malone.

THE ILLUSTRATED MAN. 1968, Warner Bros. Howard B. Kreitsek.

I'LL GET BY. 2nd rev. sht. final. 1950, Fox. No. 19. Mary Loos
      and Richard Sale.

I'LL NEVER FORGET WHAT'S 'IS NAME. 1968, Regional Film Dist. Peter
      Draper.

IMAGINATION. [1947]. No. 22. [Garson Kanin and Ruth Gordon].

*IMITATION GENERAL. 1958, MGM. William Bowers.

IMITATION OF LIFE. 1959, Universal. [John M. Stahl], Eleanore
      Griffin and Allan Scott.

THE IMMORTAL SERGEANT. 1943, Fox. Lamar Trotti. See also mate-
      rials in the John Stahl Collection, No. 11.

I'M DYING TO LIVE. And story outline and 1st draft cont. and 2nd
      draft. [1941]. [Charles E. Roberts and George Jeske].

I'M NO ANGEL. 1933, Paramount. [Mae West].

IMPACT. 1949, United Artists. No. 94. Jay Dratler and Dorothy
      Reid.

IMPASSE. 1969, United Artists. [John C. Higgins].

IN COLD BLOOD. See Interview with Richard Brooks.

IN ENEMY COUNTRY. 5 drafts. 1968, Universal. No. 27. Edward
      Anhalt and Alfred Hayes.

*IN GAY MADRID. 1930, MGM. [Bess Meredyth, Salisbury Field and
      Edwin Justus Mayer].

IN LOVE AND WAR. 3 copies. Also THE BIG WAR. 1958, Fox. No.
      41. No. 27. Edward Anhalt.

IN OLD ARIZONA. 1929, Fox. [Tom Barry].

IN OLD KENTUCKY. 1935, Fox. [Sam Hellman].

IN OLD SACRAMENTO. See FLAME OF SACRAMENTO.

IN OLD VIENNA. 1956, Republic. James A. Fitzpatrick.

IN SEARCH OF GREGORY. 1970, Universal. [Tonino Guerra and Lucille
      Laks].

INADMISSABLE EVIDENCE   TITLES INDEX

INADMISSABLE EVIDENCE. 1968, Paramount. John Osborne.

INHUMAN GROUND. [1942], [MGM]. No. 8. [Clara Beranger].

THE INNOCENTS. Rev. draft. 1961, Fox. William Archibald and
        Truman Capote. See also Interview with Jack Clayton.

INSIDE STRAIGHT. 1951, MGM. Guy Trosper.

*INSIDE STRAIGHT. 1951, MGM. Guy Trosper.

THE INSPECTOR. [1961]. No. 41. [Nelson Gidding].

INTERLOCHEN. [1940], [Paramount].

INTERNATIONAL LADY. 1941, Universal. Howard Estabrook.

*INTERRUPTED MELODY. 2 copies. 1955, MGM. No. 15. William
        Ludwig and Sonya Levien.

INTERRUPTED MELODY. 1955, MGM. William Ludwig and Sonya Levien.

INVISIBLE AVENGER. (cc). 1958, Republic. [George Bellak and Betty
        Jeffries].

*THE INVISIBLE BOY. 1957, MGM. Cyril Hume.

THE INVISIBLE INFORMER. cc. 1946, Republic. Sherman T. Lowe.

*INVITATION. 1952, MGM. Paul Osborn.

INVITATION TO A GUNFIGHTER. 1964, United Artists. No. 37. Richard
        and Elizabeth Wilson.

*INVITATION TO THE DANCE. 1956, MGM.

IRIS. [1956]. No. 50. [Max Benoff].

IRISH EYES ARE SMILING. Rev. temp. scr. 1944, Fox. No. 19. Earl
        Baldwin and John Tucker Battle.

IRON MOUNTAIN TRAIL. 2 copies. 1953, Republic. Gerald Geraghty.

*THE IRON PETTICOAT. 1956, MGM. Ben Hecht.

IS THERE A DUCHESS IN THE HOUSE? Estimating scr. [1954], [Repub-
        lic]. [Jack Townley and Lillie Hayward].

ISABEL. 1968, Paramount. Paul Almond.

ISLAND OF LOST SOULS. Orig. title LOST ISLAND. 1933, Paramount.
[Waldemar Young and Philip Wylie].

ISLAND OF THE LOST. 1st and 2nd rev. drafts. 1967, Paramount.
[Richard Carlson].

ISLE OF THE DEAD. 1945, RKO. Ardel Wray and Josef Mischel.

*IT CAN'T HAPPEN HERE. n. d., MGM.

IT COULD HAPPEN TO YOU. 1937, Republic. Samuel Ornitz and
Nathanael West.

IT HAPPENED ON FIFTH AVENUE. 1947, Allied Artists. No. 75.
Everett Freeman and [Vick Knight].

IT HAPPENED ONE NIGHT. 1934, Columbia. No. 63. [Robert Riskin].

IT HAPPENED OUT WEST. 1937, Fox. No. 68. Earle Snell and John
Roberts.

IT SEEMS THERE WERE THESE TWO IRISHMEN. [1963]. Marion Hargrove.

THE ITALIAN JOB. 1968, Paramount. Troy Kennedy Martin.

*IT'S A BIG COUNTRY. 1951, MGM. William Ludwig, Helen Deutsch, Ray
Chordes, Isobel Lennart, Allen Rivkin, Dorothy Kingsley,
Dore Schary and George Wells.

IT'S A BIG COUNTRY. See above for writers. 1951, MGM. No. 66.

IT'S A DOG'S LIFE. See BAR SINISTER. [1955].

IT'S A MAD, MAD, MAD, MAD WORLD. 2 copies. 1963, United Artists.
No. 26. No. 37. William and Tanya Rose.

*IT'S A WISE CHILD. [1931], MGM. [Laurence E. Johnson].

*IT'S ALWAYS FAIR WEATHER. 1955, MGM. Betty Comden and Adolph
Green.

*IVANHOE. 1952, MGM. Noel Langley.

JACK OF DIAMONDS. Final scr. 1967, MGM. Jack DeWitt and Sandy
Howard.

JACKASS MAIL   TITLES INDEX

*JACKASS MAIL. 1942, MGM. Lawrence Hazard.

THE JACKIE ROBINSON STORY. 1950, Eagle Lion. No. 94. Lawrence
    Taylor and Arthur Mann.

JAGUAR. 3 copies. cc. 1956, Republic. John Fenton Murray and
    Benedict Freedman.

*JAILHOUSE ROCK. 1957, MGM. Guy Trosper.

JAMBOREE. cc. 1944, Republic. Jack Townley.

JED HARRIS #1. Rough draft. [1941]. No. 8. [Irwin Shaw].

*JENNY LIND. [1931], MGM. [Hans Kraly and Claudia West].

*JEOPARDY. 1953, MGM. Mel Dinelli.

JERUSALEM JERUSALEM. [1970], [MGM]. Troy Kennedy Martin.

JESSE JAMES. Final scr. 1938, Fox. Nunnally Johnson.

JESSE JAMES AT BAY. cc. 1941, Republic. James R. Webb.

JEZEBEL. 1938, Warner Bros. Clements Ripley, Abem Finkel and John
    Huston.

JOAN OF ARC. 1948, RKO. Maxwell Anderson and Andrew Solt.

JOAN OF OZARK. 2 copies. 1942, Republic. Robert Harari, Eve
    Greene and Jack Townley.

JOANNA. 1968, Fox. [Michael Sarne].

JOE KIDD. 1972, Universal. [Elmore Leonard].

JOHN AND MARY. 1969, Fox. John Mortimer.

JOHNNY APOLLO. 1940, Fox. No. 41. Philip Dunne and Roland Brown.

THE JOHNNY BRODERICK STORY. Treatment, notes, and rev. estimating
    scr. [1950], [RKO]. [Robert H. Andrews].

JOLLY PINK JUNGLE. Final scr. [1967], [Universal]. [Charles
    Williams].

JOSETTE. Sht. final scr. 1938, Fox. No. 19. James Edward Grant.

*THE JOURNEY. 1959, MGM. George Tabori.

*JOURNEY FOR MARGARET. 1942, MGM. David Hertz and William Ludwig.

JOURNEY FOR MARGARET. 1942, MGM. David Hertz and William Ludwig.

JOURNEY TO SHILOH. Rev. final scr. 1968, Universal. Gene Coon.

THE JOY OF LIVING. 1938, RKO. No. 65. Gene Towne, Graham Baker
    and Allan Scott.

JOYRIDE. cc. 1958, Allied Artists. Christopher Knopf.

JUAREZ. 1939, Warner Bros. John Huston, Aeneas MacKenzie and Wolf-
    gang Reinhardt. See also materials in the William Dieterle
    Collection, No. 17.

JUDGE PRIEST. 1934, Fox. [I. S. Cobb].

JUDGEMENT AT NURENBERG. See Interview with Abby Mann.

*JULIA MISBEHAVES. 1948, MGM. William Ludwig, Harry Ruskin and
    Arthur Wimperis.

*JULIE. 1956, MGM. Andrew L. Stone.

*JULIUS CAESAR. 1953, MGM. Joseph L. Mankiewicz.

JULIUS CAESAR. 1953, MGM. No. 26. Play by William Shakespeare;
    sht. scr. by Joseph L. Mankiewicz.

JUMPING JACKS. 1952, Paramount. No. 37. Robert Lees, Fred
    Rinaldo and Herbert Baker.

JUPITER'S DARLING. 2 copies. 1955, MGM. No. 15. Dorothy
    Kingsley.

*JUPITER'S DARLING. And budgeting files. 1955, MGM. Dorothy
    Kingsley.

*JUST A GIGOLO. 1931, MGM. [Hans Kraly, Richard Schayer and
    Claudine West.

JUST IMAGINE. 1930, Fox. No. 19.

*JUST THIS ONCE. 1952, MGM. Sidney Sheldon.

JUVENILE JUNGLE. cc. 1958, Republic. Arthur T. Horman.

THE KANSAS CITY BOMBER   TITLES INDEX

THE KANSAS CITY BOMBER. 1972, MGM. [Thomas Rickman and Calvin
        Clements].

*KEEP YOUR POWDER DRY. 1945, MGM. Mary C. McCall, Jr. and George
        Bruce.

*KEEPING COMPANY. 1941, MGM. Harry Ruskin, James H. Hill and
        Adrian Scott.

KENNER. Orig. title THE YEAR OF THE CRICKET. 1969, MGM. Harold
        Clemins and John R. Long.

THE KENTUCKIAN. Treatment [1951]. [1955], [United Artists].
        No. 0. Irving Wallace.

KENTUCKY KERNALS. 1934, RKO. [Bert Kalmar and Harry Ruby].

KEY. See Interview with Carl Foreman.

*KEY TO THE CITY. 1950, MGM. Robert Riley Crutcher.

THE KEYS OF THE KINGDOM. 1944, Fox. Joseph L. Mankiewicz and
        Nunnally Johnson. See also materials in the John Stahl
        Collection, No. 11.

THE KID FROM CLEVELAND. cc. 1949, Republic. John Bright.

KIDNAPPED. 1938, Fox. Sonya Levien, Eleanor Harris, Ernest Pascal
        and Edwin Harvey Blum.

*KILDARE #10. [1941], MGM.

KILL A DRAGON. 1967, United Artists. George W. Schenck and
        William Marks.

*KILLER MC COY. 1947, MGM. Frederick Hazlitt Brennan.

KIND LADY. 1935, MGM. Bernard Schubert.

KIND LADY. 2 copies. 1951, MGM. Jerry Davis, Charles Bennett and
        Edward Chodorov.

THE KING AND I. Rev. final scr. 1956, Fox. No. 19. Ernest
        Lehman.

KING OF BURLESQUE. Final scr. 1935, Fox. No. 19. [Gene Markey
        and Harry Tugend].

KING OF THE RACE TRACK. cc and trailer cc. Re-issue of THAT'S MY
        MAN [1947]. 1953, Republic. Steve Fisher and Bradley King.

KING OF THE ROYAL MOUNTED. 1936, Fox. [Republic per SWG]. No. 68.
        Earle Snell and [D. Swift and Zane Grey].

*KING SOLOMON'S MINES. 1950, MGM. Helen Deutsch.

THE KING'S PIRATE. Final draft scr. 1967, Universal. Joseph Hoff-
        man, Paul Wayne and Aeneas MacKenzie.

*THE KING'S THIEF. 1955, MGM. Christopher Knopf.

KIRSTIE. n. d. No. 66. [Alan Scott].

*KISMET. Stills available in the William Dieterle Collection,
        No. 17. 1944, MGM. John Meehan.

*KISMET. 1955, MGM. Charles Lederer and Luther Davis.

*THE KISS. 1929, MGM. [Hans Kraly].

KISS ME DEADLY. 1955, United Artists. No. 94. A. I. Bezzerides.

*KISS ME KATE. 1953, MGM. Dorothy Kingsley.

KISS MY FIRM BUT PLIANT LIPS. [1967], [MGM]. [Don Greenburg and
        Ernest Pintoff].

KISS OF FIRE. 1955, Universal. Franklin Coen and Richard Collins.

KISS THEM FOR ME. Rev. final scr. 1957, Fox. No. 19. Julius J.
        Epstein.

*THE KISSING BANDIT. 1948, MGM. Isobel Lennart and John Briard
        Harding.

KITTEN ON THE KEYS. See DO YOU LOVE ME?

KITTY. 1945, Paramount. Karl Tunberg and Darrell Ware.

KITTY FOYLE. 1940, RKO. Dalton Trumbo.

KLUTE. 1971, Warner Bros. [Andy and Dave Lewis].

THE KNIFE. [1949], [MGM]. Luther Davis.

KNOCK ON ANY DOOR. 1949, Columbia. Daniel Taradash and John
     Monks, Jr.

KONA COAST. 1968, Warner Bros. Gil Ralston.

*KONGO. 1932, MGM. [Leon Gordon and John Meehan].

KOTCH. See Interview with Jack Lemmon.

KRAKATOA EAST OF JAVA. 2 copies. 1969, Cinerama. No. 37. Bernard
     Gordon and Clifford Gould.

THE KREMLIN LETTER. 1970, Fox. [John Huston and Gladys Hill].

LABYRINTH. [1970]. [Edward Hume].

LADDIE. 1940, RKO. Jerry Cady and Bert Granet.

LADIES' DAY. Synopsis and final scr. and estimating scr. and 1st
     draft cont. 1943, RKO. Charles E. Roberts and Dane
     Lussier.

LADIES'DAY. Original. 1943, RKO. Bertrand Robinson, Bob Consi-
     dine and E. C. Lilley.

LADY FOR A DAY. 1933, Columbia. No. 63. [Robert Riskin].

LADY FOR A NIGHT. cc. 1941, Republic. Isabel Dawn and Boyce
     De Gaw.

THE LADY HAS PLANS. 1942, Paramount. Harry Tugend.

LADY IN A CAGE. See Interview with Leon Barsha.

THE LADY IN CEMENT. 1968, Fox. Marvin H. Albert and Jack Guss.

THE LADY IN ERMINE. Final scr. [1947], Fox. No. 19. [Samson
     Raphaelson].

THE LADY IN THE DARK. 1944, Paramount. Frances Goodrich and Albert
     Hackett.

LADY IN THE IRON MASK. 1952, Fox. No. 94. Jack Pollexfen and
     Aubrey Wisberg.

*LADY IN THE LAKE. 1946, MGM. Steve Fisher.

*A LADY OF CHANCE. 1929, MGM. [A. P. Younger].

PRIMARY CINEMA RESOURCES: AN INDEX

*THE LADY OF SCANDAL. 1930, MGM. [Hans Kraly, Claudine West and Edwin Justus Mayer].

LADY SINGS THE BLUES. Final sht. scr. 2 copies. 1972, Paramount. [Terence McCloy, Chris Clark and Suzanne dePasse]. See also Interview with John Alonzo.

THE LADY SURRENDERS. 1930, Universal.

*A LADY TO LOVE. 1930, MGM. [Sidney Howard].

THE LADY WANTS MINK. cc. 1953, Republic. Dane Lussier and Richard Alan Simmons.

*A LADY WITHOUT PASSPORT. 1950, MGM. Howard Dimsdale.

*A LADY'S MORALS. 1930, MGM. [Hans Kraly and Claudine West].

LAKE PLACID SERENADE. cc. 1944, Republic. Dick Irving Hyland and Doris Godfrey.

LANCER SPY. 1937, Fox. No. 41. Philip Dunne.

THE LARAMIE TRAIL. cc. 1944, Republic. J. Benton Cheney.

LARCENY ON THE AIR. cc. 2 copies. 1937, Republic. Endre Bohem and Richard English.

*LASSIE COME HOME. 1943, MGM. Hugo Butler.

THE LAST ADAM. See DOCTOR BULL.

THE LAST BACHELOR. Treatment. [1950]. No. 0. Irving Wallace.

THE LAST CHALLENGE. See PISTOLERO.

*THE LAST CHANCE. 1945, MGM. [Richard Schweizer].

THE LAST COMMAND. cc. 1955, Republic. Warren Duff.

THE LAST CROOKED MILE. cc. 2 copies. 1946, Republic. Jerry Sackheim.

THE LAST ESCAPE. 1970, United Artists. [Herman Hoffman].

LAST FRONTIER UPRISING. cc. 1946, Republic. Harvey Gates.

THE LAST GANGSTER. 1937, MGM. John Lee Mahin.

*THE LAST HUNT. And budgeting files. 1956, MGM. Richard Brooks.

THE LAST MUSKETEER. cc. 1952, Republic. Arthur E. Orloff.

THE LAST OF THE BAD MEN. Rel. as THE LAST OUTLAW. 1936, RKO.
    No. 66. John Twist and Jack Townley.

THE LAST OF THE BUCCANEERS. 1950, Columbia. No. 32. Robert E.
    Kent.

LAST OF THE MOHICANS. 1936, United Artists. No. 41. Philip Dunne.

THE LAST OF THE MOHICANS. 1936, United Artists. No. 8. Philip
    Dunne and [John L. Balderston].

THE LAST OUTLAW. See THE LAST OF THE BAD MEN.

THE LAST RUN. 1971, MGM. [Alan Sharp].

THE LAST SAFARI. 1st draft. 1967, Paramount. John Gay.

THE LAST SHOT YOU HEAR. 1969, Fox. [Tim Shields].

LAST STAGECOACH WEST. cc. 2 copies. 1957, Republic. Barry
    Shipman.

THE LAST TIME I SAW PARIS. 3 copies. 1954, MGM. No. 15.
    Julius J. and Philip G. Epstein and Richard Brooks.

*THE LAST TIME I SAW PARIS. And budgeting files. 1954, MGM.
    Julius J. and Philip G. Epstein and Richard Brooks.

THE LAST TRAIN WEST. [1954]. No. 50. [Frank Davis].

THE LATE GEORGE APLEY. 1947, Fox. No. 41. Philip Dunne.

LATIN LOVERS. Budgeting files only. 1953, MGM.

LATIN QUARTER. 3 copies. n. d.

LAUGHING ANNIE. cc. 1954, Republic. Pamela Bower.

*LAUGHING BOY. 1934, MGM. [John Colton and John Lee Mahin].

*LAUGHING SINNERS. 1931, MGM. [Bess Meredyth].

LAUGHTER IN THE DARK. 1969, Lopert. Edward Bond.

LAURA. 1944, Fox. Jay Dratler and Ring Lardner, Jr.

*THE LAW AND JAKE WADE. 1958, MGM. William Bowers.

THE LAW AND THE LADY. Budgeting files only. 1951, MGM.

LAW OF THE BADLANDS. 1950, RKO. Ed Earl Repp.

LAW OF THE GOLDEN WEST. cc. 1957, Republic. Norman S. Hall.

THE LAWLESS EIGHTIES. cc. 1957, Republic. [Kenneth Gamet].

LAWLESS LAND. (cc). 1937, Republic. Andrew Bennison.

A LAWMAN IS BORN. cc. 1937, Republic. George H. Plympton.

THE LAWYER. 1969, Paramount. Sidney J. Furie and Harold Buchman.

LAY THAT RIFLE DOWN. 1955, Republic. Barry Shipman.

*LAZY RIVER. 1934, MGM. [Lucien Hubbard].

LEADVILLE GUNSLINGER. 1952, Republic. M. Coates Webster.

LEAVE HER TO HEAVEN. Final scr. 1945, Fox. Jo Swerling. See
     also materials in the John Stahl Collection, No. 11.

LEFTY GETS ON THE LEVEL WITH THE DEVIL. [1950]. No. 75. [Larry
     Hays].

THE LEGEND OF LYLAH CLARE. 1968, MGM. Hugo Butler and Jean
     Rouverol.

THE LEGEND OF ROBIN HOOD. Orig. title CHALLENGE FOR ROBIN HOOD.
     [1967], [Hammer].

LES GIRLS. Orig. story and treatment. 1957, MGM. No. 19. John
     Patrick.

*LES GIRLS. 1957, MGM. John Patrick.

LET'S LIVE A LITTLE. 1948, Eagle Lion. No. 94. Howard Irving
     Young, Edmund L. Hartmann, Albert J. Cohen and Jack Harvey.

LET'S MAKE LOVE. 2nd rev. sht. final. 1960, Fox. No. 19. Norman
     Krasna.

LET'S SING AGAIN. 1936, RKO. No. 68. Dan Jarrett.

LETTER FROM PEKING   TITLES INDEX

LETTER FROM PEKING. Outline. n. d. No. 27. [Edward Anhalt].

LIBELED LADY. 1936, MGM. Maurine Watkins and Howard Emmett Rogers.

LIFE BEGINS. [1950], [Columbia].

LIFE BEGINS AT FORTY. 1935, Fox. [Lamar Trotti].

LIFE BEGINS IN COLLEGE. Rev. final scr. 1937, Fox. No. 19. Karl
    Tunberg and Don Ettlinger.

THE LIFE OF EMILE ZOLA. 1937, Warner Bros. Norman R. Raine, Heinz
    Herald and Geza Herczeg. See also materials in the William
    Dieterle Collection, No. 17.

*A LIFE OF HER OWN. 1950, MGM. Isobel Lennart.

A LIFE OF HER OWN. 1950, MGM. Isobel Lennart.

THE LIFE OF RILEY. 1949, Universal. No. 32.

LIFEBOAT. 1944, Fox. Jo Swerling.

*THE LIGHT TOUCH. 1951, MGM. Richard Brooks.

LIGHTNIN'. 1930, Fox. [Winchell Smith].

LIGHTNIN' IN THE FOREST. cc. 1948, Republic. John K. Butler.

LIGHTS OF OLD SANTA FE. cc. 1944, Republic. Gordon Kahn and Bob
    Williams.

*LILI. And budgeting files. 1953, MGM. Helen Deutsch and Paul
    Gallico.

LILIES OF THE FIELD. 3 copies. 1963, United Artists. No. 91.
    James Poe.

LILIOM. 1930, Fox. [Ferenc Molnar].

LILLIAN RUSSELL. Sht. final scr. 1940, Fox. No. 19. William
    Anthony McGuire.

LION IN WINTER. See Interview with Anthony Harvey.

LISBON. cc. 1956, Republic. John Tucker Battle.

LITTLE ADVENTURESS. Scenario. Orig. title THE DOVER ROAD. 1927,
     Prod. Dist. Corp. No. 8.

THE LITTLE COLONEL. 1935, Fox. [Mrs. A. F. Johnston].

LITTLE FAUSS AND BIG HALSY. Final and edit. lined scr. and release
     dialogue scr. 1970, Paramount. [Charles Eastman].
     See also Interview with Gray Frederickson.

*LITTLE FOOL. 1921, Metro.

*THE LITTLE HUT. 1957, MGM. F. Hugh Herbert.

LITTLE MISS MARKER. 1934, Paramount. [William Lipman, Sam Hellman
     and Gladys Lehman].

*LITTLE MISTER JIM. 1946, MGM. George Bruce.

LITTLE WHITE BROTHER. n. d. [Paul Gerard Smith].

*LITTLE WOMEN. 1949, MGM. Andrew Solt, Sarah Y. Mason and Victor
     Heerman. See also Interview with George Cukor.

THE LITTLEST REBEL. 1935, Fox. [E. H. Peple].

THE LIVELY SET. Rev. 1st draft. 1963, Universal. Mel Goldberg and
     William Wood.

LIVES OF A BENGAL LANCER. 1935, Paramount. [Waldemar Young, John L.
     Balderston, Achmed Abdullah], Grover Jones and William
     Slavens McNutt.

LIVING BETWEEN TWO WORLDS. See Interview with Horace Jackson.

LIVING DANGEROUSLY. 1936, Gaumont-British. [Alan Rivkin].

*THE LIVING IDOL. 1957, MGM. Albert Lewin.

*LIVING IN A BIG WAY. 1947, MGM. Gregory LaCava and Irving
     Ravetch.

*LIZZIE. 1957, MGM. Mel Dinelli.

LLOYD'S OF LONDON. 2 copies. 1936, Fox. Ernest Pascal and Walter
     Ferris.

LOCKED DOORS. 1925, Paramount. [Clara Beranger].

THE LODGER. 1944, Fox. No. 92. Barre Lyndon.

LOLITA. See Interview with James B. Harris.

*LOMBARDI, LTD. 1919, Metro. [June Mathis].

*LONDON AFTER MIDNIGHT. 1927, MGM. [Waldemar Young].

LONDON BLACKOUT MURDERS. cc. 1942, Republic. Curt Siodmak.

LONE STAR RAIDERS. cc. 3 copies. 1940, Republic. Joseph Moncure
     March and Barry Shipman.

LONE STAR RANGER. cc. 3 copies. 1942, Fox. William Conselman,
     Jr. and Irving Cummings, Jr.

LONE TEXAS RANGER. cc. 2 copies. 1945, Republic. Bob Williams.

LONELY HEART BANDITS. cc and trailer cc. 1950, Republic. Gene
     Lewis.

LONESOME. 1928, Universal. [E. T. Lowe, Jr.].

THE LONG DAY'S DYING. 1968, Paramount. [Charles Wood and Alan
     White].

THE LONG DUEL. Rev. scr. 1967, Paramount. Peter Yeldham and
     Geoffrey Orme.

*THE LONG, LONG TRAILER. 1954, MGM. Frances Goodrich and Albert
     Hackett.

THE LONG SHIPS. 1964, Columbia. [Bruce Geller] [1959], Berkley
     Mather and Beverly Cross.

THE LOOKING GLASS WAR. 1970, Columbia. [Frank R. Pierson].

LOOKIN' GOOD. [1970], [MGM]. [Bruce Geller and Eugene Price].

LOOPHOLE. 1954, Allied Artists. Warren Douglas.

*LORD BYRON OF BROADWAY. 1930, MGM. [Crane Wilbut and Willard
     Mack].

LORD EPPING HAS PLANS. 2 copies and rough draft scr. and synopsis
     of new treatment. n. d. [Charles E. Roberts and George
     Jeske].

LOS SOLDADEROS. Outline and draft. n. d. No. 27. [Edward Anhalt].

LOST-A WIFE. See BANCO.

LOST ANGEL. 1943, MGM. No. 66. Isobel Lennart.

*LOST ANGEL. 1943, MGM. Isobel Lennart.

THE LOST CONTINENT. 1968, Fox. [Dennis Wheatley] and Michael Nash.

THE LOST MAN. 1969, Universal. Robert Alan Aurthur.

LOST ISLAND. See ISLAND OF LOST SOULS.

LOST PATROL. 1934, RKO. [Dudley Nichols].

LOST PLANET AIRMEN. cc. Re-ed. from KING OF THE ROCKET MEN, Serial. 1951, Republic. Royal Cole, William Lively and Sol Shor.

THE LOST ROMANCE. Scenario. 1921. No. 8. [Edward Knoblock].

THE LOST WEEKEND. 3 copies. 1945, Paramount. Charles Brackett and Billy Wilder.

THE LOTTERY LOVER. Final sht. scr. 1935, Fox. No. 19. [Franz Schulz].

LOVE AND KISSES. Rev. final. 1965, Universal. No. 19. Ozzie Nelson.

THE LOVE BOMB. 1966. No. 50. [Rafael Hayes].

THE LOVE GOD. 1969, Universal. Nat Hiken.

*LOVE IS BETTER THAN EVER. 1933, MGM. [Ruth Brooks Flippen].

LOVE IS MY PROFESSION. Loop dialogue only. 1959, Kingsley International. Jean Aurenche and Pierre Bost.

LOVE IS NEWS. 1937, Fox. No. 65. Harry Tugend and Jack Yellen.

*LOVE LAUGHS AT ANDY HARDY. 1946, MGM. Harry Ruskin and William Ludwig.

*LOVE ME OR LEAVE ME. 1955, MGM. Daniel Fuchs and Isobel Lennart.

LOVE ME TENDER. Rev. final scr. 1956, Fox. No. 19. Robert H. Buckner. See also materials in the David Weisbart Collection, No. 50.

LOVE NEST. Treatment. [1944]. No. 0. [Irving Wallace].

LOVE STORY. See Interview with Arthur Hiller.

LOVE: VAMPIRE STYLE. See Interview with Ken Del Conte.

THE LOVE-INS. 1967, Columbia. Hal Collins and Arthur Dreifuss.

*THE LOVELORN. 1927, MGM. [Beatrice Fairfax and Bradley King].

*LOVELY TO LOOK AT. 1952, MGM. George Wells and Harry Ruby.

A LOVELY WAY TO DIE. 1968, Universal. A. J. Russell.

LOVER, COME BACK. 2 copies. 1961, Universal. No. 32. Stanley Shapiro and Paul Henning.

*LOVERS. 1927, MGM.

*LOVERS COURAGEOUS. 1932, MGM. [Frederick Lonsdale].

*LOVE'S BLINDNESS. 1926, MGM. [Elinor Glyn].

THE LOVES OF MONA LISA. Treatment and 2 drafts. [1963]. [Irving Wallace].

THE LOVES OF OMAR KHAYYAM. n. d. No. 94.

*LOVEY MARY. 1926, MGM. [Agnes Christine Johnston and Charles Maigne].

LOVING. 1969, Columbia. Don Devlin.

LUCK OF GINGER COFFEE. See Interview with Irvin Kershner.

THE LUCK OF THE IRISH. 1948, Fox. No. 41. Philip Dunne.

*THE LUCKIEST GUY IN THE WORLD. [1944], MGM. [Doane Hoag].

LUCKY JORDAN. 1942, Paramount. Darrell Ware and Karl Tunberg.

THE LUCKY STIFF. 1949, United Artists. No. 94. Lewis R. Foster.

LULU BELLE. 1948, Columbia. No. 94. Everett Freeman.

LUST FOR LIFE. 1956, MGM. Norman Corwin.

*LUST FOR LIFE. And budgeting files. 1956, MGM. Norman Corwin.

LUV. 1967, Columbia. No. 94. Elliott Baker.

LUXURY LINER. Retakes only. 1948, MGM. Gladys Lehman and Richard
          Connell.

*LUXURY LINER. 1948, MGM. Gladys Lehman and Richard Connell.

LYDIA BAILEY. 1952, Fox. No. 41. Michael Blankfort and Philip
          Dunne.

M. 1951, Columbia. No. 94. Norman Reilly Raine and Leo Katcher.

*MGM PARADE. TV scripts. [1955], MGM.

MACBETH. Trailer cc. 1948, Republic. [Orson Welles].

THE MAD DOCTOR. Rel. as DESTINY. 1941, Paramount. Howard J.
          Green.

MAD LOVE. 1935, MGM. No. 8.

THE MAD ROOM. 1969, Columbia. Bernard Girard and A. Z. Martin.

*MADAM SATAN. 1930, MGM. [Jeanne Macpherson, Gladys Unger and
          Elsie Janis].

MADAME BOSS. Cont. n. d.

*MADAME BOVARY. 1949, MGM. Robert Ardrey.

*MADAME CURIE. 1943, MGM. Paul Osborn and Paul H. Rameau.

MADAME X. n. d. No. 75. [John Raphael and J. E. Nash].

MADE FOR EACH OTHER. 1971, Fox. [Renee Taylor and Joseph
          Bologna].

MADEMOISELLE FIFI. 1944, RKO. No. 49. Josef Mischel and Peter
          Ruric.

MADONNA OF THE DESERT. cc. 1948, Republic. Charles Bennett.

THE MADONNA'S SECRET. (cc) and trailer cc. 1946, Republic.
          Bradbury Foote and William Thiele.

THE MADWOMAN OF CHAILLOT   TITLES INDEX

THE MADWOMAN OF CHAILLOT. 2 treatments, 4 drafts and final. 1969, Warner Bros. No. 27. Edward Anhalt.

MAGIC FIRE. And long vers. cc, Spanish vers. and trailer cc. 1956, Republic. Bertita Harding, E. A. Dupont and David Chantler.

MAGIC TOWN. 1947, RKO. No. 63. Robert Riskin.

THE MAGNIFICENT FRAUD. 1939, Paramount. Gilbert Gabriel and Walter Ferris.

MAGNIFICENT OBSESSION. 1935, Universal. Sarah Y. Mason and Victor Heerman.

THE MAGNIFICENT ROGUE. cc. 1946, Republic. Dane Lussier.

*THE MAGNIFICENT YANKEE. 1950, MGM. Emmett Lavery.

THE MAGUS. 1968, Fox. John Fowles.

THE MAIN STREET KID. cc. 1948, Republic. Jerry Sackheim.

*MAIN STREET TO BROADWAY. 1953, MGM. Samson Raphaelson.

*MAISIE GETS HER MAN. 1942, MGM. Mary C. McCall, Jr.

THE MAJOR AND THE MINOR. 1942, Paramount. Charles Brackett and Billy Wilder.

MAJOR BELL'S IRREGULARS. n. d. No. 41. [Philip Dunne and W. H. Menger].

MAKE A WISH. 1937, RKO. No. 68. Gertrude Berg, Bernard Schubert and Earle Snell.

MAKE HASTE TO LIVE. cc. 1954, Republic. Warren Duff.

MAKE WAY FOR TOMORROW. Also YEARS ARE SO LONG. 1937, Paramount. Vina Delmar.

MAKING IT. 1971, Fox. [Peter Bart].

THE MALE ANIMAL. 1942, Warner Bros. No. 75. Julius J. and Philip G. Epstein and Stephen Morehouse Avery.

THE MALTESE FALCON. 1941, Warner Bros. John Huston.

MALVINA SWINGS IT. Final scr. [1940]. Nathaniel West and Charles E. Roberts.

MAMA LOVES PAPA. 3 vers. 1943. 1945, RKO. Charles E. Roberts, Monte Brice and [Leslie Goodwins].

MAMA RUNS WILD. 1937, Republic. Gordon Kahn and Hal Yates.

A MAN ALONE. (cc). 1955, Republic. John Tucker Battle.

A MAN BETRAYED. cc. 1937, Republic. Dorrell and Stuart McGowan.

THE MAN-EATER OF RAVALKARNA. [1963]. No. 66. [John Higgins].

MAN FROM CHEYENNE. cc. 1942, Republic. Winston Miller.

*THE MAN FROM DOWN UNDER. 1943, MGM. Wells Root and Thomas Seller.

MAN FROM FRISCO. (cc). 1944, Republic. Ethel Hill and Arnold Manoff.

MAN FROM MUSIC MOUNTAIN. cc. 1938, Republic. Bradford Ropes and J. Benton Cheney.

MAN FROM OKLAHOMA. cc and trailer cc. 1945, Republic. John K. Butler.

THE MAN FROM RAINBOW VALLEY. cc. 1946, Republic. Betty Burbridge.

THE MAN FROM THE RIO GRANDE. cc. 1943, Republic. Norman S. Hall.

THE MAN FROM THUNDER RIVER. cc. 1943, Republic. J. Benton Cheney.

MAN HUNT. 1941, Fox. Dudley Nichols.

MAN IN THE MIDDLE. 1964, Fox. No. 97. Keith Waterhouse and Willis Hall.

THE MAN IS ARMED. cc. 1956, Republic. Richard Landau and Robert C. Dennis.

MAN OF A THOUSAND FACES. 1957, Universal. No. 26. Robert Wright Campbell, Ivan Goff and Ben Roberts.

MAN OF CONQUEST. (cc). 1939, Republic. Wells Root, E. E. Paramore, Jr. and Jan Fortune.

*MAN ON FIRE. And budgeting files. 1957, MGM. Ranald MacDougall.

THE MAN ON THE TRAIN   TITLES INDEX

THE MAN ON THE TRAIN. [1950], [MGM]. [Art Cohn].

MAN OR GUN. cc. 1958, Republic. Vance Skarstedt and James J.
     Cassity.

THE MAN THEY COULD NOT HANG. 1939, Columbia. Karl Brown.

A MAN TO REMEMBER. Estimating scr. 1938, RKO. No. 66. Dalton
     Trumbo.

THE MAN WHO BROKE THE BANK AT MONTE CARLO. 1935, Fox. [H. E.
     Smith].

THE MAN WHO DIED TWICE. (cc). 1958, Republic. [Richard C.
     Sarafian].

*THE MAN WITH A CLOAK. 1951, MGM. Frank Fenton.

THE MAN WITH NINE LIVES. 1940, Columbia. Karl Brown.

MANCHURIAN CANDIDATE. See Interview with George Axelrod.

THE MANDARIN MYSTERY. cc. 1937, Republic. John Francis Larkin,
     Rex Taylor, Gertrude Orr and Courtland Fitzsimmons.

MANHANDLED. 1949, Paramount. No. 94. Lewis R. Foster and Whit-
     man Chambers.

MANHATTAN MAISIE. See OH MAISIE.

*MANHATTAN MELODRAMA. 1934, MGM. [Oliver H. P. Garrett and
     Joseph L. Mankiewicz].

MANHATTAN MERRY-GO-ROUND. cc. 1937, Republic. Harry Sauber.

MAN'S FAVORITE SPORT. 1964, Universal. John F. Murray and Steve
     McNeil.

*A MAN'S MAN. 1929, MGM. [Forrest Halsey].

*MANY RIVERS TO CROSS. And budgeting files. 1955, MGM. Harry
     Brown and Guy Trosper.

*THE MARAUDERS. 1955, MGM. Jack Leonard and Earl Felton.

THE MARAUDERS. Rel. as THE DESPERADOES. 1969, Columbia. Walter
     Brough.

*MARIANNE. 1929, MGM. [Dale Van Every].

MARGIE. Rev. final scr. 1946, Fox. No. 19. [F. Hugh Herbert].

MARIE GALANTE. 1934, Fox. [Jacques Deval].

MARNIE. 1964, Universal. Jay Presson Allen.

THE MARRIAGE CIRCLE. 1924, Warner Bros.

THE MARRIAGE MAKER. 1923, Paramount. [Edward Knoblock]. See also
        THE FAUN.

*MARRIED FLIRTS. 1924, Metro Goldwyn. [Julia Crawford Ivers].

MARRIED IN HOLLYWOOD. 1929, Fox. No. 19.

MARSHAL OF AMARILLO. cc. 1948, Republic. Bob Williams.

MARSHAL OF CEDAR ROCK. cc. 1953, Republic. Albert DeMond.

MARSHAL OF CRIPPLE CREEK. cc. 1947, Republic. Earle Snell.

MARSHAL OF LAREDO. cc. 1944, Republic. Bob Williams.

MARSHAL OF RENO. cc. 1944, Republic. Anthony Coldeway.

MARYJANE. 1968, American International. Peter L. Marshall and
        Richard Gautier.

THE MASK OF DIMITRIOS. 1944, Warner Bros. Frank Gruber.

*THE MASKS OF THE DEVIL. 1928, MGM. [Frances Marion and Jacob
        Wasserman].

*MATA HARI. 1932, MGM. [Benjamin Glazer and Leo Bersinski].

*THE MATING GAME. 1959, MGM. William Roberts.

MATTER OF INNOCENCE. Orig. title PRETTY POLLY. 1968, Universal.
        Keith Waterhouse and Willis Hal.

THE MAVERICK QUEEN. cc. 2 copies. 1956, Republic. Kenneth Gamet
        and DeVallon Scott.

THE MAYOR OF 44TH STREET. 1942, RKO. Lewis Foster and Frank Ryan.

ME, NATALIE.   TITLES INDEX

ME, NATALIE. 1969, Cinema Center. A. Martin Zweiback and Stanley
    Shapiro.

MEET JOHN DOE. 1941, Warner Bros. No. 63. Robert Riskin.

MEET ME AFTER THE SHOW. Sht. final scr. 1951, Fox. No. 19. Mary
    Loos and Richard Sale.

MEET ME IN LAS VEGAS. See WEEKEND AT LAS VEGAS.

*MEET ME IN LAS VEGAS. (WEEKEND AT LAS VEGAS). And budgeting files.
    1956, MGM. Isobel Lennart.

MEET MR. AND MRS. AMERICA. [1943]. [Charles E. Roberts].

MEET THE BOY FRIEND. cc. 1937, Republic. Bradford Ropes.

*MEET THE PEOPLE. 1944, MGM. S. M. Herzig and Fred Saidy.

MELINDA. 1972, MGM. [Lonnie Elder III].

MELODY AND MOONLIGHT. cc. 1940, Republic. Bradford Ropes.

THE MELODY LINGERS ON. 1935, United Artists. No. 41. [Ralph
    Block and Philip Dunne].

MELODY RANCH. cc. 1940, Republic. Jack Moffitt, F. Hugh Herbert,
    Bradford Ropes and Betty Burbridge.

MELODY TRAIL. cc. 1935, Republic. [Sherman Lowe].

MEMBER OF THE WEDDING. 1952, Columbia. No. 27. Edward Anhalt.

*MEMORY LANE. 1926, First National. [John M. Stahl and Benjamin
    Glazer].

*MEN CALL IT LOVE. 1931, MGM. [Doris Anderson].

*MEN IN WHITE. 1934, MGM. [Waldemar Young].

*MEN MUST FIGHT. 1933, MGM. [C. Gardner Sullivan].

MEN OF CHANCE. 1932, RKO. [Louis Weitzenkorn].

*MEN OF THE FIGHTING LADY. 1954, MGM. Art Cohn.

THE MEPHISTO WALTZ. 1971, Fox. [Ben Maddow].

MERELY MARY ANN. Final sht. scr. 1931, Fox. No. 19. [Jules
    Furthman].

*MERRY ANDREW. 1958, MGM. Isobel Lennart and I. A. L. Diamond.

*THE MERRY WIDOW. 1934, MGM. [Ernest Vajda and Samson Raphaelson.]

MERRY-GO-ROUND OF 1938. 1937, Universal. Monte Brice and A. Dorian
    Otvos.

*MERTON OF THE MOVIES. 1947, MGM. George Wells and Lou Breslow.

A MESSAGE TO GARCIA. 1936, Fox. W. P. Lipscomb and Gene Fowler.

METROPOLITAN. 2 copies. 1935, Fox. No. 19. [Bess Meredyth].

MEXICALI ROSE. cc. 1939, Republic. Gerald Geraghty.

THE MEXICAN SPITFIRE. 2 copies. 1939, RKO. Joseph A. Fields and
    Charles E. Roberts.

THE MEXICAN SPITFIRE. Outline. 1941. MEXICAN SPITFIRE SEES A
    GHOST. [1941]. Charles E. Roberts and [Jerry Cady].

THE MEXICAN SPITFIRE AND THE ELEPHANT. 1st draft cont. 1942, RKO.
    Charles E. Roberts. (Rel. as MEXICAN SPITFIRE'S ELEPHANT.)

THE MEXICAN SPITFIRE AND THE GHOST. (Rel. as MEXICAN SPITFIRE SEES
    A GHOST.) 1942, RKO. Charles E. Roberts and Monte Brice.

THE MEXICAN SPITFIRE OUT WEST. Estimating scr. and final scr.
    1940, RKO. Charles E. Roberts and Jack Townley.

THE MEXICAN SPITFIRE PLAYS CUPID. [1941], [RKO].

THE MEXICAN SPITFIRE'S BABY. 2nd draft cont. 1941, RKO. Jerry
    Cady and Charles E. Roberts.

THE MEXICAN SPITFIRE'S BLESSED EVENT. 2 vers. 1943, RKO. Charles
    E. Roberts and Dane Lussier.

THE MEXICAN SPITFIRE'S ELEPHANT. Final scr. 1942, RKO. Charles E.
    Roberts. See also THE MEXICAN SPITFIRE AND THE ELEPHANT.

THE MEXICAN SPITFIRE SEES A GHOST. See THE MEXICAN SPITFIRE'S
    SPOOK and THE MEXICAN SPITFIRE. Outline. Also THE MEXICAN
    SPITFIRE AND THE GHOST.

MEXICAN SPITFIRE'S SPOOK   TITLES INDEX

THE MEXICAN SPITFIRE'S SPOOK. Orig. title MEXICAN SPITFIRE SEES A
     GHOST. 1942, RKO. Charles E. Roberts and Monte Brice.

MICHAEL KOHLHAAS. [1968]. [Edward Bond].

THE MIDAS RUN. 1969, Cinerama. James D. Buchanan, Ronald Austin
     and Berne Giler.

MIDNIGHT MELODY. Re-issue of MURDER IN THE MUSIC HALL. cc. 1950,
     Republic. Frances Hyland and Lazlo Gorog.

MIDSUMMER MADNESS. Scenario. 1920, Paramount. No. 8.

A MIDSUMMER NIGHT'S DREAM. Sht. scr. 1935, Warner Bros. [Olga
     Printzlau].

MIGHTY BARNUM. Rev. final scr. 1934, United Artists. No. 19.
     [Gene Fowler and Bess Meredyth].

*THE MIGHTY MC GURK. 1946, MGM. William Lipman, Grant Garrett and
     Harry Clork.

MIKE. 1926, MGM. No. 65. [Charles Tannen and Tay Garnett].

MILDRED PIERCE. 2 copies. 1945, Warner Bros. Ranald MacDougall.

*MILLION DOLLAR MERMAID. 1952, MGM. Everett Freeman.

MILLION DOLLAR PURSUIT. cc. 2 copies. 1951, Republic. Albert
     DeMond and Bradbury Foote.

*MIN AND BILL. 1930, MGM. [Frances Marion and Marion Jackson].

THE MIND OF MR. SOAMES. 1970, Columbia. [Stanley Mann and John
     Hale].

THE MINE WITH THE IRON DOOR. 1936, Columbia. No. 68. Don Swift
     and Dan Jarrett.

*THE MINIVER STORY. 1950, MGM. George Froeschel and Ronald Millar.

MINNIE AND MOSKOWITZ. 1971, Universal. [John Cassavetes].

A MINUTE TO PREY, A SECOND TO DIE. 1968, Cinerama. Louis Gar-
     finkle, Ugo Liberatore and Albert Band.

A MIRACLE CAN HAPPEN. n. d. No. 94.

MIRACLE OF FATIMA. 1952, Warner Bros. No. 92. Crane Wilbur and
　　James O'Hanlon.

*THE MISFIT WIFE. 1920, Metro. [Lois Zellner and A. P. Younger].

MISS LULU BETT. Bound with WHITE YOUTH. 1921, Paramount.

MISSING WOMEN. cc. 1951, Republic. John K. Butler.

MISSLE MONSTERS. cc. 2 copies. 1958, Republic. [Ronald Davidson].

THE MISSOURIANS. cc. 1950, Republic. Arthur E. Orloff.

MR. AND MRS. AMERICA. Synopsis. [1941]. Dane Lussier and
　　Nicholas Barrows.

MR. BELL. [1948], [RKO]. No. 31.

MR. DEEDS GOES TO TOWN. 2 copies. 1936, Columbia. No. 63.
　　Robert Riskin.

MR. DISTRICT ATTORNEY. cc. 2 copies. 1947, Columbia. Ian
　　McLellan Hunter.

MR. DISTRICT ATTORNEY IN THE CARTER CASE. cc. 1941, Republic.
　　Sidney Sheldon and Ben Roberts.

MR. DOODLE KICKS OFF. 1938, RKO. Bert Granet.

MR. 880. 1950, Fox. No. 63. Robert Riskin.

MR. IMPERIUM. 1951, MGM. Edwin H. Knopf and Don Hartman.

*MR. IMPERIUM. 1951, MGM. Edwin H. Knopf and Don Hartman.

MR. JUSTICE GOES HUNTING. [1942]. No. 66. [Isobel Lennart and
　　William Kozlenko].

MR. MOTO'S GAMBLE. 1938, Fox. Charles Belden and Jerry Cady.

MISTER SEBASTIA. [1967], [Paramount]. [Gerald Vaigh-Hughes].

MR. WONG, DETECTIVE. 1938, Monogram. Houston Branch.

MR. WONG IN CHINATOWN. 1939, Monogram. Scott Darling.

*MR. WU. 1927, MGM. [Loina Woods].

MRS. BROWN YOU'VE GOT   TITLES INDEX

MRS. BROWN YOU'VE GOT A LOVELY DAUGHTER. 1968, MGM. Thaddeus Vane.

*MRS. MINIVER. 1942, MGM. Arthur Wimperis, George Froeschel, James Hilton and Claudine West.

MRS. O'MALLEY AND MR. MALONE. 1950, MGM. William Bowers.

*MRS. O'MALLEY AND MR. MALONE. 1950, MGM. William Bowers.

MRS. PARKINGTON. 1944, MGM. No. 65. Robert Thoeren and Polly James.

*MRS. PARKINGTON. 1944, MGM. Robert Thoeren and Polly James.

M'LISS. 2 copies. 1936, RKO. No. 66. Dorothy Yost.

MOBY DICK. See Interview with Ray Bradbury.

THE MODEL SHOP. 1969, Columbia. Jacques Demy.

THE MODEL WIFE. 1st draft. 1941, Universal. Charles A. Kaufman, Horace Jackson and Grant Garrett.

*MOGAMBO. 1953, MGM. John Lee Mahin.

MOJAVE FIREBRAND. cc. 2 copies. 1944, RKO. Norman S. Hall.

THE MOLLY MAGUIRES. 1969, Paramount. Walter Bernstein.

MONEY FROM HOME. 1953, Paramount. No. 8. James Allardice and Hal Kanter.

*MONEY TALKS. 1926, MGM. [Jessie Burns, Bernard Vorhaus, Frederic and Fanny Hatton].

MONSIEUR BEAUCAIRE. 1946, Paramount. Melvin Frank and Norman Panama.

MONTANA BELLE. cc. 1952, RKO. Horace McCoy and Norman S. Hall.

*MONTANA MOON. 1930, MGM. [Sylvia Thalberg and Frank Butler].

MONTE WALSH. See Interview with William Fraker.

THE MOON IS BLUE. 1953, United Artists. No. 94. F. Hugh Herbert.

MOON OVER MIAMI. Final scr. 1941, Fox. No. 19. Vincent Lawrence and Brown Holmes.

MOON ZERO TWO. [1967]. [Gavin Lyall, Frank Hardman and Martin Davidson].

*MOONFLEET. 1955, MGM. Jan Lustig and Margaret Fitts.

MOONLIGHT MASQUERADE. (cc). 1942, Republic. Lawrence Kimble.

MOONRISE. cc. 2 copies and trailer cc. 1948, Republic. Charles F. Haas.

MOONSTRUCK MELODY. Re-ed. from EARL CARROLL VANITIES. cc. 2 copies. 1945, Republic. Frank J. Gill, Jr.

MORE DEAD THAN ALIVE. 1969, United Artists. George Schenck.

MORE THAN A MIRACLE. 1967, MGM. Francesco Rosi, Tonino Guerra, Raffaele LaCapria and Peppino Patroni Griffi.

MORE THAN A SECRETARY. 1936, Columbia. Dale Van Every and Lynn Starling.

*MORGAN'S LAST RAID. 1929, MGM. [Ross Wills and Madeleine Ruthven].

THE MORNING STAR. [1942]. No. 22. [Emlyn Williams].

MOSCOW. n. d. [Charles Whittaker].

MOTHER WORE TIGHTS. Sht. final. 2 copies. 1947, Fox. No. 19. Lamar Trotti.

MOUNTAIN RHYTHM. cc. 2 copies. 1939, Republic. Gerald Geraghty.

MOURNING BECOMES ELECTRA. 1947, RKO. Play by Eugene O'Neill. Adapted by Dudley Nichols.

MOVIETONE FOLLIES OF 1930. n. d., Fox. No. 19. [William K. Wells].

THE MUMMY'S SHROUD. 1967, Fox. John Gilling.

*MURDER IN A PRIVATE CAR. 1934, MGM. [Harvey Thew, Al Boasberg and Edgar Allan Woolf].

MURDER IN THE MUSIC HALL. See MIDNIGHT MELODY.

MURDER, MY SWEET. Aka FAREWELL MY LOVELY. 1944, RKO. No. 8. John Paxton.

MURDER ON A BRIDLE PATH   TITLES INDEX

MURDER ON A BRIDLE PATH. 1936, RKO. Dorothy Yost, Thomas Lennon,
     Edmund North and James Gow.

*MUSIC FOR MILLIONS. 1944, MGM. Myles Connolly.

MUSIC IN MOONLIGHT. Re-ed. from ICE CAPADES. cc. 1941, Republic.
     Jack Townley, Robert Harari and Olive Cooper

*THE MUTINY [OF THE ELSINORE]. 1920, Metro. [A. S. Le Vino].

MUTINY. 1952, United Artists. No. 94. Philip Yordan and Sidney
     Harmon.

MY BEST GAL. (cc). 1944, Republic. Olive Cooper and Earl Felton.

MY BLUE HEAVEN. Rev. final scr. 1950, Fox. No. 19. Lamar Trotti
     and Claude Binyon.

*MY BROTHER TALKS TO HORSES. 1946, MGM. Morton Thompson.

MY BUDDY. cc. 1944, Republic. Arnold Manoff.

MY DEAR MISS ALDRICH. 1937, MGM. Herman J. Mankiewicz.

MY FAVORITE BLONDE. 1942, Paramount. Don Hartman and Frank Butler.

MY FAVORITE SPY. 1942, RKO. No. 65. Sig Herzig and William
     Bowers.

MY FRIEND IRMA. 1949, Paramount. No. 75. Cy Howard and Parke
     Levy.

MY GAL SAL. Sht. final. 1942, Fox. No. 19. Seton I. Miller,
     Darrell Ware and Karl Tunberg.

MY HEART BELONGS TO DADDY. 1942, Paramount. F. Hugh Herbert.

MY LIPS BETRAY. Final scr. 1933, Fox. No. 19. [Hans Kraly, Jane
     Storm and S. N. Behrman].

*MY MAN AND I. And budgeting files. 1952, MGM. John Fante and
     Jack Leonard.

MY PAL TRIGGER. cc. 2 copies and trailer cc. 1946, Republic.
     Jack Townley and John K. Butler.

MY SIDE OF THE MOUNTAIN. 1969, Paramount. Ted Sherdeman, Jane Klove
     and Joanna Crawford. See also Interview with Robert Radnitz.

MY WIFE'S RELATIVES. cc. 1939, Republic. Jack Townley.

*THE MYSTERIOUS ISLAND. 1929, MGM. [Lucien Hubbard].

*THE MYSTERIOUS LADY. 1928, MGM. [Bess Meredyth].

THE MYSTERIOUS MISS X. cc. 1939, Republic. Olive Cooper.

THE MYSTERIOUS MR. VALENTINE. (cc). 2 copies. 1946, Republic.
    Milton Raison.

MYSTERY BROADCAST. cc. 2 copies. 1943, Republic. Dane Lussier
    and Gertrude Walker.

MYSTERY IN MEXICO. 1948, RKO. No. 49. Lawrence Kimbel.

THE MYSTERY OF GHOST FARM. (HARDY BOYS). [1957], [MGM]. [Jackson
    Gillis].

*MYSTERY OF MR. X. 1934, MGM. [Howard Emmett Rogers].

THE MYSTERY OF THE BLACK JUNGLE. cc. 1955, Republic. Ralph
    Murphy and Jean Paul Callegari.

*MYSTERY STREET. 1950, MGM. Sydney Boehm and Richard Brooks.

*THE MYSTIC. 1925, Metro Goldwyn. [Waldemar Young].

THE NAKED CITY. 1948, Universal. Albert Maltz and Malvin Wald.

THE NAKED EDGE. 1961, United Artists. No. 97. Joseph Stefano.

THE NAKED JUNGLE. 2 copies. 1954, Paramount. No. 94. Philip
    Yordan and Ranald MacDougall.

NAKED KISS. See Interview with Stanley Cortez.

*NANCY GOES TO RIO. 1950, MGM. Sidney Sheldon.

THE NARROW MARGIN. 1952, RKO. No. 31. Earl Felton.

NATIONAL VELVET. [1936]. 1944, MGM. No. 25. Theodore Reeves
    and Helen Deutsch.

NAVAJO TRAIL RIDERS. cc and trailer cc. 1949, Republic. M. Coates
    Webster.

NAVY BLUE AND GOLD. 1937, MGM. George Bruce.

NEGATIVES   TITLES INDEX

NEGATIVES. 1968, Continental Dist. [Peter Everett and Donald Ford].

NEPTUNE'S DAUGHTER. 1949, MGM. Dorothy Kingsley.

*NEVER LET ME GO. 1953, MGM. Ronald Millar and George Froeschel.

NEW BROOMS. Bound with THE FORBIDDEN WOMAN. 1925, Paramount.
     [Clara Beranger].

A NEW LEAF. See Interview with Howard Koch.

*NEW MORALS FOR OLD. [John Van Druten, Zelda Sears and Wanda
     Tuchock].

NEXT OF KIN. See HOT SPELL.

NICE PEOPLE. 2 copies. 1922, Paramount. No. 8. [Clara Beranger].

NIGHT AND DAY. 1946, Warner Bros. Charles Hoffman, Leo Townsend
     and William Bowers.

NIGHT CLUB. 1932, Paramount. [Richard Schayer].

THE NIGHT CLUB LADY. 1932, Columbia. No. 63. [Robert Riskin].

*NIGHT COURT. 1932, MGM. [Bayard Veiller and Lenore Coffee].

THE NIGHT FIGHTERS. 1960, United Artists. No. 65. Robert Wright
     Campbell.

NIGHT FLIGHT. 1933, MGM. [Oliver H. P. Garrett].

THE NIGHT HAWK. cc. 1938, Republic. Earl Felton.

NIGHT INTO MORNING. See PEOPLE IN LOVE.

NIGHT KEY. 1937, Universal. Tristam Tupper and John C. Moffitt.

NIGHT MUST FALL. 1937, MGM. [John Van Druten].

NIGHT OF THE FOLLOWING DAY. 1969, Universal. Hubert Cornfield and
     Robert Phippeny.

NIGHT OF THE GENERALS. 1967, Columbia. Joseph Kessel and Paul
     Dehn.

*NIGHT OF THE QUARTER MOON. 1959, MGM. Frank Davis and Franklin
     Coen.

Primary Cinema Resources: An Index

NIGHT RIDERS OF MONTANA. cc. 2 copies. 1951, Republic. M. Coates Webster.

*NIGHT SHIFT. [1942], MGM. [Leonard Lee and Lawrence Bachmann].

THE NIGHT THEY RAIDED MINSKY'S. See Interview with Norman Lear.

NIGHT TIDE. See Interview with Curtis Harrington.

NIGHT TIME IN NEVADA. cc. 1948, Republic. Sloane Nibley.

NIGHT TRAIN TO MEMPHIS. cc. 1946, Republic. Dorrell and Stuart McGowan.

THE NIGHT WALKER. 1965, Universal. Robert Bloch.

THE NIGHT WATCH. [1948], [Universal]. [Robert Buckner].

NITHTSHADE. [1953]. [Ken Englund and Sidney Field].

NINE HOURS TO RAMA. See Interview with Nelson Gidding.

NO MAN IS AN ISLAND. 1962, Universal. [James Poe]. John Monks, Jr. and Richard Gladstone.

NO MAN'S WOMAN. cc. 3 copies and trailer cc. 1955, Republic. John K. Butler.

*NO MINOR VICES. 1948, MGM. Arnold Manoff.

NO PLACE TO LAND. cc. 2 copies. 1958, Republic. Vance Skarstedt.

NO TIME FOR COMEDY. 1940, Warner Bros. Julius and Philip Epstein.

NO TIME FOR LOVE. 1944, Paramount. No. 66. Claude Binyon, Robert Lees, Fred Rinaldo and [Warren Duff].

NO WAY TO TREAT A LADY. 1968, Paramount. John Gay.

NOB HILL. Sht. final. 1945, Fox. No. 19. Wanda Tuchock and Norman Reilly Raine.

NOBODY'S PERFECT. 1968, Universal. John D. F. Black.

THE NORMAN VINCENT PEALE STORY. n. d. No. 94.

*NORTH BY NORTHWEST. 1959, MGM. Ernest Lehman.

NORTHWEST MOUNTED POLICE   TITLES INDEX

NORTHWEST MOUNTED POLICE. 1940, Paramount. No. 8. Alan LeMay, Jesse Lasky, Jr. and C. Gardner Sullivan.

NORTHWEST PASSAGE. See materials in the King Vidor Collection, No. 25.

NORTHWEST STAMPEDE. Rev. final and 2nd rev. final. 1948, Eagle Lion. No. 32. Art Arthur.

NORWOOD. 1970, Paramount. [Marguerite Roberts].

THE NOT SO COOL MILLION. n. d. No. 41. [Philip Dunne].

NOTHING BUT THE TRUTH. 1941, Paramount. Don Hartman and Ken Englund.

NOTORIETY. Scenario. 1922, Weber-North/Webster. No. 8.

THE NOTORIOUS LANDLADY. 2nd estimating draft. 1962, Columbia. [Blake Edwards].

THE NOTORIOUS LANDLADY. Estimating draft. 1962, Columbia. [Larry Gelbart].

THE NOTORIOUS MR. MONKS. cc. 1958, Republic. [Richard C. Sarafan].

*NOWHERE TO GO. 1959, MGM. Seth Holt and Kenneth Tynan.

NUMBER ONE. 1969, United Artists. No. 97. David Moessinger.

THE NUMBERS MAN. See Interview with Joseph Vogel.

THE NUN'S STORY. 1959, Warner Bros. Robert Anderson.

NUTTY PROFESSOR. See Interview with Jerry Lewis.

O.S.S. 117 (IS NOT DEAD). cc. 3 copies and trailer cc. 1959, Republic. [Jacques Berland and Jean Levitte].

ODDS AGAINST TOMORROW. 1959, United Artists. No. 49. John O. Killens and Nelson Gidding.

OEDIPUS THE KING. 1968, Universal. [Michael Luke and Philip Saville].

OFFICER O'BRIEN. 1930, Pathe. No. 65. [Tom Buckingham].

*OH MAISIE. Aka MANHATTAN MAISIE. [1942], MGM. [J. Walter Ruben].

OH, SUZANNAH. cc. 1936, Republic. Oliver Drake.

OH, YEAH. 1930, Pathe. No. 65. [James Gleason and Tay Garnett].

OH, YOU BEAUTIFUL DOLL. 1949, Fox. No. 19. Albert Lewis and Arthur Lewis.

OIL FOR THE LAMPS OF CHINA. Outline. 1935, Warner Bros. [H. T. N. Hobart].

OKAY, AMERICA. 1932, Universal. No. 65. [William Anthony McGuire].

OKAY, BIG BOY. n. d. [Charles E. Roberts].

*OKLAHOMA! 1955, Magna Pictures. Sonya Levien and William Ludwig.

OKLAHOMA ANNIE. (cc) and trailer cc. 1952, Republic. Jack Townley.

OKLAHOMA BADLANDS. (cc and trailer cc). 1948, Republic. Bob Williams.

THE OLD CORRAL. cc. 1937, Republic. Sherman Lowe and Joseph Poland.

THE OLD FRONTIER. cc and trailer cc. 1950, Republic. Bob Williams.

THE OLD HOMESTEAD. cc. 1942, Republic. Dorrell and Stuart McGowan.

*OLD LADY 31. 1920, Metro. [June Mathis].

OLD LOS ANGELES. cc. 3 copies and 1 rev. 1948, Republic. Gerald Adams and Clements Ripley.

THE OLD MAID. 1939, Warner Bros. Casey Robinson.

OLD OKLAHOMA PLAINS. cc. 3 copies. 1952, Republic. Milton Raison.

OLD OVERLAND TRAIL. 1953, Republic. Milton Raison.

THE OLD SOAK. 1936, Universal. [A. E. Thomas].

O'MALLEY OF THE MOUNTED. 1936, Fox. No. 68. Dan Jarrett, Frank Howard Clark and [William S. Hart].

93

THE OMEGA MAN   TITLES INDEX

THE OMEGA MAN. n. d. No. 97.

ON A CLEAR DAY YOU CAN SEE FOREVER. 1970, Paramount. [Alan Jay
      Lerner].

ON THE AVENUE. 2 copies. 1937, Fox. No. 19. Gene Markey and
      William Conselman.

ON THE OLD SPANISH TRAIL. cc. 1947, Republic. A. Sloan Nibley.

ON THE RIVIERA. Sht. final. 1951, Fox. No. 19. Valentine Davies,
      Phoebe and Henry Ephron.

ON THE TOWN. 1949, MGM. Betty Comden and Adolph Green.

ON THE WATERFRONT. See Interview with Budd Schulberg.

ONCE UPON A ROMANCE. Final scr. n. d. [Charles E. Roberts].

*ONCE UPON A THURSDAY. Rel. as THE AFFAIRS OF MARTHA also. 1942,
      MGM. Isobel Lennart and Lee Gold.

THE ONE AND ONLY, GENUINE ORIGINAL FAMILY BAND. 1968, Buena Vista.
      Lowell S. Hawley.

ONE EXCITING WEEK. 1946, Republic. Jack Townley and John K.
      Butler.

ONE FOR THE ROAD. Sht. scr. [1952], Republic. [Irving Shulman].

ONE FRIGHTENED NIGHT. cc. n. d., Republic. [Wellyn Totman].

ONE HAPPY FAMILY. [1950]. No. 75. [James Prindle].

100 RIFLES. 1969, Fox. Clair Huffaker and Tom Gries.

ONE IN A MILLION. 1936, Fox. Leonard Praskins and Mark Kelly.

ONE IS A LONELY NUMBER. See Interview with Mel Stuart.

ONE MINUTE TO ZERO. 1952, RKO. No. 65. Milton Krims and William
      Wister Haines.

ONE MORE TOMORROW. 1946, Warner Bros. Charles Hoffman and
      Catherine Turney.

ONE NIGHT IN LISBON. 1941, Paramount. Virginia Van Upp.

ONE POTATO, TWO POTATO. See Interview with Larry Pierce.

ONE SUNDAY AFTERNOON. 1948, Warner Bros. No. 75. Robert L.
      Richards.

ONE TO GROW ON. [1954]. No. 50. [Major R. Scott].

ONE WAY PASSAGE. 1932, Warner Bros. No. 65. [Wilson Mizner and
      Joseph Jackson].

ONE-EYED JACKS. 1961, Paramount. No. 97. Guy Trosper and Calder
      Willingham. See also Interview with Karl Malden.

O'NEIL (THE GOLDEN ONES?). [1968], [Universal]. No. 41. [Philip
      Dunne].

THE ONLY GAME IN TOWN. 1969, Fox. Frank D. Gilroy.

ONLY 38. 1928, Paramount. [A. E. Thomas].

ONLY WHEN I LARF. 1968, Paramount. [John Salmon].

ONLY YESTERDAY. 1933, Universal. No. 11. [Arthur Richman and
      William Hurlbut].

OPERATION MALAYA. [1949], [MGM]. [Frank Fenton].

OPERATION MADBALL. 1957, Columbia. No. 45. Arthur Carter, Jed
      Harris and Blake Edwards.

OPERATION PETTICOAT. 1st draft scr. and 2nd draft cont. 1959,
      Universal. Stanley Shapiro and Maurice Richlin.

OPERATION ST. PETER. [1967].

*THE OPPOSITE SEX. 1956, MGM. Fay and Michael Kanin.

ORCHESTRA WIVES. Rev. final scr. 1942, Fox. No. 19. Karl Tunberg
      and Darrell Ware.

THE OREGON TRAIL. cc. 1945, Republic. Betty Burbridge.

THE ORGANIZATION. 1971, United Artists. [James R. Webb].

THE OTHER. 1972, Fox. [Thomas Tryon].

*THE OTHER LOVE. 1947, United Artists. Harry Brown and Ladislas
      Fodor.

OTLEY. 1969, Columbia. Ian LaFrenais and Dick Clement.

OUR DAILY BREAD. 1934, United Artists. No. 25.

OUR MAN FLINT. See Interview with Ray Bradbury.

OUR MOTHER'S HOUSE. 1967, MGM. Jeremy Brooks and Haya Harareet.

OUR TOWN. 1940, United Artists. No. 68. Thornton Wilder, Frank
Craven and Harry Chandlee.

*OUR VINES HAVE TENDER GRAPES. See FOR OUR VINES HAVE TENDER
GRAPES.

OUT CALIFORNIA WAY. cc. 1946, Republic. Elizabeth Burbridge.

OUT OF IT. 1969, United Artists. [Paul Williams].

OUT OF THE STORM. cc and trailer cc. 1948, Republic. John K.
Butler.

THE OUTCAST. cc. 2 copies and trailer cc. 1954, Republic. John
K. Butler and Richard Wormser.

OUTCASTS OF POKER FLAT. 1937, RKO. No. 66. John Twist and Harry
Segall.

THE OUTCASTS OF THE CITY. cc. 1958, Republic. [Stephen Longstreet].

OUTCASTS OF THE TRAIL. cc and trailer cc. 1949, Republic. Olive
Cooper.

THE OUTLANDERS. [1952], [Columbia]. [Roy Huggins].

OUTLAWS OF PINE RIDGE. cc. 1942, Republic. Norman S. Hall.

OUTLAWS OF SANTA FE. cc. 3 copies. 1944, Republic. Norman S.
Hall.

OUTLAWS OF SONORA. cc. 1938, Republic. Elizabeth Burbridge and
Edmond Kelso.

*THE OUTRIDERS. 1950, MGM. Irving Ravetch.

OVERLAND MAIL ROBBERY. cc. 1943, Republic. Robert Yost and Bob
Williams.

THE OWL AND THE PUSSYCAT. 1970, Columbia. [Buck Henry].

P. J. 1968, Universal. Philip Reisman, Jr.

PACIFIC LINER. And estimating scr. 1939, RKO. No. 66. John
    Twist, Anthony Coldeway and Henry Symonds.

PAGLIACCI. [1933]. No. 8. [Clara Beranger].

PAINTED DESERT. Final scr. 1938, RKO. John Rathmell and Oliver
    Drake.

THE PAINTED HILLS. See SHEP OF THE PAINTED HILLS.

THE PALM BEACH STORY. 1942, Paramount. Preston Sturges.

PALS OF THE GOLDEN WEST. cc. 2 copies. 1951, RKO. Albert DeMond
    and Eric Taylor.

PALS OF THE SADDLE. cc. 1938, Republic. Stanley Roberts and Betty
    Burbridge.

*PANAMA HATTIE. 1942, MGM. Jack McGowan and Wilkie Mahoney.

PANAMA SAL. cc and trailer cc. 1957, Republic. Arnold Belgard.

PANAMINT'S BAD MAN. 1938, Fox. No. 68. Luci Ward and Charles
    Arthur Powell.

*THE PARADINE CASE. 1948, Selznick. [Arthur Wimperis, Salka
    Viertel, Polly James] and David O. Selznick.

PANDORA AND THE FLYING DUTCHMAN. 1951, MGM. No. 44. Albert
    Lewin.

PANIC BUTTON. n. d. No. 66. [Albert Beich and William Wright].

PANIC IN THE STREETS. Orig. story. 1950, Fox. No. 27. Richard
    Murphy, Edna and Edward Anhalt and Daniel Fuchs.

PANIC STRICKEN. n. d. No. 94.

PAPA MARRIED A MORMON. n. d. No. 66. [Warren Duff].

PARIS BLUES. 1961, United Artists. No. 97. Jack Sher, Irene Kamp
    and Walter Bernstein. See also Interview with Irene Kamp.

PARIS DOES STRANGE THINGS. 1957, Warner Bros. No. 0. Jean Renoir.

PARLOR, BEDROOM AND BATH   TITLES INDEX

*PARLOR, BEDROOM AND BATH. 1920, Metro. [A. P. Younger and June
     Mathis].

*PARLOR, BEDROOM AND BATH. 1931, MGM. [Richard Schayer and Robert
     Hopkins].

PARNELL. 1937, MGM. [John M. Stahl], John Van Druten and S. N.
     Behrman. See also materials in the John Stahl Collection,
     No. 11.

THE PARTY. 1968, United Artists. Blake Edwards, Tom Waldman and
     Frank Waldman.

*PARTY GIRL. 1958, MGM. George Wells.

PASSION FLOWER. 1930, MGM. No. 8.

THE PASSION OF MARY MAGDALENE. Treatment, 4 outlines and draft scr.
     n. d. No. 27. [Edward Anhalt].

PASSKEY TO DANGER. cc. 2 copies. 1946, Republic. O'Leta Rhine-
     hart and Williams Hagens.

THE PATSY. 1928, MGM. No. 25. [Barry Conners].

PECK'S BAD BOY. 1934, Fox. No. 68. [M. Roberts and Bernard
     Schubert].

PECK'S BAD BOY WITH THE CIRCUS. 1938, RKO. No. 68. David Boehm,
     Al Martin and Robert Neville.

PEER GYNT. n. d. No. 44. [Albert Lewin].

PENDULUM. 2 copies. 1969, Columbia. No. 37. Stanley Niss.

*PENNY'S PARTY. [1938], MGM. [Robert Lees and Fred Rinaldo].

THE PEOPLE AGAINST O'HARA. Budgeting files only. 1951, MGM.

PEOPLE IN LOVE. Rel. as NIGHT INTO MORNING. 2 copies. 1951, MGM.
     Karl Tunberg and Leonard Spigelgass.

PEOPLE WILL TALK. 1951, Fox. Joseph L. Mankiewicz.

A PERFECT DAY FOR RASPBERRY RIPPLE. [1971]. [David Seltzer].

PERIOD OF ADJUSTMENT. See Interview with George Roy Hill.

A PERILOUS JOURNEY. 1953, Republic. Richard Wormser.

THE PERILS OF PAULINE. 1947, Paramount. P. J. Wolfson and Frank Butler.

PERILS OF PAULINE. 1967, Universal. Albert Beich.

PETE AND TILLIE. 1972, Universal. [Julius J. Epstein].

PETER PAN. 1953, RKO. No. 66. [Play by J. M. Barrie].

PETER THE GREAT. 2 drafts. n. d. No. 27. [Edward Anhalt].

THE PETRIFIED FOREST. 3 copies. 1936, Warner Bros. No. 10-1. Delmer Daves and Charles Kenyon.

PETULIA. 1968, Warner Bros. Lawrence B. Marcus.

PEYTON PLACE. 1957, Fox. John Michael Hayes.

THE PHANTOM PLAINSMAN. cc. 1942, Republic. Robert Yost and Barry Shipman.

THE PHANTOM SPEAKS. cc. 1945, Republic. John K. Butler.

THE PHANTOM STALLION. cc. 1954, Republic. Gerald Geraghty.

THE PHYNX. 1969, Warner Bros. Stan Cornyn, Bob Booker and George Foster.

THE PICASSO SUMMER. 1967, Independent. Ray Bradbury.

THE PICTURE OF DORIAN GRAY. 1945, MGM. No. 44. Albert Lewin.

PIED PIPER. 1942, Fox. Nunnally Johnson.

PIGSKIN PARADE. 2 copies. 1936, Fox. No. 19. Harry Tugend, Jack Yellen and William Conselman.

THE PILGRIM LADY. cc. 2 copies. 1947, Republic. Dane Lussier.

PILLOW TALK. See Interview with Tony Randall.

PINKY. 1949, Fox. No. 41. Philip Dunne and Dudley Nichols.

PIN-UP GIRL. Rev. final scr. 1944, Fox. No. 19. Robert Ellis, Helen Logan and Earl Baldwin.

PIONEER MARSHAL   TITLES INDEX

PIONEER MARSHAL. cc. 2 copies. 1950, Republic. Bob Williams.

*THE PIRATE. 1948, MGM. Albert Hackett and Frances Goodrich.

PISTOL PACKIN' MAMA. cc. 1943, Republic. Edward Dein and Fred
    Schiller.

PISTOLERO. Rel. as THE LAST CHALLENGE. 1967, MGM. John Sherry and
    Robert E. Ginna.

THE PITTSBURGH KID. (cc). 1941, Republic. Earl Felton and Houston
    Branch.

A PLACE FOR LOVERS. 1969, MGM. [Julian Halevy, Peter Baldwin,
    Ennio de Concini, Tonio Guerra and Cesare Zavattini].

A PLACE IN THE SUN. 2 copies, first preliminary and final scr.
    1951, Paramount. Michael Wilson and Harry Brown. See also
    Interview with Shelley Winters.

THE PLAINSMAN. 1936, Paramount. Waldemar Young, Harold Lamb and
    Lynn Riggs.

THE PLAINSMAN AND THE LADY. cc. 1946, Republic. Richard Wormser.
    See also DRUMBEATS OVER WYOMING.

PLANET OF THE APES. 1967, Fox. Michael Wilson.

THE PLASTIC MAN. [1971], [Universal]. [Douglas Heyes and B. W.
    Saxon].

PLATINUM BLONDE. 1931, Columbia. No. 63. [Robert Riskin].

PLAY IT AGAIN SAM. See Interview with Arthur Jacobs.

PLAY IT AS IT LAYS. See Interview with Joan Didion.

PLAY MISTY FOR ME. 1971, Universal. [Jo Heims and Dean Riesner].
    See also Interview with Robert Daley.

THE PLAYROOM. [1966], [MGM]. [Richard Maibaum].

THE PLAY'S THE THING. Estimating scr. [1941]. No. 66. [Bella and
    Samuel Spewack].

*PLEASE BELIEVE ME. 1950, MGM. Nathaniel Curtis.

*PLEASE GET MARRIED. 1919, Metro. [Finis Fox, James Cullen and Lewis Allen Browne].

THE PLEASURE SEEKERS. 1964, Fox. No. 50. Edith Seeker.

THE PLOUGH AND THE STARS. 1936, RKO. No. 66. Dudley Nichols.

THE PLUNDERERS. cc. 1948, Republic. Gerald Geraghty and Gerald Drayson Adams.

PLUNDERERS OF PAINTED FLATS. cc. 2 copies. 1959, Republic. Phil Shuken and John Greene.

POCKETFUL OF MIRACLES. 1961, United Artists. No. 32. Hal Kanter and Harry Tugend.

POINT BLANK. See Interview with Irwin Winkler.

THE POOR LITTLE RICH GIRL. 1936, Fox. Sam Hellman, Gladys Lehman and Harry Tugend.

POPI. 1969, United Artists. Lester and Tina Pine.

THE PORT OF FORTY THIEVES. cc. 1944, Republic. Dane Lussier.

PORTIA ON TRIAL. cc. 1937, Republic. Samuel Ornitz.

PORTNOY'S COMPLAINT. 1972, Warner Bros. [Ernest Lehman].

THE POSSESSION OF JOEL DELANEY. 1972, Paramount. [Matt Robinson and James Grice].

POST OFFICE INVESTIGATOR. Trailer cc. 1949, Republic. John K. Butler.

THE POSTMAN ALWAYS RINGS TWICE. 1946, MGM. No. 65. Harry Ruskin and Niven Busch.

POWDER RIVER RUSTLERS. And trailer cc. 1949, Republic. Richard Wormser.

THE POWER. 1968, MGM. John Gay.

*THE POWER AND THE PRIZE. 1956, MGM. Robert Ardrey.

PRAIRIE MOON. (cc). 1938, Republic. Betty Burbridge and Stanley Roberts.

THE PREACHER. n. d. No. 32.

PREHISTORIC WOMEN. 1967, Fox. Henry Younger.

THE PRESIDENT'S ANALYST. See Interviews with Pat Harrington.

THE PRESIDENT'S MYSTERY. cc. 1936, Republic. Lester Cole and
        Nathaneal West.

PRESTIGE. 1932, RKO. No. 65. [Rollo Lloyd and Tay Garnett].

THE PRETENDER. cc. 1947, Republic. Don Martin.

PRETTY POISON. See SHE LET HIM CONTINUE.

*THE PRICE OF REDEMPTION. 1920, Metro. [Florence Hein].

THE PRIDE AND THE PASSION. 2nd draft. 1957, United Artists.
        No. 27. Edna and Edward Anhalt.

PRIDE OF MARYLAND. cc. 1951, Republic. John K. Butler.

PRIDE OF THE NAVY. cc. 1939, Republic. Ben Markson and Saul
        Elkins.

PRINCE BART. [1955]. No. 50. [Arthur Ross].

PRINCE OF PLAYERS. 1955, Fox. No. 41. Moss Hart.

PRINCE OF THE PLAINS. cc. 3 copies. 1949, Republic. Louise
        Rousseau.

*PRISONER OF WAR. 1954, MGM. Allen Rivkin.

*THE PRISONER OF ZENDA. 1952, MGM. John Balderston and Noel
        Langley.

THE PRISONER OF ZENDA. 1937, United Artists. Donald Ogden Stewart,
        John Balderston and Wells Root.

PRISONERS IN PETTICOATS. cc. 3 copies. 1950, Republic. Bradbury
        Foote.

THE PRIVATE AFFAIRS OF BEL AMI. 1947, United Artists. No. 44. Al-
        bert Lewin.

A PRIVATE'S AFFAIR. See materials in the David Weisbart Collection,
        No. 50.

THE PRIZE. Early vers. 1963, MGM. No. 19. Ernest Lehman.

PRO. [1968], [United Artists]. [David Moessinger].

*THE PRODIGAL. 1955, MGM. Maurice Zimm.

PROFESSIONAL SOLDIER. 1935, Fox. No. 65. [Howard Ellis Smith and George Jessel].

PROJECT X. 1968, Paramount. Edmund Morris.

*PROSPERITY. 1932, MGM. [Zelda Sears and Eve Greene].

*THE PROUD REBEL. 1958, Buena Vista. Joseph Petracca and Lillie Hayward.

PRUDENCE AND THE PILL. 1968, Fox. Hugh Mills.

PUBLIC COWBOY NO. 1. cc. 1937, Republic. Oliver Drake.

PUBLIC DEFENDER. 1931, RKO. [Bernard Schubert].

PUBLIC ENEMIES. cc. 1941, Republic. Edward T. Lowe and Lawrence Kimble.

PUBLIC ENEMY NO. 2. See BABY FACE HARRINGTON.

THE PUBLIC EYE. 1972, Universal. [Peter Shaffer].

PUDDIN' HEAD. cc. 1941, Republic. Jack Townley and Milt Gross.

PUPPETS. Final sht. scr. [1933], Fox. No. 19. [Rowland V. Lee and Edwin Justus Mayer].

*PUPPETS OF FATE. 1921, Metro.

THE PURPLE HEART. 1944, Fox. Jerome Cady.

THE PURPLE VIGILANTES. cc. 1938, Republic. Betty Burbridge and Oliver Drake.

PURSUED. 2 copies. 1947, Warner Bros. Niven Busch.

PYGMALION. 1938, MGM. G. B. Shaw.

PYGMALION JONES. [1947]. No. 75. [Morton Thompson].

THE PYTHON PROJECT. [1968], [Universal]. No. 41. [Philip Dunne].

QUEEN CHRISTINA   TITLES INDEX

*QUEEN CHRISTINA. 1933, MGM. [Salka Viertel, Margaret F. Levin and
        H. M. Harwood].

*QUENTIN DURWARD. 1955, MGM. Robert Ardrey.

QUIET DAY AT SOUTH FORK. n. d. John Mantley.

THE QUIET MAN. (cc). 1952, Republic. Frank S. Nugent.

"QUIET PLEASE!" [1941]. F. Hugh Herbert and Hans Kraly.

QUO VADIS. [1948], [MGM]. John Lee Mahin, S. N. Behrman and Sonya
        Levien.

*QUO VADIS. [1942]. 1951, MGM. [Cyril Hume and Walter Reisch].

RABBITS. [1971], MGM. [Gene R. Kearney and Hal Dresner].

RACHEL CADE. Rel. also as THE SINS OF RACHEL CADE. 1961, Warner
        Bros. No. 27. Edward Anhalt.

*THE RACK. 1956, MGM. Stewart Stern.

RADIO CITY REVELS. 1938, RKO. Matt Brooks, Eddie Davis, Mortimer
        Offner and Anthony Veiller.

THE RAGE. See Interview with Glenn Ford.

THE RAID ON ROMMEL. 1971, Universal. [James Poe] and Richard
        Bluel.

RAIDERS OF OLD CALIFORNIA. cc. 3 copies and trailer cc. 1957,
        Republic. Sam Roeca and Thomas G. Hubbard.

RAIDERS OF SUNSET PASS. cc. 1943, Republic. John K. Butler.

RAIDERS OF THE RANGE. cc. 1942, Republic. Barry Shipman.

RAINBOW ON THE RIVER. 1936, RKO. No. 68. Harry Chandlee, Earle
        Snell and William Hurlbut.

RAINBOW OVER TEXAS. cc and trailer cc. 1946, Republic. Gerald
        Geraghty.

THE RAINS CAME. 1939, Fox. No. 41. Philip Dunne and Julien
        Josephson.

*RAINTREE COUNTY. 1957, MGM. Millard Kaufman.

RAMONA. 1936, Fox. Lamar Trotti.

*RAMROD. 1947, United Artists. Jack Moffitt, Graham Baker and
    Cecile Kramer.

RAMROD. 1947, United Artists. No. 75. Jack Moffitt, Graham Baker
    and Cecile Kramer.

*RANDOM HARVEST. 1942, MGM. George Froeschel, Claudine West and
    Arthur Wimperis.

RANGE DEFENDERS. cc. 2 copies. 1937, Republic. Joseph Poland.

RANGER OF CHEROKEE STRIP. 2 copies. 1949, Republic. Bob Williams.

*RANSOM. And budgeting files. 1956, MGM. Cyril Hume and Richard
    Maibaum.

RASCAL. 1969, Buena Vista. Harold Swanton.

THE RAT RACE. 1960, Paramount. No. 32. Garson Kanin.

RAWHIDE. 1938, Fox. No. 68. Dan Jarrett and Jack Natteford.

REAP THE WILD WIND. 1942, Paramount. Alan LeMay, Charles Bennett
    and Jesse Lasky, Jr.

REBECCA. 1940, United Artists. Robert E. Sherwood and Joan Har-
    rison.

REBECCA OF SUNNYBROOK FARM. 1932, Fox. Karl Tunberg and Don
    Ettlinger.

REBEL WITHOUT A CAUSE. 1955, Warner Bros. No. 26. Stewart Stern.

THE RECKLESS ROAD. Orig. story and dialogue. n. d. [Charles E.
    Roberts].

THE RECKONING. See THE HARP THAT ONCE.

*THE RED BADGE OF COURAGE. 1951, MGM. John Huston.

RED CANYON. 1949, Universal. Maurice Geraghty.

*THE RED DANUBE. 1949, MGM. Gina Kaus and Arthur Wimperis.

THE RED MENACE. cc. 1949, Republic. Albert DeMond and Gerald
    Geraghty.

RED PLANET   TITLES INDEX

RED PLANET. [1931]. No. 8. [John L. Balderston].

THE RED PONY. cc. 1949, Republic. John Steinbeck.

RED RIVER RANGE. cc and trailer cc. 1939, Republic. Stanley
     Roberts, Betty Burbridge and Luci Ward.

RED RIVER RENEGADES. cc. 1946, Republic. Norman S. Hall.

RED RIVER SHORE. cc. 2 copies and trailer cc. 1954, Republic.
     Arthur E. Orloff and Gerald Geraghty.

RED RIVER VALLEY. cc. 1941, Republic. Stuart and Dorrell McGowan.

RED SKY AT MORNING. 1971, Universal. [Marguerite Roberts]. See
     also Interview with James Goldstone.

REDHEADS ON PARADE. Final rev. sht. scr. 1935, Fox. No. 19.
     [Rian James and Don Hartman].

REDWOOD FOREST TRAIL. cc. 2 copies. 1950, Republic. Bradford
     Ropes.

THE REFORMER AND THE REDHEAD. 1950, MGM. Norman Panama and Melvin
     Frank.

*THE REFORMER AND THE REDHEAD. 1950, MGM. Norman Panama and Melvin
     Frank.

THE REIVERS. 1969, Cinema Center. Irving Ravetch and Harriet
     Frank, Jr.

*THE RELUCTANT DEBUTANTE. 1958, MGM. William Douglas Hume.

REMEMBER. 1939, MGM. Corey Ford and Norman Z. McLeod.

RENDEZVOUS. 1935, MGM. No. 75. [Maxwell Anderson and Andrew
     Solt].

RENDEZVOUS WITH ANNIE. See CORPORAL DOLAN GOES A.W.O.L.

RENEGADES OF SONORA. cc. 1948, Republic. M. Coates Webster.

RENO. 1939, RKO. No. 66. John Twist.

THE RETURN OF CORPORAL ADAMS. [1946], [RKO]. No. 31.

THE RETURN OF JIMMY VALENTINE. cc. 1936, Republic. Jack Natteford and Olive Cooper.

RETURN OF THE BOOMERANG. 1969, Warner Bros. Richard Fielder.

RETURN TO PARADISE. 1953, United Artists. Charles A. Kaufman.

*RHAPSODY. 1954, MGM. Fay and Michael Kanin.

RHYTHM HITS THE ICE. cc. Rev. from ICE CAPADES REVUE. 1942, Republic. Bradford Ropes and Gertrude Purcell.

RIDE A WILD MARE. n. d. No. 65. [Tay Garnett].

RIDE, RANGER, RIDE. cc. 1936, Eagle Lion. Dorrell and Stuart McGowan.

RIDE THE MAN DOWN. cc and treatment. 1952, Republic. Mary C. McCall, Jr.

RIDE WITH TERROR. [1967]. [Nicholas E. Baehr].

RIDERS OF THE BLACK HILLS. cc. 1938, Republic. Betty Burbridge.

RIDERS OF THE PURPLE SAGE. 1931, Fox. [John F. Goodrich, Philip Klein and Barry Conners].

RIDERS OF THE RIO GRANDE. cc. 1943, Republic. Albert DeMond.

RIDERS OF THE WHISTLING SKULL. (cc). 1937, Republic. Oliver Drake and John Rathmell.

*RIGHT CROSS. 1950, MGM. Charles Schnee.

*THE RIGHT OF WAY. 1920, Metro. [June Mathis?].

RING HORSE. n. d. No. 32.

RING OF BRIGHT WATER. 1969, Cinerama. Jack Couffer and Bill Travers.

RINGSIDE MAISIE. 1941, MGM. Mary C. McCall, Jr.

RIO CONCHOS. 1964, Fox. No. 50. Joseph Landon and Clair Huffaker.

RIO GRANDE RAIDERS. (cc). 1946, Republic. Norton S. Parker.

RIO RITA   TITLES INDEX

*RIO RITA. 1942, MGM. Richard Connell and Gladys Lehman.

THE RIOT. 1969, Columbia. James Poe.

RIOT ON SUNSET STRIP. 1967, American International. Orville H.
    Hampton.

RITA COVENTRY. Rel. as DON'T CALL IT LOVE. 1923, Paramount.
    [J. L. Street].

THE RIVER. 1928, Fox. [Tristam Tupper and Dwight Cummins].

RIVERBOAT RHYTHM. Synopsis, final (2) and rev. final. 1946, RKO.
    Charles E. Roberts.

*THE ROAD AWAY FROM HOME. [1942], MGM. [Dan Totheroh].

THE ROAD BACK. 1937, Universal. R. C. Sherriff and Charles
    Kenyon.

*THE ROAD HOME. Treatment. [1942], MGM. [Lili Hatvany and James
    Hill].

ROAD TO ALCATRAZ. (cc). 1945, Republic. Dwight V. Babcock and
    Jerry Sackheim.

THE ROAD TO DENVER. 1955, Republic. Horace McCoy and Allen
    Rivkin.

ROAD TO RIO. 1947, Paramount. No. 94. Edmund Beloin and Jack
    Rose.

ROBBERS ALL. n. d., [Universal]. No. 41. [Philip Dunne].

THE ROBE. 1953, Fox. No. 41. Philip Dunne.

ROBIN AND THE SEVEN HOODS. 1964, Warner Bros. David R. Schwartz.

ROBIN HOOD OF TEXAS. cc. 1947, Republic. John K. Butler and Earle
    Snell.

ROBINSON CRUSOE OF CLIPPER ISLAND. cc. 1936, Republic. Barry
    Shipman, Maurice Geraghty and John Rathmell.

RODEO KING AND THE SENORITA. cc. 1951, Republic. John K. Butler.

ROGER "THE TERRIBLE" TOUHY. n. d. No. 66. [Bennet Kaye].

*ROGUE COP. And budgeting files. 1954, MGM. Sydney Boehm.

ROGUE'S GALLERY. 1968, Paramount. Steve Fisher.

*ROGUE'S MARCH. 1952, MGM. Leon Gordon.

ROLL ALONG, COWBOY. 1937, Fox. No. 68. Dan Jarrett, [H. B. Wright and Earle Snell].

ROLL ON TEXAS MOON. cc. 3 copies. 1946, Republic. Paul Gangelin and Mauri Grashin.

ROMANCE AND RHYTHM. Re-ed. from HIT PARADE OF 1941. cc and trailer cc. 1940, Republic. Bradford Ropes, F. Hugh Herbert and Maurice Leo.

ROMANCE IN HIGH C. [1947]. No. 75. [Philip and Julius Epstein and I. A. L. Diamond].

*THE ROMANCE OF ROSY RIDGE. 1947, MGM. Lester Cole.

ROMANCE ON THE RUN. cc. 1938, Republic. Jack Townley.

ROMANOFF AND JULIET. Rev. 1st draft. 1961, Universal. Peter Ustinov.

ROMEO AND JULIET. 2 copies. 1936, MGM. Talbot Jennings.

*ROOKIES. 1927, MGM. [E. Richard Schayer, Philip Klein and Byron Morgan].

ROOTIN' TOOTIN' RHYTHM. 1937, Republic. Jack Natteford.

ROSALIE. 1937, MGM. William Anthony McGuire.

ROSE MARIE. 1936, MGM. Albert Hackett, Frances Goodrich and Alice Duer Miller.

ROSEMARY'S BABY. 1968, Paramount. Roman Polanski. See also Interview with Roman Polanski.

ROSIE! 1967, Universal. Samuel A. Taylor.

ROSITA FROM RIO. Estimating scr. [1952], Republic. [Arthur T. Horman].

ROUGH NIGHT IN JERICHO. 1967, Universal. Sydney Boehm and Marvin H. Albert.

ROUGH RIDERS OF CHEYENNE   TITLES INDEX

ROUGH RIDERS OF CHEYENNE. cc. 1945, Republic. Elizabeth Beecher.

ROUGH RIDERS OF DURANGO. cc. 1951, Republic. M. Coates Webster.

ROUGH RIDERS' ROUND-UP. cc. 1939, Republic. Jack Natteford.

ROUGHLY SPEAKING. 1945, Warner Bros. Louise Randall Pierson.

ROUND-UP TIME IN TEXAS. (cc). 1937, Republic. Oliver Drake.

ROVIN' TUMBLEWEEDS. cc. 1939, Republic. Betty Burbridge, Dorrell
     and Stuart McGowan.

ROYAL HUNT OF THE SUN. See Interview with Irving Lerner.

RUGGLES OF RED GAP. 1934, Paramount. [Walter DeLeon and Harlan
     Thompson].

RUN FOR COVER. 1955, Paramount. No. 8. Winston Miller and
     [Michael Fessier].

RUN SHADOW RUN. 1969, Fox. No. 31. George Wells.

RUN SILENT, RUN DEEP. See materials in the Robert Wise Collection,
     No. 49.

RUSS. n. d. No. 41. [Philip Dunne].

THE RUSSIANS ARE COMING, THE RUSSIANS ARE COMING. 1966, United
     Artists. William Rose.

RUSTLERS OF DEVIL'S CANYON. cc. 1947, Republic. Earle Snell.

RUSTLERS ON HORSEBACK. (cc) and trailer cc. 1950, Republic.
     Richard Wormser.

SOS TIDAL WAVE. (cc). 1939, Republic. Maxwell Shane and Gordon
     Kahn.

SAADIA. Budgeting files only. 1953, MGM.

*SABOTAGE. Treatment. [1940], MGM. [J. Hockfilder and E. M.
     Adler.

SACCO AND VENZETTI. 2 copies. [1963]. No. 31. No. 27.
     [Edward Anhalt].

SADDLE PALS. cc and trailer cc. 1947, Republic. Bob Williams and
Jerry Sackheim.

*SADDLE THE WIND. 1958, MGM. Rod Serling.

*THE SAFECRACKER. 1958, MGM. Paul Monash.

THE SAGEBRUSH TROUBADOR. cc. 1935, Republic. [Oliver Drake and
Joseph Poland].

*SAIGON. [1943], MGM. [Harry Hervey].

SAILOR BEWARE. 1951, Paramount. No. 37. James Allardice and Martin Rackin.

ST. LOUIS BLUES. Partial scr. only. 1958, Paramount. No. 37.
Robert Smith and Ted Sherdeman.

THE SAINT MEETS THE TIGER. cc. 1943, Republic. Leslie Arliss,
Wolfgang Wilhelm and James Seymour.

THE SAINT STRIKES BACK. 1939, RKO. No. 66. John Twist.

THE ST. VALENTINE'S DAY MASSACRE. 1967, Fox. Howard Browne.

SALLY, IRENE AND MARY. Rev. final scr. 1938, Fox. No. 19. Harry
Tugend and Jack Yellen.

SALT AND PEPPER. 1968, United Artists. Michael Pertwee.

SALT LAKE RAIDERS. cc. 2 copies and trailer cc. 1950, Republic.
M. Coates Webster.

*SALUTE TO THE MARINES. 1943, MGM. George Bruce.

THE SALZBURG CONNECTION. 4 drafts and final. 1972. No. 27.
Oscar Millard.

SAM HOUSTON. Draft. [1951]. No. 66. Wells Root. See also
materials in the King Vidor Collection, No. 25.

SAMSON AND DELILAH. 1949, Paramount. No. 8. Jesse Lasky, Jr. and
Fredric M. Frank.

SAMSON AND DELILAH. 1949, Paramount. Jesse Lasky, Jr. and Fredric
M. Frank.

SAN ANTONE   TITLES INDEX

SAN ANTONE. cc. 2 copies and trailer cc. 1953, Republic. Steve
      Fisher.

SAN ANTONE AMBUSH. cc. 1949, Republic. Norman S. Hall.

THE SAN ANTONIO KID. 2 copies. 1944, Republic. Norman S. Hall.

SAN FERNANDO VALLEY. cc. 1944, Republic. Dorrell and Stuart
      McGowan.

THE SAND PEBBLES. 1966, Fox. No. 49. Robert Anderson.

SANDS OF IWO JIMA. 1949, Republic. Harry Brown and James Edward
      Grant.

SANTA FE PASSAGE. cc and trailer cc. 1955, Republic. Lillie
      Hayward.

SANTA FE SADDLEMATES. (cc). 1945, Republic. Bennett Cohen.

SANTA FE SCOUTS. cc. 1943, Republic. Morton Grant and Betty
      Burbridge.

SANTA FE UPRISING. cc. 1946, Republic. Earle Snell.

*SAPHEAD. 1921, Metro. [Victor Mapes and Winchell Smith].

SATAN'S SATELLITES. cc. 1958, Republic. [Ronald Davidson].

SATURDAY NIGHT AND SUNDAY MORNING. 1961, Continental Dist. Alan
      Sillitoe.

SAVAGE FRONTIER. cc. 3 copies and cc. 1953, Republic. Dwight
      Babcock and Gerald Geraghty.

SAVAGE MESSIAH. 1972, MGM. [Christopher Logue].

SAY ONE FOR ME. Sht. final. 1959, Fox. No. 19. Robert O'Brien.

THE SCALPHUNTERS. 1968, United Artists. William Norton.

SCANDAL INCORPORATED. 1956, Republic. Milton Mann.

*THE SCAPEGOAT. 1959, MGM. Robert Hamer.

SCARAMOUCHE. 1952, MGM.

SCARED STIFF. 1945, Paramount. No. 94. Geoffrey Homes and Maxwell Shane.

*THE SCARLET COAT. 1955, MGM. Karl Tunberg.

*THE SCARLET LETTER. 1926, MGM. [Francis Marion].

THE SCAVENGERS. 1st draft scr. THE JACKALS? [1966]. Harold Medford.

*SCENE OF THE CRIME. 1949, MGM. Charles Schnee.

SCENE OF THE CRIME. 1949, MGM. Charles Schnee.

A SCREAM IN THE DARK. 1943, Republic. Gerald Schnitzer and Anthony Coldeway.

SCREAMING TEENS. n. d. [Robert M. Young, William Idelson and Joseph Cranston].

SEA OF GRASS. 1947, MGM. Marguerite Roberts and Vincent Lawrence.

SEA RACKETEERS. (cc). 1937, Republic. Dorrell and Stuart McGowan.

SEANCE ON A WET AFTERNOON. See Interview with Bryan Forbes.

*THE SEARCH. 1948, MGM. Richard Schweizer and David Wechsler.

SECOND FIDDLE. Rev. final scr. 1939, Fox. No. 19. Harry Tugend.

SECRET CEREMONY. 1968, Universal. George Tabori.

*THE SECRET GARDEN. 1949, MGM. Robert Ardrey.

*THE SECRET HEART. 1946, MGM. Whitfield Cook and Anne Morrison Chapin.

*THE SECRET LAND. Documentary. 1948, MGM. Harvey Haislip and William C. Park (narration).

SECRET LIFE OF AN AMERICAN WIFE. 1968, Fox. George Axelrod.

SECRET VALLEY. 1936, Fox. No. 68. Earle Snell, Dan Jarrett, Paul Franklin and [H. B. Wright].

SECRET VENTURE. And Spanish vers. 1955, Republic. Paul Erickson.

SECRET WAR OF HARRY FRIGG   TITLES INDEX

THE SECRET WAR OF HARRY FRIGG. Combined cont. 1968, Universal.
      Peter Stone and Frank Tarloff.

SECRETS OF SCOTLAND YARD. cc. 1944, Republic. Dennison Clift.

SECRETS OF THE UNDERGROUND. 1943, Republic. Robert Tasker and
      Geoffrey Homes.

*SEE HERE, PRIVATE HARGROVE. 1944, MGM. Harry Kurnitz.

SEPARATE TABLES. 1958, United Artists. No. 22. Terence Rattigan
      and John Gay.

SEPTEMBER AFFAIR. 1950, Paramount. Robert Thoeren. See also
      materials in William Dieterle Collection, No. 17.

SERENADE FOR SUZETTE. [1949], [MGM]. [George Wells and Sy Gomberg].

THE SET-UP. 1949, RKO. No. 49. Art Cohn.

*SEVEN BRIDES FOR SEVEN BROTHERS. 1954, MGM. Albert Hackett,
      Frances Goodrich and Dorothy Kingsley.

*THE SEVEN HILLS OF ROME. 1958, MGM. Art Cohn and Giorgio
      Prosperi.

THE SEVEN MINUTES. 1969, Fox. No. 31. [Marvin Albert].

SEVEN SINNERS. 1940, Universal. No. 65. John Meehan and Harry
      Tugend.

*THE SEVENTH CROSS. 1944, MGM. Helen Deutsch.

*THE SEVENTH SIN. 1957, MGM. Karl Tunberg.

77 SOUTH. See Interview with Booker McClay.

SHADOWS OF TOMBSTONE. 1953, Republic. Gerald Geraghty.

SHADOWS OVER CHINATOWN. 1946, Monogram. Raymond L. Schrock.

SHAFT. 1971, MGM. [Ernest Tidyman and John D. F. Black].

SHAKE HANDS WITH THE DEVIL. 1959, United Artists. No. 97. Ivan
      Goff and Ben Roberts.

THE SHAKIEST GUN IN THE WEST. 1968, Universal. Jim Fritzell and
      Everett Greenbaum.

SHALAKO. 1968, Cinerama Rel. J. J. Griffith, Hal Hopper and Scot
      Finch.

THE SHANGHAI STORY. cc. 1954, Republic. Seton I. Miller and Steve
      Fisher.

SHARED WIFE. n. d. No. 66. [Dane Lussier and Robert Crutcher].

SHE COULDN'T TAKE IT. 1935, Columbia. No. 65.

SHE LET HIM CONTINUE. Rel. as PRETTY POISON. 1968, Fox. Lorenzo
      Semple, Jr.

*THE SHEEPMAN. 1958, MGM. William Bowers and James Edward Grant.

SHEIK OF BUFFALO BUTTES. [1941]. [B. Cheney and Bernard McCon-
      ville].

SHEP OF THE PAINTED HILLS. Rel. as THE PAINTED HILLS. 1951, MGM.
      True Boardman.

SHERIFF OF CIMARRON. cc and trailer cc. 1945, Republic. Bennett
      Cohen.

SHERIFF OF LAS VEGAS. cc. 1944, Republic. Norman S. Hall.

SHERIFF OF SUNDOWN. cc. 1944, Republic. Norman S. Hall.

SHERIFF OF WICHITA. cc. 1949, Republic. Bob Williams.

SHE'S WORKING HER WAY THROUGH COLLEGE. 1952, Warner Bros. No. 75.
      Peter Milne.

A SHIPMENT OF TARTS. [1968]. [Melville Shavelson and Mort Lach-
      man].

THE SHOCKING MISS PILGRIM. Sht. final. 1947, Fox. No. 19. George
      Seaton.

SHOOT OUT. 1971, Universal. [Marguerite Roberts].

SHOOTING STAR. [1935]. No. 66. [Jock Sayre and John Twist].

*SHORE ACRES. 1920, Metro. [James A. Hearne].

*SHOULD A WOMAN TELL. [1928], MGM. [Finis Fox].

SHOW BOAT. 1951, MGM.

*THE SHOW-OFF. 1946, MGM. George Wells.

SHOWDOWN. (Orig. and rev. scr. [1972], [Universal]. [Theodore Taylor].

THE SILENCERS. 2nd and 3rd rev. final draft. 1966, Columbia. No. 37. Oscar Saul.

SILENT RUNNING. See Interview with Doug Trumbull.

*SILK STOCKINGS. 1957, MGM. Leonard Gershe and Leonard Spigelgass.

SILVER CITY KID. 1944, Republic. Taylor Caven.

SILVER DOLLAR. 1932, First National. [David Karsner].

THE SILVER STREAK. 1934, RKO. [Roger Rolt-Wheeler].

SINCERELY YOURS. 1955, Warner Bros. No. 0. Irving Wallace.

SING, BOY, SING. Rev. final scr. 1958, Fox. No. 19. Claude Binyon.

SING, NEIGHBOR, SING. 1944, Republic. Dorrell and Stuart McGowan.

SINGING GUNS. 1950, Republic. Dorrell and Stuart McGowan.

THE SINGING HILL. 1941, Republic. Olive Cooper.

*SINGIN' IN THE RAIN. 1952, MGM. Betty Comden and Adolph Green.

THE SINGING VAGABOND. cc. 1935, Republic. [Oliver Drake and Betty Burbridge].

*SINNERS IN SILK. 1924, Metro Goldwyn. [Carey Wilson and Benjamin Glazer].

THE SINS OF RACHEL CADE. See RACHEL CADE.

SIS HOPKINS. cc. 1941, Republic.

SITTING PRETTY. Sht. final. 1948, Fox. F. Hugh Herbert.

SITTING TARGET. 1972, MGM. [Alexander Jacobs].

SIX TO ONE. n. d. No. 94.

SKIDDING. [1937], [MGM]. [Kay Van Riper].

SKIDOO. 1968, Paramount. Doran William Cannon.

SKIN GAME. 1971, Warner Bros. [Pierre Marton].

SKIRTS AHOY. 1952, MGM. No. 26. Isobel Lennart.

SKULLDUGGERY. 1969, Universal. Nelson Gidding.

SKYJACKED. n. d. No. 97.

SKYLINE. 1931, Fox. [Felix Riesenberg].

*SLANDER. 1956, MGM. Jerome Weidman.

SLAVE SHIP. 2 copies. 1937, Fox. No. 65. Sam Hellman, Lamar
    Trotti and Gladys Lehman.

SLEEPY-TIME GAL. 1942, Republic. Art Arthur, Albert Duffy and Max
    Lief.

*SLIDE, KELLY, SLIDE. 1927, MGM. [A. P. Younger].

A SLIGHT CASE OF LARCENY. Budgeting files only.

SLIGHTLY HONORABLE. 1940, United Artists. No. 65. Ken Englund.

SLIGHTLY SCARLET. See BLACKBIRDS.

SMALL TOWN GIRL. 1936, MGM. John Lee Mahin, Frances Goodrich,
    Albert Hackett and Edith Fitzgerald.

SMALL WONDER. n. d. No. 94.

SMASHING TIME. 1967, Paramount. George Melly.

SMILIN' THROUGH. 1941, MGM. No. 8. Donald Ogden Stewart and John
    Balderston.

SMITH! 1969, Buena Vista. Louis Pelletier.

THE SNAKE PIT. 1948, Fox. Frank Partos and Millen Brand.

*THE SNATCHING OF BOOKIE BOB. [1942], MGM. [Earl Baldwin].

THE SNIPER. 1952, Columbia. No. 27. Harry Brown.

SNOW BLINDNESS. n. d. No. 75. [Katherine Newlin Burt].

SNOW JOB. 1972, Warner Bros. [Ken Kolb and Jeffrey Bloom].

SNOW WHITE AND THE SEVEN DWARFS. Spanish vers. 1937, RKO. Trans-
    lated by Rafael MacClure Elizalde.

SNOW WHITE AND THE THREE STOOGES. 1961, Fox. No. 19. Noel
    Langley and Elwood Ullman.

SO BIG. 1953, Warner Bros. No. 49. John Twist.

...SO I LEFT...TO AVOID A HOLOCAUST. [1970]. [Michael Graham and
    Peter Kass.

SO RED THE ROSE. See materials in the King Vidor Collection,
    No. 25.

SO THIS IS NEW YORK. 1948, United Artists. No. 31. Carl Foreman
    and Herbert Baker. See also Interview with George Glass.

SOBRIETY HOUSE. [1939]. No. 66. [Dalton Trumbo].

SOL MADRID. 1968, MGM. David Karp.

SOLDIERS THREE. 1951, MGM. No. 65. Marguerite Roberts, Tom Reed
    and Malcolm Stuart Boylan.

SOLOMON AND SHEBA. See materials in the King Vidor Collection,
    No. 25.

*SOMBRERO. 1953, MGM. Josefina Niggli and Norman Foster.

*SOME CAME RUNNING. 1958, MGM. John Patrick and Arthur Sheekman.

SOME DAY SOON. [1937], [MGM]. [Richard Goldstone].

SOME GIRLS DO. [1968]. [David Osborn and Liz Charles-Williams].

SOME KIND OF A NUT. 1969, United Artists. Garson Kanin.

SOME LIKE IT HOT. 1959, United Artists. Billy Wilder and I. A. L.
    Diamond.

SOME RAIN MUST FALL. n. d. No. 94.

SOMEBODY UP THERE LIKES ME. 1956, MGM. No. 49. Ernest Lehman.

*SOMEBODY UP THERE LIKES ME. 1956, MGM. Ernest Lehman.

SOMETHING FOR THE BOYS. Rev. final scr. 1944, Fox. No. 19.
     Robert Ellis, Helen Logan and Frank Gabrielson.

*SOMETHING OF VALUE. 1957, MGM. Richard Brooks.

SOMETIMES A GREAT NOTION. 1971, Universal. [John Gay].

*SOMEWHERE I'LL FIND YOU. 1942, MGM. Marguerite Roberts.

SON OF FRANKENSTEIN. 1939, Universal. Willis Cooper.

SON OF FURY. 1942, Fox. No. 41. Philip Dunne.

SON OF SINBAD. 1955, RKO. Aubrey Wisberg and Jack Pollexfen.

A SONG FOR MISS JULIE. cc. 2 copies. 1945, Republic. Rowland
     Leigh.

SONG OF ARIZONA. 1946, Republic. M. Coates Webster.

THE SONG OF BERNADETTE. 1943, Fox. George Seaton.

*SONG OF LOVE. 1947, MGM. Ivan Tors, Irmagard Von Cube, Allen
     Vincent and Robert Ardrey.

SONG OF MEXICO. (cc). 1946, Republic. John Fitzpatrick.

SONG OF THE CITY. 1937, MGM. Michael Fessier.

SONG OF THE ISLANDS. Sht. final. 1942, Fox. No. 19. Joseph
     Schrank, Robert Pirosh, Robert Ellis and Helen Logan.

*SONG OF THE THIN MAN. 1947, MGM. Steve Fisher and Nat Perrin.

SONG OF YOUTH. Sht. scr. [1951], Republic. [Alan LeMay].

SONS OF ADVENTURE. cc and trailer cc. 1948, Republic. Franklyn
     Adreon and Sol Shor.

SONS OF THE PIONEERS. cc. 3 copies. 1942, Republic. M. Coates
     Webster, Mauri Grashin and Robert T. Shannon.

SORRY, WRONG NUMBER. 1948, Paramount. Lucille Fletcher.

*SOULS FOR SALE. 1923, Goldwyn. [Rupert Hughes].

THE SOUND OF GLORY. n. d. No. 40. [Fred Freiberger].

THE SOUND OF MUSIC   TITLES INDEX

THE SOUND OF MUSIC. 1965, Fox. No. 49. Ernest Lehman.

SOUNDER. See Interview with John Alonzo.

SOUTH OF CALIENTE. 1951, Republic. Eric Taylor.

SOUTH OF RIO. (cc). 1949, Republic. Norman S. Hall.

SOUTH OF SANTA FE. cc. 1942, Republic. James R. Webb.

SOUTH OF THE BORDER. cc. 1939, Republic. Betty Burbridge and
     Gerald Geraghty.

SOUTH PACIFIC. 1958, Magna Pictures. No. 19. Paul Osborn.

SOUTH PACIFIC TRAIL. cc. 1952, Republic. Arthur E. Orloff.

THE SOUTHERN STAR. 1969, Columbia. David Pursall and Jack Seddon.

*A SOUTHERN YANKEE. 1948, MGM. Harry Tugend.

SOYLENT GREEN. 1973, MGM. No. 97.

THE SPACE CHILDREN. 1958, Paramount. No. 94. Bernard C. Schoen-
     feld.

THE SPANISH MAIN. 1945, RKO. George Worthing Yates and Herman J.
     Mankiewicz.

SPECTER OF THE ROSE. 1946, Republic. Ben Hecht.

SPEED IS OF THE ESSENCE. See BELIEVE IN ME.

SPEEDWAY. 1968, MGM. Philip Shuken.

THE SPIRAL ROAD. 1st draft scr. 1962, Universal. Neil Paterson
     and John Lee Mahin.

THE SPLIT. 1968, MGM. Robert Sabaroff.

SPLIT SECOND. 1953, RKO. No. 0. William Bowers and Irving
     Wallace.

SPOILERS OF THE FOREST. 1957, Republic. Bruce Manning.

SPOILERS OF THE NORTH. 1947, Republic. Milton Raison.

SPOILERS OF THE PLAINS. cc. 1951, Republic. Sloan Nibley.

A SPORTING CHANCE. cc. 2 copies. 1945, Republic. Dane Lussier.

SPRING AND PORT WINE. [1967]. No. 19. [Bill Naughton].

SPRING CLEANING. Bound with MEN AND WOMEN. [1924]. [Clara Beranger].

SPRING MAGIC. Bound with MEN AND WOMEN. n. d. [Clara Beranger].

SPRINGTIME FOR HENRY. 1934, Fox. [Keene Thompson and Frank Tuttle].

SPRINGTIME IN THE ROCKIES. cc. 1937, Republic. Gilbert Wright and Betty Burbridge.

SPRINGTIME IN THE ROCKIES. 1942, Fox. No. 19. Walter Bullock and Ken Englund.

*SPUR OF PRIDE. [1939], MGM. [James K. McGuinness].

STAGECOACH TO DENVER. cc. 2 copies. 1946, Republic. Earle Snell.

STAGECOACH TO MONTEREY. (cc). 1944, Republic. Norman S. Hall.

STAIRCASE. 1969, Fox. Charles Dyer.

STAND UP AND SING. Re-ed. from EARL CARROLL VANITIES. 2 copies. 1945, Republic. Frank J. Gill, Jr.

STAND-IN. 1937, United Artists. No. 65. Gene Towne and Graham Baker.

STANLEY AND LIVINGSTON. 1939, Fox. No. 41. Philip Dunne and Julien Josephson.

THE STAR. 1953, Fox. No. 94. Katherine Albert and Dale Eunson.

STAR! 2 copies. 1968, Fox. No. 49. No. 94. William Fairchild.

A STAR IS BORN. Rev. estimating scr. and final. 1954, Warner Bros. Moss Hart.

STAR SPANGLED RHYTHM. 1942, Paramount. Harry Tugend.

STARDUST AND SWEET MUSIC. Re-ed. from CALENDAR GIRL. cc. 1947, Republic. Mary Loos, Richard Sale and Lee Loeb.

STARDUST ON THE SAGE. cc. 1942, Republic. Betty Burbridge.

STARS AND GUITARS   TITLES INDEX

STARS AND GUITARS. Re-ed. from BRAZIL. cc and trailer cc. 1944,
     Republic. Frank J. Gill, Jr. and Laura Kerr.

STARS AND STRIPES FOREVER. 1952, Fox. No. 19. Lamar Trotti.

STARS IN MY CROWN. 1950, MGM. Margaret Fitts Scott.

*STARS IN MY CROWN. 1950, MGM. Margaret Fitts Scott.

STATE FAIR. 1933, Fox. Sonya Levien and Paul Green.

STATE FAIR. 1945, Fox. Oscar Hammerstein II.

STATE FAIR. 1945, Fox. No. 19. Oscar Hammerstein II.

STATE FAIR. 1962, Fox. No. 19. Richard Breen.

STATE FARM. n. d. David E. Durston.

*STATE OF THE UNION. 1948, MGM. Anthony Veiller and Myles
     Connolly.

STATE OF THE UNION. 1948, MGM. Anthony Veiller and Myles Connolly.

STAY AWAY, JOE. 1968, MGM. Michael A. Hoey.

STEELYARD BLUES. 1973, Warner Bros. [David S. Ward].

STELLA DALLAS. 2 copies. 1937, United Artists. No. 25. Victor
     Heerman and Sarah Y. Mason.

STEP LIVELY, JEEVES! 1937, Fox. Frank Fenton and Lynn Root.

STEPPIN' IN SOCIETY. (cc). 1945, Republic. Bradford Ropes.

THE STERILE CUCKOO. 1969, Paramount. Alvin Sargent.

STILETTO. 1969, AE. A. J. Russell.

THE STORK CLUB. 2 copies. 1945, Paramount. No. 75. B. G.
     DeSylva and John McGowan.

STORMBOUND. 2 copies. 1951, Republic. [Comenico Meccoli, Fulvio
     Palmieri and Corrado Pavolini].

STORMY WEATHER. 1943, Fox. No. 19. Frederick Jackson and Ted
     Koehler.

THE STORY OF A WOMAN. 1969, Universal. Leonardo Bercovici.

THE STORY OF DR. EHRLICH'S MAGIC BULLET. Rel. as DR. EHRLICH'S
     MAGIC BULLET. 1940, Warner Bros. No. 17. John Huston,
     Heinz Herald and Norman Burnside.

THE STORY OF DR. WASSELL. 2 copies. 1944, Paramount. No. 8.
     Alan Lemay and Charles Bennett.

THE STORY OF IRENE. [1947]. No. 8. [John Balderston].

THE STORY OF LOUIS PASTEUR. 2 copies. 1935, Warner Bros. Pierre
     Collings and Sheridan Gibney. Stills available in the
     William Dieterle Collection, No. 17.

*THE STORY OF THREE DOVES. 1953, MGM. John Collier, Jan Lustig and
     George Froeschel.

STOWAWAY. 1936, Fox. William Conselman, Arthur Sheekman and Nat
     Perrin.

STRANDED. 1935, Warner Bros. [F. W. Weade].

A STRANGE ADVENTURE. (cc). 1956, Republic. Houston Branch.

THE STRANGE AFFAIR. 1968, Paramount. Stanley Mann.

STRANGE BEDFELLOWS. 1st draft scr. 1964, Universal. Melvin Frank
     and Michael Pertwee.

THE STRANGE CASE OF DR. MANNING. 1958, Republic. [Paul Tabori and
     Bill Luckwell].

STRANGE IMPERSONATION. 1946, Republic. Mindret Lord.

*STRANGE INTERLUDE. 1932, MGM. [Bess Meredyth and C. Gardner
     Sullivan].

THE STRANGER. 1968, Paramount. George Conchon, Suso Cecchi d'Amico
     and Luchino Visconti.

STRANGER AT MY DOOR. cc and trailer cc. 1956, Republic. Barry
     Shipman.

STRANGER AT SOLDIER SPRINGS. n. d. No. 94.

STRANGER IN THE HOUSE. [1966]. [From the novel by Georges
     Simenon].

STRANGERS IN THE NIGHT   TITLES INDEX

STRANGERS IN THE NIGHT. 1944, Republic. Bryant Ford and Paul
     Gangelin.

STRANGERS IN TOWN. n. d.

STREET BANDITS. 1951, Republic. Milton Raison.

STREET OF DARKNESS. 1958, Republic. [Malvin Wald and Maurice
     Tombragel].

THE STREET WITH NO NAME. 2nd rev. sht. final. 1948, Fox. Harry
     Kleiner.

A STREETCAR NAMED DESIRE. 2 copies. 1951, Warner Bros. Tennessee
     Williams.

STREETS OF SAN FRANCISCO. 1949, Republic. John K. Butler.

STRICTLY DISHONORABLE. And budgeting files. 1951, MGM. Melvin
     Frank and Norman Panama.

THE STRIP. 2 copies. 1951, MGM. Allen Rivkin.

STRONGER THAN TRUTH. n. d. No. 75. [Vera Caspary and I. G. Gold-
     smith].

*THE STUDENT PRINCE. 1954, MGM. William Ludwig and Sonya Levien.

THE SUBJECT WAS ROSES. 1968, MGM. Frank D. Gilroy.

SUCH GOOD FRIENDS. 1971, Paramount. [Esther Dale].

SUEZ. 1938, Fox. No. 41. Philip Dunne and Julien Josephson.

SUICIDE SQUADRON. 2 copies. 1942, Republic. Terence Young.

SULLIVAN'S TRAVELS. 1941, Paramount. Preston Sturges.

SUMMER STOCK. 2 copies. 1950, MGM. George Wells and Sy Gomberg.

*SUMMER STOCK. 1950, MGM. George Wells and Sy Gomberg.

*THE SUN COMES UP. 1949, MGM. William Ludwig and Margaret Fitts.

SUN IN THE MORNING. [1948]. No. 66. [William Ludwig and Margaret
     Fitts Scott].

THE SUN SHINES BRIGHT. 2 copies. 1953, Republic. Laurence Stallings.

SUN VALLEY CYCLONE. cc. 1946, Republic. Earle Snell.

SUNDAYS AND CYBELE. See Interviews with Serge Bourguignon.

SUNDOWN AT SANTA FE. 2 copies. 1948, Republic. Norman S. Hall.

SUNNYSIDE UP. 1929, Fox. No. 19. [G. B. De Sylva and Brown and Henderson].

SUNSET BOULEVARD. 1950, Paramount. Billy Wilder, Charles Brackett and D. M. Marshman, Jr.

SUNSET IN EL DORADO. 2 copies. 1945, Republic. John K. Butler.

SUNSET IN WYOMING. cc. 1941, Republic. Ivan Goff and Anne Morrison Chapin.

SUNSET ON THE DESERT. cc. 1942, Republic. Gerald Geraghty.

SUNSET SERENADE. cc. 1942, Republic. Earl Felton.

SUPPOSE THEY GAVE A WAR AND NOBODY CAME. 1969, Cinerama. Don McGuire and Hal Hauser.

SURRENDER. cc. 1950, Republic. Sloan Nibley and James Edward Grant.

SUSQUATCH. [1962]. [Chris Allen].

*THE SWAN. And budgeting files. 1956, MGM. John Dighton.

SWANEE RIVER. 1939, Fox. No. 41. John Taintor Foote and Philip Dunne.

SWEET AND LOW-DOWN. 1944, Fox. No. 19. Richard English.

SWEET BIRD OF YOUTH. See Interview with Ed Begley.

THE SWEET RIDE. 1968, Fox. Tom Mankiewicz.

SWEET ROSIE O'GRADY. 2 copies. 1943, Fox. No. 19. Ken Englund.

SWEETHEARTS ON PARADE. cc. 1953, Republic. Houston Branch.

THE SWIMMER. 2 copies. 1968, Columbia. Eleanor Perry.

SWING FEVER   TITLES INDEX

SWING FEVER. 1943, MGM. Nat Perrin and Warren Wilson.

SWINGIN' ON A RAINBOW. (cc). 1945, Republic. Olive Cooper and
        John Grey.

SWISS FAMILY ROBINSON. 1940, RKO. Walter Ferris, Gene Towne and
        Graham Baker.

SYLVIA. See Interview with Martin Poll.

THE SYMPHONY STORY. Rel. as UNFAITHFULLY YOURS. 1948, Fox.
        Preston Sturges.

THX 1138. See Interview with George Lucas.

TAKE A LETTER, DARLING. 1942, Paramount. Claude Binyon.

*TAKE ME OUT TO THE BALL GAME. 1949, MGM. Harry Tugend and George
        Wells.

*TAKE THE HIGH GROUND. 1953, MGM. Millard Kaufman.

TAKE THE MONEY AND RUN. 1969, Cinerama. Woody Allen and Mickey
        Rose.

TAKING A CHANCE. 1929, Fox. [A. H. Halprin].

A TALENT FOR LOVING. [1968], [Paramount]. [Jack Rose].

*TALK ABOUT A STRANGER. 1952, MGM. Margaret Fitts.

*THE TALL TARGET. 1951, MGM. George Worthing Yates and Art Cohn.

THE TALL TARGET. 1951, MGM. George Worthing Yates and Art Cohn.

TAMING SUTTON'S GAL. 1957, Republic. Thames Williamson and Fred-
        eric Louis Fox.

TARAS BULBA. 1962, United Artists. No. 37. Waldo Salt and Karl
        Tunberg.

TARGET HONG KONG. 1952, Columbia. Herbert R. Purdum.

TARGET ZERO. 1955, Warner Bros. No. 66. Sam Rolfe and [James
        Warner Bellah].

TARGETS. See Interview with Peter Bogdanovich.

TARNISHED. 1950, Republic. John K. Butler.

TARTU. See THE ADVENTURES OF TARTU.

*TARZAN NO. 3. TARZAN'S NEW YORK ADVENTURE? [1941], MGM. [Myles Connolly].

*TARZAN NO. 4. [1946].

*TARZAN AGAINST THE WORLD. [1941], MGM. [Myles Connolly and William Lipman].

*TARZAN AND HIS MATE. 1934, MGM.

*TARZAN AND THE LOST SAFARI. 1957, MGM. Montgomery Pittman and Lillie Hayward.

*TARZAN, KING OF THE SEA. Treatment. [1940], MGM.

*TARZAN THE APE MAN. 1932, MGM. [Cyril Hume and Ivor Novello].

TARZAN THE FEARLESS. 1933, Principal. No. 68. [W. L. Wright, B. Dickey and George Plympton].

*TARZAN'S FIGHT FOR LIFE. 1958, MGM. Thomas Hal Philips.

TARZAN'S REVENGE. 1938, Fox. No. 68. Robert Lee Johnson and Jay Vann.

A TASTE OF HONEY. 1st draft scr. 1962, Continental Dist. Shelagh Delaney and Tony Richardson.

*TEA AND SYMPATHY. 1956, MGM. Robert Anderson.

TEACH ME HOW TO CRY. n. d. No. 94.

*THE TEAHOUSE OF THE AUGUST MOON. 1956, MGM. John Patrick.

THE TEAHOUSE OF THE AUGUST MOON. 2 copies. 1956, MGM. John Patrick.

TELL IT TO A STAR. (cc). 1945, Republic. John K. Butler.

TELL ME THAT YOU LOVE ME, JUNIE MOON. 1970, Paramount. [Marjorie Kellogg].

*THE TEMPTRESS. 1926, MGM. [Dorothy Farnum].

THE TEN COMMANDMENTS. 1956, Paramount. Aeneas MacKenzie, Jesse L. Lasky, Jr., Jack Gariss and Fredric M. Frank.

TEN NORTH FREDERICK. 1958, Fox. No. 41. Philip Dunne.

*TEN THOUSAND BEDROOMS. 1957, MGM. Laslo Vadnay, Art Cohn, William Ludwig and Leonard Spigelgass.

THE TENDER HOURS. [1950], [MGM]. [Dorothy Kingsley and John Larkin].

*THE TENDER TRAP. And budgeting files. 1955, MGM. Julius Epstein.

*TENNESSEE CHAMP. 1954, MGM. Art Cohn.

*TENNESSEE JOHNSON. 1942, MGM. John L. Balderston and Wells Root. Stills available in the William Dieterle Collection, No. 17.

TENSION. 1949, MGM. No. 66. Allen Rivkin.

TENTH AVENUE. 2 copies. Scenario. Bound with THE FORBIDDEN WOMAN. 1928, Pathe. No. 8. [Douglas Doty].

*TENTH AVENUE ANGEL. 1948, MGM. Harry Ruskin and Eleanore Griffin.

TENTH AVENUE KID. cc. 1938, Republic. Gordon Kahn.

TERROR AT MIDNIGHT. cc and trailer cc. 1956, Republic. John K. Butler.

TERROR OF TINY TOWN. 1933, Columbia. No. 68.

*TERRY MALLOY. Treatment. [1941], MGM. [Hans Kafka].

*TESS OF THE D'URBERVILLES. 1924, Metro Goldwyn. [Dorothy Farnum].

TESS OF THE STORM COUNTRY. 1932, Fox. [S. N. Behrman and Sonya Levien.

TEST 606. Rel. as DR. EHRLICH'S MAGIC BULLET.

A TEXAN RIDES. cc. 1937, Republic. Charles Francis Royal.

*TEXAS CARNIVAL. And budgeting files. 1951, MGM. Dorothy Kingsley.

TEXAS GUINAN. [1942]. No. 66. [Claude Binyon].

THE TEXAS RANGERS. 1936, Paramount. No. 25. Louis Stevens.

THE TEXAS UPRISING. Re-ed. from THE FABULOUS TEXAN. cc. 1947, Republic. [Lawrence Hazard and Horace McCoy].

THANK YOU, JEEVES. 1936, Fox. Joseph Hoffman and Stephen Gross.

THANKS A MILLION. 2 copies. 1935, Fox. No. 19. [Nunnally Johnson].

THANKS GOD, I'LL TAKE IT FROM HERE. [1945]. No. 75. [Andrew Solt].

THAT BRENNAN GIRL. cc and trailer cc. 1946, Republic. Doris Anderson.

THAT CERTAIN LADY. 1941, Republic.

THAT MAN FROM ISTANBUL. See Interview with Horst Buchholz.

*THAT MIDNIGHT KISS. 1949, MGM. Bruce Manning and Tamara Hovey.

THAT NIGHT IN RIO. 1941, Fox. No. 19. George Seaton, Bess Meredyth and Hal Long.

THAT TOUCH OF MINK. 1962, Universal. Stanley Shapiro and Nate Monaster.

*THAT WAS NO LADY. [1941], MGM. [William Ludwig and David Hertz].

*THAT'S HIS STORY. n. d., MGM.

THAT'S MY BOY. Orig. story. 1951, Paramount. [Cy Howard].

THAT'S MY GAL. 1947, Republic. Joseph Hoffman.

THAT'S MY MAN. Filed under MY. 1947, Republic. Steve Fisher and Bradley King. See also KING OF THE RACE TRACK.

THAT'S MY POP. n. d. No. 32.

THERE GOES THE GROOM. Rel. as DON'T FORGET TO REMEMBER. 1937, RKO. S. K. Lauren, Dorothy Yost and Harold Kusell.

THERE WAS A CROOKED MAN... 1969, Lopert. David Newman and Robert Benton.

THERE'S NO BUSINESS LIKE SHOW BUSINESS. 1954, Fox. No. 19. Henry and Phoebe Ephron and Lamar Trotti.

THESE CRAZY PEOPLE. See materials in the King Vidor Collection,
    No. 25.

THESE THOUSAND HILLS. 1959, Fox. No. 31. Alfred Hayes. See also
    materials in the David Weisbart Collection, No. 50.

*THESE WILDER YEARS. 1956, MGM. Frank Fenton.

*THEY LIVE BY NIGHT. [1941], MGM. [Jane Hall].

THEY LIVE BY NIGHT. 1948, RKO. Charles Schnee and Nicholas Ray.

THEY ONLY KILL THEIR MASTERS. 1972, MGM. [Lane Slate].

THEY SELL SAILORS ELEPHANTS. [1951]. No. 75. [Chester Erskine].

*THEY SHALL NOT MARCH ALONE. [1943], MGM. [Hamilton MacFadden and
    Lesser Samuels].

THEY SHOOT HORSES, DON'T THEY? See Interview with Sydney Pollack.

THEY WENT THAT-A-WAY. n. d. No. 32.

*THEY WERE EXPENDABLE. 1945, MGM. Frank Wead.

THEY'RE PLAYING OUR SONG. [1961]. No. 50. [Luther Davis].

THE THIEF WHO CAME TO DINNER. 1973, Warner Bros. [Walter Hill].

THIEVES MARKET. [1960-1969]. No. 50. [Liam O'Brian].

THIN ICE. 1937, Fox. Boris Ingster and Milton Sperling.

THE THIN KNIFE. Budgeting files only.

*THE THIN MAN GOES HOME. 1944, MGM. Robert Riskin and Dwight
    Taylor.

THE THIN MAN GOES HOME. (cc). 1944, MGM. No. 63. Robert Riskin
    and Dwight Taylor.

THE THIRTEENTH CHAIR. 2 copies. 1937, MGM. Marion Parsonnet.

30 IS A DANGEROUS AGE, CYNTHIA. 1968, Columbia. Dudley Moore,
    Joseph McGrath and John Wells.

THIRTY SECONDS OVER TOKYO. 1944, MGM. No. 75. Dalton Trumbo.

*THIRTY SECONDS OVER TOKYO. 1944, MGM. Dalton Trumbo.

THIS COULD BE THE NIGHT. 1957, MGM. No. 49. Isobel Lennart.

*THIS COULD BE THE NIGHT. 1957, MGM. Isobel Lennart.

THIS GUN FOR HIRE. 2 copies. 1942, Paramount. Albert Maltz,
     William Burnett and [Frank Tuttle].

THIS IS KOREA. (cc). 1951, Republic. Supervised by John Ford.

THIS IS MY WIFE. [1937], [MGM]. [Harry Ruskin, Donald H. Clarke
     and James E. Grant].

THIS IS NEW YORK. See TWO KINDS OF WOMEN.

THIS MAD WORLD. 2 rev. copies. 1930, MGM. No. 8.

THIS MAN REUTERS. Rel. as DISPATCH FROM REUTERS.

*THIS MAN'S NAVY. 1945, MGM. Borden Chase.

*THIS TIME FOR KEEPS. 1947, MGM. Gladys Lehman.

THOROUGHBREDS. (cc). 1944, Republic. Wellyn Totman.

THOROUGHBREDS ALL. [1935]. No. 66. [F. Clark, J. Hutchison and
     Ferdinand Reyher].

THOROUGHLY MODERN MILLIE. 1967, Universal. Richard Morris.

A THOUSAND CLOWNS. See Interview with Herb Gardner.

THE THOUSAND DOLLAR MARRIAGE. [1940], [RKO]. [Charles E. Roberts].

A THOUSAND DOLLARS A MINUTE. cc. [1935], [Republic]. [Joseph
     Fields].

THREE BRAVE MEN. 1957, Fox. No. 41. Philip Dunne.

*THREE DARING DAUGHTERS. 1948, MGM. Albert Mannheimer, Frederick
     Kohner, Sonya Levien and John Meehan.

THREE FACES WEST. 1940, Republic. F. Hugh Herbert, Joseph Moncure
     March and Samuel Ornitz.

THREE FOR BEDROOM C. 1952, Warner Bros. No. 94. Milton Bren.

THREE GODFATHERS   TITLES INDEX

*THREE GODFATHERS. 1948, MGM. Laurence Stallings and Frank Nugent.

365 NIGHTS IN HOLLYWOOD. Final sht. scr. 1934, Fox. No. 19.
        [William Conselman and Henry Johnson].

THREE INTO TWO WON'T GO. 1969, Universal. Edna O'Brien.

THREE LITTLE GIRLS IN BLUE. 2 copies. 1946, Fox. No. 19. Valen-
        tine Davies.

THREE LITTLE SISTERS. cc. 1944, Republic. Olive Cooper.

*THREE LITTLE WORDS. 1950, MGM. George Wells.

THE THREE MESQUITEERS. cc. 1936, Republic. Jack Natteford.

THREE MUSKETEERS. 1935, RKO. Dudley Nichols and Rowland V. Lee.

THREE SECRETS. 1950, Warner Bros. No. 49. Martin Rackin and Gina
        Kaus.

3:10 TO YUMA. See Interview with Delmer Daves.

THREE WISE FOOLS. 1923, Goldwyn. No. 25. [Austin Strong].

THREE WISE GIRLS. 1932, Columbia. No. 63. [Robert Riskin].

THREE'S A CROWD. 2 copies. 1945, Republic. Dane Lussier.

THUNDER BAY. 1953, Universal. Gil Doud and John Michael Hayes.

THUNDER IN GOD'S COUNTRY. 1951, Republic. Arthur E. Orloff.

THUNDER MOUNTAIN. 1935, Fox. No. 68. [Zane Grey, Don Swift and
        Dan Jarrett].

THUNDER OVER ARIZONA. cc. 1956, Republic. Sloan Nibley.

THUNDERBIRD SIX. [1968], [United Artists]. [Gerry and Sylvia
        Anderson].

THE TIGER MAKES OUT [IN THE BIG CITY WITH A GIRL FROM SUBURBIA HE
        MEETS ON THE WAY]. 1967, Columbia. Murray Schisgal. See
        also Interview with Eli Wallach.

THE TIGER MAN. Rev. from THE LADY AND THE MONSTER. cc. 1944,
        Republic. Dane Lussier and Frederick Kohner.

*TILL THE CLOUDS ROLL BY. 1946, MGM. Myles Connolly and Jean
    Holloway.

TILLIE THE TOILER. 1941, Columbia. Karen de Wolf and Francis J.
    Martin.

TIMBERJACK. (cc). 1955, Republic. Allen Rivkin.

A TIME TO SING. 1968, MGM. Robert E. Kent and Orville H. Hampton.

*TIN HATS. 1926, MGM. [Donald W. Lee and Lew Lipton].

TIN PAN ALLEY. 1940, Fox. No. 19. Robert Ellis and Helen Logan.

*TIP ON A DEAD JOCKEY. And budgeting files. 1957, MGM. Charles
    Lederer.

THE TITANS. n. d. [Cornell Wilde?].

TO BEAT THE BAND. 1935, RKO. [George Marion, Jr. and Dorothy Yost].

TO EACH HIS OWN. 1946, Paramount. Charles Brackett and Jacques
    Thery.

TO HIPPOCRATES--WITH LOVE. n. d. No. 40. [Fred Freiberger].

TO KILL A MOCKINGBIRD. 1962, Universal. No. 37. Horton Foote.
    See also Interview with Elmer Bernstein.

TO MARY, WITH LOVE. 1936, Fox. Richard Sherman and Howard Ellis
    Smith.

TO PLEASE A LADY. And rev. final. 1950, MGM. Barré Lyndon and
    Marge Decker.

*THE TOAST OF NEW ORLEANS. 1950, MGM. Sy Gomberg and George Wells.

THE TOAST OF NEW ORLEANS. 1950, MGM. Sy Gomberg and George Wells.

TOBOR THE GREAT. cc. 2 copies. 1954, Republic. Philip MacDonald
    and Richard Goldstone.

TOM, DICK, AND HARRY. 1941, RKO. No. 66. Paul Jarrico.

TOM JONES. See Interview with Lou Greenspan.

*TOM THUMB. 1958, MGM. Ladislas Fodor.

TOMAHAWK. 1951, Universal. No. 32. Silvia Richards and Maurice
    Geraghty.

TOMORROW'S ALMOST OVER   TITLES INDEX

TOMORROW'S ALMOST OVER. n. d. [Oscar Boetticher, Jr.].

TONIGHT AND EVERY NIGHT. 2 copies. 1945, Columbia. Lesser Samuels and Abem Finkel.

TONIGHT WE SING. 1953, Fox. No. 19. Harry Kurnitz and George Oppenheimer.

TONY ROME. 1967, Fox. Richard Breen.

TOO LATE FOR TEARS. 2 copies. 1949, United Artists. Roy Huggins.

TOO MANY WIVES. 1937, RKO. Dorothy Yost, Lois Eby and John Grey.

TOP DOG. [1956]. No. 32.

TOP OF THE WORLD. 1955, United Artists. No. 66. John D. Klorer and N. Richard Nash.

THE TOPEKA TERROR. cc.. 1945, Republic. Patricia Harper and Norman S. Hall.

TORA! TORA! TORA! See materials in the Richard Fleischer Collection, No. 31.

TORPEDO. [1958]. No. 49. [John Gay].

*TORPEDO RUN. 1958, MGM. Richard Sale and William Wister Haines.

*TORTILLA FLAT. 1942, MGM. John Lee Mahin and Benjamin Glazer.

TORTURE GARDEN. 1968, Columbia. Robert Bloch.

THE TOUCHABLES. 1968, Fox. [Ian Le Frenais].

TOUGH GIRL. Re-ed. from THAT BRENNAN GIRL. 1951, Republic. Doris Anderson.

THE TOUGHEST MAN IN ARIZONA. Trailer cc. 1952, Republic. John K. Butler.

TOWN WITHOUT PITY. See Interview with Gottfried Reinhardt.

THE TOWN'S WOMAN. n. d. [Thomson Burtis].

TRACK OF THE SEVENTEEN. n. d. No. 40. [Fred Freiberger].

TRACK THE MAN DOWN. cc and trailer cc. 1956, Republic. Paul
    Erickson.

TRADE WINDS. 1938, United Artists. No. 65. Dorothy Parker, Alan
    Campbell and Frank R. Adams.

*TRADER HORN. 1931, MGM. [Dale Van Every, John Thomas Neville,
    Richard Schayer, John Howard Lawson and Jim Tully].

TRAIL TO SAN ANTONE. cc. 1947, Republic. Jack Natteford and Luci
    Ward.

TRAIN TO ALCATRAZ. cc. 1948, Republic. Gerald Geraghty.

THE TRAITOR WITHIN. cc. 1942, Republic. Jack Townley.

TRAP FOR A MAN. [1964], [Fox]. No. 31. [John Paxton].

TRAPPED. 1949, Eagle Lion. No. 31. Earl Felton.

THE TRAVELING LADY. n. d. No. 94.

TRAVELS WITH MY AUNT. 1972, MGM. [Jay Presson Allen and Hugh
    Wheeler].

TREE ON THE PARKWAY. [1956]. [George Tibbles].

TRENT'S LAST CASE. cc. 1953, Republic. Pamela Bower.

*TRIAL. And budgeting files. 1955, MGM. Don M. Mankiewicz.

*TRIBUTE TO A BAD MAN. 1956, MGM. Michael Blankfort. See also
    materials in the Robert Wise Collection, No. 19.

THE TRIGGER TRIO. cc. 1937, Republic. Joseph Poland and Oliver
    Drake.

TRIPLE CROSS. 1967, Warner Bros. Rene Hardy.

TRIUMPH OVER PAIN. See GREAT WITHOUT GLORY.

TROCADERO. cc. 1944, Republic.

TROPICAL HEAT WAVE. cc and trailer cc. 1952, Republic. Arthur T.
    Horman.

TROUBLE IN THE GLEN. cc. 2 copies. 1954, Republic. Frank S.
    Nugent.

TROUBLE MAN

TROUBLE MAN. 1972, Fox. [John D. F. Black].

TUMBLING TUMBLEWEEDS. 1935, Republic. [Ford Beebe].

*THE TUNNEL OF LOVE. 1958, MGM. Joseph Fields.

12 ANGRY MEN. 1957, United Artists. Reginald Rose.

TWELVE CROWDED HOURS. 1939, RKO. No. 66. John Twist.

TWENTY THOUSAND LEAGUES UNDER THE SEA. 1954, Buena Vista. No. 31.
     Earl Felton.

THE TWENTY-FIFTH HOUR. 1967, MGM. Henri Verneuil, Francois Boyer
     and Wolf Mankowitz.

TWILIGHT FOR THE GODS. 1958, Universal. No. 32. Ernest K. Gann.

TWILIGHT ON THE RIO GRANDE. cc. 1947, Republic. Dorrell and
     Stuart McGowan.

TWIN BEDS. 1942, United Artists. Curtis Kenyon, Kenneth Earl and
     E. Edwin Moran.

THE TWINKLE IN GOD'S EYE. cc. 3 copies. 1955, Republic. P J.
     Wolfson.

A TWIST OF SAND. 1968, United Artists. Marvin H. Albert.

*TWISTS OF FATE. [1941], MGM. [Robert Lopez].

TWO FLAGS WEST. 1950, Fox. No. 49. Casey Robinson.

TWO FOR THE ROAD. 1967, Fox. Frederic Raphael.

TWO FOR THE SEESAW. 1962, United Artists. No. 49. Isobel Lennart.

*TWO GIRLS AND A SAILOR. 1944, MGM. Richard Connell and Gladys
     Lehman.

TWO KINDS OF WOMEN. Orig. THIS IS NEW YORK. Bound with THE FOR-
     BIDDEN WOMAN. 1932, Paramount. [Benjamin Glazer].

TWO MULES FOR SISTER SARA. 2 copies. 1970, Universal. Albert
     Maltz.

TWO YEARS BEFORE THE MAST. 1946, Paramount. No. 94. Seton I.
     Miller and George Bruce.

U.S.S. MARBLEHEAD. And estimating scr. and rev. estimating scr. [1952]. No. 66. [Harold Medford].

THE UGLY AMERICAN. Rev. 2nd draft. 1963, Universal. Stewart Stern.

THE UMBRELLA. [1937], [MGM]. [George Oppenheimer].

*UNCHARTED SEAS. 1921, Metro.

UNCLE ANDY HARDY. [1946]. No. 66. [Harry Ruskin and William Ludwig].

UNCONQUERED. 1947, Paramount. No. 8. Charles Bennett, Fredric M. Frank and Jesse Lasky, Jr.

THE UNDEFEATED. 1969, Fox. James Lee Barrett.

UNDER COLORADO SKIES. cc. 1947, Republic. Louise Rousseau.

UNDER MEXICALI STARS. cc. 1950, Republic. Bob Williams.

UNDER TWO FLAGS. 1936, Fox. W. P. Lipscomb and Walter Ferris.

UNDER WESTERN STARS. cc. 3 copies. 1938, Republic. Dorrell and Stuart McGowan and Betty Burbridge.

UNDERCOVER MAN. 1932, Paramount.

THE UNDERCOVER WOMAN. cc. 1946, Republic. Jerry Sackheim and Sherman T. Lowe.

*UNDERCURRENT. 1946, MGM. Edward Chodorov.

UNDERGROUND. 1968, Warner Bros. [Ron Bishop].

UNDERGROUND SPY. cc and trailer cc. Rev. from THE RED MENACE. [1949], Republic. [Albert DeMond and Gerald Geraghty].

*UNDERSTANDING HEART. 1927, MGM. [Edward T. Lowe, Jr.].

*UNDERWATER WARRIOR. 1958, MGM. Gene Levitt.

UNEXPECTED UNCLE. 1941, RKO. No. 65. Delmer Daves and Noel Langley.

UNFAITHFULLY YOURS. See also THE SYMPHONY STORY. 1948, Fox. No. 19. Preston Sturges.

*THE UNFINISHED DANCE. 1947, MGM. Myles Connolly.

UNION PACIFIC. 1939, Paramount. No. 8. Walter DeLeon, C. Gardner
    Sullivan and Jesse Lasky, Jr.

THE UNKILLABLES. [1967]. [Andy White].

*THE UNKNOWN MAN. 1951, MGM. Ronald Millar and George Froeschel.

UNMASKED. cc. 1950, Republic. Albert DeMond and Norman S. Hall.

THE UNSINKABLE MOLLY BROWN. See materials in the Lawrence Wein-
    garten Collection, No. 59.

*UNTAMED. 1929, MGM. [Sylvia Thalberg and Frank Butler].

UNTAMED HEIRESS. 1954, Republic. Barry Shipman.

*UNTIL THEY SAIL. And budgeting files. 1957, MGM. Robert Anderson.

UNTIL THEY SAIL. 1957, MGM. No. 49. Robert Anderson.

UNTITLED COLUMBIA NO. 5. n. d. Autographed by Boris Karloff.

UNTITLED COLUMBIA NO. 81. n. d.

UNTITLED REPUBLIC NO. 958. [1940].

UNTITLED REPUBLIC NO. 988. [1941].

UNTITLED. Treatment. Roy Rogers feature. [1945]. [Clarence Upson
    Young].

UP THE JUNCTION. 1968, Paramount. Roger Smith.

*UPSTAGE. 1926, MGM. [Lorna Moon].

UTAH. cc. 2 copies. 1945, Republic. Jack Townley and John K.
    Butler.

UTAH WAGON TRAIN. cc. 3 copies and trailer cc. 1951, Republic.
    John K. Butler.

THE UTAH WAR. n. d. No. 66. [Richard Vetterli and Ruth Hale].

VALERIE. 1957, United Artists. No. 94. Leonard Heideman and
    Emmett Murphy.

THE VALLEY OF DECISION. 1945, MGM. No. 65. John Meehan and Sonya Levien.

VALLEY OF HUNTED MEN. cc. 2 copies. 1942, Republic. Albert DeMond and Morton Grant.

VALLEY OF THE DOLLS. 1967, Fox. No. 50. Helen Deutsch and Dorothy Kingsley.

*VALLEY OF THE KINGS. 1954, MGM. Robert Pirosh and Karl Tunberg.

VALLEY OF THE SUN. 1942, RKO. No. 66. Horace McCoy and [Bartlett Cormack].

THE VANISHING AMERICAN. 1955, Republic. Alan LeMay.

VANISHING POINT. 1971, Fox. [Guillermo Cain].

THE VANISHING WESTERNER. cc. 2 copies. 1950, Republic. Bob Williams.

VARSITY SHOW. 1937, Warner Bros. Jerry Wald and Richard Macaulay.

THE VENGEANCE OF SHE. 1968, Fox. Peter O'Donnell.

VERA CRUZ. 2 copies. 1954, United Artists. No. 94. Roland Kibbee and James R. Webb.

VICTORY. 2 copies. 1940, Paramount. No. 8. John Balderston.

THE VIEW FROM POMPEY'S HEAD. 1955, Fox. No. 41. Philip Dunne.

VIGILANTE HIDEOUT. 1950, Republic. Richard Wormser.

VIGILANTES OF BOOMTOWN. (cc). 1947, Republic. Earle Snell.

VIGILANTES OF DODGE CITY. 1944, Republic. Norman S. Hall and Anthony Coldeway.

THE VIKING QUEEN. 1967, Fox. Clarke Reynolds.

THE VIKINGS. 1958, United Artists. No. 31. Calder Willingham.

THE VILLAGE DOCTOR. Treatment. [1954], Republic. [Alfred Hayes].

VILLAGE TALE. 1935, RKO. [Allan Scott].

VILLAIN. 1971, MGM. [Dick Clement and Ian Le Frenais].

VILLA RIDES   TITLES INDEX

VILLA RIDES. 1968, Paramount. Robert Towne and Sam Peckinpah.

*THE VINTAGE. 1957, MGM. Michael Blankfort.

THE VIOLENT HOUR. See DIAL 1119.

VIOLENT SATURDAY. 1955. Fox. No. 31. Sydney Boehm.

VIPERS. See Interview with Baird Bryant.

VIRTUE. 1932, Columbia. No. 63. [Robert Riskin].

*VISA. [1949], MGM. [Howard Dimsdale].

VIVA MAX. 1969, Commonwealth United. [Elliott Baker].

*VIVA VILLA! 1934, MGM.

VIVA ZAPATA! 1952, Fox. John Steinbeck.

VON RYAN'S EXPRESS. 1965, Fox. No. 91. Wendell Mayes and Joseph
        Landon.

THE VOODOO EYE. n. d.

WABASH AVENUE. 1950, Fox. No. 19. Harry Tugend and Charles
        Lederer.

WAC FROM WALLA WALLA. cc. 1952, Republic. Arthur T. Horman.

THE WAFFLE IRON. See ARE ALL MEN ALIKE?

WAIT UNTIL DARK. 1967, Warner Bros. Robert and Jane Howard
        Carrington.

WAKE UP AND LIVE. 2 copies. 1937, Fox. No. 19. Harry Tugend
        and Jack Yellen.

A WALK IN THE SPRING RAIN. 1970, Columbia. [Stirling Silliphant].

WALK ON THE WILD SIDE. 1962, Columbia. No. 37. John Fante and
        Edmund Morris.

A WALK WITH LOVE AND DEATH. 1969, Fox. Dale Wasserman.

THE WALKING DEAD. 1936, Warner Bros. Ewart Adamson.

*WALK-OFFS. 1920, Metro. [A. P. Younger].

A WALL FOR SAN SEBASTIAN. [1967], [MGM]. [James R. Webb].

WALL STREET COWBOY. 1939, Republic. Gerald Geraghty and Norman S. Hall.

THE WALLS OF JERICHO. 1948, Fox. Lamar Trotti.

WANDA. See Interview with Barbara Loden.

WAR BETWEEN MEN AND WOMEN. See Interview with Mel Shavelson.

WAR IN SPACE. Dubbing scr. n. d. Shinichi Sekizawa.

WAR LORD. WEST OF SHANGHAI, aka CORNERED. 1937, Warner Bros. Crane Wilbur.

THE WAR LORD. 1965, Universal. No. 97. John Collier and Millard Kaufman.

*WAR PAINT. 1926. [Charles Maigne].

THE WAR WAGON. 1967, Universal. Clair Huffaker.

WATCH ON THE RHINE. 1943, Warner Bros. Dashiell Hammett.

*WATCH YOUR STEP. 1922, Goldwyn. [Julien Josephson].

WATERFRONT ANGEL. Outline. n. d. Charles E. Roberts.

WATERHOLE NO. 3. 1967, Paramount. Joseph T. Steck and R. R. Young.

WAY DOWN EAST. 1935, Fox. William Hurlbut.

WAY DOWN SOUTH. 1939, RKO. No. 68. Clarence Muse and Langston Hughes.

WAY OF A GAUCHO. 1952, Fox. No. 41. Philip Dunne.

THE WAY TO THE GOLD. See materials in the David Weisbart Collection, No. 50.

THE WAY WEST. 2 copies. 1967, United Artists. No. 37. Ben Maddow and Mitch Lindeman.

THE WAYWARD BUS. 1957, Fox. Ivan Moffat and [Victor Vicas].

THE WAYWARD GIRL. (cc). 1957, Republic. Houston Branch and Frederic Louis Fox.

WE ARE ALL CHRIST   TITLES INDEX

WE ARE ALL CHRIST. See Interview with Tom Laughlin.

WE ARE NOT ALONE. 1939, Warner Bros. James Hilton and Milton Krims.

WE FOOLS OF NATURE. n. d. No. 44. [Albert Lewin].

WE, THE JURY. [1936], [RKO]. [Franklin Coen].

THE WEB OF DANGER. (cc). 1947, Republic. David Lang and Milton
     Raison.

WEE WILLIE WINKIE. 1937, Fox. Ernest Pascal and Julien Josephson.

WEEKEND AT LAS VEGAS. Rel. as MEET ME IN LAS VEGAS. 1956, MGM.
     No. 26. Isobel Lennart.

*WEEKEND AT THE WALDORF. 1945, MGM. Bella and Samuel Spewack.

WEEKEND FOR THREE. 1941. RKO. No. 65. Dorothy Parker and Alan
     Campbell.

WEEKEND IN HAVANA. 1941, Fox. No. 19. Karl Tunberg and Darrell
     Ware.

WELCOME HOME SOLDIER BOYS. 1972, Fox. [Guerdon Trueblood].

THE WELL. 1951, United Artists. No. 94. Russell Rouse and
     Clarence Greene.

WELLS FARGO. 1937, Paramount. Paul Schofield, Gerald Geraghty and
     Frederick Jackson.

WELLS FARGO GUNMASTER. cc. 3 copies. 1951, Republic. M. Coates
     Webster.

WEST OF ABILINE. Rel. as AFTER THE JAMES GANG. 1940, Columbia.
     Paul Franklin.

WEST OF CIMARRON. cc. 1941, Republic. Albert DeMond and Don Ryan.

WEST OF SHANGHAI. See WAR LORD.

WEST OF THE PECOS. 1944, RKO. Norman Houston.

THE WEST SIDE KID. 1943, Republic. Albert Beich and Anthony
     Coldeway.

WEST SIDE STORY. 1961, United Artists. No. 91. Ernest Lehman.
See also Interview with Irwin Kostal. See also materials in
the Robert Wise Collection, No. 49.

WESTERN AFFAIR. 1954, Republic. [Gene Lewis].

WESTERN GOLD. 1937, Fox. No. 68. Earle Snell, Forrest Barnes and
[Harold Bell Wright].

WESTERN JAMBOREE. 1938, Republic. Gerald Geraghty.

WESTERN LIMITED. Outline. n. d. George Jeske and Charles E.
Roberts.

THE WESTERN STORY. [1948], [Universal]. [William Bowers and Oscar
Brodney].

WESTWARD HO. cc. 1942, Republic. Morton Grant and Doris Schroeder.

WHAT A LIFE. 1939, Paramount. Charles Brackett and Billy Wilder.

WHAT EVER HAPPENED TO AUNT ALICE? 1969, Cinerama. Theodore Apstein.

WHAT EVERY GIRL WANTS. [1963]. No. 66. [Arthur Sheekman].

WHAT EVERY WOMAN KNOWS. Scenario. 1921, Paramount. No. 8.

WHATEVER HAPPENED TO BABY JANE. See Interview with Robert Aldrich.

WHAT'S THE RUSH? Outline. [1944]. [Charles E. Roberts and Charles
R. Marion].

*WHEN A FELLER NEEDS A FRIEND. 1932, MGM. [Sylvia Thalberg and
Frank Butler].

WHEN A MAN'S A MAN. 1935, Fox. No. 68. [Harold Bell Wright].

WHEN GANGLAND STRIKES. cc. 2 copies. 1956, Republic. John K.
Butler and Frederic Louis Fox.

WHEN I GROW UP. 1951, Eagle Lion. No. 94. Michael Kanin.

*WHEN IN ROME. 1952, MGM. Charles Schnee and Dorothy Kingsley.

WHEN MY BABY SMILES AT ME. 1948, Fox. No. 19. Lamar Trotti. See
also BURLESQUE.

WHEN THE LEGENDS DIE   TITLES INDEX

WHEN THE LEGENDS DIE. Also WHEN LEGENDS DIE. 1972, Fox. Robert
     Dozier.

WHEN YOU'RE IN LOVE. 1937, Columbia. No. 63. Robert Riskin.

WHERE DOES IT HURT? 1972, Cinerama. [Rod Amateau and Budd Robin-
     son].

WHERE THE BOYS ARE. 1960, MGM. George Wells.

WHERE'S JACK? 1969, Paramount. [Rafe and David Newhouse].

WHISKEY'S RENEGADES. [1968]. [William W. Norton].

WHISPERERS. See Interview with Ronald Shedlo.

WHISPERING SMITH SPEAKS. 1935, Fox. No. 68. [F. Spearman, Don
     Swift and Dan Jarrett].

THE WHITE ANGEL. See materials in the William Dieterle Collection,
     No. 17.

*WHITE CARGO. 1942, MGM. Leon Gordon.

*THE WHITE CLIFFS OF DOVER. 1944, MGM. Claudine West, Jan Lustig
     and George Froeschel.

WHITE COLLARS. [1929], [MGM]. No. 8. [Clara Beranger].

WHITE FANG. 1936, Fox. Gene Fowler, Hal Long and S. G. Duncan.

*THE WHITE SISTER. 1933, MGM. [Donald Ogden Stewart and Leonard
     Praskins].

WHITE YOUTH. 1920, Universal. [Clara Beranger and Forrest Halsey].

WHO KILLED AUNT MAGGIE? 2 copies. 1940, Republic. Stuart Palmer.

THE WHOLE TOWN'S TALKING. 1935, Columbia. No. 63. [Robert Riskin
     and Jo Swerling].

WHO'S AFRAID OF VIRGINIA WOOLF? 1966, Warner Bros. Ernest Lehman.
     See also materials in the Ernest Lehman Collection, No. 19.

WHY WAS I BORN? Treatment. [1955]. No. 0. [Irving Wallace].

THE WILD BLUE YONDER. (cc). 1951, Republic. Richard Tregaskis.

WILD BRIAN KENT. 1936, RKO. No. 68. James Gruen, Earle Snell and
    [Harold Bell Wright].

THE WILD FRONTIER. cc. 1947, Republic. Albert DeMond.

WILD GEESE CALLING. 1941, Fox. Horace McCoy.

THE WILD GOOSE CHASE. Scenario. 1915. No. 8.

WILD HARVEST. 1947, Paramount. No. 65. John Monks, Jr.

WILD HORSE AMBUSH. cc. 3 copies. 1952, Republic. William Lively.

WILD IN THE COUNTRY. 1961, Fox. No. 41. Clifford Odets.

WILD IN THE STREETS. 1968, American International. Robert Thom.

WILD RIVER. 1960, Fox. Paul Osborn.

THE WILD SEED. 1965, Universal. No. 96. Les Pine and [Ike Jones].

WILL PENNY. 2 copies. 1968, Paramount. No. 96. Tom Gries.

WILLIE WONKA AND THE CHOCOLATE FACTORY. See Interview with David
    Lipton.

*THE WILLOW TREE. 1920, Metro. [June Mathis].

WILSON. Rev. final scr. 1944, Fox. Lamar Trotti.

WINDS OF THE WASTELAND. 1936, Republic. Joe Poland.

WINGED VICTORY. Final scr. 1944, Fox. Moss Hart.

*THE WINGS OF EAGLES. 1957, MGM. Frank Fenton and William Wister
    Haines.

WINNING. Outline, 5 drafts and final. 1969, Universal. Howard
    Rodman. See also Interview with James Goldstone.

WINTER SERENADE. cc. 3 copies. Re-ed. from LAKE PLACID SERENADE.
    n. d. Republic. [Dick Irving Hyland and Doris Gilbert].

WINTER WONDERLAND. cc and trailer cc. 1947, Republic. Peter
    Goldbaum, David Chandler, Arthur Marx and Gertrude Purcell.

WINTERTIME. 1943, Fox. No. 19. E. Edwin Moran, Jack Jevne and
    Lynn Starling.

WITCH IN THE WILDERNESS   TITLES INDEX

WITCH IN THE WILDERNESS. [1939]. No. 25. [David Mertz and
        Laurence Stallings].

*WITCH OF WILDERNESS. [1940], MGM. [Laurence Stallings].

WITH A SONG IN MY HEART. 1952, Fox. No. 19. Lamar Trotti.

WITHOUT HONOR. 1st draft. 2 copies. 1949, United Artists. James
        Poe.

*WITHOUT LOVE. 1945, MGM. Donald Ogden Stewart.

WITHOUT RESERVATIONS. 1946, RKO. No. 75. Andrew P. Solt.

WITHOUT WARNING. 1952, United Artists. Bill Raynor.

WIVES AND LOVERS. Draft and final scr. 1963, Paramount. No. 27.
        Edward Anhalt.

THE WIZARD OF OZ. See materials in the King Vidor Collection,
        No. 25.

WOLF OF NEW YORK. cc. 1940, Republic. Lionel Houser.

WOMAN FROM HEADQUARTERS. cc. 1950, Republic. [Andrew Solt].

WOMAN IN THE DARK. cc. 1952, Republic. Albert DeMond.

*A WOMAN OF AFFAIRS. 1929, MGM. [Bess Meredyth].

THE WOMAN THEY ALMOST LYNCHED. cc. 1953, Republic. Steve Fisher.

A WOMAN'S DEVOTION. cc. 1956, Republic. Robert Hill.

WOMEN IN LOVE. See Interview with Larry Kramer.

*WOMEN LOVE DIAMONDS. 1927, MGM. [Edmund Goulding and Edwin
        Justis Mayer].

WOMEN OF GLAMOR. 2nd draft. 1937, Columbia. Lynn Starling and
        Mary C. McCall, Jr.

*THE WONDER OF WOMEN. 1929, MGM. [Bess Meredyth and James Forbes].

THE WONDERFUL COUNTRY. 3 copies. 1959, United Artists. No. 32.
        Robert Ardrey.

THE WONDERFUL YEARS. Treatment, outline, drafts, final and rev.
    final scr. n. d. No. 27. [Edward Anhalt].

WORDS AND MUSIC. 1948, MGM. No. 19. Fred Finkelhoffe.

*WORDS AND MUSIC. 1948, MGM. Fred Finkelhoffe.

WORK... IS A FOUR LETTER WORD. 1968, Universal. Jeremy Brooks.

WORKING OUR WAY THROUGH COLLEGE. Treatment. 1949. No. 0.
    [Irving Wallace].

*THE WORLD, THE FLESH, AND THE DEVIL. 1959, MGM. Ranald
    MacDougall.

THE WORLD'S APPLAUSE. 1923, Paramount. [Clara Beranger].

THE WORM BURNS. Dialogue treatment and synopsis. n. d. [Charles
    E. Roberts and George Jeske].

THE WRATH OF GOD. 1972, MGM. [Ralph Nelson].

A WREATH FOR PETROFF'S GRAVE. Synopsis. [1950]. [Clare Booth
    Luce].

THE WRECK OF THE MARY DEARE. 1959, MGM. Eric Ambler.

THE WRECKING CREW. (THE HOUSE OF JOYS). 1968, Columbia. No. 37.
    William McGivern.

THE WRONG ROAD. cc. 1937, Republic. Gordon Rigby and Eric Taylor.

WYLIE. [1968], [Universal]. [Joseph Stefano].

WYOMING. 1940, MGM. Jack Jevne and Hugo Butler.

WYOMING. cc. 1947, Republic. Lawrence Hazard and Gerald Geraghty.

THE WYOMING BANDIT. (cc). 1949, Republic. M. Coates Webster.

X MARKS THE SPOT. cc. 1942, Republic. Stuart Palmer.

A YANK IN THE R. A. F. 1941, Fox. Karl Tunberg and Darrell Ware.

A YANK ON THE BURMA ROAD. See CHINA CARAVAN.

YANKS IN TANKS. Treatment. [1943]. [Robert T. Shannon].

THE YEAR OF THE CRICKET   TITLES INDEX

THE YEAR OF THE CRICKET. See KENNER.

THE YEAR OF THE TIGER. See Interview with Marshall Thompson.

*THE YEARLING. 1946, MGM. Paul Osborn.

YEARS ARE SO LONG. See MAKE WAY FOR TOMORROW.

*THE YELLOW CAB MAN. 1950, MGM. Albert Beich and Devery Freeman.

YELLOW SUBMARINE. 1968, United Artists. Lee Minoff, Al Brodax,
    Jack Mendelsohn, and Erich Segal. See also Interview with
    Al Brodax.

YELLOWNECK. cc. 1955, Republic. Nat S. Linden.

YODELIN' KID FROM PINE RIDGE. cc. 1937, Republic. Jack Natteford,
    Stuart and Dorrell McGowan.

YOKEL BOY. 1942, Republic. Isabel Dawn.

YOU CAME ALONG. 2 copies. 1945, Paramount. No. 75. Robert
    Smith and Ayn Rand.

YOU CAN'T HAVE EVERYTHING. 2 copies. 1937, Fox. No. 19. Harry
    Tugend, Jack Yellen and Karl Tunberg.

YOU CAN'T TAKE IT WITH YOU. 1938, Columbia. No. 63. Robert
    Riskin.

YOU CAN'T WIN 'EM ALL. 1970, Columbia. [Leo V. Gordon].

YOU WERE MEANT FOR ME. 1948, Fox. No. 19. Elick Moll and Valen-
    tine Davies.

YOU TOUCHED ME! [1950]. [Montgomery Clift and Kevin McCarthy].

YOU'LL LIKE MY MOTHER. Rev. and final rev. scr. 1972, Universal.
    [Jo Heims].

YOUNG AND WILD. cc. 1958, Republic. Arthur T. Horman.

THE YOUNG ANIMALS. Aka BORN WILD. 1968, American International.
    James Gordon White.

YOUNG BILL HICKOK. cc. 1940, Republic. Norton S. Parker and
    Olive Cooper.

148

YOUNG BUFFALO BILL. 1940, Republic.

THE YOUNG LIONS. Treatment and final scr. 1958, Fox. No. 27.
     Edward Anhalt.

*YOUNG MAN WITH IDEAS. 1952, MGM. Arthur Sheekman.

YOUNG MR. LINCOLN. 1939, Fox. Lamar Trotti.

YOUNG ROMANCE. Scenario. 1914, Paramount. No. 8. [William
     DeMille].

THE YOUNG RUNAWAYS. 1968, MGM. Orville H. Hampton.

THE YOUNG SAVAGES. 3 drafts and final. 1961, United Artists.
     No. 27. Edward Anhalt and J. P. Miller.

YOU'RE MY EVERYTHING. 1949, Fox. No. 19. Lamar Trotti and Will
     Hays, Jr.

YOURS, MINE AND OURS. See Interview with Mel Shavelson.

YOUTH ON PARADE. cc. 1942, Republic. George Carleton Brown.

ZANZABUKU. cc. 1956, Republic. Ronald Davidson.

ZORRO RIDES AGAIN. cc. 3 copies. 1959, Republic. Barry Shipman,
     John Rathmell, Franklyn Adreon, Ronald Davidson and Morgan
     Cox.

SHORT SUBJECTS

The following is a list of screenplays for the short subjects in the collection. These short subjects are from the files of Metro-Goldwyn-Mayer, Republic Studios, and Radio-Keith-Orpheum (RKO) Studios and are arranged alphabetically by title under the headings of their producing studios. Writing credits and further information are much more difficult to obtain reliably and have not been provided in this list.

M-G-M shorts (1942-1957)

Camera Sleuth
Crashing the Movies
Curious Contests
Darkness into Light
Did'ja Know?
Do Someone A Favor
The Fabulous Fraud
The Fall Guy
Global Quiz
Going to Blazes
Historical Oddities
I Love My Wife, But...
Jubilee Overture
Just Suppose
Just What I Needed
Madero of Mexico
Main Street Today
Make Mine Freedom
Martin Block's Musical
    Merry-Go-Round
Mr. Whitney Had A Notion
Neighbor Pests
Operation Teahouse

Penny Wise
Pest Control
Pigskin Packers
Pigskin Skill
Poet and Peasant Overture
Screen Actors
Sea for Yourself
Slang
Souvenir of Death
Sports Oddities
Tale of the Navajos
That's His Story
Underground News
Wanted: One Egg
Water Trix
We Can Dream, Can't We?
The Wedding in Monaco
Why Is It?
Why Play Leapfrog
A Wife's Life
Wrong Son
Wrong Way Butch
You Can't Win

SHORT SUBJECTS

Republic Shorts (1935-1941?)

    Land of Opportunity--"The Mardi Gras" cc
    Meet the Stars (1940-41)--8 shorts
    Smart Set (1935-38)--13 shorts
    Stories of the Century: 9 cc's
        Clay Allison and Ben Thompson
        Joaquin Murietta and Chief Crazy Horse
        Johnny Ringo and Doc Holliday
        Little Britches and the Doolin Gang
        Quantrill and His Raiders and Belle Starr
        Sam Bass and Frank and Jesse James
        Tiburcio Vasques and Black Bart
        Tom Horn and Black Jack Ketchum
        The Wild Bunch of Wyoming and Harry Tracy
    Superba--9 scripts including drafts
    This World of Ours--16 shorts on individual countries

RKO Comedy Shorts, which featured:

    Leon Errol--34 scripts plus drafts
    Edgar Kennedy--52 scripts plus drafts (1935-1947)
    Ray Whitley--19 scripts plus drafts (1939-1942)
    Bert Wheeler and Robert Woolsey--3 scripts plus drafts plus
        estimating scripts (1935-1936)

SCREENWRITERS AND FILM PERSONALITIES INDEX

This section lists alphabetically all screenwriters with credits in the Title Index and includes any additional credited screenplays in the USC Screenplay Collection. All titles, to the best of our ability, are cited as release titles. If the screenplay is filed in the collection under an alternate title, cross references have been made to the shelf title under which it is filed.

Following the same procedure as in the Titles Index, cross references to individuals other than screenwriters are also included. These cross references are to individual collections in the Special Collections area and to specific interviews. Cross references for individuals participating in panel discussions are not included.

This index enables the researcher to determine quickly whether there is material relating to any individual who may be a subject of his investigations. Further information concerning identification of movies referred to in this Index may be found in the Titles Index.

ABDULLAH, ACHMED.
    Lives of A Bengal Lancer

ABERBACH, HY. See Interviews on
    Tape.

ABRAHAMS, MORT. See Interviews
    on Tape.

ADAMS, FRANK R.
    Trade Winds

ADAMS, GERALD DRAYSON.
    Armoured Car Robbery
    California Outpost
    Frontier Rangers
    The Gallant Legion
    Old Los Angeles
    The Plunderers

ADAMSON, EWART.
    The Walking Dead

ADLER, E. M.
    Sabotage

ADREON, FRANKLYN
    The Fighting Devil Dogs
    Sons of Adventure
    Zorro Rides Again

AINSLEE, MARION.
    Foreign Devils

AKINS, ZOE
    Desire Me

ALBERT, KATHERINE
    The Star

ALBERT, MARVIN H.
    The Lady in Cement
    Rough Night in Jericho
    The Seven Minutes
    A Twist of Sand

ALDRICH, ROBERT. See also Inter-
    views on Tape.
    4 for Texas

ALEXANDER, RONALD.
    Billie

ALLARDICE, JAMES.
    Money From Home
    Sailor Beware

ALLEN, CHRIS.
    Susquatch

ALLEN, GRACIE. Collection No. 24.

ALLEN, JAY PRESSON.
    Marnie
    Travels With My Aunt

ALLEN, STEVE. Collection No. 64.

ALLEN, WOODY.
    Take the Money and Run

ALMOND, PAUL.
    Isabel

ALONZO, JOHN. See Interviews on
    Tape.

ALTMAN, ROBERT. See Interviews
    on Tape.

AMATEAU, ROD.
    Hook, Line, and Sinker
    Where Does It Hurt?

AMBLER, ERIC.
    The Wreck of the Mary
    Deare

ANDERSON, DORIS.
    Men Call It Love
    That Brennan Girl
    Tough Girl

ANDERSON, GERRY and SYLVIA.
    Doppel Ganger
    Thunderbird Six

ANDERSON, MAXWELL.
    Joan of Arc
    Rendezvous

ANDERSON, ROBERT.
    The Nun's Story
    The Sand Pebbles
    Tea and Sympathy
    Until They Sail

ANDERSON, WALT. See Interviews
    on Tape.

ANDREWS, ROBERT D.
    Bataan
    Before I Hang
    Cross of Lorraine
    The Edge of Running
        Water

ANDREWS, ROBERT H.
    The Johnny Broderick
        Story

ANGELL, BUCKLEY.
    The Hired Gun

ANHALT, EDNA
    Panic in the Streets
    The Pride and the Pas-
        sion

ANHALT, EDWARD. Collection
    No. 27.
    The Affair in Arcady
    The Ark of Dr. Hollister
    Becket
    The Big Kill
    Boeing-Boeing
    The Boston Strangler
    Bugsy Siegel
    Day of the Champion
    Decision at Delphi
    The Devil's Advocate

ANHALT, EDWARD. (cont.)
    The Fifth Estate
    The Flesh is Strong
    A Girl Named Tomiko
    The Golden Journey
    Hour of the Gun
    In Enemy Country
    In Love and War
    Letter from Peking
    Los Soldaderos
    The Madwoman of
    Member of the Wedding
    Panic in the Streets
    Passion of Mary Magdalene
    Peter the Great
    The Pride and the Passion
    Sacco and Venzetti
    Sins of Rachel Cade
    A Time for Killing
    Wives and Lovers
    The Wonderful Years
    The Young Lions
    The Young Savages

ANTHONY, JOHN J. Collection
    No. 86

ANTROBUS, JOHN.
    The Bed Sitting Room

APSTEIN, THEODORE.
    What Ever Happened to
        Aunt Alice?

ARCHIBALD, WILLIAM.
    The Innocents

ARDREY, ROBERT.
    The Green Years
    Madame Bovary
    The Power and the Prize
    Quentin Durward
    The Secret Garden
    Song of Love
    The Wonderful Country

ARGENTO, DARIO.
    Five Man Army

ARLEN, MICHAEL.
    The Heavenly Body

ARLISS, LESLIE.
    The Saint Meets the
       Tiger

ARNOLD, JOHN. See Interviews
    on Tape.

ARTHUR, ART.

    Northwest Stampede
    Sleepy-Time Gal

ASTAIRE, FRED. Collection
    No. 70.

AURENCHE, JEAN.
    Love is My Profession

AURTHUR, ROBERT ALAN.
    The Lost Man

AUSTIN, RONALD.
    The Midas Run.

AVERY, STEPHEN MOREHOUSE.
    The Male Animal

AXELROD, GEORGE. See also In-
    terviews on Tape.
    Secret Life of an
       American Wife

AXELROD, JONATHAN.
    Every Little Crook
       and Nanny

AYERS, JERRY. See Interviews
    on Tape.

BABCOCK, DWIGHT V.
    Road to Alcatraz
    Savage Frontier

BACH, RICHARD. See Interviews
    on Tape.

BACHMANN, LAWRENCE.
    Night Shift

BACKUS, JIM & HENNY. Collection
    No. 26.

BADARACCO, JACOB A. See Inter-
    views on Tape.

BAEHR, NICHOLAS E.
    Ride With Terror

BAILY, JOHN. See Interviews on
    Tape.

BAINTER, FAY. Collection No. 77.

BAKALEINIKOFF, MISCHA. Collection
    No. 9.

BAKER, ELLIOTT.
    Luv
    Viva Max

BAKER, GRAHAM.
    Eternally Yours
    The Joy of Living
    Ramrod
    Stand-in
    Swiss Family Robinson

BAKER, HERBERT.
    The Ambushers
    The Big Leaguer
    Dream Wife
    The Girl Can't Help It
    Hammerhead
    Jumping Jacks
    So This is New York

BALDERSTON, JOHN L.
    Andrew Jackson
    Berkeley Square
    Bride of Frankenstein
    Cargo of Innocents
    Christian of the Bounty
    Gaslight
    Green Mansions

BALDERSTON, JOHN L. (cont.)
    He Who Gets Slapped
    The Last of the
      Mohicans
    Lives of A Bengal
      Lancer
    The Prisoner of Zenda
    Red Planet
    Smilin' Through
    The Story of Irene
    Tennessee Johnson
    Victory

BALDWIN, EARL.
    Greenwich Village
    Irish Eyes Are Smiling
    Pin-Up Girl
    The Snatching of
      Bookie Bob

BALDWIN, PETER.
    A Place for Lovers

BALSHOFER, FRED J. See Interviews on Tape.

BAND, ALBERT.
    A Minute to Prey, A
      Second to Die

BARNES, FORREST.
    Western Gold

BARON, ALLEN. See Interviews
on Tape.

BARRETT, ALLAN. See Interviews
on Tape.

BARRETT, JAMES LEE.
    Bandolero!
    Fools' Parade
    The Green Berets
    The Undefeated

BARRETT, TONY.
    Good Times

BARRIE, JAMES M.
    Doctor's Secret [Half an
      Hour]

BARROWS, NICHOLAS.
    Mr. and Mrs. America

BARRY, TOM.
    In Old Arizona

BARRYMORE, ETHYL. See Interviews
on Tape.

BARSHA, LEON. See Interviews on
Tape.

BART, PETER.
    Making It

BARTLETT, HALL. See Interviews on
Tape.

BARTLETT, JEANNE.
    Gallant Bess

BARTLETT, SY.
    Che!

BASSANI, GIORGIO.
    Don Juan's Night of Love

BAST, WILLIAM.
    Hammerhead

BATT, BERT.
    Frankenstein Must Be Des-
      troyed

BATTLE, JOHN TUCKER.
    Irish Eyes Are Smiling
    Lisbon
    A Man Alone

BAVA, MARIO.
    Danger: Diabolik

BEAUCHAMP, DANIEL D.
    For the Love of Mike

BEEBE, FORD.
    Tumbling Tumbleweeds

BEECHER, ELIZABETH.
    Rough Riders of
      Cheyenne

BEGLEY, ED. See Interviews on
    Tape.

BEHN, HARRY.
    Frozen River

BEHRMAN, S. N.
    My Lips Betray
    Parnell
    Quo Vadis
    Tess of the Storm
      Country

BEICH, ALBERT.
    The Bride Goes Wild
    Gangs of the Water-
      front
    Gay Blades
    Panic Button
    Perils of Pauline
    The West Side Kid
    The Yellow Cab Man

BELDEN, CHARLES S.
    Charlie Chan at the
      Opera
    Mr. Moto's Gamble

BELGARD, ARNOLD.
    Panama Sal

BELLAH, JAMES WARNER.
    Target Zero

BELLAKI, GEORGE.
    Invisible Avenger

BELOIN, EDMUND.
    A Connecticut Yankee
      in King Arthur's
      Court

BELOIN, EDMUND (cont.)
    The Harvey Girls
    Road to Rio

BENCHLEY, NATHANIEL.
    The Great American Pastime

BENEDEK, LAZLO. See Interviews on
    Tape.

BENNET, SPENCER. See Interviews
    on Tape.

BENNETT, CHARLES.
    Cause for Alarm
    Kind Lady
    Madonna of the Desert
    Reap the Wild Wind
    The Story of Dr. Wassell
    Unconquered

BENNISON, ANDREW.
    Lawless Land

BENOFF, MAX
    Iris

BENSON, SALLY.
    Conspirator
    The Farmer Takes A Wife

BENTON, ROBERT.
    Bonnie and Clyde
    There Was a Crooked Man...

BERANGER, CLARA. See Collection
    No. 8.
    The Bar Sinister
    The Bedroom Window
    The Blemish
    Carmen
    Craig's Wife
    The Fear Market
    The Forbidden Woman
    The Gift Horse
    Grumpy
    Icebound
    Idle Rich

BERANGER, CLARA (cont.)
   Inhuman Ground
   Locked Doors
   New Brooms
   Nice People
   Pagliacci
   Spring Cleaning
   Spring Magic
   White Collars
   White Youth
   The World's Applause

BERCOVICI, ERIC.
   Change of Habit
   Culpepper Cattle Co.
   The Evil Gun

BERCOVICI, LEONARDO.
   The Bishop's Wife
   The Story of a Woman

BERG, GERTRUDE.
   Make A Wish

BERGEN, POLLY. See Interviews
   on Tape.

BERKELEY, MARTIN.
   Fall Guy
   Gypsy Colt

BERLAND, JACQUES
   O.S.S. 117 Is Not Dead

BERN, MICHAEL.
   Crack in the Mirror

BERNSTEIN, ELMER. See Interviews on Tape.

BERNSTEIN, WALTER.
   The Molly Maguires
   Paris Blues

BERSINSKI, LEO.
   Mata Hari

BEST, WILLIAM.
   Gwangi the Great

BEZZERIDES, A. I.
   Angry Hills
   Kiss Me Deadly

BIDDELL, SIDNEY.
   Appointment on "A" Deck

BILL, TONY. See Interviews on
   Tape.

BINYON, CLAUDE.
   Down About the Sheltering
      Palms
   Holiday Inn
   I Met Him At Paris
   My Blue Heaven
   No Time For Love
   Sing, Boy, Sing
   Take A Letter, Darling
   Texas Guinan ·

BISHOP, RON.
   Underground

BLACK, JOHN. See Interviews on
   Tape.

BLACK, JOHN D. F.
   Nobody's Perfect
   Shaft
   Trouble Man

BLACKTON, MARIAN CONSTANCE.
   Becky

BLANKFORT, HENRY.
   Humphrey Takes A Chance

BLANKFORT, MICHAEL.
   Adam Had Four Sons
   Blind Alley
   Dark Past
   Humphrey Takes A Chance
   Lydia Bailey

BLANKFORT, MICHAEL (cont.)
    Tribute to a Bad Man
    The Vintage

BLATTY, WILLIAM PETER.
    I Am Legend

BLAUGH, LOUIS. See Interviews
    on Tape.

BLEES, ROBERT.
    High School Confiden-
        tial

BLOCH, ROBERT.
    Torture Garden
    The Night Walker

BLOCK, RALPH.
    The Melody Lingers On

BLOOM, HAROLD JACK.
    Arena

BLOOM, JEFFERY.
    Snow Job

BLUEL, RICHARD.
    The Raid on Rommel

BLUM, EDWIN HARVEY.
    The Great American
        Broadcast
    Kidnapped

BLUMOFE, ROBERT F. See Inter-
    views on Tape.

BOARDMAN, TRUE.
    The Painted Hills

BOASBERG, AL.
    Murder in a Private
        Car

BODEEN, DEWITT.
    The Curse of the Cat
        People
    The Enchanted Cottage

BOEHM, DAVID.
    Peck's Bad Boy With the
        Circus

BOEHM, SYDNEY.
    The High Wall
    Mystery Street
    Rogue Cop
    Rough Night in Jericho
    Violent Saturday

BOETTICHER, BUDD. See Interviews
    on Tape.

BOETTICHER, OSCAR, JR.
    Tomorrow's Almost Over

BOGDANOVICH, PETER. See Inter-
    views on Tape.

BOHEM, ENDRE.
    House of a Thousand
        Candles
    Larceny on the Air

BOLLINGER, HENRI. See Interviews
    on Tape.

BOLOGNA, JOSEPH.
    Made For Each Other

BOLTON, G. R.
    Delicious

BOLTON, GUY.
    Dollar Bill

BOLTON, MURIEL ROY.
    Grissly's Millions
    Henry Aldrich, Editor

BOND, EDWARD.
    Laughter in the Dark
    Michael Kohlhaas

BOOKER, BOB.
    The Phynx

BOOLOOTIAN, DR. R. A. See
    Interviews on Tape.

BOROWSKY, MARVIN.
    Alias Mike Fury

BOST, PIERRE.
    Love is my Profession

BOURGUIGNON, SERGE. See Inter-
    views on Tape.

BOWER, PAMELA.
    Laughing Annie
    Trent's Last Case

BOWERS, WILLIAM. See also
    Interviews on Tape.
    The Best Things in
        Life Are Free
    Imitation General
    The Law and Jake Wade
    Mrs. O'Malley and Mr.
        Malone
    My Favorite Spy
    Night and Day
    The Sheepman
    Split Second
    The Western Story

BOYER, FRANCOIS.
    The Twenty-fifth Hour

BOYLAN, MALCOLM STUART.
    Hell Divers
    Soldiers Three

BRABIN, CHARLES
    The Great Meadow

BRACKETT, CHARLES.
    A Foreign Affair
    The Girl in the Red Vel-
        vet Swing
    The Lost Weekend
    The Major and the Minor
    Sunset Boulevard
    To Each His Own
    What A Life

BRACKETT, LEIGH.
    The Big Sleep

BRACKMAN, CLYDE.
    The Cameraman

BRADBURY, RAY. See also Inter-
    views on Tape.
    The Picasso Summer

BRANCH, GERARD.
    The Fearless Vampire Kil-
        lers, Or Pardon Me But
        Your Teeth Are in My
        Neck

BRANCH, HOUSTON.
    Bal Tabarin
    City of Shadows
    Fighting Chance
    Girls of the Big House
    Mr. Wong, Detective
    The Pittsburgh Kid
    A Strange Adventure
    Sweethearts on Parade
    The Wayward Girl

BRAND, MILLEN.
    The Snake Pit

BREECHER, IRVING. Collection
    No. 30.
    Best Foot Forward
    DuBarry Was a Lady
    The Life of Riley

BREEN, RICHARD L.
    Captain Newman, M.D.
    A Foreign Affair
    State Fair
    Tony Rome

BREN, MILTON.
    Three for Bedroom C

BRENNAN, FREDERICK HAZLITT.
    Adventure
    Killer McCoy

BRESLOW, LOU.
    Abbott and Costello in
        Hollywood
    15 Maiden Lane
    Merton of the Movies

BRICE, MONTE.
    Eadie Was A Lady
    Mama Loves Papa
    Merry-Go-Round of 1938
    The Mexican Spitfire
        Sees a Ghost

BRICUSSE, LESLIE.
    Dr. Dolittle

BRICKER, GEORGE
    If I'm Lucky

BRIDGES, JAMES. See also
    Interviews on Tape.
    Colossus: The Forbin
        Project

BRIGHT, JOHN.
    The Kid From Cleveland

BRISKIN, MORT.
    The Damned

BROADHURST, G. H.
    Bought and Paid For

BRODAX, AL. See also Interviews
    on Tape.
    Yellow Submarine

BRODIE, MEL. See Interviews on
    Tape.

BRODNEY, OSCAR.
    Abbott and Costello Meet
        the Killer
    Harvey
    The Western Story

BROOKS, JEREMY.
    Our Mother's House
    Work...Is A Four Letter
        Word

BROOKS, MATT
    Radio City Revels

BROOKS, RICHARD. See also Inter-
    views on Tape.
    Any Number Can Play
    Battle Circus
    The Blackboard Jungle
    The Brothers Karamazov
    Cat on a Hot Tin Roof
    The Last Hunt
    The Last Time I Saw Paris
    The Light Touch
    Mystery Street
    Something of Value

BROUGH, WALTER.
    The Desperadoes

BROUN, HEYWOOD.
    The Boy Who Grew Older

BROWN, BERT.
    Counterfeit

BROWN, GEORGE CARLETON.
    Atlantic City Honeymoon
    Youth on Parade

BROWN, HARRY.
    All the Brothers Were
      Valiant
    Arch of Triumph
    Many Rivers to Cross
    The Other Love
    A Place in the Sun
    Sands of Iwo Jima
    The Sniper

BROWN, KARL.
    The Calling of Dan
      Matthews
    Fast Workers
    Gangs of Chicago
    The Man They Could Not
      Hang
    The Man with Nine
      Lives

BROWN, LEWIS ALLEN.
    Please Get Married

BROWN, ROLAND.
    Johnny Apollo

BROWN, ROSCOE LEE. See Inter-
    views on Tape.

BROWNE, ARTHUR, JR.
    Clambake

BROWNE, HOWARD.
    The St. Valentine's
      Day Massacre

BRUCE, GEORGE.
    Fiesta
    Keep Your Powder Dry
    Little Mister Jim
    Navy Blue and Gold
    Salute to the Marines
    Two Years Before the
      Mast

BRULE, CLAUDE.
    The Champagne Murders

BRYANT, BAIRD. See Interviews on
    Tape.

BUCHANAN, JAMES D.
    The Midas Run

BUCHANAN, LARRY. See Interviews
    on Tape.

BUCHHOLZ, HORST. See Interviews
    on Tape.

BUCHMAN, HAROLD.
    Cynthia
    The Lawyer

BUCHMAN, SIDNEY.
    Cleopatra

BUCKINGHAM, TOM.
    Officer O'Brien

BUCKNER, ROBERT.
    Love Me Tender
    The Night Watch

BUFFINGTON, ADELE.
    Circus Girl

BULLOCK, WALTER.
    The Farmer Takes A Wife
    The Gang's All Here
    Golden Girl
    Greenwich Village
    The I Don't Care Girl
    Springtime in Alaska

BURBRIDGE, BETTY.
    Alias Billy the Kid
    Heroes of the Hills
    The Man from Rainbow
      Valley
    Melody Ranch
    The Oregon Trail
    Pals of the Saddle
    Prairie Moon
    The Purple Vigilantes
    Red River Range

BURBRIDGE, BETTY (cont.)
     Riders of the Black
          Hills
     Rovin' Tumbleweeds
     Santa Fe Scouts
     The Singing Vagabond
     South of the Border
     Springtime in the
          Rockies
     Stardust on the Sage
     Under Western Stars

BURBRIDGE, ELIZABETH.
     Out California Way
     Outlaws of Sonora

BURCH, RUTH. See Interviews
     on Tape.

BURKE, EDWIN.
     Bad Girl

BURNETT, WILLIAM.
     This Gun For Hire

BURNS, GEORGE. Collection
     No. 24.

BURNS, JESSIE.
     Money Talks

BURNSIDE, NORMAN.
     Dr. Ehrlich's Magic
          Bullet

BURT, FRANK.
     Flame of Youth

BURT, KATHERINE NEWLIN.
     Snow Blindness

BURTIS, THOMSON.
     The Town's Woman

BURTON, JAY. Collection
     No. 28.

BURTON, VAL.
     Glamour Boy #2
     Henry Aldrich, Editor

BUSCH, NIVEN.
     Daybreak
     The Postman Always Rings
          Twice
     Pursued

BUTLER, DAVID.
     Bright Eyes
     Bottoms Up

BUTLER, FRANK.
     Aloma of the South Seas
     Going My Way
     Montana Moon
     My Favorite Blonde
     The Perils of Pauline
     Untamed
     When a Feller Needs a
          Friend

BUTLER, HUGO.
     Lassie Come Home
     The Legend of Lylah Clare
     Wyoming
     A Yank on the Burma Road

BUTLER, JOHN K.
     Affair in Reno
     Down Dakota Way
     G.I. War Brides
     The Girl Who Dared
     Headline Hunters
     Hell's Crossroads
     I Cover the Underworld
     Lightnin' in the Forest
     Man from Oklahoma
     Missing Women
     My Pal Trigger
     No Man's Woman
     One Exciting Week
     Out of the Storm
     The Outcast
     The Phantom Speaks
     Post Office Investigator

BUTLER, JOHN K. (cont.)
    Pride of Maryland
    Raiders of Sunset Pass
    Robin Hood of Texas
    Rodeo King and the
        Senorita
    Streets of San
        Francisco
    Sunset in El Dorado
    Tarnished
    Tell It to a Star
    Terror At Midnight
    The Toughest Man in
        Arizona
    Utah
    Utah Wagon Train
    When Gangland Strikes

CACOYANNIS, MICHAEL. See
    Interviews on Tape.

CADY, JERRY.
    Five Came Back
    Full Confession
    Laddie
    The Mexican Spitfire's
        Baby
    Mr. Moto's Gamble
    The Purple Heart

CAESER, ARTHUR.
    Anne of the Indies

CAIN, GUILLERMO.
    Vanishing Point

CALLEGARI, JEAN PAUL.
    The Mystery of the
        Black Jungle

CAMPANILE, PASQUALE FESTA.
    The Girl and the
        General

CAMPBELL, ALAN.
    Trade Winds
    Weekend for Three

CAMPBELL, ROBERT WRIGHT.
    Man of a Thousand Faces
    The Night Fighters

CANFIELD, MARK.
    Crack in the Mirror

CANNING, VICTOR.
    The Assassin

CANNON, DORAN WILLIAM.
    The Innocents

CAPOTE, TRUMAN.
    The Innocents

CAPRA, FRANK. See Interviews on
    Tape.

CARLINO, LEWIS JOHN.
    The Brotherhood

CARLOCK, MARVIN and MARY. Collec-
    tion No. 84.

CARLSON, RICHARD.
    Island of the Lost

CAROTHERS, A. J.
    The Happiest Millionaire

CARR, ALAN. See Interviews on
    Tape.

CARR, RICHARD.
    Heaven With A Gun

CARRERAS, MICHAEL.
    Creatures the World Forgot

CARRINGTON, ROBERT and JANE-HOWARD.
    Wait Until Dark

CARROLL, JUNE.
    An Angel Comes to Brooklyn

CARROLL, RICHARD.
    The Ape

CARSON, ROBERT.
    Action of the Tiger
    Beau Geste

CARTER, ARTHUR.
    Operation Madball

CASE, JAMES. See Interviews on
    Tape.

CASE, ROBERT ORMOND.
    The Girl from Alaska

CASPARY, VERA.
    Stronger than Truth

CASSITY, JAMES J.
    Man or Gun

CASSAVETES, JOHN.
    Minnie and Moskowitz

CAVEN, TAYLOR.
    Silver City Kid

CAVETT, FRANK.
    Going My Way

CHAMBERS, WHITMAN.
    Manhandled

CHAMIE, AL. See Interviews on
    Tape.

CHAMPLIN, CHARLES. See Inter-
    views on Tape.

CHANDLEE, HARRY.
    Our Town
    Rainbow on the River

CHANDLER, DAVID.
    Winter Wonderland

CHANTLER, DAVID.
    Magic Fire

CHAPIN, ANNE MORRISON.
    The Big City
    The Secret Heart
    Sunset in Wyoming

CHAPIN, ROBERT.
    Checkers

CHAPLIN, SAUL. Collection No. 15.

CHAPMAN, TEDWELL.
    The Fabulous Suzanne

CHARLES-WILLIAMS, LIZ.
    Some Girls Do

CHASE, BORDEN.
    Coming at You
    The Fighting Seabees
    This Man's Navy

CHASE, MARY C.
    Harvey

CHENEY, B.
    Sheik of Buffalo Buttes

CHENEY, J. BENTON.
    The Laramie Trail
    Man from Music Mountain
    The Man from Thunder River

CHODOROV, EDWARD.
    Kind Lady
    Undercurrent

CHODOROV, JERRY.
    Dancing Feet

CHORDES, RAY
    It's A Big Country

CHRISTIAN-JACQUE
    The Foxiest Girl in Paris

CLARK, CHRIS
    Lady Sings the Blues

CLARK, F.
    Thoroughbreds All

CLARK, FRANK HOWARD.
    O'Malley of the
      Mounted

CLARK, KENNETH B.
    Daddy's Gone A-Hunting

CLARKE, CHARLES G. See Interviews on Tape.

CLARKE, DONALD H.
    This Is My Wife

CLARKE, THOMAS E. B.
    All at Sea
    The Half-Way House

CLAWSON, ELLIOT.
    Body and Soul
    California

CLAYTON, JACK. See Interviews
on Tape.

CLEMENT, DICK.
    Hannibal Brooks
    Otley
    Villain

CLEMENTS, CALVIN
    The Kansas City Bomber

CLEMENTS, COLIN.
    Elizabeth Blackwell

CLEMINS, HAROLD.
    Kenner

CLIFT, DENNISON.
    End of the Road
    Secrets of Scotland
      Yard

CLIFT, MONTGOMERY.
    You Touched Me!

CLORK, HARRY.
    Broadway Rhythm
    The Mighty McGurk

COBB, I. S.
    Judge Priest

COEN, FRANKLIN.
    Forged Passport
    The Golden Ones
    Kiss of Fire
    Night of the Quarter Moon
    We, the Jury

COFFEE, LENORE.
    Arsene Lupin
    Night Court

COGHILL, NEVILL.
    Doctor Faustus

COHEN, ALBERT J.
    Let's Live A Little

COHEN, BENNETT.
    The Border Patrolman
    Santa Fe Saddlemates
    Sheriff of Cimarron

COHEN, HERMAN.
    Berserk!

COHEN, LARRY.
    Daddy's Gone A-Hunting

COHEN, RONALD M.
    Blue

COHN, A. A.
    The Cisco Kid

COHN, ART.
    Carbine Williams
    The Girl Who Had Everything
    Glory Alley
    The Man on the Train
    Men of the Fighting Lady
    The Set-Up

COHN, ART (cont.)
    The Seven Hills of Rome
    The Tall Target
    Ten Thousand Bedrooms
    Tennessee Champ

COLDEWAY, ANTHONY.
    Code of the Prairie
    Death Valley Manhunt
    A Gentleman of Leisure
    Marshall of Reno
    Pacific Liner
    A Scream in the Dark
    Vigilantes of Dodge
      City
    The West Side Kid

COLE, LESTER.
    Charlie Chan's Great-
      est Case
    Fiesta
    Follow Your Heart
    The High Wall
    The President's
      Mystery
    The Romance of Rosy
      Ridge

COLE, ROYAL K.
    Exposed
    Ghost of Zorro
    Lost Planet Airmen

COLEMAN, PATRICIA.
    Delilah

COLLINGS, PIERRE.
    The Story of Louis
      Pasteur

COLLIER, JOHN.
    Deception
    Her Conscience
    The Story of Three
      Loves
    The War Lord

COLLINS, HAL.
    Best of Luck
    For Singles Only
    The Love-Ins

COLLINS, RICHARD.
    The Badlanders
    Kiss of Fire

COLT, SAMUEL. Collection No. 18.

COLTON, JOHN.
    Call of the Flesh
    Laughing Boy

COMDEN, BETTY.
    The Band Wagon
    The Barkleys of Broadway
    Good News
    It's Always Fair Weather
    On the Town
    Singin' in the Rain

CONCHON, GEORGE.
    The Stranger

CONNELL, RICHARD.
    Her Highness and the Bell-
      Boy
    Luxury Liner
    Rio Rita
    Two Girls and a Sailor

CONNELLY, MARC.
    Green Pastures

CONNERS, BARRY.
    The Patsy
    Riders of the Purple Sage

CONNOLLY, MYLES.
    Music for Millions
    State of the Union
    Tarzan Against the World
    Till the Clouds Roll By
    The Unfinished Dance

CONSELMAN, WILLIAM.
    Business and Pleasure
    The Connecticut Yankee
    On the Avenue
    Pigskin Parade
    Stowaway
    365 Nights in Hollywood

CONSELMAN, WILLIAM, JR.
    Lone Star Ranger

CONSIDINE, BOB.
    Hoodlum Empire
    Ladies' Day

COOK, FIEDLER. See Interviews
    on Tape.

COOK, PETER.
    Bedazzled

COOK, WHITFIELD.
    The Big City
    The Secret Heart

COON, GENE.
    Journey to Shiloh

COOPER, DOROTHY.
    A Date with Judy
    The Duchess of Idaho

COOPER, GLADYS. Collection
    No. 22.

COOPER, JOHN C.
    The First Man in Space
    The Haunted Stranger

COOPER, OLIVE.
    Affairs of Jimmy
        Valentine
    Dancing Feet
    Down Mexico Way
    The Great Train Robbery
    Hearts in Bondage
    Ice Capades
    Idaho

COOPER, OLIVE (cont.)
    Music in Moonlight
    My Best Gal
    The Mysterious Miss X
    Outcasts of the Trail
    The Return of Jimmy Val-
        entine
    The Singing Hill
    Swingin' On A Rainbow
    Three Little Sisters
    Young Bill Hickok

COOPER, WILLIS.
    Son of Frankenstein

COPELAND, JACK. See Interviews on
    Tape.

COPPEL, ALEC.
    The Black Knight
    The Bliss of Mrs. Blossom

COPPOLA, FRANCIS FORD.
    The Godfather

CORMACK, BARTLETT
    Valley of the Sun

CORNELL, KATHERINE. See Inter-
    views on Tape.

CORNFIELD, HUBERT.
    Night of the Following Day

CORNYN, STAN.
    The Phynx

CORRELL, CHARLES. Collection
    No. 7.

CORRINGTON, JOHN WILLIAM.
    I Am Legend

CORTEZ, STANLEY. See Interviews
    on Tape.

CORWIN, NORMAN.
    The Blue Veil
    Lust for Life

COUFFER, JACK.
    Ring of Bright Water

COWARD, NOEL P.
    Cavalcade

COX, JUDD. See Interviews on
    Tape.

COX, MORGAN.
    Zorro Rides Again

CRANE, HARRY.
    The Harvey Girls

CRANSTON, JOSEPH.
    Screaming Teens

CRAVEN, FRANK.
    Our Town

CRAWFORD, JOANNA.
    My Side of the
      Mountain

CRITTENDEN, JORDAN.
    Get to Know Your
      Rabbit

CROSS, BEVERLY.
    Half A Sixpence
    The Long Ships

CROTHERS, RACHEL.
    Nice People

CRUTCHER, ROBERT RILEY
    Key to the City
    Shared Wife

CUKOR, GEORGE. Collection
    No. 1. See also Inter-
    views on Tape.

CULLEN, JAMES.
    Please Get Married

CUMMINGS, IRVING, JR.
    Lone Star Ranger

CUMMINGS, RUTH.
    Daybreak

CUMMINS, DWIGHT.
    The River

CUNNINGHAM, JACK.
    Captain Salvation
    A Gentleman of Leisure

CURTIS, NATHANIEL.
    The Harvey Girls
    Please Believe Me

CURTIS, TONY. See Interviews on
    Tape.

DALE, ESTHER.
    Such Good Friends

DALEY, ROBERT. See Interviews on
    Tape.

DALMAS, HERBERT.
    An American Romance

D'AMICO, SUSO CECCHI.
    The Stranger

DANIELS, WILLIAM H. (BILL). See
    Interviews on Tape.

D'ANTONI, PHIL. See Interviews on
    Tape.

DARLING, SCOTT.
    Charlie Chan at the Opera
    Fatal Hour
    Mr. Wong in Chinatown

DAVES, DELMER. See also
    Interviews on Tape.
    Clear All Wires
    The Dark Passage
    Divorce in the Family
    The Petrified Forest
    Unexpected Uncle

DAVID, MACK. Collection
    No. 37.

DAVIDSON, MARTIN.
    Moon Zero Two

DAVIDSON, RONALD.
    Black Hills Ambush
    The Fighting Devil
       Dogs
    Missile Monsters
    Satan's Satellites
    Zanzabuku
    Zorro Rides Again

DAVIES, HUNTER.
    Here We Go Round The
       Mulberry Bush

DAVIES, VALENTINE.
    On the Riviera
    Three Little Girls
       in Blue
    You Were Meant For Me

DAVIS, EDDIE.
    Radio City Revels

DAVIS, FRANK.
    Are Husbands Necessary?
    The Last Train West
    Night of the Quarter
       Moon

DAVIS, JEROME L.
    Apache War Smoke
    The Duchess of Idaho

DAVIS, JERRY.
    The Devil Makes Three
    Kind Lady

DAVIS, KEVIN.
    The Hoax

DAVIS, LUTHER. Collection No. 21.
    B. F.'s Daughter
    Black Hand
    Holiday For Lovers
    The Hucksters
    Kismet
    The Knife
    They're Playing Our Song

DAVIS, WRAY. See Interviews on
    Tape.

DAWN, ISABEL.
    Goodnight, Sweetheart
    Lady For a Night
    Yokel Boy

DECKER, MARGE.
    To Please A Lady

DE FELITTA, FRANK.
    The Color of Love

DEFORE, DON. Collection No. 75.

DEGAS, BRIAN.
    Danger: Diabolik

DE GAW, BOYCE.
    Lady For a Night

DEHN, PAUL.
    Night of the Generals

DEIN, EDWARD.
    Pistol Packin' Mama

DELANEY, SHELAGH.
    Charlie Bubbles
    A Taste of Honey

DEL CONTE, KEN. See Interviews
    on Tape.

DELEON, WALTER.
    Ruggles of Red Gap
    Union Pacific

DELMAR, VINA.
    Bad Boy
    Make Way For Tomorrow

DEMETRAKAS, JOHANNA. See
    Interviews on Tape.

DEMILLE, WILLIAM C. Collection
    No. 8.
    Carmen
    Hollywood and Return
    Young Romance

DEMOND, ALBERT.
    Code of the Prairie
    Duke of Chicago
    Federal Agent at
        Large
    Gangs of Sonora
    Gauchos of El Dorado
    Marshal of Cedar Rock
    Million Dollar Pursuit
    Pals of the Golden
        West
    The Red Menace
    Riders of the Rio
        Grande
    Underground Spy
    Unmasked
    Valley of Hunted Men
    West of Cimarron
    The Wild Frontier
    Woman in the Dark

DEMY, JACQUES. See also
    Interviews on Tape.
    The Model Shop

DENNIS, ROBERT C.
    The Man Is Armed

DE PASSE, SUZANNE.
    Lady Sings the Blues

DERN, BRUCE. See Interviews on
    Tape.

DE SYLVA, B. G.
    Bottoms Up
    The Stork Club
    Sunnyside Up

DEUTSCH, HELEN.
    Flame and the Flesh
    Forever Darling
    Glass Slipper
    It's A Big Country
    King Solomon's Mines
    Lili
    National Velvet
    The Seventh Cross
    Valley of the Dolls

DEVAL, JACQUES.
    Cafe Metropole
    Her Cardboard Lover
    Marie Galante

DEVINE, ANDY. Collection No. 80.

DEVLIN, DON.
    Loving

DEWITT, JACK.
    Jack of Diamonds

DE WOLF, KAREN.
    Checkers
    The Cockeyed Miracle
    Tillie the Toiler

DIAMOND, I. A. L.
    Merry Andrew
    Romance in High C
    Some Like It Hot

DICKEY, B.
    Tarzan the Fearless

DICKEY, JAMES.
  Deliverance

DIDION, JOAN. See Interviews
  on Tape.

DIETERLE, WILLIAM. Collection
  No. 17.

DIETZ, HOWARD.
  Hollywood Party

DIGHTON, JOHN.
  The Swan

DIMSDALE, HOWARD.
  A Lady Without Pass-
    port
  Visa

DINELLI, MEL.
  Cause For Alarm
  Jeopardy
  Lizzie

DMYTRYK, EDWARD. See Interviews on Tape.

DONIGER, WALTER. Collection
  No. 34.
  The Desperate Search

DONLEY, ROBERT M.
  Andy Hardy Comes Home

DONNER, RICHARD. See Interviews on Tape.

DOTY, DOUGLAS.
  Tenth Avenue

DOUD, GIL.
  Thunder Bay

DOUGLAS, NATHAN.
  The Defiant Ones

DOUGLAS, WARREN.
  Loophole

DOYLE, LAIRD.
  Hell Below

DOZIER, ROBERT.
  When Legends Die

DRAKE, OLIVER.
  Arizona Legion
  Boots and Saddles
  Heart of the Rockies
  Oh, Suzannah
  Painted Desert
  Public Cowboy #1
  The Purple Vigilantes
  Riders of the Whistling
    Skull
  Round-Up Time in Texas
  The Sagebrush Troubador
  The Singing Vagabond
  The Trigger Trio

DRAPER, PETER.
  I'll Never Forget What's
    'is Name

DRATLER, JAY.
  Impact
  Laura

DREIFUSS, ARTHUR.
  For Singles Only
  The Love-Ins

DRESNER, HAL.
  The April Fools
  The Extraordinary Seaman
  Rabbits

DRUMGOLD, GEORGE.
  Celebrity

DUFF, WARREN.
  Alias Mike Fury
  Angel in Furs
  Each Dawn I Die

DUFF, WARREN (cont.)
    The Last Command
    Make Haste to Live
    No Time for Love
    Papa Married A Mormon

DUFFY, ALBERT.
    Blind Alley
    Dark Past
    Down Mexico Way
    Sleepy-Time Gal

DUFFY, JESSE.
    Bordertown Trail

DUNCAN, S. G.
    White Fang

DUNING, GEORGE. See Interviews
    on Tape.

DUNNE, JOHN GREGORY. See
    Interviews on Tape.

DUNNE, PHILIP. Collection
    No. 41.
    The Agony and the
      Ecstasy
    The Angel Rum
    Anne of the Indies
    The Audubon Eyrie
    Blindfold
    Blue Denim
    David and Bathsheba
    Demetrius and the
      Gladiators
    The Diehards
    The Egyptian
    Escape
    Forever Amber
    The Ghost and Mrs.
      Muir
    The Golden Ones
    Graduation at Gettys-
      burg
    A Gross of Pink Tele-
      phones
    Her Majesty's Cannibals

DUNNE, PHILIP (cont.)
    Hilda Crane
    The Horrible and Unnatural
      Rebellion of Daniel
      Shays
    How Green Was My Valley
    Johnny Apollo
    Lancer Spy
    The Last of the Mohicans
    The Late George Apley
    The Luck of the Irish
    Lydia Bailey
    Major Bell's Irregulars
    The Melody Lingers On
    The Not So Cool Million
    O'Neil
    Pinky
    The Python Project
    The Rains Came
    Robbers All
    The Robe
    Russ
    Son of Fury
    Stanley and Livingston
    Suez
    Swanee River
    Ten North Frederick
    Three Brave Men
    The View From Pompey's
      Head
    Way of A Gaucho

DUPONT, E. A.
    Magic Fire

DURANTE, JIMMY. Collection
    No. 78.

DURSTON, DAVID E.
    State Farm

DURYEA, DAN. Collection No. 69.

DYER, CHARLES.
    Staircase

EARL, KENNETH
    Twin Beds

EASTMAN, CHARLES
    Little Fauss and Big
        Halsy

EBY, LOIS.
    Too Many Wives

EDDY, NELSON. Collection
    No. 55.

EDENS, ROGER. Collection
    No. 73.

EDERER, BERNARD.
    Deadline for Devlon

EDESON, ARTHUR. See Inter-
    views on Tape.

EDWARDS, BLAKE. See also
    Interviews on Tape.
    The Notorious Landlady
    Operation Madball
    The Party

EDWARDS, GEORGE. See Inter-
    views on Tape.

EILERS, SALLY. Collection
    No. 33.

EISINGER, JO.
    Bedevilled

EISNER, LOTTE. See Interviews
    on Tape.

ELDER, JOHN.
    Dracula Has Risen from
        the Grave

ELDER, LONNIE, III.
    Melinda

ELDRIDGE, JOHN.
    Decision Against Time

ELINSON, IRVING.
    Belle of New York

ELKINS, SAUL.
    Pride of the Navy

ELLIOTT, PEGGY.
    Come Back, Charleston Blue

ELLIS, EDITH.
    The Easiest Way
    The Great Meadow

ELLIS, ROBERT.
    Charlie Chan at the
        Olympics
    Charlie Chan at the Race
        Track
    Do You Love Me?
    Footlight Serenade
    Four Jills in a Jeep
    The Great American
        Broadcast
    Hello, Frisco, Hello
    Iceland
    If I'm Lucky
    Pin-Up Girl
    Something for the Boys
    Song of the Islands
    Tin Pan Alley

ELLIS, SYD. See Interviews on
    Tape.

EMERSON, JOHN.
    The Girl from Missouri

EMMANUEL, JACQUES.
    The Foxiest Girl in Paris

ENDERS, ROBERT. See Interviews on
    Tape

175

ENGLISH   SCREENWRITERS INDEX

ENGLISH, RICHARD.
    Larceny on the Air
    Sweet and Low-Down

ENGLUND, KEN.
    Androcles and the Lion
    Nightshade
    Nothing But the Truth
    Slightly Honorable
    Springtime in the
        Rockies
    Sweet Rosie O'Grady

EPHRON, PHOEBE.
    The Best Things in Life
        Are Free

EPHRON, PHOEBE & HENRY.
    Captain Newman, M.D.
    Carousel
    Daddy Long Legs
    On the Riviera
    There's No Business
        Like Show Business

EPSTEIN, JEROME.
    The Adding Machine

EPSTEIN, JULIUS J.
    Fanny
    Kiss Them For Me
    Pete and Tillie
    The Tender Trap
    (See also Epstein,
        Julius J. and
        Philip G.)

EPSTEIN, JULIUS J. and PHILIP G.
    Arsenic and Old Lace
    The Last Time I Saw
        Paris
    The Male Animal
    No Time for Comedy
    Romance in High C

ERICKSON, PAUL.
    The Green Buddha
    Secret Venture
    Track the Man Down

ERSKINE, CHESTER
    Androcles and the Lion
    They Sell Sailors Ele-
        phants

ERSKINE, JOHN.
    Bachelor of Arts

ESSEX, HARRY.
    Bodyguard
    Dragnet

ESTABROOK, HOWARD.
    Dawns Early Light
    The Human Comedy
    International Lady

ESTRADA, ART.
    Blueprint for Crime

ESWAY, ALEXANDER.
    Cross of Lorraine

ETTLINGER, DON.
    The Great American Broad-
        cast
    Life Begins in College
    Rebecca of Sunnybrook Farm

EUNSON, DALE.
    The Star

EUNSON, DALE & KATHERINE.
    Eighteen and Anxious

EVANS, VINCENT V.
    Battle Hymn

EVERETT, PETER
    Negatives

FADIMAN, WILLIAM. See Interviews
    on Tape.

FAIRCHILD, WILLIAM.
    Star!

FAIRE, RUDY. See Interviews on
    Tape.

FAIRFAX, BEATRICE.
    The Lovelorn

FAIRLIE, GERARD.
    Conspirator

FANTE, JOHN
    My Man and I
    Walk on the Wild Side

FARAGOH, FRANCIS EDWARDS.
    The Crime of Sylvestre
        Bonnard
    Easy Come, Easy Go

FARNUM, DORTHY.
    Bardelys, the Magni-
        ficent
    Call of the Flesh
    The Divine Woman
    Dream of Love
    The Temptress
    Tess of the D'Urbe-
        villes

FARNUM, WILLIAM.   Collection
No. 6.

FARROW, JOHN.
    Around the World in
        Eighty Days

FAULKNER, WILLIAM.
    The Big Sleep

FAUST, FREDERICK
    Daughter of the Regi-
        ment

FAYE, RANDALL.
    The Fabulous Suzanne
    The Ghost Goes Wild
    Great Stagecoach Robbery

FELTON, EARL.
    Armoured Car Robbery
    Bandido
    Calling All Marines
    The Happy Time
    Heart of the Golden West
    The Marauders
    My Best Gal
    The Narrow Margin
    The Night Hawk
    The Pittsburgh Kid
    Sunset Serenade
    Trapped
    Twenty Thousand Leagues
        Under the Sea

FELSEN, HENRY GREGOR.
    Fever Heat

FENTON, FRANK.
    Checkers
    Escape From Fort Bravo
    Garden of Evil
    Highways by Night
    The Man With A Cloak
    Operation Malaya
    Step Lively, Jeeves!
    These Wilder Years
    The Wings of Eagles

FERGUSON, HARVEY.
    Hot Saturday

FERGUSON, RON.
    The Double Cross

FERRAR, JOSE.
    The Great Man

FERRIS, WALTER.
    Heidi
    Lloyd's of London
    The Magnificent Fraud

FERRIS, WALTER (cont.)
    Swiss Family Robinson
    Under Two Flags

FERRY, JEAN.
    The Foxiest Girl in
        Paris

FESSIER, MICHAEL.
    Run for Cover
    Song of the City

FIELD, SALISBURY.
    In Gay Madrid

FIELD, SIDNEY.
    Nightshade

FIELDER, RICHARD.
    Return of the Boomerang

FIELDS, JOSEPH.
    The Farmer Takes A
        Wife
    Flower Drum Song
    Gentleman from
        Louisiana
    The Girl From Mexico
    The Mexican Spitfire
    A Thousand Dollars A
        Minute
    The Tunnel of Love

FINCH, SCOT.
    Catlow
    Shalako

FINE, MORTON. Collection
    No. 25.
    Hot Summer Night

FINK, HARRY JULIAN.
    Dirty Harry

FINK, R. M.
    Dirty Harry

FINKEL, ABEM.
    Jezebel
    Tonight and Every Night

FINKELHOFFE, FRED F.
    Best Foot Forward
    For Me and My Gal
    Girl Crazy
    Words and Music

FISHER, BOB.
    Eight on the Lam

FISHER, MICHAEL.
    Buckskin

FISHER, STEVE.
    Arizona Bushwackers
    The Golden Herd
    Hell's Half Acre
    Hostile Guns
    King of the Race Track
    Lady in the Lake
    Rogue's Gallery
    San Antone
    The Shanghai Story
    Song of the Thin Man
    That's My Man
    The Woman They Almost
        Lynched

FITTS, MARGARET. See SCOTT,
    MARGARET FITTS.

FITZGERALD, EDITH.
    Five and Ten
    Small Town Girl

FITZPATRICK, JAMES A.
    In Old Vienna

FITZPATRICK, JOHN.
    Song of Mexico

FITZSIMMONS, COURTLAND.
    The Mandarin Mystery

FLEISCHER, RICHARD. Collec-
    tion No. 31.

FLEISCHMAN, STANLEY. See
    Interviews on Tape.

FLETCHER, LUCILLE.
    Sorry, Wrong Number

FLICKER, THEODORE. Collec-
    tion No. 61.

FLIPPEN, RUTH BROOKS.
    Love Is Better Than
      Ever

FLOURNOY, RICHARD.
    The Affairs of Susan

FODOR, LADISLAS.
    The Great Sinner
    The Other Love
    Tom Thumb

FOLSEY, GEORGE J. See Inter-
    views on Tape.

FOOTE, BRADBURY.
    Homicide for Three
    The Madonna's Secret
    Million Dollar Pursuit
    Prisoners in Petti-
      coats

FOOTE, HORTON.
    Hurry Sundown
    To Kill A Mockingbird

FOOTE, JOHN TAINTOR.
    Swanee River

FORBES, BRYAN. See also
    Interviews on Tape.
    Deadfall

FORBES, JAMES.
    The Wonder of Women

FORD, BRYANT.
    Strangers in the Night

FORD, COREY.
    Remember

FORD, DONALD.
    Negatives

FORD, GLENN. See Interviews on
    Tape.

FOREMAN, CARL. See also Inter-
    views on Tape.
    Champion
    The Clay Pigeon
    High Noon
    Home of the Brave
    So This is New York

FOREMAN, JACK. See Interviews on
    Tape.

FORRESTER, IZOLA.
    The Four Flusher

FORTUNE, JAN.
    Exit Leading Lady
    Man of Conquest

FOSTER, GEORGE.
    The Phynx

FOSTER, LEWIS R.
    Armored Car
    I Wonder Who's Kissing Her
      Now
    The Lucky Stiff
    Manhandled
    The Mayor of 44th Street

FOSTER, MAURICE.
    Assignment K

FOSTER, NORMAN.
    Sombrero

FOWLER, GENE. See also
    Interviews on Tape.
    A Message to Garcia
    Mighty Barnum
    White Fang

FOWLER, MARJORIE. See Inter-
    views on Tape.

FOWLES, JOHN.
    The Magus

FOX, FINIS.
    Alias Jimmy Valentine
    Please Get Married
    Should A Woman Tell

FOX, FREDERICK LOUIS.
    Dakota Incident
    Eighty Steps to Jonah
    Headline Hunters
    High Iron
    Taming Sutton's Gal
    The Wayward Girl
    When Gangland Strikes

FRAKER, WILLIAM. See Inter-
    views on Tape.

FRANK, FREDRIC M.
    Appointment on "A"
        Deck
    The Greatest Show on
        Earth
    Samson and Delilah
    The Ten Commandments
    Unconquered

FRANK, HARRIET, JR.
    A Case of Need
    The Cowboys
    The Reivers

FRANK, MELVIN.
    Above and Beyond
    Buona Sera, Mrs.
        Campbell
    Callaway Went Thataway

FRANK, MELVIN (cont.)
    Happy Go Lucky
    Monsieur Beaucaire
    The Reformer and the Red-
        head
    Strange Bedfellows
    Strictly Dishonorable

FRANK, MILO, JR.
    The High Cost of Living

FRANKENHEIMER, JOHN. See Inter-
    views on Tape.

FRANKLIN, CHESTER.
    Detectives

FRANKLIN, PAUL.
    Secret Valley
    West of Abilene

FRANKOVICH, MICHAEL. See Inter-
    views on Tape.

FRASSINETTI, AUGUSTO.
    Don Juan's Night of Love

FREDERICKSON, GRAY. See Inter-
    views on Tape.

FREED, ARTHUR. Collection No. 62.
    See also Interviews on
        Tape.

FREED, BERT. See Interviews on
    Tape.

FREEDMAN, BENEDICT.
    The Atomic Kid
    Jaguar

FREEMAN, DEVERY.
    The Yellow Cab Man

FREEMAN, EVERETT.
    It Happened on Fifth
        Avenue

FREEMAN, EVERETT (cont.)
    Lulu Belle
    Million Dollar Mermaid

FREEMAN, LEONARD.
    Hang 'Em High

FREEMAN, Y. FRANK. Collection
    No. 72.

FREIBERGER, FRED. Collection
    No. 40.
    Blood Arrow
    The Daring and the
        Damned
    Eighteen and Anxious
    Fever Pitch
    The Sound of Glory
    To Hippocrates--With
        Love
    Track of the Seven-
        teen

FRIEDKIN, DAVID.
    Hot Summer Night

FRIEDKIN, WILLIAM. See Inter-
    views on Tape.

FRIEDMAN, TULLY. See Inter-
    views on Tape.

FRINGS, KETTI.
    About Mrs. Leslie

FRITZELL, JIM.
    The Shakiest Gun in
        the West

FROELICH, ANNE.
    Easy Come, Easy Go

FROESCHEL, GEORGE.
    Command Decision
    The Miniver Story
    Mrs. Miniver
    Never Let Me Go
    Random Harvest

FROESCHEL, GEORGE (cont.)
    The Story of Three Loves
    The Unknown Man
    The White Cliffs of Dover

FROUG, WILLIAM. See Interviews on
    Tape.

FRY, CHRISTOPHER.
    Barabbas

FUCHS, DANIEL.
    Love Me or Leave Me
    Panic in the Streets

FULLER, SAMUEL.
    Explosion
    Gangs of New York
    Hell and High Water

FULTON, MAUD.
    The Brat

FURIE, SIDNEY J.
    The Lawyer

FURTHMAN, C.
    Hard Rock Harrigan

FURTHMAN, JULES.
    The Big Sleep
    Merely Mary Ann

GABRIEL, GILBERT
    The Magnificent Fraud

GABRIELSON, FRANK.
    Flight of the Doves
    Something for the Boys

GALLICO, PAUL.
    Lili

GAMET, KENNETH.
    Devil's Island
    The Fighting Coast Guard
    Hell's Outpost

GAMET, KENNETH (cont.)
    The Lawless Eighties
    The Maverick Queen

GANGELIN, PAUL.
    The Big Bonanza
    Roll on Texas Moon
    Strangers in the Night

GANN, ERNEST K.
    Twilight for the Gods

GANNAWAY, AL.
    Hidden Guns

GARDNER, HERB. See Interviews
on Tape.

GARFEIN, JACK. See Interviews
on Tape.

GARFINKLE, LOUIS.
    A Minute to Prey, A
      Second to Die

GARISS, JACK.
    The Ten Commandments

GARNETT, TAY. Collection
    No. 65.
    Celebrity
    The Delta Factor
    The Fireball
    The Flying Fool
    Mike
    Oh, Yeah
    Prestige
    Ride a Wild Mare

GARRETT, GRANT.
    Bad Bascomb
    Clarence
    The Mighty McGurk
    The Model Wife

GARRETT, OLIVER H. P.
    Duel in the Sun
    A Farewell to Arms

GARRETT, OLIVER H. P. (cont.)
    Manhattan Melodrama
    Night Flight

GARRISON, GREG. Collection No. 48.

GARSTIN, CROSBIE.
    China Seas

GATES, HARVEY.
    Heaven on Earth
    Hell Divers
    Last Frontier Uprising

GATES, TUDOR.
    Danger: Diabolik

GAUTIER, RICHARD.
    Maryjane

GAY, JOHN.
    The Last Safari
    No Way to Treat A Lady
    The Power
    Separate Tables
    Sometimes A Great Notion
    Torpedo

GEISEL, THEODOR S. and HELEN.
    Design for Death

GELBART, LARRY.
    The Notorious Landlady

GELLER, BRUCE.
    The Long Ships
    Lookin' Good

GEORGE, WILLIAM.
    Banderas

GERAGHTY, GERALD.
    Blue Montana Skies
    Come On Rangers
    Down Laredo Way
    Mexicali Rose
    Mountain Rhythm
    The Phantom Stallion

GERAGHTY, GERALD (cont.)
  The Plunderers
  Rainbow Over Texas
  The Red Menace
  Red River Shore
  Savage Frontier
  Shadows of Tombstone
  South of the Border
  Sunset on the Desert
  Train to Alcatraz
  Underground Spy
  Wall Street Cowboy
  Wells Fargo
  Western Jamboree
  Wyoming

GERAGHTY, MAURICE.
  Apache Trail
  Red Canyon
  Robinson Crusoe of
      Clipper Island
  Tomahawk

GERARD, MERWIN.
  Eldorado

GERSHE, LEONARD.
  Silk Stockings

GIBNEY, SHERIDAN.
  Cheers for Miss Bishop
  The Story of Louis
      Pasteur

GIBSON, TOM.
  The Climbers

GIDDING, NELSON. See also
  Interviews on Tape.
  The Andromeda Strain
  Battle!
  The Haunting
  I Want To Live!
  The Inspector
  Odds Against Tomorrow
  Skullduggery

GIESLER, ABNER. See Interviews on
  Tape.

GILBERT, DORIS.
  Atlantic City Honeymoon
  Winter Serenade

GILER, BERNE.
  The Midas Run

GILL, FRANK J., JR.
  Atlantic City Honeymoon
  Beyond the Border
  Casanova in Burlesque
  Change of Heart
  Earl Carroll Sketchbook
  Earl Carroll Vanities
  Geraldine
  Moonstruck Melody
  Stand Up and Sing
  Stars and Guitars

GILLING, JOHN.
  The Mummy's Shroud

GILLIS, JACKSON
  The Mystery of Ghost Farm

GILROY, FRANK D.
  Beau Geste
  The Only Game in Town
  The Subject Was Roses

GINNA, ROBERT E.
  The Last Challenge

GIRARD, BERNARD.
  The Mad Room

GLADSTONE, RICHARD.
  No Man Is An Island

GLASMON, KUBEC.
  The Glass Key

GLASS, GEORGE. See Interviews on
  Tape.

183

GLAZER, BENJAMIN.
    A Farewell to Arms
    Flesh and the Devil
    The Gay Deceiver
    Mata Hari
    Memory Lane
    Sinners in Silk
    Tortilla Flat
    Two Kinds of Women

GLEASON, JAMES.
    Oh, Yeah

GLYN, ELINOR.
    Love's Blindness

GODARD, JEAN-LUC. See Interviews on Tape.

GODFREY, DORIS.
    Lake Placid Serenade

GOETZ, RUTH and AUGUSTUS.
    Carrie
    The Heiress

GOFF, IVAN.
    Goodbye My Fancy
    Green Fire
    Man of a Thousand Faces
    Shake Hands With the
        Devil
    Sunset in Wyoming

GOLD, ERNEST. See Interviews on Tape.

GOLD, HERBERT. See Interviews on Tape.

GOLD, LEE.
    Once Upon A Thursday

GOLD, LEON. See Interviews on Tape.

GOLDBAUM, PETER.
    Winter Wonderland

GOLDBECK, WILLIS.
    Calling Dr. Gillespie
    Diamond Handcuffs
    Dr. Kildare's Triple X
    The Enemy

GOLDBERG, MEL.
    Hang 'Em High
    The Lively Set

GOLDING, DAVID. See Interviews on Tape.

GOLDMAN, LES. See Interviews on Tape.

GOLDMAN, WILLIAM.
    Hot Rock

GOLDSMITH, I. G.
    Stronger Than Truth

GOLDSTEIN, EMANUEL. See Interviews on Tape.

GOLDSTONE, DINA. See Interviews on Tape.

GOLDSTONE, JAMES. See Interviews on Tape.

GOLDSTONE, RICHARD.
    Some Day Soon
    Tobor the Great

GOMBERG, SY. See also Interviews on Tape.
    The Bloodhounds of Broad-
        way
    Serenade for Suzette
    Summer Stock
    The Toast of New Orleans

GOODHART, WILLIAM.
    Generation

GOODMAN, HAL. Collection No. 35.

GOODRICH, FRANCES.
    Diary of Anne Frank
    Easter Parade
    Father of the Bride
    Father's Little Divi-
       dend
    Fugitive Lovers
    Gaby
    Give a Girl a Break
    Hide-Out
    The Hitler Gang
    In the Good Old Summer-
       time
    The Lady in the Dark
    The Long, Long Trailer
    The Pirate
    Rose Marie
    Seven Brides for Seven
       Brothers
    Small Town Girl

GOODRICH, JOHN F.
    Riders of the Purple
       Sage

GOODWINS, LESLIE.
    Double Trouble
    Mama Loves Papa

GORDON, BERNARD.
    Custer of the West
    Krakatoa East of Java

GORDON, JAMES B.
    The File of the Golden
       Goose

GORDON, LEO V.
    You Can't Win 'Em All

GORDON, LEON.
    His Brother's Wife
    Kongo
    Rogue's March
    White Cargo

GORDON, RICHARD.
    Doctor at Sea

GORDON, RUTH. See also Interviews
    on Tape.
    Adam's Rib
    Imagination

GOROG, LAZLO.
    The Affairs of Susan
    Midnight Melody

GOSDEN, FREEMAN. Collection No. 7.

GOTTLIEB, CARL. See Interviews on
    Tape.

GOULD, CLIFFORD.
    Krakatoa East of Java

GOULDING, EDMUND.
    Women Love Diamonds

GOW, JAMES.
    Murder on A Bridle Path

GRANET, BERT.
    Career
    The Day the Bookies Wept
    Glamour Boy #2
    Laddie
    Mr. Doodle Kicks Off

GRANT, JAMES EDWARD.
    Bullfighter and the Lady
    Josette
    Sands of Iwo Jima
    The Sheepman
    Surrender
    This Is My Wife

GRANT, JOHN.
    Abbott and Costello Meet
       the Killer

GRANT, MORTON.
    Santa Fe Scouts
    Valley of Hunted Men
    Westward Ho

GRASHIN, MAURI.
    Roll on Texas Moon
    Sons of the Pioneers

GRASSOFF, ALEX. See Interviews
    on Tape.

GRAUMAN, WALTER. Collection
    No. 83.
    See also Interviews on
        Tape.

GRAY, HUGH.
    Helen of Troy

GRAYSON, CHARLES.
    Battle Hymn

GREEN, ADOLPH.
    The Band Wagon
    The Barkleys of Broad-
        way
    Good News
    It's Always Fair
        Weather
    On the Town
    Singin' in the Rain

GREEN, HOWARD J.
    The Mad Doctor

GREEN, PAUL.
    Doctor Bull
    State Fair

GREENBAUM, EVERETT.
    The Shakiest Gun in
        the West

GREENBERG, HENRY. See Inter-
    views on Tape.

GREENBURG, DON.
    Kiss My Firm But Pliant
        Lips

GREENE, CLARENCE.
    The Well

GREENE, EVE.
    Beauty For Sale
    Born to Kill
    Joan of Ozark
    Prosperity

GREENE, GRAHAM.
    The Comedians

GREENE, JOHN.
    Plunderers of Painted
        Flats

GREENSPAN, LON. See Interviews on
    Tape.

GREY, JOHN.
    Swingin' On a Rainbow
    Too Many Wives

GREY, ZANE.
    King of the Royal Mounted
    Thunder Mountain

GRICE, JAMES.
    The Possession of Joel
        Delaney

GRIES, THOMAS S. See also Inter-
    views on Tape.
    100 Rifles
    Will Penny

GRIFFIN, ELEANORE.
    Imitation of Life
    Tenth Avenue Angel

GRIFFITH, J. J.
    Catlow
    Shalako

GRIFFITHS, LEON.
    The Grissom Gang

GROSS, MILT.
    Puddin' Head

GROSS, STEPHEN.
    Thank You, Jeeves

GRUBER, FRANK.
    The French Key
    The Mask of Dimitrias

GRUEN, JAMES.
    Wild Brian Kent

GRUNWALD, ANATOLE DE.
    Doctor's Dilemma

GUERRA, TONINO.
    In Search of Gregory
    More Than A Miracle
    A Place for Lovers

GUEST, VAL.
    Assignment K

GUIOL, FRED.
    Giant

GUNN, GILBERT.
    Chamber of Horrors

GUNZBURG, MILTON.
    The Edge of Running
      Water

GUSS, JACK.
    The Lady in Cement

HAAS, CHARLES F.
    Moonrise

HACKETT, ALBERT.
    Diary of Anne Frank
    Easter Parade
    Father of the Bride
    Father's Little Divi-
      dend
    Fugitive Lovers
    Gaby
    Give a Girl a Break
    Hide-Out
    The Hitler Gang

HACKETT, ALBERT (cont.)
    In the Good Old Summertime
    The Lady in the Dark
    The Long, Long Trailer
    The Pirate
    Rose Marie
    Seven Brides for Seven
      Brothers
    Small Town Girl

HAEBEL, MRS. OTTO. Collection
    No. 71.

HAGEN, EARLE. See Interviews on
    Tape.

HAGENS, WILLIAMS.
    Passkey to Danger

HAINES, WILLIAM WISTER.
    One Minute to Zero
    Torpedo Run
    The Wings of Eagles

HAISLIP, H. S.
    Cargo of Innocents

HAL, WILLIS.
    Matter of Innocence

HALE, JOHN.
    The Mind of Mr. Soames

HALE, RUTH.
    The Utah War

HALEVY, JULIAN.
    Custer of the West
    A Place For Lovers

HALL, JANE.
    They Live By Night

HALL, NORMAN S.
    Corpus Christi Bandits
    Death Valley Manhunt
    Fugitive From Sonora
    Law of the Golden West

HALL, NORMAN S. (cont.)
  The Man from the Rio
      Grande
  Mojave Firebrand
  Montana Belle
  Outlaws of Pine Ridge
  Outlaws of Santa Fe
  Red River Renegades
  San Antone Ambush
  The San Antonio Kid
  Sheriff of Las Vegas
  Sheriff of Sundown
  South of Rio
  Stagecoach to Monterrey
  Sundown at Santa Fe
  The Topeka Terror
  Unmasked
  Vigilantes of Dodge
      City
  Wall Street Cowboy

HALL, WILLIS.
  Man in the Middle

HALPRIN, A. H.
  Taking A Chance

HALSEY, FORREST.
  A Man's Man
  White Youth

HAMER, ROBERT.
  The Scapegoat

HAMILBURG, MICHAEL. See Interviews on Tape.

HAMILTON, HENRY.
  Best of Luck

HAMILTON, WILLIAMS
  Call Out the Marines

HAMMERSTEIN, OSCAR, II.
  State Fair

HAMMETT, DASHIELL.
  Watch On the Rhine

HAMMOND, LEN.
  Cause For Alarm

HAMNER, ROBERT. Collection
  No. 42.

HAMPTON, ORVILLE H.
  Riot on Sunset Strip
  A Time to Sing
  The Young Runaways

HANDLER, KEN. See Interviews on
  Tape.

HANEMANN, H. W.
  House of a Thousand
      Candles

HANKS, A.
  Billions

HANLEY, WILLIAM.
  The Gypsy Moths

HANSARD, WILLIAM. See Interviews
  on Tape.

HANSERT, BURT. See Interviews on
  Tape.

HANSFORD, BILL. See Interviews
  on Tape.

HANSON, CURTIS LEE.
  The Dunwich Horror

HARAREET, HAYA.
  Our Mother's House

HARARI, ROBERT.
  Ice Capades
  Joan of Ozark
  Music in Moonlight

HARBURG, E. Y.
  Finian's Rainbow

HARDING, BERTITA.
    Magic Fire

HARDING, JOHN BRIARD.
    The Kissing Bandit

HARDMAN, FRANK.
    Moon Zero Two

HARDY, RENE.
    Triple Cross

HARGREAVES, LANCE Z.
    Battle Beneath the
        Earth
    The First Man in Space

HARGROVE, MARION.
    It Seems There Were
        These Two Irish-
        men

HARMON, SIDNEY.
    Graduation at Gettys-
        burg
    The Horrible and Un-
        natural Rebellion
        of Daniel Shays
    Mutiny

HARPER, PATRICIA.
    The Topeka Terror

HARRINGTON, CURTIS. See
    Interviews on Tape.

HARRINGTON, PAT. See Inter-
    views on Tape.

HARRIS, ELEANOR.
    Kidnapped

HARRIS, ELMER.
    The Barbarian
    Feast of Reason

HARRIS, JAMES B. See Inter-
    views on Tape.

HARRIS, JED.
    Operation Madball

HARRIS, SNAG.
    Four Jills in a Jeep

HARRISON, CHARLES F.
    The Awakening of John
        Slater

HARRISON, JOAN.
    Rebecca

HART, MOSS.
    Gentleman's Agreement
    Prince of Players
    A Star is Born
    Winged Victory

HART, WILLIAM S.
    O'Malley of the Mounted

HARTE, BETTY. Collection No. 47.

HARTMAN, DON.
    Mr. Imperium
    My Favorite Blonde
    Nothing But the Truth
    Redheads on Parade

HARTMANN, EDMUND L.
    Let's Live A Little

HARVEY, ANTHONY. See Interviews
    on Tape.

HARVEY, JACK.
    Let's Live a Little

HARWOOD, H. M.
    Queen Christina

HARWOOD, ROOVE and RONALD.
    Diamonds for Breakfast

HATTON, FREDERICK & FANNY.
    The Auction Block
    Money Talks

HATVANY, LILI.
     Between Two Nights
     8 Little Black Boys
     The Road Home

HAUSER, HAL.
     Suppose They Gave a War
        and Nobody Came

HAWKS, HOWARD. See Interviews
     on Tape.

HAWLEY, LOWELL S.
     The One and Only,
        Genuine Original
        Family Band

HAYES, ALFRED.
     The Double Man
     In Enemy Country
     These Thousand Hills
     The Village Doctor

HAYES, DOUGLAS.
     The Chalk Garden

HAYES, JOHN MICHAEL.
     The Chalk Garden
     It's A Dog's Life
     Peyton Place
     Thunder Bay

HAYES, RAFAEL.
     The Love Bomb

HAYS, LARRY.
     Lefty Gets on the Level
        with the Devil

HAYS, WILL, JR.
     You're My Everything

HAYWARD, LILLIE.
     Aloma of the South Seas
     Blood on the Moon
     Child of Divorce
     Follow Me Quietly
     Heart of the Rio Grande

HAYWARD, LILLIE (cont.)
     Is There A Duchess in the
        House?
     The Proud Rebel
     Santa Fe Passage
     Tarzan and the Lost Patrol

HAZARD, LAWRENCE.
     The Fabulous Texan
     Gentle Annie
     Jackass Mail
     The Texas Uprising
     Wyoming

HEAD, EDITH. See Interviews on
     Tape.

HEARNE, JAMES A.
     Shore Acres

HECHT, BEN.
     Broken Soil
     Comrade X
     The Iron Petticoat
     Specter of the Rose

HEERMAN, VICTOR.
     Little Women
     Magnificent Obsession
     Stella Dallas

HEIDEMAN, LEONARD.
     Valerie

HEIMS, JO.
     Play Misty For Me
     You'll Like My Mother

HEIN, FLORENCE.
     Are All Men Alike?
     The Price of Redemption

HELLINGER, MARK.
     Broadway Bill

HELLMAN, SAM.
     In Old Kentucky
     Little Miss Marker

HELLMAN, SAM (cont.)
> The Poor Little Rich
> > Girl
> The Slave Ship

HENNING, PAUL.
> Bedtime Story
> Lover, Come Back

HENRY, BUCK.
> Catch-22
> The Graduate
> The Owl and the Pussy-
> > cat

HERALD, HEINZ.
> Dr. Ehrlich's Magic
> > Bullet
> The Great Flamarion
> The Life of Emile
> > Zola

HERBERT, F. HUGH.
> Baby Mine
> Dark Command
> The Little Hut
> Margie
> Melody Ranch
> The Moon Is Blue
> My Heart Belongs To
> > Daddy
> Quiet Please
> Romance and Rhythm
> Sitting Pretty
> Three Faces West

HERBERT, JOHN.
> Fortune and Men's Eyes

HERCZEG, GEZA.
> The Life of Emile
> > Zola

HERMAN, JEAN.
> Farewell Friend

HERTZ, DAVID.
> Blackmail
> Journey for Margaret
> That Was No Lady

HERVEY, HARRY.
> Saigon

HERZIG, SIG M.
> I Dood It
> Meet the People
> My Favorite Spy

HESTON, CHARLTON. See Interviews
> on Tape.

HEYES, DOUGLAS.
> The Alien
> Beau Geste
> The Plastic Man

HIGGINS, JOHN C.
> The File of the Golden
> > Goose
> Impasse
> The Man-Eater of Raval-
> > karna

HIKEN, NAT.
> The Love God?

HILL, ELIZABETH.
> H. M. Pulham, Esq.

HILL, ETHEL.
> Man From Frisco

HILL, GEORGE ROY. See Interviews
> on Tape.

HILL, GLADYS.
> The Kremlin Letter

HILL, JAMES.
> The Hoodlum Saint
> The Road Home

HILL, JAMES H.
        Keeping Company

HILL, ROBERT.
        A Woman's Devotion

HILL, WALTER.
        The Thief Who Came to
            Dinner

HILLER, ARTHUR. See Interviews
        on Tape.

HILTON, ARTHUR. See Interviews
        on Tape.

HILTON, JAMES.
        We Are Not Alone
        Mrs. Miniver

HIRSCHMAN, HERBERT. See
        Interviews on Tape.

HOAG, DOANE.
        The Luckiest Guy in
            the World

HOBART, H. T. N.
        Oil For the Lamps of
            China

HOBSON, LAURA Z.
        Her 12 Men

HOCKFILDER, J.
        Sabotage

HODGES, HORACE
        Grumpy

HOERL, ARTHUR.
        The Great Adventures of
            Captain Kidd

HOEY, MICHAEL A.
        Stay Away, Joe

HOFFENSTEIN, SAMUEL.
        An American Tragedy
        Carnival in Costa Rica
        Cluny Brown
        Give My Regards to Broad-
            way

HOFFMAN, CHARLES.
        Night and Day
        One More Tomorrow

HOFFMAN, HERMAN.
        The Hoaxters
        The Last Escape

HOFFMAN, JOSEPH.
        The King's Pirate
        Thank You, Jeeves
        That's My Gal

HOLLOWAY, JEAN.
        Till the Clouds Roll By

HOLMES, BROWN.
        Moon Over Miami

HOLSOPPLE, TED. See Interviews on
        Tape.

HOLT, SETH.
        Nowhere to Go

HOMES, GEOFFREY.
        Scared Stiff
        Secrets of the Underground

HOPGOOD, AVERY.
        Fair and Warmer

HOPKINS, GEORGE JAMES. Collection
        No. 4.

HOPKINS, HENRY. See Interviews on
        Tape.

HOPKINS, ROBERT E.
        Caught Short
        Parlor, Bedroom and Bath

HOPPER, DENNIS. See Interviews
on Tape.

HOPPER, HAL.
Shalako

HORMAN, ARTHUR T.
Call A Messenger
Gobs and Gals
Juvenile Jungle
Rosita from Rio
Tropical Heat Wave
WAC From Walla Walla
Young and Wild

HOROVITZ, ISRAEL.
Believe in Me.

HOUSER, LIONEL.
Condemned Woman
Courage of Lassie
Dark Command
Faithful in My Fashion
The Girl From Mexico
Ground Crew
Hold High the Torch
Wolf of New York

HOUSTON, NORMAN.
Frisco Waterfront
West of the Pecos

HOVEY, TAMARA.
That Midnight Kiss

HOWARD, CY.
Every Little Crook and
Nanny
My Friend Irma
That's My Boy

HOWARD, SANDY.
Jack of Diamonds

HOWARD, SIDNEY.
Gone With the Wind
A Lady to Love

HOWE, JAMES WONG. See Interviews
on Tape.

HOWELL, DOROTHY.
The Big Timer

HUBBARD, LUCIEN.
Lazy River
The Mysterious Island

HUBBARD, THOMAS G.
Andrassy U+60
Daniel Boone, Trail Blazer
Raiders of Old California

HUFFAKER, CLAIR. See also Inter-
views on Tape.
Flaming Star
Hellfighters
100 Rifles
Rio Conchos
The War Wagon

HUGGINS, ROY.
The Outlanders
Too Late For Tears

HUGHES, ADELAIDE & RUPERT.
Gimme!

HUGHES, LANGSTON.
Way Down South

HUGHES, RUPERT.
Souls For Sale

HUME, CYRIL.
The Chicago Method
Daybreak
Forbidden Planet
The Invisible Boy
Quo Vadis
Ransom
Tarzan the Ape Man

HUME, EDWARD
Labyrinth

HUME, WILLIAM DOUGLAS.
        The Reluctant Debutant

HUMPHREY, HAL. Collection
        No. 76.

HUNTER, IAN.
        A Dream of Kings

HUNTER, IAN MC LELLAN.
        Fisherman's Wharf
        Mr. District Attorney

HURLBUT, WILLIAM.
        Adam Had Four Sons
        Only Yesterday
        Rainbow on the River
        Way Down East

HUSTON, JOHN.
        The Asphalt Jungle
        Dr. Ehrlich's Magic
            Bullet
        Jezebel
        Juarez
        The Kremlin Letter
        The Maltese Falcon
        The Red Badge of
            Courage

HUTCHISON, J.
        Thoroughbreds All

HUTSHING, EDWARD E.
        Andy Hardy Comes Home

HYLAND, DICK IRVING.
        Lake Placid Serenade
        Winter Serenade

HYLAND, FRANCES.
        The Castaway (aka The
            Cheaters
        Flame of Sacramento
        Gallant Thoroughbred
        Midnight Melody

IDELSON, WILLIAM.
        Screaming Teens

IMHOFF, ROGER. Collection No. 57.

INGE, WILLIAM.
        Bus Riley's Back in Town

INGSTER, BORIS.
        Thin Ice

ISHERWOOD, CHRISTOPHER.
        Diane
        The Great Sinner

IVERS, JULIA CRAWFORD.
        Married Flirts

IVORY, JAMES.
        The Guru

JACKSON, FREDERICK.
        Stormy Weather
        Wells Fargo

JACKSON, HORACE. See also Inter-
        views on Tape.
        The Model Wife

JACKSON, JOSEPH.
        One Way Passage

JACKSON, LARRY.
        Blueprint for Crime

JACKSON, MARION.
        Min and Bill

JACOBS, ALEXANDER.
        Sitting Target

JACOBS, ARTHUR P. Collection
        No. 90.
        See also Interviews on
            Tape.

JACOBY, MICHAEL.
        Doomed to Die

JAMES, POLLY.
    Mrs. Parkington
    The Paradine Case

JAMES, DONALD.
    Doppel Ganger

JAMES, RIAN.
    Redheads on Parade

JANIS, ELSIE.
    Madam Satan

JAPRISOT, SEBASTIAN.
    Farewell Friend

JARRE, MAURICE. Collection
    No. 20.

JARRETT, DAN.
    The Border Patrolman
    The Calling of Dan
        Matthews
    Hard Rock Harrigan
    Hawaiian Buckaroo
    Let's Sing Again
    The Mine with the Iron
        Door
    O'Malley of the
        Mounted
    Rawhide
    Roll Along, Cowboy
    Secret Valley
    Thunder Mountain
    Whispering Smith
        Speaks

JARRICO, PAUL.
    Tom, Dick, and Harry

JASON, JAY
    Caprice

JEFFRIES, BETTY
    Invisible Avenger

JENNINGS, TALBOT.
    Across the Wide Missouri
    Frenchman's Creek
    The Good Earth
    Romeo and Juliet

JENNINGS, WILLIAM DALE.
    The Cowboys

JESKE, GEORGE.
    The Day the Bookies Wept
    I'm Dying to Live
    Lord Epping Has Plans
    Western Limited
    The Worms Burns

JESSEL, GEORGE.
    Professional Soldier

JESSUP, RICHARD.
    Chuka

JEVNE, JACK.
    Wintertime
    Wyoming

JEWISON, NORMAN. See Interviews
    on Tape.

JOHNSON, BOBBY. See Interviews on
    Tape.

JOHNSON, HENRY.
    365 Nights in Hollywood

JOHNSON, LAMONT. See Interviews
    on Tape.

JOHNSON, LAWRENCE E.
    Bachelor Father
    It's A Wise Child

JOHNSON, NUNNALLY.
    Baby Face Harrington
    Banjo on My Knee
    Everybody Does It
    Flaming Star

JOHNSON, NUNNALLY (cont.)
  How to be Very, Very
    Popular
  Jesse James
  The Keys of the Kingdom
  Pied Piper
  Thanks A Million

JOHNSON, ROBERT LEE.
  Girl from God's Country
  Tarzan's Revenge

JOHNSTON, AGNES CHRISTINE.
  Altars of Desire
  Andy Hardy's Blonde
    Trouble
  Andy Hardy's Double
    Life
  Demi-Bride
  The Enemy
  Lovey Mary

JONES, CHARLES M. See Interviews on Tape.

JONES, GROVER.
  Captain Fury
  Dark Command
  Lives of A Bengal
    Lancer

JONES, HENRY ARTHUR.
  The Cheater

JONES, IKE.
  The Wild Seed

JONES, ROBERT. See Interviews
  on Tape.

JOSEPHSON, JULIEN.
  Disraeli
  Heidi
  Hungry Hearts
  The Rains Came
  Stanley and Livingston
  Suez

JOSEPHSON, JULIEN (cont.)
  Watch Your Step
  Wee Willie Winkie

JOSEPHY, ALVIN M., JR.
  The Captive City

JULIAN, ARTHUR.
  The Happy Road

KAFKA, HANS.
  Terry Malloy

KAHN, BERNARD.
  Busman's Holiday

KAHN, GORDON.
  An American Romance
  Lights of Old Santa Fe
  Mama Runs Wild
  SOS Tidal Wave
  Tenth Avenue Kid
  A Yank on the Burma Road

KALMAR, BERT.
  Kentucky Kernals

KAMB, KARL.
  The Captive City

KAMINS, BERNIE. See Interviews on
  Tape.

KAMP, IRENE. See also Interviews
  on Tape.
  Paris Blues

KAMP, LOUIS. See Interviews on
  Tape.

KANDEL, ABEN.
  Berserk!

KANIN, FAY and MICHAEL. See also
  Michael Kanin.
  The Opposite Sex
  Rhapsody

196

KANIN, GARSON.
    Adam's Rib
    Imagination
    The Rat Race
    Some Kind of a Nut

KANIN, MICHAEL. See also Fay
    and Michael Kanin.
    Cross of Lorraine
    When I Grow Up

KANTER, HAL.
    About Mrs. Leslie
    Money From Home
    Pocketful of Miracles

KANTOR, MAC KINLAY.
    Battle Hymn

KARP, DAVID.
    Sol Madrid

KARPF, STEVEN.
    Caravans

KARSNER, DAVID.
    Silver Dollar

KARTARIUM, ARAM. See Inter-
    views on Tape.

KASS, PETER.
    ...So I Left...To Avoid
    a Holocaust

KATCHER, LEO.
    M

KAUFMAN, CHARLES A.
    Cynthia
    The Golden Ones
    The Model Wife
    Return to Paradise

KAUFMAN, MILLARD. Collection
    No. 38.
    See also Interviews on
    Tape.
    Bad Day at Black Rock
    Raintree County
    Take the High Ground
    The War Lord

KAUFMAN, PHILIP.
    The Great Northfield,
    Minnesota Raid

KAUS, GINA.
    The Red Danube
    Three Secrets

KAYE, BENNET.
    Roger "The Terrible"
    Touhy

KEARNEY, GENE R.
    Rabbits

KEITH, CARLOS.
    The Body Snatcher

KELLER, SHELDON.
    Buona Sera, Mrs. Campbell

KELLOGG, MARJORIE.
    Tell Me That You Love Me,
    Junie Moon

KELLY, MARK.
    One in a Million

KELSO, EDMOND.
    Outlaws of Sonora

KENT, ROBERT E.
    The Fastest Guitar Alive
    Fifty-two Miles to Terror
    The Last of the Buccaneers
    A Time to Sing

KENYON, CHARLES.
    The Petrified Forest
    The Road Back

KENYON, CURTIS.
    Twin Beds

KERR, LAURA.
    Grounds for Marriage
    Stars and Guitars

KERSHNER, IRVIN. See Inter-
    views on Tape.

KESSEL, JOSEPH.
    Night of the Generals

KIBBEE, ROLAND.
    Vera Cruz

KILLENS, JOHN O.
    Odds Against Tomorrow

KIMBLE, LAWRENCE.
    Angel on the Amazon
    The Avengers
    Criminal Court
    Diary of A Bride
    The Flame
    Moonlight Masquerade
    Mystery in Mexico

KIN, MU. See Interviews on
    Tape.

KING, BRADLEY.
    Diamond Handcuffs
    King of the Race Track
    The Lovelorn
    That's My Man

KINGSLEY, DOROTHY.
    Angels in the Outfield
    Broadway Rhythm
    Can-Can
    A Date With Judy
    Don't Go Near the
        Water
    Easy to Wed
    Green Mansions
    It's A Big Country
    Jupiter's Darling

KINGSLEY, DOROTHY (cont.)
    Kiss Me Kate
    Neptune's Daughter
    Seven Brides for Seven
        Brothers
    The Tender Hours
    Texas Carnival
    Valley of the Dolls
    When in Rome

KINOY, ERNEST.
    Brother John
    Buck and the Preacher

KINSOLVING, WILLIAM LEE.
    A Fan's Notes

KIRGO, GEORGE.
    Don't Make Waves

KLANE, ROBERT.
    Every Little Crook and
        Nanny

KLAUBER, MARCEL.
    Code Two

KLEIN, LARRY. Collection No. 35.

KLEIN, PHILIP.
    Dante's Inferno
    Riders of the Purple Sage
    Rookies

KLEINER, HARRY.
    Carmen Jones
    Fantastic Voyage
    The Street With No Name

KLORER, JOHN D.
    Top of the World

KLOVE, JANE.
    My Side of the Mountain

KNEALE, NIGEL.
      The Entertainer
      Five Million Years to
          Earth

KNIGHT, ARTHUR. Collection
      No. 3.
      See also Interviews on
          Tape.

KNIGHT, VICK.
      It Happened on Fifth
          Avenue

KNOBLOCK, EDWARD.
      The Lost Romance
      Marriage Maker

KNOPF, CHRISTOPHER.
      Joyride
      The King's Thief

KNOPF, EDWIN H.
      Mr. Imperium

KOBER, ARTHUR.
      Hollywood Party

KOCH, HOWARD. See Interviews
      on Tape.

KOEHLER, TED.
      Stormy Weather

KOHNER, FREDERICK.
      Three Daring Daughters
      The Tiger Man

KOLB, KEN.
      Snow Job

KOSTAL, IRWIN. See Interviews
      on Tape.

KOVACS, ERNIE. Collection
      No. 45.

KOZLENKO, WILLIAM.
      Mr. Justice Goes Hunting

KRALY, HANS.
      A Desperate Adventure
      Jenny Lind
      Just A Gigolo
      The Kiss
      The Lady of Scandal
      A Lady's Morals
      My Lips Betray
      Quiet Please

KRAMER, CECILE.
      Ramrod

KRAMER, LARRY. See Interviews on
      Tape.

KRAMER, STANLEY. See Interviews
      on Tape.

KRANTZ, STEVE. See Interviews on
      Tape.

KRANZE, DON. See Interviews on
      Tape.

KRASNA, NORMAN.
      The Big Hangover
      Let's Make Love

KREITSEK, HOWARD B.
      The Illustrated Man

KRIMS, MILTON.
      A Dispatch from Reuters
      One Minute to Zero
      We Are Not Alone

KRISMAN, SERGE. See Interviews on
      Tape.

KUBRICK, STANLEY. See Interviews
      on Tape.

KURNITZ, HARRY.
    Goodbye Charlie
    The Happy Road
    See Here, Private
       Hargrove
    Tonight We Sing

KUSELL, HAROLD.
    Don't Forget to Remmber

LA CAVA, GREGORY.
    Living in A Big Way

LACHMAN, MORT.
    A Shipment of Tarts

LAIDLAW, WILLIAM R.
    Command Decision

LAKS, LUCILLE.
    In Search of Gregory

LAMB, HAROLD.
    The Buccaneer
    The Crusades
    The Plainsman

LANDAU, RICHARD.
    Fever Pitch
    The Man Is Armed

LANDIS, ADRIAN.
    Everything's On Ice

LANDON, JOSEPH.
    Rio Conchos
    Von Ryan's Express

LANG, CHARLES. See Interviews
    on Tape.

LANG, DAVID.
    The Hired Gun
    The Web of Danger
    A Yank on the Burma
      Road

LANG, FRITZ. See Interviews on
    Tape.

LANGLEY, NOEL.
    Ivanhoe
    The Prisoner of Zenda
    Snow White and the Three
      Stooges

LANGTRY, KENNETH.
    I Was A Teenage Franken-
      stein

LARDNER, RING, JR.
    Cross of Lorraine
    Forever Amber
    Laura

LARKIN, JOHN.
    Carnival in Costa Rica
    The Dolly Sisters
    The Tender Hours

LARKIN, JOHN FRANCIS.
    The Mandarin Mystery

LARNER, JEREMY.
    The Candidate

LARSON, CHARLES.
    Dark Violence

LASKO, EDWARD, JR.
    Gentle Giant

LASKY, JESSE, JR. See also Inter-
    views on Tape.
    Back in the Saddle
    Hell and High Water
    Northwest Mounted Police
    Reap the Wild Wind
    Samson and Delilah
    The Ten Commandments
    Unconquered
    Union Pacific

LAUGHLIN, TOM. See Interviews on
    Tape.

LAUREN, JERRY.
    Deadline for Devlon

LAUREN, S. K.
    Don't Forget to
    Remember

LAVEN, ARNOLD. See Interviews
    on Tape.

LAVERY, EMMET G.
    Bright Road
    The Magnificent Yankee

LAWRENCE, VINCENT.
    Adventure
    The Bugle Blows at
      Midnight
    Cimarron
    Moon Over Miami
    Sea of Grass

LAWSON, JOHN HOWARD.
    Trader Horn

LAY, BEIRNE, JR.
    Above and Beyond

LAZZARINO, TONY.
    Counter Force

LEAR, NORMAN. See Interviews
    on Tape.

LEDER, HERBERT J.
    Fiend Without a Face

LEDERER, CHARLES.
    Broken Soil
    Can-Can
    Comrade X
    Gaby
    Gentlemen Prefer
      Blondes
    Kismet
    Tip on a Dead Jockey
    Wabash Avenue

LEE, DONALD W.
    Tin Hats

LEE, JAMES.
    Change of Habit
    Counterpoint

LEE, LEONARD.
    Night Shift

LEE, NORMAN.
    Chamber of Horrors

LEE, ROBERT N.
    Armored Car

LEE, ROWLAND V.
    Puppets
    Three Musketeers

LEES, ROBERT.
    The Black Cat
    Jumping Jacks
    No Time For Love
    Penny's Party

LE FRENAIS, IAN.
    Hannibal Brooks
    The Touchables
    Villain

LEHMAN, ERNEST. Collection No. 14.
    Are You There?
    Baby Take A Bow
    Executive Suite
    The Gay Retreat
    The King and I
    North by Northwest
    Portnoy's Complaint
    The Prize
    Somebody Up There Likes Me
    The Sound of Music
    West Side Story
    Who's Afraid of Virginia
      Woolf?

LEHMAN, GLADYS.
    Golden Girl
    Her Highness and the
       Bellboy
    Little Miss Marker
    Luxury Liner
    The Poor Little Rich
       Girl
    Rio Rita
    Slave Ship
    This Time For Keeps
    Two Girls and a Sailor

LEIGH, ROWLAND.
    A Song For Miss Julie

LEMAY, ALAN.
    I Dream of Jeannie
    Northwest Mounted
      Police
    Reap the Wild Wind
    Song of Youth
    The Story of Dr.
      Wassell
    The Vanishing American

LEMMON, JACK. See Interviews
on Tape.

LENNART, ISOBEL. See also
    Interviews on Tape.
    Anchors Aweigh
    East Side, West Side
    The Girl Next Door
    Holiday in Mexico
    It's A Big Country
    The Kissing Bandit
    A Life of Her Own
    Lost Angel
    Love Me or Leave Me
    Meet Me in Las Vegas
    Merry Andrew
    Mr. Justice Goes Hunt-
      ing
    Once Upon a Thursday
    Skirts Ahoy
    This Could Be the Night
    Two for the Seesaw

LENNON, THOMAS.
    Murder on a Bridle Path

LEO, MAURICE.
    Romance and Rhythm

LEONARD, ELMORE.
    Joe Kidd

LEONARD, JACK.
    Cry of the Hunted
    The Marauders
    My Man and I

LERNER, ALAN JAY.
    An American in Paris
    Brigadoon
    Gigi
    On a Clear Day You Can See
      Forever

LERNER, IRVING. See Interviews
on Tape.

LESIS, TOM.
    Cause For Alarm

LESSER, SOL. Collection No. 68.
    See also Interviews on
      Tape.

LESTER, SEELEG.
    Eldorado

LEVIEN, SONYA.
    Bhowani Junction
    The Country Doctor
    Daddy Long Legs
    The Great Caruso
    The Green Years
    Hit the Deck
    The Hunchback of Notre
      Dame
    I Hear You Calling Me
    Interrupted Melody
    Kidnapped
    Oklahoma!
    Quo Vadis

LEVIEN, SONYA (cont.)
State Fair
The Student Prince
Tess of the Storm
Country
Three Daring Daughters
The Valley of Decision

LEVIN, BORIS. See Interviews
on Tape.

LEVIN, MARGARET F.
Queen Christina

LE VINO, A. S.
Burning Daylight
The Four Flusher
The Hope
The Mutiny of the
Elsinore

LEVITT, ALFRED LEWIS.
Dream Wife

LEVITT, GENE.
Underwater Warrior

LEVITTE, JEAN.
O.S.S. 117 Is Not Dead

LEVY, JULES. See Interviews on
Tape.

LEVY, PARKE.
Earl Carroll Sketchbook
My Friend Irma

LEWIN, ALBERT E. Collection
No. 44.
The Actress
Call Me Mister
Diana at Midnight
Down About the Shelter-
ing Palms
Eight on the Lam
The Living Idol
Pandora and the Flying
Dutchman

LEWIN, ALBERT E. (cont.)
Peer Gynt
The Picture of Dorian Gray
The Private Affairs of Bel
Ami
We Fools of Nature

LEWIS, ALBERT and ARTHUR.
Oh, You Beautiful Doll

LEWIS, ANDY & DAVE.
Klute

LEWIS, GENE.
Lonely Heart Bandits
Western Affair

LEWIS, H. CLYDE.
Fisherman's Wharf

LEWIS, JERRY. Collection No. 52.
See also Interviews on
Tape.
The Big Mouth

LEWIS, ROGER.
The Big Bam Boo

LIBERATORE, UGO.
A Minute to Prey, A Second
to Die

LIBOTT, ROBERT YALE.
Flame of Youth

LIEF, MAX.
Sleepy-Time Gal

LILLEY, E. C.
Ladies' Day

LINDEMAN, MITCH.
The Way West

LINDEN, NAT S.
Yellowneck

LINDER, CARL. See Interviews
on Tape.

LIPMAN, WILLIAM R.
Alias A Gentleman
Bad Bascomb
The Bugle Blows at
Midnight
Little Miss Marker
The Mighty McGurk
Tarzan Against the
World

LIPTON, DAVID. See Interviews
on Tape.

LIPTON, LEW.
Baby Mine
The Cameraman
Tin Hats

LIPSCOMB, W. P.
A Message to Garcia
Under Two Flags

LITTLEFIELD, CONSTANCE. Collection No. 14.

LIVELY, WILLIAM.
The Dakota Kid
Daughter of the Jungle
Ghost of Zorro
Lost Planet Airmen
Wild Horse Ambush

LIVINGSTON, DAVID. See Interviews on Tape.

LIVINGSTON, HAROLD.
The Hell With Heroes

LLOYD, ROLLO.
Prestige

LODEN, BARBARA. See Interviews
on Tape.

LOEB, LEE.
Forged Passport
Stardust and Sweet Music

LOGAN, HELEN.
Charlie Chan at the
Olympics
Charlie Chan at the Race
Track
Do You Love Me?
Footlight Serenade
Four Jills in a Jeep
The Great American Broad-
cast
Hello, Frisco, Hello
Iceland
If I'm Lucky
Pin-Up Girl
Something for the Boys
Song of the Islands
Tin Pan Alley

LOGUE, CHRISTOPHER.
Savage Messiah

LOMBARD, HENRY. See Interviews on
Tape.

LONG, HAL.
Folies Bergere de Paris
That Night in Rio
White Fang

LONG, JOHN R.
Kenner

LONGSTREET, STEPHEN.
The Outcasts of the City

LONSDALE, FREDERICK.
The Fast Set
Lovers Courageous

LOOS, ANITA.
The Barbarian
Biography of a Bachelor
Girl
Blondie of the Follies

LOOS, ANITA (cont.)
    Blossoms in the Dust
    Burnt Fingers
    The Girl from Missouri

LOOS, MARY.
    The Big Gamble
    Corporal Dolan Goes
      A.W.O.L.
    I'll Get By
    Meet Me After the Show
    Stardust and Sweet
      Music

LOPEZ, ROBERT.
    Twists of Fate

LORD, JACK. Collection No. 79.

LORD, MINDRET.
    Strange Impersonation

LORD, ROBERT.
    Annie Laurie

LOWE, EDWARD T., JR.
    Big Game
    Broadway
    Charlie Chan at the
      Race Track
    The Girl From Alaska
    Lonesome
    Public Enemies
    Understanding Heart

LOWE, ELLEN.
    Emperor Concerto

LOWE, SHERMAN T.
    Everything's On Ice
    The Invisible Informer
    Melody Trail
    The Old Corral
    The Undercover Woman

LOY, NONNIE. See Interviews on
    Tape.

LUBIN, A. RONALD. See Interviews
    on Tape.

LUCAS, GEORGE. See Interviews on
    Tape.

LUCAS, JOHN MEREDYTH.
    Dark City

LUCE, CLARE BOOTH.
    A Wreath for Petroff's
      Grave

LUCKWELL, BILL.
    The Strange Case of Dr.
      Manning

LUDWIG, JERRY.
    Fade In

LUDWIG, WILLIAM.
    An American Romance
    Andy Hardy's Blonde
      Trouble
    Athena
    Blackmail
    Boys' Ranch
    The Great Caruso
    Gun Glory
    Hills of Home
    Hit the Deck
    Interrupted Melody
    It's A Big Country
    Journey for Margaret
    Julia Misbehaves
    Love Laughs at Andy Hardy
    Oklahoma!
    The Student Prince
    The Sun Comes Up
    Sun in the Morning
    Ten Thousand Bedrooms
    That Was No Lady
    Uncle Andy Hardy

LUKE, MICHAEL.
    Oedipus the King

LUSSIER, DANE.
    Ladies' Day
    The Lady Wants Mink
    The Magnificent Rogue
    The Mexican Spitfire's
       Blessed Event
    Mr. and Mrs. America
    Mystery Broadcast
    The Pilgrim Lady
    The Port of Forty
       Thieves
    Shared Wife
    A Sporting Chance
    Three's A Crowd
    The Tiger Man

LUSTIG, JAN.
    Moonfleet!
    The Story of Three
       Loves
    The White Cliffs of
       Dover

LYCELL, GAVIN.
    Moon Zero Two

LYNDON, BARRE.
    The Greatest Show on
       Earth
    The Lodger
    To Please A Lady

LYONS, REGGIE. See Interviews
    on Tape.

MAC ARTHUR, CHARLES.
    Get Rich Quick Walling-
       ford

MACAULAY, RICHARD.
    Born to Kill
    Dragnet
    Hello, Frisco, Hello
    Varsity Show

MAC CANN, RICHARD DYER. See
    Interviews on Tape.

MAC DONALD, JOHN.
    The Executioners

MAC DONALD, PHILIP.
    Blind Alley
    The Body Snatcher
    Dark Past
    Tobor the Great

MAC DOUGALL, RANALD.
    Cleopatra
    The Hasty Heart
    Man on Fire
    Mildred Pierce
    The Naked Jungle
    The World, The Flesh, and
       the Devil

MAC FADDEN, HAMILTON.
    They Shall Not March Alone

MACK, WILLARD.
    Broadway to Hollywood
    Caught Short
    His Glorious Night
    Lord Byron of Broadway

MAC KENZIE, AENEAS.
    The Avengers
    The Fighting Seabees
    Juarez
    The King's Pirate
    The Ten Commandments

MAC PHERSON, JEANNE.
    The Devil's Brother
    Madam Satan

MADDOW, BEN. See also Interviews
    on Tape.
    The Asphalt Jungle
    The Chairman
    The Mephisto Waltz
    The Way West

MAHIN, JOHN LEE.
    The Last Gangster
    Laughing Boy

MAHIN, JOHN LEE (cont.)
    Mogambo
    Quo Vadis
    Small Town Girl
    The Spiral Road
    Tartu
    Tortilla Flat

MAHONEY, WILKIE.
    Panama Hattie

MAIBAUM, RICHARD. See also
    Interviews on Tape.
    The Playroom
    Ransom

MAIGNE, CHARLES.
    Lovey Mary
    War Paint

MAIURI, DINO.
    Danger: Diabolik

MALDEN, KARL. See Interviews
on Tape.

MALERBE, LUIGI.
    The Girl and the
      General

MALONE, JOEL.
    Illegal Entry

MALTZ, ALBERT.
    The Naked City
    This Gun For Hire
    Two Mules For Sister
      Sara

MAMOULIAN, ROUBEN. See Interviews on Tape.

MANBER, DAVID.
    Hail Hero

MANDEL, LORING.
    Countdown

MANKIEWICZ, DON W.
    The House of Numbers
    I Want to Live!
    Trial

MANKIEWICZ, HERMAN J.
    Another Language
    Cause For Alarm
    The Enchanted Cottage
    My Dear Miss Aldrich
    The Spanish Main

MANKIEWICZ, JOSEPH L.
    Alice in Wonderland
    All About Eve
    Cleopatra
    Guys and Dolls
    Julius Caesar
    The Keys of the Kingdom
    Manhattan Melodrama
    People Will Talk

MANKIEWICZ, TOM.
    The Sweet Ride

MANKOWITZ, WOLF.
    The Twenty-fifth Hour

MANN, ABBY. Collection No. 60.
    See also Interviews on
      Tape.

MANN, ARTHUR.
    The Jackie Robinson Story

MANN, GRAHAM. See Interviews on
    Tape.

MANN, MILTON.
    Scandal Incorporated

MANN, STANLEY.
    The Mind of Mr. Soames
    The Strange Affair

MANNING, BRUCE.
    Flame of the Islands
    Hoodlum Empire

MANNING, BRUCE (cont.)
    Spoilers of the Forest
    That Midnight Kiss

MANNHEIMER, ALBERT.
    Finishing School
    Three Daring Daughters

MANOFF, ARNOLD.
    Man From Frisco
    My Buddy
    No Minor Vices

MANTLE, BURUS.
    A Dark Lantern

MANTLEY, JOHN.
    Quiet Day at South Fork

MANULIS, MARTIN. See Inter-
    views on Tape.

MAPES, VICTOR.
    Saphead

MARCH, JOSEPH MONCURE.
    Lone Star Raiders
    Three Faces West

MARCUS, LAWRENCE B.
    Dark City
    Going Home
    Petulia

MARGULIES, STAN. See Inter-
    views on Tape.

MARION, CHARLES R.
    Goin' To Town
    What's the Rush?

MARION, FRANCES. See also
    Interviews on Tape.
    The Beloved Adventuress
    Big House
    Blondie of the Follies
    Dinner at Eight
    The Masks of the Devil

MARION, FRANCES (cont.)
    Min and Bill
    The Scarlet Letter

MARION, GEORGE, JR.
    To Beat the Band

MARISCHKA, ERNST.
    Embezzled Heaven

MARKEY, GENE.
    As You Desire Me
    The Floradora Girl
    Girls' Dormitory
    King of Burlesque
    On the Avenue

MARLEY, JOHN. See Interviews on
    Tape.

MARKS, WILLIAM.
    Barquero
    Kill A Dragon

MARKSON, BEN
    Pride of the Navy

MARLOWE, DEREK.
    A Dandy in Aspic

MARQUETTE, DESMOND. See Inter-
    views on Tape.

MARSHALL, GARRY.
    How Sweet It Is!

MARSHALL, PETER L.
    Maryjane

MARSHMAN, D. M., JR.
    Sunset Boulevard

MARTIN, A. Z.
    The Mad Room

MARTIN, AL.
    A Gentle Gangster
    Peck's Bad Boy With
        the Circus

MARTIN, CHARLES.
    If He Hollers, Let Him
        Go

MARTIN, DON.
    Double Jeopardy
    The Pretender

MARTIN, FRANCIS J.
    Tillie the Toiler

MARTIN, TROY KENNEDY.
    The Italian Job
    Jerusalem, Jerusalem

MARTON, PIERRE.
    Skin Game

MARX, ARTHUR.
    Eight on the Lam
    Winter Wonderland

MASCOT, LAWRENCE. See Inter-
    views on Tape.

MASINO, STEVE.
    Blueprint for Crime

MASON, SARAH Y.
    Alias Jimmy Valentine
    The Girl Said No
    Held in Trust
    Little Women
    Magnificent Obsession
    Stella Dallas

MATHER, BERKLEY.
    The Long Ships

MATHESON, RICHARD.
    The Beat Generation
    De Sade
    The Devil's Bride

MATHIS, JUNE.
    Dangerous to Men
    Greed
    Hearts are Trumps
    Lombardi Ltd.
    Old Lady 31
    Parlor, Bedroom and Bath
    The Right of Way
    The Willow Tree

MATTHAU, WALTER. See Interviews
    on Tape.

MAXWELL, ROBERT.
    The Bushbaby

MAYER, ARTHUR. See Interviews on
    Tape.

MAYER, EDWIN JUSTUS.
    The Buccaneer
    In Gay Madrid
    The Lady of Scandal
    Puppets
    Women Love Diamonds

MAYER, GERALD. See Interviews on
    Tape.

MAYES, WENDELL.
    The Hanging Tree
    Von Ryan's Express

MC CALL, MARY C., JR.
    Keep Your Powder Dry
    Maisie Gets Her Man
    Ride the Man Down
    Ringside Maisie
    Woman of Glamor

MC CARTHY, KEVIN.
    You Touched Me!

MC CLAIN, JOHN.
    Cairo

MC CLAY, BOOKER. See Interviews
    on Tape.

MC CLOY, TERENCE.
    Lady Sings the Blues

MC CONVILLE, BERNARD.
    The Sheik of Buffalo
      Buttes

MC COY, HORACE.
    The Fabulous Texan
    The Fireball
    Montana Belle
    The Road to Denver
    The Texas Uprising
    Valley of the Sun
    Wild Geese Calling

MC EVEETY, JOSEPH L.
    The Computer Wore
      Tennis Shoes

MC GANN, WILLIAM. See Inter-
    views on Tape.

MC GIVERN, WILLIAM.
    The Wrecking Crew

MC GOWAN, DORRELL and STUART.
    The Big Bonanza
    Git Along Little Dogies
    Hellfire
    Hi Neighbor
    Hollywood Stadium
      Mystery
    A Man Betrayed
    Night Train to Memphis
    The Old Homestead
    Red River Valley
    Ride, Ranger, Ride
    Rovin' Tumbleweeds
    San Fernando Valley
    Sea Racketeers
    Sing, Neighbor, Sing
    Singing Guns
    Twilight on the Rio
      Grande
    Under Western Stars
    Yodelin' Kid from Pine
      Ridge

MC GOWAN, JACK.
    Broadway Melody
    Panama Hattie

MC GOWAN, JOHN.
    The Stork Club

MC GRATH, HAROLD.
    The Goose Girl

MC GRATH, JOHN.
    The Bofors Gun
    The Reckoning

MC GRATH, JOSEPH.
    30 Is A Dangerous Age,
      Cynthia

MC GREEVEY, JOHN
    Hello Down There

MC GUINNESS, JAMES K.
    Spur of Pride

MC GUIRE, DON.
    Suppose They Gave a War
      and Nobody Came

MC GUIRE, WILLIAM ANTHONY.
    Lillian Russell
    Okay, America
    Rosalie

MC HUGH, JIMMY. Collection No. 36.

MC LEOD, NORMAN Z.
    Remember

MC NEIL, STEVE.
    Man's Favorite Sport

MC NUTT, PATTERSON
    George White's Scandals of
      1935

MC NUTT, WILLIAM SLAVENS.
    Lives of A Bengal Lancer

MC NUTTY, JOHN.
Easy Come, Easy Go

MECCOLI, COMENICO.
Stormbound

MEDFORD, HAROLD.
Berlin Express
The Scavengers
U.S.S. Marblehead

MEEHAN, ELIZABETH.
Girl From God's Country

MEEHAN, JOHN.
The Divorcee
Free Souls
His Brother's Wife
Kismet
Kongo
Seven Sinners
Three Daring Daughters
The Valley of Decision

MELICK, WELDON.
Escape to Paradise

MELLY, GEORGE.
Smashing Time

MELTZER, LEWIS.
The Beat Generation
High School Confiden-
tial

MENDELSOHN, JACK.
Yellow Submarine

MENGER, W. H.
Blindfold
A Gross of Pink Tele-
phones
Major Bell's Irregu-
lars

MEREDYTH, BESS.
Ben-Hur
Chasing Rainbows

MEREDYTH, BESS (cont.)
Folies Bergere de Paris
In Gay Madrid
Laughing Sinners
Metropolitan
Mighty Barnum
The Mysterious Lady
Strange Interlude
That Night in Rio
A Woman of Affairs
The Wonder of Women

MERTZ, DAVID.
Witch in the Wilderness

MEYER, RICH. See Interviews on
Tape.

MILESTONE, LEWIS. See also Interviews on Tape.
Arch of Triumph

MILLAR, RONALD.
The Miniver Story
Never Let Me Go
The Unknown Man

MILLARD, OSCAR.
The Salzburg Connection

MILLER, ALICE DUER.
Rose Marie

MILLER, ARTHUR C. See Interviews
on Tape.

MILLER, HERMAN.
Coogan's Bluff

MILLER, J. P.
The Young Savages

MILLER, JONATHAN. See Interviews
on Tape.

MILLER, SETON I.
Charlie Chan's Courage
My Gal Sal

MILLER, SETON I. (cont.)
    The Shanghai Story
    Two Years Before the
        Mast

MILLER, VIRGIL. See Interviews
    on Tape.

MILLER, WINSTON.
    April Love
    Heart of the Rio Grande
    Man From Cheyenne
    Run for Cover

MILLS, HUGH.
    Prudence and the Pill

MILNE, PETER.
    Geraldine
    She's Working Her Way
        Through College

MILNER, VICTOR. See Interviews
    on Tape.

MINOFF, LEE.
    Yellow Submarine

MISCHEL, JOSEF.
    Isle of the Dead
    Mademoiselle Fifi

MITCHELL, GEORGE. See Inter-
    views on Tape.

MIZNER, WILSON.
    One Way Passage

MOESSINGER, DAVID.
    Number One

MOFFAT, IVAN.
    Bhowani Junction
    Giant
    The Wayward Bus

MOFFIT, JOHN C.
    Night Key

MOFFITT, JACK.
    Melody Ranch
    Ramrod

MOHR, HAL. See Interviews on
    Tape.

MOLL, ELICK.
    You Were Meant For Me

MOLNAR, FERENC.
    Liliom

MONASH, PAUL.
    The Safecracker

MONASTER, NATE.
    Band of Gold
    That Touch of Mink

MONKS, JOHN, JR.
    Dial 1119
    Knock on any Door
    No Man is an Island
    Wild Harvest

MONROE, THOMAS.
    The Affairs of Susan

MOON, LORNA.
    Upstage

MOORE, DUDLEY.
    30 Is A Dangerous Age,
        Cynthia

MORAN, CHARLES.
    Exposed

MORAN, E. EDWIN.
    Twin Beds
    Wintertime

MORGAN, AL.
    The Great Man

MORGAN, BYRON.
    All at Sea
    The Fair Co-Ed
    Fast Life
    Rookies

MORGAN, HENRY. See Interviews
    on Tape.

MORHAIM, JOSEPH.
    The Happy Road

MORRIS, EDMUND.
    Project X
    Walk on the Wild Side

MORRIS, RICHARD.
    Thoroughly Modern
        Millie

MORRISSEY, PAUL. See Inter-
    views on Tape.

MORROW, VIC. See Interviews
    on Tape.

MORTIMER, JOHN.
    A Flea in Her Ear
    John and Mary

MULLIGAN, ROBERT. See Inter-
    views on Tape.

MURFIN, JANE.
    Andy Hardy Grows Up
    Dawns Early Light

MURPHY, EMMETT.
    Valerie

MURPHY, RALPH.
    The Mystery of the
        Black Jungle

MURPHY, RICHARD.
    Back in the Saddle
    Boomerang!
    Panic in the Streets

MURRAY, JOHN FENTON.
    The Atomic Kid
    Did You Hear the One About
        the Traveling Sales-
        lady?
    Jaguar
    Man's Favorite Sport

MUSE, CLARENCE.
    Way Down South

MYTON, FRED.
    Gun Lords of Stirrup Basin

NACHMANN, KURT
    The Congress Dances

NASH, J. E.
    Madame X

NASH, MICHAEL.
    The Lost Continent

NASH, N. RICHARD.
    Top of the World

NATHAN, ROBERT.
    The Clock

NATTEFORD, JACK.
    Boots and Saddles
    Come on Rangers
    Heart of the Rockies
    Rawhide
    The Return of Jimmy Valen-
        tine
    Rootin' Tootin' Rhythm
    Rough Riders Round-Up
    The Three Mesquiteers
    Trail to San Antone
    Yodelin' Kid from Pine
        Ridge

NAUGHTON, BILL.
    Spring and Port Wine

NELSON, OZZIE.
    Love and Kisses

NELSON, PETER. See Interviews
     on Tape.

NELSON, RALPH. See also Inter-
     views on Tape.
     Flight of the Doves
     The Wrath of God

NESBITT, JOHN.
     The Amazing Mr. Nordill

NEUMANN, KURT.
     The Deerslayer

NEVILLE, JOHN THOMAS.
     Trader Horn

NEVILLE, ROBERT.
     The Black Cat
     Peck's Bad Boy With
          the Circus

NEWHOUSE, RAFE and DAVID.
     Where's Jack?

NEWLEY, ANTHONY.
     Can Heironymous Merkin
          Ever Forget Mercy
          Humpe and Find True
          Happiness?

NEWMAN, ALFRED.   Collection
     No. 74.

NEWMAN, DAVID.
     Bonnie and Clyde
     There Was A Crooked
          Man...

NEWMAN, WALTER.
     Captain and the Jolly
          Roger
     Cat Ballou

NIBLEY, A. SLOANE.
     Down Dakota Way
     Eyes of Texas
     The Far Frontier

NIBLEY, A. SLOANE (cont.)
     Hostile Guns
     Night Time in Nevada
     On the Old Spanish Trail
     Spoilers of the Plains
     Surrender
     Thunder Over Arizona

NIBLO, FRED, JR.
     Bodyguard

NICHOLS, DUDLEY.
     For Whom the Bell Tolls
     Lost Patrol
     Man Hunt
     Mourning Becomes Electra
     Pinky
     The Plough and the Stars
     Three Musketeers

NICHOLSON, JACK.
     Head

NIGGLI, JOSEFINA.
     Sombrero

NISS, STANDLEY.
     Pendulum

NOBLE, BILL.
     Faculty Row

NORDEN, DENIS.
     The Best House in London
     The Bliss of Mrs. Blossom
     Buona Sera, Mrs. Campbell

NORTH, EDMUND H.
     The Day the Earth Stood
          Still
     Murder on A Bridle Path

NORTON, WILLIAM W.
     The Scalphunters
     Whiskey's Renegades

NOVARESE, VITTORIO NINO.
     Don Juan's Night of Love

NOVELLO, IVOR.
    But the Flesh is Weak
    Tarzan the Ape Man

NUGENT, FRANK S.
    The Quiet Man
    Three Godfathers
    Trouble in the Glen

OAKIE, JACK. Collection
    No. 32.

OBOLER, ARCH.
    The Arnelo Affair

O'BRIAN, LIAM.
    Thieves Market

O'BRIEN, EDNA.
    Three Into Two Won't
      Go

O'BRIEN, ROBERT.
    Belle of New York
    Say One For Me

O'BRINE, PADDY MANNING.
    The Avenger of the
      Desert

O'DEA, JOHN.
    Fugitive Lady

ODETS, CLIFFORD.
    Wild in the Country

O'DONNELL, PETER.
    The Vengeance of She

OFFNER, MORTIMER.
    Radio City Revels

O'HANLON, JAMES.
    The Harvey Girls
    Miracle of Fatima

O'HARA, GEORGE.
    Honeymoon

OLIANSKY, JOEL.
    Counterpoint

OLIVIER, LAWRENCE.
    Henry V

OLSEN, DALE. See Interviews on
    Tape.

OLSEN, OLE. Collection No. 85.

O'NEAL, CHARLES.
    Golden Girl

O'NEILL, E. G.
    Anna Christie

OPPENHEIMER, GEORGE.
    Tonight We Sing
    The Umbrella

ORLOFF, ARTHUR E.
    El Paso Stampede
    The Last Musketeer
    The Missourians
    Red River Shore
    South Pacific Trail
    Thunder in God's Country

ORME, GEOFFREY.
    The Long Duel

ORNITZ, SAM[UEL].
    Follow Your Heart
    The Hit Parade
    It Could Happen To You
    Portia on Trial
    Three Faces West

ORR, GERTRUDE.
    The Mandarin Mystery

OSBORN, DAVID.
    Some Girls Do

OSBORN, PAUL.
    Cry Havoc
    Homecoming

OSBORN, PAUL (cont.)
    Invitation
    Madame Curie
    South Pacific
    Wild River
    The Yearling

OSBORNE, JOHN.
    The Entertainer
    Inadmissable Evidence

OTROS, A. DORIAN.
    Merry-Go-Round of 1938

OURY, GERARD.
    The Brain

OVERBAUGH, RAY. See Interviews
    on Tape.

OWEN, SEENA.
    Aloma of the South Seas
    Clarence

PAGE, ELIZABETH.
    Dawns Early Light

PAGE, MANN.
    The Four Flusher

PALEY, STANLEY.
    An Angel Comes to
        Brooklyn

PALMER, CHARLES "CAP". See
    Interviews on Tape.

PALMER, STUART.
    Hollywood Stadium
        Mystery
    Who Killed Aunt Maggie?
    X Marks the Spot

PALMIERI, FULVIO.
    Stormbound

PANAMA, NORMAN.
    Above and Beyond
    Callaway Went Thataway
    Happy Go Lucky
    Monsieur Beaucaire
    The Reformer and the Red-
        head
    Strictly Dishonorable

PARAMORE, E. E., JR.
    Man of Conquest

PARKER, DOROTHY. See also Inter-
    views on Tape.
    Trade Winds
    Weekend for Three

PARKER, JEFFERSON.
    A Gentle Gangster

PARKER, NORTON S.
    Rio Grande Raiders
    Young Bill Hickok

PARROTT, URSULA.
    Gentleman's Fate

PARSONNET, MARION.
    Dangerous Partners
    Dawns Early Light
    The Thirteenth Chair

PARSONS, LOUELLA. Collection
    No. 29.

PARTOS, FRANK.
    Daughter of the Regiment
    The Snake Pit

PASCAL, ERNEST.
    Falling Stars
    Kidnapped
    Lloyd's of London
    Wee Willie Winkie

PASTERNAK, JOE. Collection No. 81.

PATERSON, NEIL.
    The Spiral Road

PATRICK, JACK.
    Daniel Boone, Trail
        Blazer

PATRICK, JOHN.
    15 Maiden Lane
    High Society
    Les Girls
    Some Came Running
    The Teahouse of the
        August Moon

PAUL, FRANK.
    Adorable

PAVOLINI, CORRADO.
    Stormbound

PAXTON, JOHN.
    The Cobweb
    Murder, My Sweet
    Trap For A Man

PECK, GREGORY. See Interviews
    on Tape.

PECKINPAH, SAM.
    Villa Rides

PELLETIER, LOUIS.
    Smith!

PEPLE, E. H.
    The Littlest Rebel

PEPPER, DAN.
    The Enemy General

PERELMAN, S. J.
    Around the World in
        Eighty Days

PERKINS, HARRY. See Interviews
    on Tape.

PERRIN, NAT.
    Abbott and Costello in
        Hollywood
    Dimples
    Hullabaloo
    Song of the Thin Man
    Stowaway
    Swing Fever

PERRY, BEN.
    The Boss

PERRY, ELEANOR.
    The Swimmer

PERTWEE, MICHAEL.
    Finders Keepers
    Salt and Pepper
    Strange Bedfellows

PETER, WILLIAM.
    The Great Bank Robbery

PETERS, ELEANOR.   Collection
    No. 12.

PETRACCA, JOSEPH.
    The Proud Rebel

PETRAKIS, HARRY MARK.
    A Dream of Kings

PETTUS, KEN.
    The Day of the Land-
        grabbers

PEYSER, ARNOLD and LOIS.
    The Chautauqua

PHILIPS, HERBERT.
    Dr. Joseph Goebbels, His
        Life and Loves

PHILIPS, THOMAS HAL.
    Tarzan's Fight for Life

PHIPPENY, ROBERT.
    Night of the Following Day

PHYSIOC, LEWIS. See Interviews
  on Tape.

PICARD, BURT.
  The Enemy General

PIERCE, LARRY. See Interviews
  on Tape.

PIERSON, ARTHUR.
  Hometown Story

PIERSON, LOUISE RANDALL.
  Roughly Speaking

PIERSON, FRANK R.
  Cat Ballou
  Cop
  The Looking Glass War

PINE, LESTER.
  Popi
  The Wild Seed

PINE, TINA.
  Popi

PINTER, HAROLD.
  The Birthday Party
  The Go-Between

PINTOFF, ERNEST.
  Kiss My Firm But Pliant
  Lips

PIROSH, ROBERT.
  Battleground
  Go for Broke
  Song of the Islands
  Valley of the Kings

PITTMAN, MONTGOMERY.
  Come Next Spring
  Tarzan and the Lost
  Safari

PLYMPTON, GEORGE H.
  The Gambling Terror
  The Great Adventures of
  Captain Kidd
  Gun Lords of Stirrup Basin
  A Lawman is Born
  Tarzan the Fearless

POE, JAMES.
  Around the World in Eighty
  Days
  The Big Knife
  Cat On A Hot Tin Roof
  Hot Spell
  Lilies of the Field
  No Man Is an Island
  The Raid on Rommel
  The Riot
  Without Honor

POGOSTIN, S. LEE. See also Interviews on Tape.
  Hard Contract

POLAND, JOSEPH.
  The Old Corral
  Range Defenders
  The Sagebrush Troubadors
  The Trigger Trio
  Winds of the Wasteland

POLANSKI, ROMAN. See also Inter-
  views on Tape.
  The Fearless Vampire Kil-
  lers, or Pardon Me But
  Your Teeth are in My
  Neck
  Rosemary's Baby

POLL, MARTIN. See Interviews on
  Tape.

POLLACK, BARRY.
  Cool Breeze

POLLACK, SYDNEY. See Interviews
  on Tape.

POLLEXFEN, JACK.
    Back to Nature
    Lady in the Iron Mask
    Son of Sinbad

POST, TED. See Interviews on
    Tape.

POULIOT, STEVE. See Interviews
    on Tape.

POWELL, CHARLES ARTHUR.
    Panamint's Bad Man

POWELL, ELEANOR. Collection
    No. 67.

POWERS, JAMES. See Interviews
    on Tape.

PRASKINS, LEONARD.
    Doll Face
    Emma
    Gentleman's Fate
    One in a Million
    The White Sister

PRATT, JAMES. See Interviews
    on Tape.

PRENTISS, GREGORY.
    Culpepper Cattle
    Company

PRICE, EUGENE.
    Lookin' Good

PRINDLE, JAMES.
    One Happy Family

PRINTZLAU, OLGA.
    Conrad in Quest of his
        Youth
    Midsummer Madness

PROSPERI, GIORGIO.
    The Seven Hills of
    Rome

PROUSE, DEREK.
    The Champagne Murders

PURCELL, GERTRUDE.
    Ice Capades Review
    Rhythm Hits the Ice
    Winter Wonderland

PURDUM, HERBERT R.
    Target Hong Kong

PURSALL, DAVID.
    The Southern Star

PUZO, MARIO.
    The Godfather

RACKIN, MARTIN. See also Inter-
    views on Tape.
    The Clown
    The Great Diamond Robbery
    Sailor Beware
    Three Secrets

RADNITZ, ROBERT. See Interviews
    on Tape.

RAINE, NORMAN REILLY.
    A Bell for Adano
    Each Dawn I Die
    The Life of Emile Zola
    M
    Nob Hill

RAISON, MILTON.
    Counterfeit
    The Double Cross
    The Mysterious Mr. Valen-
        tine
    Old Oklahoma Plains
    Old Overland Trail
    Spoilers of the North
    Street Bandits
    The Web of Danger

RAJANAN, INDO. See Interviews on
    Tape.

RAKSIN, DAVID. See Interviews
    on Tape.

RALEIGH, CECIL.
    Best of Luck

RALSTON, GIL.
    Kona Coast

RAMEAU, PAUL H.
    Madame Curie

RAMRUS, AL.
    Halls of Anger

RAND, AYN.
    You Came Along
    The Fountainhead

RANDALL, TONY. See Interviews
    on Tape.

RANSOHOFF, MARTIN. See Inter-
    views on Tape.

RAPELSON, BOB.
    Head

RAPHAEL, FREDERIC
    Two For the Road

RAPHAEL, JOHN.
    Madame X

RAPHAELSON, SAMSON.
    Green Dolphin Street
    The Harvey Girls
    Lady In Ermine
    Main Street to Broadway
    The Merry Widow

RAPPER, IRVING. See Interviews
    on Tape.

RATHMELL, JOHN.
    Painted Desert
    Riders on the Whistling
        Skull

RATHMELL, JOHN (cont.)
    Robinson Crusoe of Clipper
        Island
    Zorro Rides Again

RATTIGAN, TERENCE.
    Separate Tables

RAUCHER, HERMAN.
    Can Heironymous Merkin
        Ever Forget Mercy
        Humpe and Find True
        Happiness?

RAVETCH, IRVING.
    A Case of Need
    The Cowboys
    Living in a Big Way
    The Outriders
    The Reivers

RAY, NICHOLAS.
    They Live By Night

RAYFIEL, DAVID.
    Castle Keep

RAYNOR, BILL.
    Without Warning

READ, JAN.
    The Haunted Strangler

REED, TOM.
    Soldiers Three

REEVES, THEODORE.
    Bernadine
    The Doctor and the Girl
    National Velvet

REIN, DOROTHY.
    Impact

REINER, CARL.
    The Comic
    Enter Laughing

REINHARDT, ELIZABETH.
    Carnival in Costa Rica
    Cluny Brown
    Give My Regards to
      Broadway

REINHARDT, GOTTFRIED. See
    Interviews on Tape.

REINHARDT, WOLFGANG.
    Juarez

REISCH, WALTER.
    Gaslight
    The Girl in the Red
      Velvet Swing
    The Heavenly Body
    Quo Vadis

REISMAN, PHILIP, JR.
    P. J.

RELPH, MICHAEL.
    The Assassination
      Bureau

RENNAHAN, RAY. See Interviews
    on Tape.

RENOIR, JEAN.
    Paris Does Strange
      Things

REPP, ED EARL.
    Law of the Badlands

REYHER, FERDINAND.
    Don't Turn 'Em Loose
    Thoroughbreds All

REYNOLDS, CLARKE.
    The Viking Queen

REYNOLDS, SHELDON.
    Assignment to Kill

REYNOLDS, WILLIAM. See Inter-
    views on Tape.

RHINEHART, O'LETA.
    Passkey to Danger

RICHARDS, MARC.
    Five Man Army

RICHARDS, ROBERT L.
    Act of Violence
    One Sunday Afternoon

RICHARDS, SILVIA.
    Tomahawk

RICHARDSON, TONY.
    A Taste of Honey

RICHLIN, MAURICE.
    Operation Petticoat

RICHMAN, ARTHUR.
    Only Yesterday

RICHMOND, BILL.
    The Big Mouth

RICKMAN, THOMAS.
    The Kansas City Bomber

RIENITS, REX.
    Cross Channel

RIESENBERG, FELIX.
    Skyline

RIESNER, DEAN.
    Coogan's Bluff
    Dirty Harry
    Play Misty For Me

RIGBY, GORDON.
    Gentleman From Louisiana
    The Wrong Road

RIGGS, LYNN.
    The Plainsman

RINALDO, FRED.
 The Black Cat
 Jumping Jacks
 No Time For Love
 Penny's Party

RIPLEY, CLEMENTS.
 California Outpost
 Jezebel
 Old Los Angeles

RISKIN, ROBERT. See also Fay
 Wray Collection, No. 63.
 American Madness
 Ann Carver's Profes-
  sion
 The Big Timer
 Broadway Bill
 Carnival
 It Happened One Night
 Lady for a Day
 Magic Town
 Meet John Doe
 Mr. Deeds Goes to Town
 Mr. 880
 The Night Club Lady
 Platinum Blonde
 The Thin Man Goes Home
 Three Wise Girls
 Virtue
 When You're in Love
 The Whole Town's Talk-
  ing
 You Can't Take It With
  You

RITT, MARTIN. See Interviews
 on Tape.

RIVER, W. L.
 The Great Man's Lady

RIVERS, JOHNNY. Collection
 No. 43.

RIVKIN, ALLEN. See also Inter-
 views on Tape.
 The Admiral Hoskins Story
 The Big Operator
 Dancing Lady
 The Eternal Sea
 Grounds for Marriage
 It's A Big Country
 Living Dangerously
 Prisoner of War
 The Road to Denver
 The Strip
 Tension
 Timberjack

ROACH, HAL. Collection No. 10.

ROBERTS, BEN.
 Goodbye My Fancy
 Green Fire
 Man of a Thousand Faces
 Mr. District Attorney in
  the Carter Case
 Shake Hands With the Devil

ROBERTS, CHARLES E.
 Come Share My Love
 Cuban Fireball
 Double Trouble
 The Fabulous Senorita
 Glamour Boy #2
 Goin' to Town
 Havana Rose
 Honeychile
 How to Be a Wolf
 I'm Dying to Live
 Ladies' Day
 Lord Epping Has Plans
 Malvina Swings It
 Mama Loves Papa
 Meet Mr. and Mrs. America
 The Mexican Spitfire
 The Mexican Spitfire Out
  West
 The Mexican Spitfire Sees
  a Ghost
 The Mexican Spitfire's
  Baby

ROLFE

ROLFE, SAM.
    Target Zero

ROLT-WHEELER, ROGER.
    The Silver Streak

ROOT, LYNN.
    Checkers
    Highways by Night
    Step Lively, Jeeves!

ROOT, WELLS.
    Hell Ship Mutiny
    The Man From Down
        Under
    Man of Conquest
    The Prisoner of Zenda
    Sam Houston
    Tennessee Johnson

ROPES, BRADFORD.
    Circus Girl
    Flame of Youth
    Glamour Boy #2
    The Hit Parade
    Ice Capades Review
    Man from Music Mountain
    Meet the Boy Friend
    Melody and Moonlight
    Melody Ranch
    Redwood Forest Trail
    Rhythm Hits the Ice
    Romance and Rhythm
    Steppin' in Society

ROSE, JACK.
    Road to Rio
    A Talent for Loving

ROSE, MICKEY.
    Take the Money and Run

ROSE, REGINALD.
    12 Angry Men

ROSE, TANYA.
    It's a Mad, Mad, Mad,
        Mad World

ROSE, WILLIAM.
    Davy
    Decision Against Time
    Guess Who's Coming to
        Dinner
    It's a Mad, Mad, Mad, Mad
        World
    The Russians Are Coming,
        The Russians Are
        Coming

ROSENBAUM, HENRY.
    The Dunwich Horror

ROSENBERG, FRANK P. See Interviews on Tape.

ROSENMAN, LEONARD. See Interviews on Tape.

ROSENSWEIG, BARNEY. See Interviews on Tape.

ROSENTHAL, LAURENCE. See Interviews on Tape.

ROSHER, CHARLES. See Interviews on Tape.

ROSS, ARTHUR.
    Double Trouble
    Prince Bart

ROSS, HERBERT. See Interviews on Tape.

ROSSEN, ROBERT. See Interviews on Tape.

ROSSON, HAROLD. See Interviews on Tape.

ROSTEN, LEO. See Interviews on Tape.

ROUSE, RUSSELL.
    The House of Numbers
    The Well

ROUSSEAU, LOUISE.
    Prince of the Plains
    Under Colorado Skies

ROUVEROL, AUSANIA.
    Dance Fools Dance

ROUVEROL, JEAN.
    The Legend of Lylah
      Clare

ROYAL, CHARLES FRANCIS.
    Gangs of New York
    A Texan Rides

ROZOV, VICTOR.
    Cranes Are Flying

RUBEN, J. WALTER.
    Oh Maisie

RUBIN, BENNY. Collection
    No. 88.

RUBIN, EDWARD. See Interviews
    on Tape.

RUBIN, RONALD. See Interviews
    on Tape.

RUBIN, STANLEY. See Inter-
    views on Tape.

RUBY, HARRY. Collection
    No. 39.
    Kentucky Kernals
    Lovely to Look At

RUDDY, ALBERT S. See Inter-
    views on Tape.

RUNYON, DAMON.
    Professional Soldier

RURIC, PETER.
    Mademoiselle Fifi

RUSKIN, HARRY.
    Andy Hardy Grows Up
    Andy Hardy's Blonde
      Trouble
    Between Two Women
    Calling Dr. Gillespie
    Doctor Kildare's Triple X
    The Happy Years
    Julia Misbehaves
    Keeping Company
    Love Laughs at Andy Hardy
    The Postman Always Rings
      Twice
    Tenth Avenue Angel
    This Is My Wife
    Uncle Andy Hardy

RUSSELL, A. J.
    A Lovely Way to Die
    Stiletto

RUSSELL, KEN.
    The Boyfriend
    The Devils

RUTHVEN, MADELEINE.
    Morgan's Last Raid

RUTTENBERG, JOSEPH. See Inter-
    views on Tape.

RYAN, DON.
    Devils's Island
    West of Cimarron

RYAN, FRANK.
    Call Out the Marines
    The Mayor of 44th Street

RYDELL, MARK. See Interviews on
    Tape.

RYERSON, FLORENCE.
    Casino Murder Case
    Elizabeth Blackwell
    Everybody Sing

RYON, THOMAS C.
    Hurry Sundown

SABAROFF, ROBERT.
    The Split

SACKHEIM, JERRY.
    Fatal Witness
    Heart of Virginia
    The Last Crooked Mile
    The Main Street Kid
    Road to Alcatraz
    Saddle Pals
    The Undercover Woman

SAGOR, FREDERICA.
    Flesh and the Devil

SAIDY, FRED.
    Finian's Rainbow
    I Dood It
    Meet the People

ST. JOHN, THEODORE.
    The Greatest Show on
      Earth

SALE, RICHARD.
    The Big Gamble
    Corporal Dolan Goes
      A.W.O.L.
    I'll Get By
    Meet Me After the Show
    Stardust and Sweet
      Music
    Torpedo Run

SALKOWITZ, SY.
    The Biggest Bundle of
      Them All

SALMON, JOHN.
    Only When I Larf

SALT, WALDO.
    Taras Bulba

SALTER, CLAUDIA.
    Ace Eli and Rodger of the
      Skies

SALTER, JAMES.
    The Appointment
    Downhill Racer

SAMUELS, LESSER.
    They Shall Not March Alone
    Tonight and Every Night

SANFORD, JOHN.
    Honky Tonk

SARAFIAN, RICHARD C.
    The Man Who Died Twice
    The Notorious Mr. Monks

SARGENT, ALVIN.
    The Sterile Cuckoo

SARNE, MICHAEL.
    Joanna

SAUBER, HARRY.
    Manhattan Merry-Go-Round

SAUL, OSCAR.
    The Silencers

SAUNDERS, JOHN MONK. See Fay
    Wray Collection, No. 63.

SAVILLE, PHILIP.
    Oedipus the King

SAVOIR, ALFRED.
    Lost--A Wife

SAXON, B. W.
    The Plastic Man

SAYRE, JOCK.
    Shooting Star

SCHARF, WALTER. See Interviews on
    Tape.

SCHARY, DORE.
It's A Big Country

SCHAYER, E. RICHARD.
Across to Singapore
The Actress
Children of Pleasure
Dance Fools Dance
The Flying Fleet
Honeymoon
Just a Gigolo
Night Club
Parlor, Bedroom and
Bath
Rookies
Trader Horn

SCHENCK, GEORGE W.
Barquero
Kill a Dragon
More Dead than Alive

SCHEUER, STANLEY K.   Collection
No. 91.

SCHILDKRAUT, JOSEPH.   Collection No. 46.

SCHILLER, FRED.
Pistol Packin' Mama

SCHISGAL, MURRAY.
The Tiger Makes Out

SCHLESINGER, JOHN. See Interviews on Tape.

SCHNEE, CHARLES.
The Bad and the
Beautiful
Bannerline
Right Cross
Scene of the Crime
They Live By Night
When in Rome

SCHNITZER, GERALD.
A Scream in the Dark

SCHOENFELD, BERNARD C.
The Space Children

SCHOFIELD, PAUL.
Wells Fargo

SCHRANK, JOSEPH.
The Clock
Song of the Islands

SCHROCK, RAYMOND L.
Happy Go Lucky
Hard Rock Harrigan
Hell Below
Shadows Over Chinatown

SCHROEDER, DORIS.
Gangs of Sonora
Hopalong Cassidy
Westward Ho

SCHUBERT, BERNARD.
The Dude Ranger
Fisherman's Wharf
Four Walls
Hearts in Bondage
Kind Lady
Make a Wish
Peck's Bad Boy
Public Defender

SCHULBERG, BUDD. See Interviews
on Tape.

SCHULMAN, ARNOLD.
A Hole in the Head

SCHULZ, FRANZ.
The Lottery Lover

SCHWARTZ, DAVID R.
Robin and the Seven Hoods

SCHWARTZ, MARVIN.
Her Majesty's Cannibals

SCHWEIG, BONTCHE.
    Come Back Charleston
      Blue

SCHWEITZER, RICHARD.
    The Last Chance

SCHWEITZER, S. S.
    Chance of Habit

SCHWEIZER, RICHARD.
    The Search

SCODINAK, CURT. See Interviews
    on Tape.

SCOLA, KATHRYN.
    Alexander's Ragtime
      Band
    The Glass Key

SCOTT, ADRIAN.
    Keeping Company

SCOTT, ALLAN.
    The Guy Who Sank the
      Navy
    Imitation of Life
    The Joy of Living
    Kirstie
    Village Tale

SCOTT, BARBARA FITTS.
    Stars in My Crown

SCOTT, DeVALLON.
    Hell Ship Mutiny
    The Maverick Queen

SCOTT, MAJOR R.
    One to Grow On

(SCOTT) FITTS, MARGARET.
    Moonfleet
    The Sun Comes Up
    Sun in the Morning
    Talk About a Stranger

SEARS, ZELDA.
    Beauty for Sale
    Daybreak
    New Morals for Old
    Prosperity

SEATON, GEORGE. See also Inter-
    views on Tape.
    Billy Rose's Diamond
      Horseshoe
    Coney Island
    The Country Girl
    The Eve of St. Mark
    The Shocking Miss Pilgrim
    The Song of Bernadette
    That Night in Rio

SEDDON, JACK.
    The Southern Star

SEEKER, EDITH.
    The Pleasure Seekers

SEGAL, ERICH.
    Yellow Submarine

SEGALL, HARRY.
    Don't Turn 'Em Loose
    Outcasts of Poker Flat

SEITZ, GEORGE B.
    Fugitive Lovers

SEITZ, JOHN. See Interviews on
    Tape.

SEKIZAWA, SHINICHI.
    War in Space

SELLER, THOMAS.
    The Man From Down Under

SELTZER, DAVID.
    A Perfect Day for Rasp-
      berry Ripple

SELZNICK, DAVID O.
    Duel in the Sun
    The Paradine Case

SEMPLE, LORENZO JR.
    Daddy's Gone A-Hunting
    Fathom
    Pretty Poison

SERLING, ROD.
    Saddle the Wind

SEYMOUR, JAMES.
    The Saint Meets the
        Tiger

SHAFFER, PETER.
    The Public Eye

SHAGAN, STEVE. See Interviews
    on Tape

SHANE, MAXWELL.
    Federal Manhunt
    Scared Stiff
    SOS Tidal Wave

SHANE, TED.
    Across to Singapore

SHANER, JOHN.
    Halls of Anger

SHANNON, ROBERT T.
    The Great Train Rob-
        bery
    Sons of the Pioneers
    Yanks in Tanks

SHAPIRO, STANLEY.
    Band of Gold
    Bedtime Story
    Lover, Come Back
    Me, Natalie
    Operation Petticoat
    That Touch of Mink

SHARP, ALAN.
    The Last Run

SHARP, HENRY. See Interviews on
    Tape.

SHARTIN, ARNOLD. See Interviews
    on Tape.

SHAVELSON, MELVILLE. See also
    Interviews on Tape.
    A Shipment of Tarts

SHAW, GEORGE BERNARD.
    Pygmalion

SHAW, IRWIN.
    The Big Gamble
    Jed Harris

SHEDLO, RONALD. See Interviews on
    Tape.

SHEEKMAN, ARTHUR.
    Call Me Madam
    Dear Ruth
    Dimples
    Some Came Running
    Stowaway
    What Every Girl Wants
    Young Man With Ideas

SHELDON, NORMAN.
    The El Paso Kid

SHELDON, SIDNEY.
    Annie Get Your Gun
    Dream Wife
    Easter Parade
    Just This Once
    Mr. District Attorney in
        the Carter Case
    Nancy Goes to Rio

SHEPARD, RICHMOND. Collection
    No. 89.

SHER, JACK.
     Paris Blues

SHERDEMAN, TED.
     My Side of the Mountain
     St. Louis Blues

SHERMAN, RICHARD.
     For Me and My Gal
     To Mary, With Love

SHERMAN, TEDDI.
     4 for Texas

SHERRIFF, R. C.
     Cargo of Innocents
     The Road Back

SHERRY, JOHN.
     The Last Challenge

SHERWIN, DAVID.
     If

SHERWOOD, ROBERT E.
     The Best Years of Our
          Lives
     The Bishop's Wife
     Rebecca

SHIELDS, TIM.
     The Last Shot You Hear

SHIPMAN, BARRY.
     Carolina Cannonball
     The Fighting Devil Dogs
     Gunfire at Indian Gap
     Hell's Crossroads
     Last Stagecoach West
     Lay That Rifle Down
     Lone Star Raiders
     The Phantom Plainsman
     Raiders of the Range
     Robinson Crusoe of
          Clipper Island
     Stranger at My Door
     Untamed Heiress
     Zorro Rides Again

SHOLEM, LEE. See Interviews on
     Tape.

SHOR, SOL.
     The Fighting Devil Dogs
     Ghost of Zorro
     Lost Planet Airmen
     Sons of Adventure

SHUKEN, PHILIP.
     Plunderers of Painted
          Flats
     Speedway

SHULMAN, IRVING.
     One for the Road

SHULMAN, MAX.
     Confidentially Connie
     Half a Hero

SHUMATE, HAROLD.
     The Forest Rangers

SHURLOCK, GEOFFREY. See Inter-
     views on Tape.

SIEGEL, DON. See Interviews on
     Tape.

SILKOSKY, RONALD.
     The Dunwich Horror

SILLIPHANT, STIRLING. See also
     Interviews on Tape.
     A Walk in the Spring Rain

SILLITOE, ALAN.
     Saturday Night and Sunday
          Morning

SILVERS, SID.
     Bottoms Up
     For Me and My Gal

SILVERSTEIN, DAVID.
     15 Maiden Lane
     Flight from Glory

SILVERSTEIN, ELLIOT. See
    Interviews on Tape.

SIMES, JOHN. See Interviews
    on Tape.

SIMMONS, RICHARD ALAN.
    Beachhead
    The Lady Wants Mink

SIMPSON, N. F.
    Diamonds for Breakfast

SINGER, ALEXANDER. See Inter-
    views on Tape.

SIODMAK, CURT.
    The Ape
    Black Friday
    False Faces
    London Blackout Murders

SISK, ROBERT. Collection
    No. 66.

SKARSTEDT, VANCE.
    Man or Gun
    No Place to Land

SLATE, LANE.
    They Only Kill Their
        Masters

SLESINGER, TESS.
    Are Husbands Necessary?
    The Good Earth

SMALL, EDWARD. Collection
    No. 82.

SMITH, H. E.
    The Man Who Broke the
        Bank at Monte Carlo

SMITH, HARRY JAMES.
    Blackbirds

SMITH, HOWARD ELLIS.
    Professional Soldier
    To Mary, With Love

SMITH, PAUL GERARD.
    Hurry, Charlie, Hurry
    Little White Brother

SMITH, HAROLD J.
    The Defiant Ones

SMITH, ROBERT.
    The Big Operator
    The Big Wheel
    I Was Kidnapped
    St. Louis Blues
    You Came Along

SMITH, ROGER. See also Interviews
    on Tape.
    Up the Junction

SMITH, WALTON HALL.
    Huddle

SMITH, WINCHELL.
    Lightnin'
    Saphead

SNELL, EARLE.
    Alias Billy the Kid
    Days of Jesse James
    Homesteaders of Paradise
        Valley
    It Happened Out West
    King of the Royal Mounted
    Make a Wish
    Marshal of Cripple Creek
    Rainbow on the River
    Robin Hood of Texas
    Roll Along, Cowboy
    Rustler's of Devil's
        Canyon
    Santa Fe Uprising
    Secret Valley
    Stagecoach to Denver
    Vigilantes of Boomtown

SNELL, EARLE (cont.)
    Western Gold
    Wild Brian Kent

SNYDER, HOWARD.
    Abbott and Costello
        Meet the Killer
    Don't Get Personal

SOLDATI, MARIO.
    Don Juan's Night of
        Love

SOLT, ANDREW P.
    For the First Time
    Joan of Arc
    Little Women
    Rendezvous
    Thanks God, I'll Take
        It from Here
    Without Reservations

SOMMER, EDITH.
    Blue Denim

SOTHERN, ANN. Collection
    No. 87.

SPEARMAN, F.
    Whispering Smith
        Speaks

SPENCE, RALPH.
    Fast Life

SPERLING, MILTON.
    Thin Ice

SPEWACK, BELLA and SAMUEL.
    Boy Meets Girl
    Clear All Wires
    The Play's the Thing
    Weekend at the Waldorf

SPIES, ADRIAN.
    Dark of the Sun

SPIGELGASS, LEONARD. Collection
    No. 5.
    See also Interviews on
        Tape.
    Athena
    Because You're Mine
    Deep in My Heart
    Night Into Morning
    Silk Stockings
    Ten Thousand Bedrooms

SPITZER, MARIAN.
    The Dolly Sisters

STAHL, JOHN M. Collection No. 11.
    Imitation of Life
    Memory Lane
    Parnell

STALLINGS, LAURENCE.
    Fast Workers
    The Sun Shines Bright
    Three Godfathers
    Witch of the Wilderness

STARLING, LYNN.
    Footlight Serenade
    More than a Secretary
    Wintertime
    Women of Glamor

STECK, JOSEPH T.
    Waterhole #3

STEFANO, JOSEPH.
    Black Orchid
    The Naked Edge
    Wylie

STEIN, JOSEPH.
    Enter Laughing

STEINBECK, JOHN.
    The Red Pony
    Viva Zapata

STERN, EZRA E. See Interviews on
    Tape.

STERN, STEWART. See also
    Interviews on Tape.
    The Rack
    Rebel Without a Cause
    The Ugly American

STEVENS, GEORGE. See Inter-
    views on Tape.

STEVENS, LEITH. See Inter-
    views on Tape.

STEVENS, LESLIE. See Inter-
    views on Tape.

STEVENS, LOUIS.
    The Texas Rangers

STEVENSON, WILLIAM H.
    The Bushbaby

STEWART, DONALD OGDEN.
    Another Language
    Barretts of Wimpole
      Street
    Cass Timberlane
    Edward, My Son
    The Prisoner of Zenda
    Smilin' Through
    The White Sister
    Without Love

STONE, ANDREW L.
    Cry Terror
    The Decks Ran Red
    The Great Waltz
    Julie

STONE, PETER.
    The Big Brass
    The Secret War of
      Harry Frigg

STONE, ROBERT.
    A Hall of Mirrors

STORM, JANE.
    Doctor Bull
    My Lips Betray

STREET, J. L.
    Rita Coventry

STRONG, AUSTIN.
    Three Wise Fools

STRUSS, KARL. See Interviews on
    Tape.

STRUTTON, BILL.
    Assignment K

STUART, MALCOLM. See Interviews
    on Tape.

STUART, MEL. See Interviews on
    Tape.

STULBERG, GORDON. See Interviews
    on Tape.

STURGES, JOHN. See Interviews on
    Tape.

STURGES, PRESTON.
    The Great Moment
    The Palm Beach Story
    Sullivan's Travels
    Unfaithfully Yours

STYLER, BURT.
    Call Me Mister
    Down About the Sheltering
      Palms
    Eight on the Lam

SULLIVAN, C. GARDNER.
    The Buccaneer
    The Cuban Love Song
    Huddle
    Men Must Fight
    Northwest Mounted Police
    Strange Interlude
    Union Pacific

SWANTON, HAROLD.
    Ballad of Josie
    Rascal

SWERDLOFF, ART. See Interviews
    on Tape.

SWERLING, JO.
    Leave Her to Heaven
    Lifeboat
    The Whole Town's Talk-
        ing

SWIFT, DON.
    The Calling of Dan
        Matthews
    King of the Royal
        Mounted
    The Mine with the Iron
        Door
    Whispering Smith
        Speaks
    Thunder Mountain

SYMONDS, HENRY.
    Pacific Liner

TABORI, GEORGE.
    The Journey
    Secret Ceremony

TABORI, PAUL.
    The Strange Case of Dr.
        Manning

TAFFEL, BESS.
    Elopement

TANNEN, CHARLES.
    Mike

TANNURA, PHILLIP. See Inter-
    views on Tape.

TARADASH, DANIEL.
    Castle Keep
    Hawaii
    Knock on any Door

TARLOFF, FRANK.
    The Double Man
    The Secret War of Harry
        Frigg

TASHLIN, FRANK.
    Caprice
    The Girl Can't Help It

TASKER, ROBERT.
    The Affairs of Jimmy Val-
        entine
    Secrets of the Underground

TAYLOR, DWIGHT.
    The Thin Man Goes Home

TAYLOR, ERIC.
    The Black Cat
    Black Friday
    Pals of the Golden West
    South of Caliente
    The Wrong Road

TAYLOR, LAWRENCE.
    The Jackie Robinson Story

TAYLOR, RENEE.
    Made for Each Other

TAYLOR, REX.
    The Mandarin Mystery

TAYLOR, SAMUEL A.
    Rosie!

TAYLOR, THEODORE.
    Showdown

TAYLOR, TOM.
    A Dispatch from Reuters

TELFORD, FRANK.
    Hello Down There

THALBERG, SYLVIA.
    Montana Moon
    Untamed
    When a Feller Needs a
        Friend

THAN, JOSEPH.
    Deception
    Her Conscience

THEW, HARVEY.
    Murder in a Private Car

THERY, JACQUES.
    To Each His Own

THIELE, WILLIAM.
    Finishing School
    The Madonna's Secret

THOEREN, ROBERT.
    The Chicago Method
    Mrs. Parkington
    September Affair

THOM, ROBERT.
    Angel, Angel, Down We
        Go
    Bloody Mama
    Wild in the Streets

THOMAS, A. E.
    The Old Soak
    Only 38

THOMPSON, HARLAN.
    Ruggles of Red Gap

THOMPSON, J. LEE. See Interviews on Tape.

THOMPSON, KEENE.
    Springtime for Henry

THOMPSON, MARSHALL. See Interviews on Tape.

THOMPSON, MORTON.
    My Brother Talks to Horses
    Pygmalion Jones

THOMPSON, THOMAS.
    Cattle King

THOROBY, WILLIAM. See Interviews on Tape.

TIBBLES, GEORGE.
    Tree on the Parkway

TIDYMAN, ERNEST. See also Interviews on Tape.
    The French Connection
    High Plains Drifter
    Shaft

TIOMKIN, DMITRI. Collection No. 51.
    See also Interviews on Tape.

TOGAWA, NAOKI. See Interviews on Tape.

TOMBRAGEL, MAURICE.
    Street of Darkness

TORS, IVAN.
    In the Good Old Summertime
    Song of Love

TOTHEROH, DAN.
    The Road Away from Home

TOTMAN, WELLYN.
    Dancing Feet
    Gangs of New York
    One Frightened Night
    Thoroughbreds

TOWNE, GENE.
    The Joy of Living
    Eternally Yours
    Stand-in
    Swiss Family Robinson

TOWNE, ROBERT.
  Villa Rides

TOWNLEY, JACK.
  Bells of Rosarita
  The Chicago Kid
  The Crooked Circle
  Cuban Fireball
  The Fabulous Senorita
  Faces in the Fog
  Goodnight, Sweetheart
  Grandpa Goes to Town
  Havana Rose
  Hitchhike to Happiness
  Honeychile
  Ice Capades
  Is There a Duchess in
    the House?
  Jamboree
  Joan of Ozark
  The Last Outlaw
  The Mexican Spitfire
    Out West
  Music in Moonlight
  My Pal Trigger
  My Wife's Relatives
  Oklahoma Annie
  One Exciting Week
  Puddin' Head
  Romance on the Run
  The Traitor Within
  Utah

TOWNSEND, LEO.
  Counterfeit
  Night and Day

TRAUBE, SHEPARD.
  Goose Step
  Hitler: Beast of Berlin

TRAVERS, BILL.
  Ring of Bright Water

TREGASKIS, RICHARD.
  The Wild Blue Yonder

TRIVERS, BARRY.
  A Desperate Adventure

TROSPER, GUY.
  Crossroads
  The Devil's Doorway
  Eyes in the Night
  Inside Straight
  Jailhouse Rock
  Many Rivers to Cross
  One-Eyed Jacks

TROTTER, THOMAS. See Interviews
  on Tape.

TROTTI, LAMAR.
  Alexander's Ragtime Band
  A Bell for Adano
  The Immortal Sergeant
  Life Begins at Forty
  Mother Wore Tights
  My Blue Heaven
  Ramona
  Slave Ship
  Stars and Stripes Forever
  There's No Business Like
    Show Business
  The Walls of Jericho
  When My Baby Smiles at Me
  Wilson
  With a Song in My Heart
  Young Mr. Lincoln
  You're My Everything

TRUEBLOOD, GUERDON.
  Welcome Home Soldier Boys

TRUMBO, DALTON.
  Career
  Five Came Back
  The Fixer
  A Guy Named Joe
  Hawaii
  Kitty Foyle
  A Man to Remember
  Our Vines Have Tender
    Grapes

TRUMBO, DALTON (cont.)
    Sobriety House
    Thirty Seconds Over
      Tokyo

TRUMBULL, DOUGLAS. See Inter-
    views on Tape.

TRYON, THOMAS.
    The Other

TUCHOCH, WANDA.
    Gay Illiterate
    Hawaii Calls
    New Morals for Old
    Nob Hill

TUGEND, HARRY.
    King of Burlesque
    The Lady Has Plans
    Love is News
    Pigskin Parade
    Pocketful of Miracles
    The Poor Little Rich
      Girl
    Sally, Irene and Mary
    Second Fiddle
    Seven Sinners
    A Southern Yankee
    Star Spangled Rhythm
    Take Me Out to the Ball
      Game
    Wabash Avenue
    Wake Up and Live
    You Can't Have Every-
      thing

TULLY, JIM.
    Trader Horn

TUNBERG, KARL.
    Ben-Hur
    Beau Brummell
    Because You're Mine
    Count Your Blessings
    Down Argentine Way
    Kitty
    Life Begins in College

TUNBERG, KARL (cont.)
    Lucky Jordan
    My Gal Sal
    Orchestra Wives
    Night Into Morning
    Rebecca of Sunnybrook Farm
    The Scarlet Coat
    The Seventh Sin
    Taras Bulba
    Valley of the Kings
    Week End in Havana
    A Yank in the R.A.F.
    You Can't Have Everything

TUPPER, TRISTAM.
    Night Key
    The River

TURMAN, LAWRENCE. See Interviews
    on Tape.

TURNEY, CATHERINE.
    One More Tomorrow

TUTTLE, FRANK.
    Springtime for Henry
    This Gun for Hire

TWIST, JOHN.
    Flight from Glory
    Helen of Troy
    The Last Outlaw
    Outcasts of Poker Flat
    Pacific Liner
    Reno
    The Saint Strikes Back
    Shooting Star
    So Big
    Twelve Crowded Hours

TYNAN, KENNETH.
    Nowhere to Go

ULLMAN, ELWOOD.
    Snow White and the Three
      Stooges

UNGER, GLADYS.
    Madam Satan

URIS, LEON.
        Gunfight at the O.K.
        Corral

USTINOV, PETER.
        Hot Millions
        Romanoff and Juliet

VADNAY, LESLIE.
        The Big Show-Off

VADRAY, LASLO.
        The Great Diamond Rob-
            bery
        Ten Thousand Bedrooms

VAIGH-HUGHES, GERARD.
        Mister Sebastia

VAJDA, ERNEST.
        Barretts of Wimpole
            Street
        The Merry Widow

VANCE, LEIGH.
        Crossplot

VAN DRUTEN, JOHN.
        Gaslight
        New Morals for Old
        Night Must Fall
        Parnell

VAN DYKE, W. S.
        California

VANE, THADDEUS.
        Mrs. Brown, You've Got a
            Lovely Daughter

VAN EVERY, DALE.
        Marianne
        More Than a Secretary
        Trader Horn

VAN RIPER, KAY.
        Skidding

VAN RONKEL, RIP.
        The High Cost of Living

VAN TREES, JAMES. See Interviews
        on Tape.

VAN UPP, VIRGINIA.
        One Night in Lisbon

VANN, JAY.
        Tarzan's Revenge

VARDA, AGNES. See also Interviews
        on Tape.
        Cleo from 5 to 7

VEILLER, ANTHONY.
        Her Cardboard Lover
        Radio City Revels
        State of the Union

VEILLER, BAYARD.
        Arsene Lupin
        Night Court

VERNEVIL, HENRI.
        The Twenty-fifth Hour

VETTERLI, RICHARD.
        The Utah War

VICAS, VICTOR.
        The Wayward Bus

VIDAL, GORE.
        The Catered Affair
        I Accuse

VIDOR, KING. Collection No. 25.
        See also Interviews on
            Tape.
        The Crowd
        H. M. Pulman, Esq.

238

VIERTEL, SALKA.
    The Paradine Case
    Queen Christina

VINCENT, ALLEN.
    The Girl in White
    Song of Love

VISCONTI, LUCHINO.
    The Stranger

VOGEL, JOSEPH. See Interviews
    on Tape.

VOGEL, PAUL. See Interviews on
    Tape.

VON CUBE, IRMAGARD.
    The Girl in White
    Song of Love

VON STROHEIM, ERICH.
    Greed

VORHAUS, BERNARD.
    Money Talks

WALD, JERRY. See also Inter-
    views on Tape.
    Varsity Show

WALD, MARVIN.
    The Naked City
    Street of Darkness

WALDMAN, TOM and FRANK.
    High Time
    The Party

WALKER, GERTRUDE.
    End of the Road
    Mystery Broadcast

WALKER, JOE. See Interviews on
    Tape.

WALLACE, IRVING.
    According to Hoyle
    Aerial Cinematography
    American Legion
    Anything for a Laugh
    The Burning Hills
    Hotel for Terror
    The Kentuckian
    The Last Bachelor
    Love Nest
    The Loves of Mona Lisa
    Sincerely Yours
    Split Second
    Working Our Way Through
      College
    Why Was I Born?

WALLACH, ELI. See Interviews on
    Tape.

WALLACH, IRA.
    Boys Night Out
    Don't Make Waves
    Hot Millions

WALSH, DAVID. See Interviews on
    Tape.

WALTER, JESSICA. See Interviews
    on Tape.

WARD, DAVID S.
    Steelyard Blues

WARD, LUCI.
    Panamint's Bad Man
    Red River Range
    Trail to San Antone

WARE, DARRELL.
    Down Argentine Way
    Kitty
    Lucky Jordan
    My Gal Sal
    Orchestra Wives
    Week End in Havana
    A Yank in the R.A.F.

SCREENWRITERS INDEX

WARREN, CHARLES M.
    The Evil Gun

WARRENTON, GILBERT. See Inter-
    views on Tape.

WASSERMAN, DALE.
    A Walk With Love and
        Death

WASSERMAN, JACOB.
    The Masks of the Devil

WATERHOUSE, KEITH.
    Man in the Middle
    Matter of Innocence

WATKINS, MAURINE.
    Behold the Bridegroom
    Libeled Lady

WATT, HARRY.
    For Those in Peril

WAYNE, PAUL.
    The King's Pirate

WEAD, FRANK.
    The Beginning or the
        End
    The Hoodlum Priest
    They Were Expendable

WEADE, F. W.
    Stranded

WEBB, JAMES R.
    Cape Fear
    Jesse James at Bay
    The Organization
    South of Santa Fe
    Vera Cruz
    A Wall for San
        Sebastian

WEBSTER, M. COATES.
    Black Hills Ambush
    Captive of Billy the Kid

WEBSTER, M. COATES (cont.)
    Desert of Lost Men
    Frisco Tornado
    Leadville Gunslinger
    Navajo Trail Riders
    Night Riders of Montana
    Renegades of Sonora
    Rough Riders of Durango
    Salt Lake Raiders
    Song of Arizona
    Sons of the Pioneers
    Wells Fargo Gunmaster
    The Wyoming Bandit

WECHSLER, DAVID.
    The Search

WEDLOCK, HUGH, JR.
    Abbott and Costello Meet
        the Killer
    Don't Get Personal

WEIDMAN, JEROME.
    Slander

WEIL, RICHARD.
    Behind City Lights
    The Big Show-Off
    The Great Flamarion

WEINGARTEN, ARTHUR.
    Busman's Holiday

WEINGARTEN, LAWRENCE. Collection
    No. 59.
    See also Interviews on
        Tape.

WEISBART, DAVID. Collection No.
    50.
    See also Interviews on
        Tape.
    Absent Without Love
    The Affair
    Amgo
    The Hearing

WEISSMAN, MURRAY. See Interviews on Tape.

WEITZENKORN, LEWIS.
Men of Chance

WELLES, HALSTEAD.
The Hanging Tree
The Hell With Heroes

WELLES, ORSON. See also Interviews on Tape.
Macbeth

WELLS, GEORGE.
Angels in the Outfield
Ask Any Girl
Designing Woman
Don't Go Near the Water
Excuse My Dust
Everything I Have Is
Yours
The Gazebo
I Love Melvin
It's a Big Country
Lovely to Look At
Merton of the Movies
Party Girl
Run Shadow Run
Serenade for Suzette
The Show-Off
Summer Stock
Take Me Out to the Ball
Game
Three Little Words
The Toast of New
Orleans
Where the Boys Are

WELLS, JOHN.
30 Is a Dangerous Age,
Cynthia

WELLS, WILLIAM K.
Movietone Follies of
1930

WENDKOS, PAUL. See Interviews on Tape.

WERRIS, SNAG.
If I'm Lucky

WERTY, QUENTIN.
Dark of the Sun

WEST, CLAUDIA.
Jenny Lind

WEST, CLAUDINE.
Barretts of Wimpole
Street
The Good Earth
Just a Gigolo
The Lady of Scandal
A Lady's Morals
Mrs. Miniver
Random Harvest
The White Cliffs of Dover

WEST, MAE. See also Interviews
on Tape.
I'm No Angel

WEST, NATHANAEL.
Born to be Wild
Five Came Back
Follow Your Heart
It Could Happen to You
Malvina Swings It
The President's Mystery

WESTCOTT, E. N.
David Harum

WESTON, GARNETT.
The Great Train Robbery

WESTON, JAY. See Interviews on
Tape.

WESTON, SAM. See Interviews on
Tape.

WEXLER, HASKELL. See Inter-
    views on Tape.

WHEATLEY, DENNIS.
    The Lost Continent

WHEELER, HUGH.
    Travels With My Aunt

WHEELWRIGHT, RALPH.
    Fast Workers

WHITE, ALAN.
    The Long Day's Dying

WHITE, ANDY.
    Africa--Texas Style!
    Gentle Giant
    The Unkillables

WHITE, JAMES GORDON.
    The Young Animals

WHITE, ROBERT A.
    Deadline for Devlon

WHITE, ROBERTSON.
    Footloose Heiress

WHITMORE, STANFORD.
    Glory Boy

WHITTAKER, CHARLES.
    Moscow

WHITTINGHAM, JACK.
    The Divided Heart

WICKI, BERNHARD. See Inter-
    views on Tape.

WIGTON, ANNE.
    The Great Flamarion

WILBUR, CRANE.
    Miracle of Fatima
    War Lord

WILBUT, CRANE.
    Lord Byron of Broadway

WILDE, CORNELL. See also Inter-
    views on Tape.
    The Titans

WILDER, BILLY.
    A Foreign Affair
    The Lost Weekend
    The Lottery Lover
    The Major and the Minor
    Some Like It Hot
    Sunset Boulevard
    What a Life

WILDER, THORNTON.
    Our Town

WILHELM, WOLFGANG.
    The Saint Meets the Tiger

WILK, MAX.
    Don't Raise the Bridge,
        Lower the River

WILLIAMS, BOB.
    Bordertown Trail
    Lights of Old Santa Fe
    Lone Texas Ranger
    Marshal of Amarillo
    Marshal of Laredo
    The Old Frontier
    Overland Mail
    Pioneer Marshal
    Ranger of Cherokee Strip
    Saddle Pals
    Sheriff of Wichita
    Under Mexicali Stars
    The Vanishing Westerner

WILLIAMS, CHARLES.
    Don't Just Stand There
    Jolly Pink Jungle

242

WILLIAMS, DAVID ODELL.
    Dealing, or the
        Berkeley-to-Boston
        Forty Brick Lost-
        Bag Blues

WILLIAMS, EMLYN.
    The Morning Star

WILLIAMS, PAUL.
    Out of It

WILLIAMS, ROBERT CREIGHTON.
    The Denver Kid
    Desperadoes of Dodge
        City
    Duel at Apache Wells
    Frontier Investigation

WILLIAMS, TENNESSEE.
    Baby Doll
    Boom
    A Streetcar Named
        Desire

WILLIAMSON, THAMES.
    Taming Sutton's Gal

WILLINGHAM, CALDER. See also
    Interviews on Tape.
    The Graduate
    One-Eyed Jacks
    The Vikings

WILLS, ROSS.
    The Heart of a Child
    Morgan's Last Raid

WILSON, CAREY.
    Arsene Lupin
    Ben-Hur
    Faithless
    Sinners in Silk

WILSON, JOHN. See Interviews
    on Tape.

WILSON, MICHAEL.
    An American Tragedy
    Che!
    Friendly Persuasion
    A Place in the Sun
    The Planet of the Apes

WILSON, RICHARD and ELIZABETH.
    See also Interviews on Tape.
    Invitation to a Gunfighter

WILSON, WARREN.
    Swing Fever

WIMPERIS, ARTHUR.
    Calling Bulldog Drummond
    If Winter Comes
    Julia Misbehaves
    Mrs. Miniver
    The Paradine Case
    Random Harvest
    The Red Danube

WINDSOR, CLAIRE. Collection
    No. 54.

WINKLER, IRWIN. See Interviews on
    Tape.

WINTERS, SHELLEY. See Interviews
    on Tape.

WISBERG, AUBREY.
    Lady in the Iron Mask
    Son of Sinbad

WISE, ROBERT. Collection No. 49.
    See also Interviews on
        Tape.

WOLFSON, P. J.
    Dancing Lady
    The Perils of Pauline
    The Twinkle in God's Eye

WOOD, CHARLES.
    The Long Day's Dying

WOOD, WILLIAM.
    The Lively Set

WOODS, LOINA.
    Mr. Wu

WOOLF, EDGAR ALLAN.
    Broadway to Hollywood
    Casino Murder Case
    Everybody Sing
    Murder in a Private Car

WORMSER, RICHARD.
    Captive of Billy the
       Kid
    Drumbeats over Wyoming
    Fort Dodge Stampede
    The Outcast
    A Perilous Journey
    The Plainsman and the
       Lady
    Powder River Rustlers
    Rustlers on Horseback
    Vigilante Hideout

WORTH, BARBARA.
    Dragnet

WRAY, ARDEL.
    Isle of the Dead

WRAY, FAY. Collection No. 63.

WRIGHT, GILBERT.
    The Californian
    Springtime in the
       Rockies

WRIGHT, HAROLD BELL.
    Roll Along, Cowboy
    Secret Valley
    Western Gold
    When a Man's a Man
    Wild Brian Kent

WRIGHT, W. L.
    Tarzan the Fearless

WRIGHT, WILLIAM H.
    Her Cardboard Lover
    Panic Button

WYLER, WILLIAM. See Interviews on
    Tape.

WYLIE, PHILIP.
    Island of Lost Souls

YATES, GEORGE WORTHINGTON.
    The Spanish Main
    The Tall Target

YATES, HAL.
    Mama Runs Wild

YATES, PETER. See Interviews on
    Tape.

YELDHAM, PETER.
    The Long Duel

YELLEN, JACK.
    Love is News
    Pigskin Parade
    Sally, Irene and Mary
    Wake Up and Live
    You Can't Have Everything

YORDAN, PHILIP.
    For Your Eyes Only
    Houdini
    Mutiny
    The Naked Jungle

YORKIN, BUD. See Interviews on
    Tape.

YOST, DOROTHY.
    Don't Forget to Remember
    M'liss
    Murder on a Bridle Path
    To Beat the Band
    Too Many Wives

YOST, ROBERT.
 Overland Mail Robbery
 The Phantom Plainsman

YOUNG, CARROLL.
 The Deerslayer

YOUNG, CLARENCE UPSON.
 Untitled Treatment-
  1945-(Roy Rogers'
  Feature)

YOUNG, HOWARD IRVING.
 Let's Live a Little

YOUNG, R. R.
 Waterhole #3

YOUNG, ROBERT M.
 Screaming Teens

YOUNG, TERENCE.
 Suicide Squadron

YOUNG, WALDEMAR.
 Island of Lost Souls
 Lives of a Bengal
  Lancer
 London After Midnight
 Men in White
 The Mystic
 The Plainsman

YOUNGER, A. P.
 Alias Jimmy Valentine
 Brown of Harvard
 Flying High
 A Lady of Chance
 The Misfit Wife
 Parlor, Bedroom and
  Bath
 Slide, Kelly, Slide
 Walk-Offs

YOUNGER, HENRY.
 Prehistoric Women

YOUNGSTEIN, MAX E. See Interviews
 on Tape.

YU, KIM. See Interviews on Tape.

ZAVATTINI, CESARE.
 A Place for Lovers

ZELLNER, LOIS.
 The Misfit Wife

ZIESLER, ALFRED.
 Dr. Joseph Goebbels, His
  Life and Loves

ZIMM, MAURICE.
 The Prodigal

ZIMMER, BERNARD.
 Caravan

ZWEIBACK, A. MARTIN.
 Me, Natalie

INTERVIEWS AND MATERIALS ON TAPE

There have been three main sources for the taped interviews which are listed below: Arthur Knight's classes, Sol Lesser's classes, and the American Society of Cinematographers.

Arthur Knight, noted critic and author of The Liveliest Art, has been recording interviews of producers, writers, directors, performers, and executives in his weekly classes at USC since 1961. The format for these interviews occasionally varies, but generally Arthur Knight introduces his guest and begins a short discussion with him concerning the movie to be shown that evening. The interview is continued after the screening, many times using the particular film only as a jumping-off point for larger issues. The discussion is soon turned over to the class and the students ask questions of the guest.

Sol Lesser, the successful film producer of Tarzan epics and many other features, has been teaching a class at USC since 1967 in Motion Picture Business. His guests tend to be specialists in the problems of studio operation, production, distribution, exhibition, and legal procedures relating to motion pictures. His interview format coincides with Arthur Knight's, although no films are shown.

The ASC tapes featuring interviews with cameramen were collected by the American Society of Cinematographers and the tapes on file at USC were dubbed from the Society's collection.

The citations of the taped materials include the name of the interviewee or speaker, date, person conducting the interview, film or subject discussed and tape catalogue number.

Written transcriptions of these interviews are currently unavailable.

ABERBACH   INTERVIEWS ON TAPE

ABERBACH, HY. Feb. 25, 1965, Knight. Ensign O'Toole (TV). T169

ABRAHAMS, MORT (p). Feb. 10, 1972, Knight. T433

AHERNE, BRIAN (a). Mar. 17, 1968, Vivien Leigh Dinner. T386

ALDRICH, ROBERT (d). Feb. 21, 1963, Knight. Whatever Happened to
    Baby Jane? T119

ALONZO, JOHN (c). Apr. 6, 1972, Panel. The Technology of Survival
    (Film conf.). C-2

ALONZO, JOHN (c). Sept. 28, 1972, Knight. Sounder. T463

ALONZO, JOHN (c). Fall, 1972, Knight. Lady Sings the Blues. T467

ALTMAN, ROBERT (d). Apr. 4, 1963, Knight. Combat (TV). T124

ANDERSON, JUDITH (a). Apr. 17, 1968, Vivien Leigh Dinner. T386

ANDERSON, WALT. Feb. 25, 1965, Knight. Ensign O'Toole (TV). T169

ARKOFF, SAM (p). Mar. 18, 1971, Panel. Film and Finance (Film
    conf.). T445-1

ARNOLD, JOHN. n. d., ASC. T407

ASTAIRE, FRED (a). Feb. 12, 1967, Cole Porter Dinner. T275

AXELROD, GEORGE (w). 1963, Knight. Manchurian Candidate. T114

AXELROD, JONATHAN (d). Apr. 8, 1972, Panel. The Young Film Maker
    and the Future (Film conference). C-6

AYERS, JERRY (p). Oct. 22, 1964, Knight. T162

AYERS, JERRY (p). Oct. 20, 1966, Knight. T216

BACH, RICHARD (nov). Mar. 11, 1965, Knight. Avalanche. T170

BADARACCO, JACOB A. n. d., ASC. T425

BAILY, JOHN. Feb. 18, 1965, Knight. T168

BALSHOFER, FRED J. n. d., ASC. T408

BARON, ALLEN (d). Apr. 2, 1964, Knight. Pie in the Sky. T148

248

BARRETT, ALLAN. Sept. 28, 1961, Knight. Blast of Silence. T85

BARRETT, RONA (columnist). Jan. 16, 1961, Panel. Hollywood Trade Papers. T41

BARRYMORE, ETHYL (See Colt, Ethyl Barrymore)

BARSHA, LEON (e). Oct. 19, 1962, Knight. T108

BARSHA, LEON (e). May 21, 1964, Knight. Lady in a Cage. T157

BARTLETT, HALL (p). May 16, 1963, Knight. The Caretakers. T128

BARTLETT, HALL (p). Apr. 10, 1969, Knight. Changes. T290

BAXTER, FRANK (a). Mar. 23, 1969, Helen Keller Dinner. T388

BEGLEY, ED (a). Mar. 28, 1963, Knight. Sweet Bird of Youth. T123

BENEDEK, LAZLO (d). May 24, 1966, Knight. T203

BENNET, SPENCER (d). n. d., ASC. T403

BERGEN, EDGAR (a). Oct. 24, 1960, Panel. Comedy. T38

BERGEN, POLLY (a). May 16, 1963, Knight. The Caretakers. T128

BERNSTEIN, ELMER (co). Jan., 1963, Knight. To Kill A Mockingbird. T116

BILL, TONY (a). Fall, 1972, Knight. Deadhead Miles. T468

BLACK, JOHN. Apr. 4, 1963, Knight. Combat (TV). T124

BLAUGH, LOUIS (law). Jan. 23, 1964, Knight. Dr. Strangelove... T140

BLAUGH, LOUIS (law). Feb. 27, 1964, Knight. Dr. Strangelove... T143

BLOOM, CLAIRE (a). Mar. 17, 1968, Vivien Leigh Dinner. T386

BLUMOFE, ROBERT F. (p). Sept. 29, 1966, Knight. T213

BOCH, JERRY (co). May 5, 1961, Panel. Musical Comedy. T72

BOETTICHER, BUDD (d). Jan. 9, 1969, Knight. T279

Primary Cinema Resources: An Index

BOGDANOVICH   INTERVIEWS ON TAPE

BOGDANOVICH, PETER (d). Apr. 6, 1968, Panel. The Art of Survival
    (Film conference). C-1

BOGDANOVICH, PETER (d). May 3, 1968, Knight. Targets. T263

BOGDANOVICH, PETER (d). Feb. 28, 1968, Panel. Jean-Luc Godard.
    T297

BOLLINGER, HENRI. Oct. 22, 1970, Knight. Fools. T320

BOOLOOTIAN, R. A., MD. Oct. 12, 1970, Lesser. The Medical film.
    T318

BOURGUIGNON, SERGE (d). Jun. 4, 1964, Knight. Sundays and Cybele.
    T158

BOURGUIGNON, SERGE (d). May 6, 1965, Knight. T179

BOWERS, WILLIAM (w-p). May 17, 1971, Lesser. T362

BRADBURY, RAY (w). Oct. 26, 1961, Knight. Moby Dick. T88

BRADBURY, RAY (w). Nov. 2, 1962, Knight. T89

BRADBURY, RAY (w). Nov. 21, 1963, Knight. Moby Dick. T90

BRADBURY, RAY (w). Nov. 12, 1964, Knight. How Not to be a Snob.
    T164

BRADBURY, RAY (w). May 26, 1965, Knight. T182

BRADBURY, RAY (w). Jan. 20, 1966, Knight. Our Man Flint. T194

BRADBURY, RAY (w). Dec. 1966, Knight. T254

BRADBURY, RAY (w). May 10, 1970, Knight. T454

BRADBURY, RAY (w). Mar. 4, 1971, Knight. The Andromeda Strain.
    T337

BRADBURY, RAY (w). Mar. 19, 1971, Panel. Film technology and the
    audience (Film conference). T445-3

BRIDGES, JAMES (w-d). Oct. 1, 1970, Knight. The Baby Maker. T313

BRODAX, AL (p). Oct. 19, 1968, Knight. The Yellow Submarine. T258

BRODIE, MEL (w). Sept. 28, 1961, Knight. Blast of Silence. T85

250

BROOKS, RICHARD (d). Jan. 4, 1967, Knight. <u>In Cold Blood</u>. T261

BROWN, ROSCOE LEE (a). Fall, 1972, Knight. <u>The Cowboys</u>. T441

BRYANT, BAIRD. Apr. 1, 1971, Knight. <u>Celebration at Big Sur</u>. T360

BRYANT, BAIRD. May 5, 1967, Knight. <u>Vipers</u>. T273

BUCHANAN, LARRY. Feb. 25, 1971, Knight. <u>Strawberries Need Rain</u>.
   T335

BUCHHOLZ, HORST (a). Nov. 18, 1965, Knight. <u>That Man From Istanbul</u>.
   T190

BURCH, RUTH. Dec. 4, 1967, Lesser. T230

CACOYANNIS, MICHAEL (d). Jan. 1963, Knight. T115

CACOYANNIS, MICHAEL (d). Jan. 14, 1965, Knight. T167

CAPRA, FRANK (d). Oct. 31, 1972, Knight. T458

CAPRA, FRANK (d). Apr. 17, 1972, Lecture. Given at Cal Tech. T479

CARR, ALAN. Sept. 24, 1970, Knight. <u>C.C. and Co</u>. T312

CASE, JAMES (Man. KCET-TV). Nov. 4, 1965, Knight. T188

CHAMIE, AL. Oct. 9, 1967, Lesser. T223

CHAMPLIN, CHARLES (cr). Apr. 8, 1972, Panel. Critics and the Sym-
      biosis of Survival (Film conference). C-5

CHAMPLIN, CHARLES (cr). Dec. 14, 1970, Lesser. T343

CHAMPLIN, CHARLES (cr). Mar. 18, 1971, Panel. Film Criticism and
      the Audience (Film conf). T445-2

CHAMPLIN, CHARLES (cr). Mar. 4, 1971, Mayer. T338

CHAMPLIN, CHARLES (cr). Mar. 17, 1968. Vivien Leigh Dinner. T386

CLARKE, CHARLES G. n. d., ASC. T415

CLAYTON, JACK (p-d). Dec. 14, 1961, Knight. <u>The Innocents</u>. T96

COLT, ETHYL BARRYMORE (a). Oct. 20, 1960, Tusher. The Professional
      Life of Show Girls. T37

CONNALLY, MIKE. Jan. 16, 1961, Panel. Hollywood Trade Papers. T41

COOK, FIEDLER (d). Jun. 1965, Knight. T178

COOPER, GLADYS (a). Mar. 17, 1968, Vivien Leigh Dinner. T386

COPELAND, JACK. Nov. 20, 1967, Lesser. T228

COPELAND, JACK. Mar. 4, 1968, Lesser. T257

COPELAND, JACK. 1971, Lesser. T253

CORMAN, ROGER (d). Feb. 28, 1968, Panel. Jean-Luc Godard. T297

CORNELL, KATHERINE (a). n. d., Francis. The Miracle Worker, the
    stage play. T398

CORTEZ, STANLEY (c). Nov. 9, 1961, Knight. T91

CORTEZ, STANLEY (c). Apr. 1, 1965, Knight. Naked Kiss. T177

COTTEN, JOSEPH (a). Mar. 17, 1968, Vivien Leigh Dinner. T386

COTTEN, JOSEPH (a). Mar. 23, 1969, Helen Keller Dinner. T388

COX, JUDD. Mar. 29, 1971, Lesser. T351

CUKOR, GEORGE (d). Mar. 18, 1965, Aldous Huxley Dinner. T174

CUKOR, GEORGE (d). Mar. 17, 1968, Vivien Leigh Dinner. T386

CUKOR, GEORGE (d). Aug. 13, 1961, Harvey. Ethyl Barrymore. T154

CUKOR, GEORGE (d). Jan. 9, 1959, Adam's Rib. T69

CUKOR, GEORGE (d). May 25, 1961, Knight. Little Women. T70

CUKOR, GEORGE (d). Nov. 1966, Knight. T253

CUKOR, GEORGE (d). Feb. 17, 1970, Knight. T304

CURTIS, TONY (a). Sept. 20, 1961, Knight. T83

CURTIS, TONY (a). Mar. 3, 1968, Knight. The Boston Strangler.
    T284

DALEY, ROBERT. Sept. 22, 1971, Knight. Play Misty For Me. T364

DAMON, MARK. Jan. 16, 1961, Panel. Hollywood Trade Papers. T41

DANIELS, WILLIAM H. (c). n. d., ASC. T401

D'ANTONI, PHIL (p). Nov. 14, 1968, Knight. Bullitt. T276

D'ANTONI, PHIL (p). Nov. 4, 1971, Knight. The French Connection.
    T369

DAVES, DELMER (w-p-d). Nov. 15, 1964, Knight. 3:10 to Yuma. T165

DAVES, DELMER (w-p-d). Sept. 20, 1969, History of the Western.
    T299

DAVIS, LUTHER (w). May 21, 1964, Knight. Lady in a Cage. T157

DAVIS, WRAY. Oct. 30, 1963, Knight. The Year of the Tiger. T136

DEL CONTE, KEN (a). Dec. 4, 1971, Knight. Love: Vampire Style.
    T372

DEMETRAKAS, JOHANNA (a). Apr. 1, 1971, Knight. Celebration at Big
    Sur. T360

DEMY, JACQUES (d). Dec. 5, 1967, Knight. T456/7

DEMY, JACQUES (d). Jan. 14, 1969, Knight. T280

DERN, BRUCE (a). Apr. 6, 1972, Panel. The Art of Survival (Film
    conference). C-1

DERN, BRUCE (a). Fall, 1972, Knight. The Cowboys. T441

DIDION, JOAN (nov). Oct. 19, 1972, Knight. Play It As It Lays.
    T460

DMYTRYK, EDWARD (d). Nov. 16, 1967, Knight. T240

DMYTRYK, EDWARD (d). Jan. 2, 1969, Knight. T278

DONNER, RICHARD (d). Mar. 23, 1962, Knight. T102

DUNING, GEORGE (co). Oct. 12, 1961, Knight. T87

DUNNE, IRENE (a). Mar. 23, 1969, Helen Keller Dinner. T388

DUNNE, JOHN GREGORY (w). Oct. 19, 1972, Knight. Play It As It
    Lays. T460

EBERT   INTERVIEWS ON TAPE

EBERT, ROGER (cr). Apr. 8, 1972, Panel. Critics and the Symbiosis
    of Survival (Film conference). C-5

EDESON, ARTHUR (c). n. d., ASC. T417

EDWARDS, BLAKE (w-p-d). Apr. 7, 1972, Lecture. The Economics of
    Survival (Film conf). C-3

EDWARDS, GEORGE (p). Oct. 12, 1967, Knight. Games. T236

EISNER, LOTTE (cr). Mar. 29, 1969, Knight. T198

ELDER, LONNIE (w). Mar. 20, 1971, Panel. Now Movies and the Audi-
    ence (Film conf). T445-3

ELLIS, SYD (w). Sept. 28, 1970, Lesser. T315

ENDERS, ROBERT (p). Dec. 3, 1970, Knight. How Do I Love Thee.
    T329

FADIMAN, WILLIAM (story editor). Feb. 12, 1968, Lesser. T221

FADIMAN, WILLIAM (story editor). Sept. 25, 1967, Lesser. T222

FAIRE, RUDY (e). Apr. 14, 1966, Knight. T199

FARBER, MANNY (cr). Apr. 8, 1972, Panel. Critics and the Symbiosis
    of Survival (Film Conference). C-5

FARBER, STEPHEN. Mar. 18, 1971, Panel. Film Criticism and the
    Audience (Film conf). T445-2

FLEISCHMAN, STANLEY (law). Apr. 28, 1966, Knight. Censorship.
    T200

FOLSEY, GEORGE J. (c). n. d., ASC. T409

FOLSEY, GEORGE J. (c). Feb. 24, 1970, Knight. T305

FONDA, HENRY (a). Apr. 4, 1971, Oscar Hammerstein Dinner. T453

FORBES, BRYAN (d). Nov. 19, 1964, Knight. Seance on a Wet After-
    noon. T175

FORD, GLENN (a). Nov. 30, 1967, Knight. The Rage. T241

FOREMAN, CARL (w-p-d). Jan. 2, 1964, Knight. Key. T142

FOREMAN, JACK (studio manager). Oct. 19, 1970, Lesser. T319

FOREMAN, JACK (studio manager). Mar. 15, 1971, Lesser. T348

FOWLER, GENE (e). Oct. 26, 1962, Knight. Angel's Flight. T109

FOWLER, GENE (e). Oct. 10, 1963, Knight. A Child is Waiting. T133

FOWLER, GENE (e). Oct. 29, 1964, Knight. Choice. T163

FOWLER, MARJORIE (w). 1962, Knight. T97

FOWLER, MARJORIE and GENE. Apr. 30, 1964, Knight. T154

FRAKER, WILLIAM (c-d). Nov. 19, 1970, Knight. Monte Walsh. T327

FRANKENHEIMER, JOHN (d). Nov. 30, 1961, Panel. Cinema Symposium. T95

FRANKENHEIMER, JOHN (d). 1963, Knight. Manchurian Candidate. T114

FRANKOVICH, MICHAEL (p). Feb. 27, 1964, Knight. Dr. Strangelove... T143

FREDERICKSON, GRAY. Oct. 24, 1970, Knight. Little Fauss and Big Halsey. T322

FREED, ARTHUR (p). Jan. 11, 1972, Knight. T375

FREED, BERT (a). Oct. 21, 1971, Knight. The Actor as Worker & Artist. T367

FRIEDKIN, WILLIAM (d). Dec. 18, 1968, Knight. The Birthday Party. T277

FRIEDMAN, TULLY (law). Nov. 2, 1970, Lesser. Legal end of documentary films. T323

FROUG, WILLIAM (w). Apr. 8, 1972, Lecture. The Young Film Maker and the Future (Film Conference). C-6

FULLER, SAM (d). Feb. 28, 1968, Panel. Jean-Luc Godard. T297

GARDNER, HERB (dramatist). Jan. 13, 1966, Knight. A Thousand Clowns. T193

GARFEIN, JACK (d). Feb. 13, 1969, Lecture. Film directing tech. T281

INTERVIEWS ON TAPE

GARFEIN, JACK (d). Mar. 6, 1969, Lecture. Film directing tech.
    T285

GARFEIN, JACK (d). Mar. 20, 1969, Lecture. Film directing tech.
    T289

GARFEIN, JACK (d). Apr. 10, 1969, Lecture. Film directing tech.
    T291

GARFEIN, JACK (d). Nov. 1970, Lecture. Film directing tech. T446

GARSON, GREER (a). Mar. 17, 1968, Vivien Leigh Dinner. T386

GIDDING, NELSON (w). Mar. 21, 1963, Knight. Nine Hours to Rama.
    T122

GIESLER, ABNER. Mar. 12, 1964, Knight. T145

GLASS, GEORGE. Nov. 5, 1970, Knight. So This is New York. T324

GLAZER, BARNEY. Jan. 16, 1961, Panel. Hollywood Trade Papers. T41

GODARD, JEAN-LUC (d). Feb. 26, 1968, Lippincott. T259

GODARD, JEAN-LUC (d). Feb. 27, 1968, Lippincott. T296

GODARD, JEAN-LUC (d). Feb. 28, 1968, Panel. Jean-Luc Godard. T297

GODARD, JEAN-LUC (d). Feb. 29, 1968, Youngblood. Young film
    makers. T298

GOLD, ERNEST (co). Apr. 18, 1963, Knight. T125

GOLD, HERBERT. Dec. 16, 1962, Lecture. At UC, Berkeley. T22

GOLD, LEON. Apr. 10, 1971, Lesser. T359

GOLDING, DAVID (publicist). Nov. 11, 1965, Knight. Guys and Dolls.
    T189

GOLDMAN, LES. Jan. 6, 1966, Knight. Animation. T192

GOLDSTEIN, EMANUEL. Nov. 2, 1971, Knight. T368

GOLDSTONE, DINA (a). Fall, 1972, Knight. Deadhead Miles. T468

GOLDSTONE, JAMES (d). May 1, 1969, Knight. Winning. T295

GOLDSTONE, JAMES (d). Apr. 22, 1971, Knight. <u>Red Sky at Morning</u>.
   T352

GOMBERG, SY (w). May 10, 1971, Knight. The blacklist. T356

GOMBERG, SY (w). Apr. 28, 1970, Knight. The blacklist. T311

GORDON, MICHAEL (d). Nov. 30, 1961, Panel. Cinema symposium. T95

GORDON, RUTH (a). Mar. 17, 1966, Knight. T197

GORDON, RUTH (a). Mar. 23, 1969, Helen Keller Dinner. T388

GOTTLIEB, CARL. Apr. 1, 1971, Knight. <u>Celebration at Big Sur</u>.
   T360

GRASSOFF, ALEX. Oct. 19, 1967, Knight. <u>The Young Americans</u>. T237

GRAUMAN, WALTER (d). May 21, 1964, Knight. <u>Lady in a Cage</u>. T157

GREENBERG, HENRY. Oct. 5, 1961, Knight. <u>Al Capone</u>. T86

GREENSPAN, LON. Oct. 17, 1963, Knight. <u>Tom Jones</u>. T134

GRIES, THOMAS S. (d). Oct. 22, 1970, Knight. <u>Fools</u>. T320

HAGEN, EARLE (co). May 24, 1966, Knight. T202

HAMILBURG, MICHAEL (ag). Apr. 29, 1971, Knight. <u>Derby</u>. T354

HANDLER, KEN. Oct. 5, 1972, Knight. <u>Bad Blood</u>. T459

HANSARD, WILLIAM. Nov. 3, 1970, Lesser. Front projection. T341

HANSERT, BURT. Oct. 22, 1964, Knight. T162

HANSFORD, BILL. Apr. 3, 1971, Lesser. T358

HARRINGTON, CURTIS (d). Apr. 20, 1961, Knight. <u>Night Tide</u>. T79

HARRINGTON, CURTIS (d). Oct. 12, 1967, Knight. <u>Games</u>. T236

HARRINGTON, PAT (a). Feb. 1, 1968, Knight. <u>The President's Ana-
   lyst</u>. T243

HARRIS, JAMES B. (p). Mar. 13, 1963, Knight. <u>Lolita</u>. T121

HARVEY   INTERVIEWS ON TAPE

HARVEY, ANTHONY (d-e). Mar. 18, 1969, Knight. Lion in Winter.
    T287

HAWKS, HOWARD (d). Sept. 7, 1969, History of the Western. T300

HAYES, HELEN (a). Mar. 23, 1969, Helen Keller Dinner. T388

HEAD, EDITH (dress design). Feb. 1972, DKA banquet honoring her.
    T438

HEAD, EDITH (dress design). May 7, 1972. T480

HESTON, CHARLTON (a). Jan. 4, 1961, Knight. T71

HESTON, CHARLTON (a). Mar. 23, 1969, Helen Keller Dinner. T388

HILL, GEORGE ROY (d). Oct. 5, 1962, Knight. Period of Adjustment.
    T106

HILLER, ARTHUR (d). Apr. 9, 1964, Knight. Americanization of Emily.
    T150

HILLER, ARTHUR (d). Jan. 21, 1971, Knight. Love Story. T333

HILTON, ARTHUR. Nov. 13, 1967, Lesser. T227

HIRSCHMAN, HERBERT. Jan. 4, 1963, Knight. In His Image. T117

HITCHCOCK, ALFRED (d). Feb. 1972, DKA banquet honoring him. T438

HOLSOPPLE, TED. Dec. 4, 1967, Lesser. T230

HOPKINS, HENRY. Apr. 28, 1966, Knight. Censorship. T200

HOPPER, DENNIS (a). Apr. 20, 1961, Knight. Night Tide. T79

HOWE, JAMES WONG (c). n. d., ASC. T400

HOWE, JAMES WONG (c). Mar. 30, 1967, Knight. T271

HUFFAKER, CLAIR (w). Oct. 8, 1970, Knight. Flap. T314

HYDE-WHITE, WILFRED (a). Mar. 17, 1968, Vivien Leigh Dinner. T386

JACKSON, HORACE (w). Jan. 9, 1964, Knight. Living Between Two
    Worlds. T141

JACOBS, ARTHUR P. (p). May 17, 1972, Knight. Play It Again, Sam. T469

JEWISON, NORMAN (d). Dec. 7, 1962, Knight. Forty Pounds of Trouble. T112

JEWISON, NORMAN (d). Sept. 24, 1969, Knight. Gaily, Gaily. T301

JOHNSON, BOBBY (p). Jan. 9, 1964, Knight. Living Between Two Worlds. T141

JOHNSON, LAMONT (d). May 20, 1971, Knight. A Gunfight. T363

JONES, CHARLES M. (Animator). Jan. 6, 1966, Knight. His cartoons. T192

JONES, ROBERT (e). Jan. 21, 1971, Knight. Love Story. T333

KAMINS, BERNIE (publicist). Dec. 7, 1970, Lesser. T342

KAMP, IRENE and LOUIS (w). Oct. 12, 1962, Knight. Paris Blues. T107

KANIN, GARSON (w). Feb. 12, 1967, Cole Porter Dinner. T275

KARTARIUM, ARAM. Apr. 20, 1961, Knight. Night Tide. T79

KAUFFMAN, MILLARD (w). Mar. 16, 1962, Knight. Reprieve. T101

KERSHNER, IRVIN (d). Oct. 1, 1964, Knight. Luck of Ginger Coffey. T160

KELLY, GENE (a). Feb. 12, 1967, Cole Porter Dinner. T275

KELLY, GENE (a). Apr. 4, 1971, Oscar Hammerstein Dinner. T453

KIN, MU (a). Nov. 14, 1963, Knight. T137

KNIGHT, ARTHUR (cr). Mar. 21, 1971, Panel. Film and its Audiences (Film conference). T445-4

KNIGHT, ARTHUR (cr). Nov. 18, 1971, Panel. Motion Picture Advertising and Publicity. T371

KNIGHT, ARTHUR (cr). Jan. 6, 1972, Lecture. The Apostrophe: Whose Film is it? T434

KNIGHT   INTERVIEWS ON TAPE

KNIGHT, ARTHUR (cr). Nov. 16, 1972, Lecture. The Extreme Close-up.
     T462

KNIGHT, ARTHUR (cr). Feb. 14, 1963, Lecture. Film criticism. T118

KNIGHT, ARTHUR (cr). Dec. 5, 1963, Lecture. Film criticism. T138

KNIGHT, ARTHUR (cr). Oct. 8, 1964, Lecture. Film criticism. T161

KOCH, HOWARD (w). Mar. 21, 1971, A New Leaf. T445-5

KOSTAL, IRWIN (co). Oct. 1971, Lecture. West Side Story. T365

KRAMER, LARRY (p). Apr. 3, 1970, Knight. Women in Love. T308

KRAMER, STANLEY (p-d). Oct. 8, 1971, Knight. Bless the Beasts and
     Children. T366

KRAMER, STANLEY (p-d). Jan. 7, 1960. MacCann. T66

KRAMER, STANLEY (p-d). Sept. 1961, Knight. dubbed from TV. T83

KRAMER, STANLEY (p-d). Nov. 30, 1961, Panel. Cinema Symposium.
     T95

KRAMER, STANLEY (p-d). May 13, 1965, Knight. T180

KRAMER, STANLEY (p-d). Dec. 14, 1966, Knight. T219

KRAMER, STANLEY (p-d). Mar. 17, 1968, Vivien Leigh Dinner. T386

KRANTZ, STEVE (p). Aug. 8, 1972, Knight. Fritz the Cat. C-8

KRANZE, DON (d). Jun. 7, 1971, Lesser. T357

KRANZE, DON (d). Oct. 5, 1970, Lesser. T317

KRISMAN, SERGE (art dir.). May 12, 1966, Knight. T201

KUBRICK, STANLEY (p-d). Jan. 23, 1964, Knight. by phone. T190

LANCHESTER, ELSA (a). Mar. 17, 1968, Vivien Leigh Dinner. T386

LANG, CHARLES (c). May 4, 1972, Knight. Butterflies Are Free.
     T465

LANG, FRITZ (d). Apr. 23, 1972, none. T480

LASKY, JESSE, JR. (p). Apr. 6, 1961, Knight. T77

LAUGHLIN, TOM (a). Feb. 23, 1961, Knight. We Are All Christ. T73

LAVEN, ARNOLD (d). Oct. 16, 1967, Lesser. T262

LEAR, NORMAN (w-p). May 23, 1963, Knight. Come Blow Your Horn.
T129

LEAR, NORMAN (w-p). Dec. 12, 1968, Knight. The Night They Raided
Minsky's. T264

LEIGH, VIVIEN. Mar. 17, 1968, Vivien Leigh Memorial Dinner. T386

LEMMON, JACK (a). Dec. 9, 1971, Knight. Kotch. T374

LEMMON, JACK (a). Nov. 9, 1962, Knight. Days of Wine and Roses.
T110

LENNART, ISOBEL (w). Sept. 26, 1968, Knight. T233

LERNER, ALAN JAY (co). Feb. 12, 1967, Cole Porter Dinner. T275

LERNER, IRVING (p-d). Dec. 7, 1962, Knight. To Be A Man. T113

LERNER, IRVING (p-d). Jan. 1963, Knight. T115

LERNER, IRVING (p-d). Oct. 3, 1969, The Royal Hunt of the Sun.
T302.

LERNER, IRVING (p-d). Apr. 7, 1970, Knight. American documentary.
T309

LE ROY, MERVYN (d). Mar. 17, 1968, Vivien Leigh Dinner. T386

LESSER, SOL (p). Dec. 10, 1959, MacCann. T65

LESSER, SOL (p). Sept. 18, 1967, Lecture. Film production. T268

LESSER, SOL (p). Feb. 5, 1968, Lecture. Film production. T266

LESSER, SOL (p). Sept. 29, 1970, Lecture. Film production. T316

LESSER, SOL (p). Feb. 8, 1971, Lecture. Film production. T346

LEVIN, BORIS (art dir.). Mar. 4, 1971, Knight. The Andromeda
Strain. T337

LEVY   INTERVIEWS ON TAPE

LEVY, JULES (p). Oct. 16, 1967, Lesser. T262

LEVY, JULES (p). Feb. 19, 1968, Lesser. T232

LEVY, JULES (p). Dec. 7, 1970, Lesser. T342

LEWIS, JERRY (a-d-p). May 2, 1963, Knight. The Nutty Professor.
    T126

LINDER, CARL (c). Oct. 22, 1968, The Devil is Dead. T293

LIPTON, DAVID (ex). Mar. 1, 1971, Lesser. T336

LIVINGSTON, DAVID. May 7, 1971, Knight. Willie Wonka and the
    Chocolate Factory. T355

LODEN, BARBARA (d-w-a). Mar. 25, 1971, Knight. Wanda. T350

LOMBARD, HENRY (ex). Apr. 13, 1961, Knight. T78

LOY, NONNIE (d). Mar. 7, 1963, Knight. Four Days of Naples. T120

LUBIN, A. RONALD (d). Sept. 29, 1962, Knight. Billy Budd. T105

LUCAS, GEORGE (d). Mar. 20, 1971, Panel. Now Movies and the Audi-
    ence (Film conf). T445-4

LUCAS, GEORGE (d). Mar. 20, 1971, THX1138. T445-5

LYONS, REGGIE (c). n. d., ASC. T418

MAC CANN, RICHARD (cr-hist). Nov. 14, 1963, Knight. T137

MADDOW, BEN (w-d). n. d., MacCann. T68

MAIBAUM, RICHARD (w-p). Jul. 29, 1972. T480

MALDEN, KARL (a). May 1961, Knight. One-Eyed Jacks. T81

MAMOULIAN, ROUBEN (d). Feb. 29, 1972, Knight. T435

MAMOULIAN, ROUBEN (d). Apr. 6, 1972, Lecture. The Art of Survival
    (Film conference). C-1

MAMOULIAN, ROUBEN (d). Dec. 9, 1969. T449

MANN, ABBY (w). Oct. 24, 1963, Knight. Judgement at Nurenberg.
    T135

MANN, ABBY (w). Mar. 30, 1971, Panel. Now Movies and the Audience (Film Conf). T445-4

MANN, GRAHAM (e). Oct. 29, 1964, Knight. Choice. T163

MANULIS, MARTIN (p-d). Nov. 16, 1962, Knight. T111

MARGULIES, STAN (p). May 7, 1971, Knight. Willie Wonka and the Chocolate Factory. T355

MARGULIES, STAN (p). Dec. 7, 1962, Knight. Forty Pounds of Trouble. T112

MARION, FRANCES (w). Oct. 6, 1966, Knight. T215

MARLEY, JOHN (a). Jan. 21, 1971, Knight. Love Story. T333

MARQUETTE, DESMOND. Apr. 27, 1961, Sloan. Storm Over Eden. T80

MASCOT, LAWRENCE. Dec. 1966, Knight. T251

MATTHAU, WALTER (a). Feb. 1972, DKA banquet honoring him. T438

MATTHAU, WALTER (a). Mar. 21, 1971. A New Leaf. T445-5

MATTHAU, WALTER (a). Mar. 17, 1968, Vivien Leigh Dinner. T386

MAYER, ARTHUR (dist). Nov. 16, 1961, Knight. Connection. T93

MAYER, ARTHUR (dist). Mar. 19, 1971, Panel. Film Education and the Audience (Film conf). T445-3

MAYER, ARTHUR (dist). Fall, 1972, Lectures. Motion Picture Business. T470/T478

MAYER, ARTHUR (dist). Spring, 1972, Lectures. Motion Picture Business. T444-1 thru 9

MAYER, GERALD (p-d). May 9, 1968, Knight. T248

MC CLAY, BOOKER (p). Feb. 27, 1969, Knight. 77 South. T283

MC CLAY, BOOKER (p). Mar. 13, 1969, Knight. Hell in the Pacific. T286

MC GANN, WILLIAM (c-d). n. d. T274

MC GANN, WILLIAM (c-d). Spring, 1966, Knight. T207

MERMAN INTERVIEWS ON TAPE

MERMAN, ETHYL (a). Feb. 12, 1967, Cole Porter Dinner. T275

MERCER, JOHNNY. Apr. 4, 1971, Oscar Hammerstein Dinner. T453

MILESTONE, LEWIS (d). n. d., MacCann. T60

MILESTONE, LEWIS (d). Feb. 1959, Mackey. MA thesis interview. T63

MILIUS, JOHN (w-d). Apr. 8, 1972, Panel. The Young Film Maker and the Future (Film Conference). C-6

MILLER, ARTHUR C. (c). n. d., ASC. T402

MILLER, ARTHUR C. (c). n. d., ASC. T415

MILLER, ARTHUR C. (c). n. d., ASC. T409

MILLER, JONATHAN. Feb. 17, 1972, Knight. T436

MILLER, VIRGIL (c). n. d., ASC. T402

MITCHELL, GEORGE (c). n. d., ASC. T414

MOHR, HAL (c). n. d., ASC. T419

MOHR, HAL (c). Apr. 3, 1971, Lesser. T358

MOHR, HAL (c). Jan. 11, 1971, Lesser. T345

MORGAN, HENRY (a). Nov. 5, 1970, Knight. So This is New York. T324

MORRISSEY, PAUL (d). Oct. 16, 1972, Knight. Heat. T466

MORROW, VIC (a-w-d). Apr. 4, 1963, Knight. Combat (TV). T124

MORROW, VIC (a-w-d). Oct. 7, 1965, Knight. Genet's Death Watch. T186

MULLIGAN, ROBERT (d). Jan. 1963, Knight. To Kill A Mockingbird. T116

MURPHY, ART (cr). Mar. 18, 1971, Panel. Film criticism and the Audience (Film conference). T445-2

MURPHY, ART (cr). Apr. 7, 1972, Panel. The Economics of Survival (Film conf). C-3

MURPHY, ART (cr). Apr. 8, 1972, Panel. Critics and the Symbiosis
    of Survival (Film Conference). C-5

NELSON, PETER (p). May 11, 1962, Knight. T104

NELSON, RALPH (d-p). Mar. 23, 1968, Knight. Charly. T249

NEWHART, BOB (a). Oct. 24, 1960, Panel. Comedy. T38

OLSEN, DALE (publicist). Oct. 22, 1964, Knight. T162

OVERBAUGH, RAY (c). n. d., ASC. T410

PALMER, CHARLES "CAP" (p). Oct. 3, 1967, Lesser. T225

PALMER, CHARLES "CAP" (p). Jan. 4, 1971, Lesser. Non-theatrical
    film. T344

PARKER, DOROTHY (w). Apr. 25, 1962, Knutson/Durbin. T13

PARSONS, LOUELLA (columnist). "Hollywood Hotel", 21 tapes of radio
    program. PAC 1

PECK, GREGORY (a). n. d., ASC. T416

PECK, GREGORY (a). Jan. 1963, Knight. To Kill A Mockingbird. T116

PERKINS, HARRY. Nov. 23, 1970, Lesser. T328

PHYSIOC, LEWIS. n. d., ASC. T405

PIERCE, LARRY (d). Jan. 7, 1965, Knight. One Potato, Two Potato.
    T166

POGOSTIN, S. LEE (w-d). Apr. 24, 1969, Knight. Hard Contract.
    T294

POLANSKI, ROMAN (d). Mar. 13, 1969, Knight. Rosemary's Baby. T282

POLL, MARTIN (p). Dec. 5, 1968, Knight. Sylvia. T265

POLL, MARTIN (p). Mar. 18, 1969, Knight. Lion in Winter. T287

POLLACK, SYDNEY (d). Feb. 17, 1966, Knight. T196

POLLACK, SYDNEY (d). Dec. 18, 1969, They Shoot Horses, Don't They?
    T303

POLLACK   INTERVIEWS ON TAPE

POLLACK, SYDNEY (d). Apr. 6, 1972, Panel. The Art of Survival
    (Film Conference). C-1

POST, TED (p-d). Feb. 17, 1962, MacCann. T67

POULIOT, STEVE. Apr. 12, 1971, Lesser. T340

POWERS, JAMES. Jan. 15, 1968, Lesser. T231

PRATT, JAMES. Oct. 23, 1967, Lesser. T224

PREMINGER, OTTO (d). Nov. 30, 1961, Panel. Cinema Symposium. T95

PRINCE, HAROLD (co). May 5, 1961, Panel. Musical comedy. T72

RACKIN, MARTY (w). May 26, 1966, Knight. T204

RADNITZ, ROBERT (p). Sept. 28, 1972, Knight. Sounder. T463

RADNITZ, ROBERT (p). Mar. 23, 1961, Knight. A Dog of Flanders.
    T76

RADNITZ, ROBERT (p). May 7, 1964, Knight. T155

RADNITZ, ROBERT (p). Apr. 7, 1972, Panel. Who Goes to the Movies,
    and Why? (Film conf). C-3

RADNITZ, ROBERT (p). Apr. 17, 1969, Knight. My Side of the Moun-
    tain. T272

RADNITZ, ROBERT (p). Mar. 18, 1971, Panel. Film and Finance (Film
    conf). T445-1

RADNITZ, ROBERT (p). Mar. 23, 1972, Knight. Film marketing. T443

RAITT, JOHN (a). Apr. 4, 1971, Oscar Hammerstein Dinner. T453

RAJANAN, INDO (w). Feb. 15, 1966, Knight. T195

RAKSIN, DAVID (co). Sept. 22, 1961, Knight. T72

RANDALL, TONY (a). Feb. 20, 1964, Knight. Pillow Talk. T152

RANSOHOFF, MARTIN (ex). Sept. 30, 1965, Knight. Cincinnati Kid.
    T176

RANSOHOFF, MARTIN (ex). Mar. 18, 1971, Panel. Film and Finance
    (Film conference). T445-1

RAPPER, IRVING (d). Mar. 19, 1970, Knight. T307

REINHARDT, GOTTFRIED (p-w). May 4, 1961, Knight. Town Without Pity. T82

RENNAHAN, RAY (c). n. d., ASC. T428

REYNOLDS, WILLIAM (e). Mar. 25, 1965, Knight. Compulsion. T172

REYNOLDS, WILLIAM (e). Apr. 18, 1968, Knight. T247

RITT, MARTIN (d). Sept. 28, 1972, Knight. Sounder. T463

RITT, MARTIN (d). Mar. 5, 1972. T480

RITT, MARTIN (d). Oct. 1963, Knight. Edge of the City. T131

RIVKIN, ALLEN (w). Oct. 2, 1967, Lesser. T269

RIVKIN, ALLEN (w). Mar. 18, 1971, Panel. Film Criticism and the Audience (Film conf). T445

ROBSON, MARK (d-p). Feb. 1959, Mackey. MA thesis interview. T63

ROSENBERG, FRANK P. (p). May 1961, Knight. One-Eyed Jacks. T81

ROSENMAN, LEONARD (co). Apr. 30, 1970, Knight. Film music. T310

ROSENSWEIG, BARNEY. Apr. 20, 1972, Knight. Who Fears the Devil? T447

ROSENTHAL, LAURENCE (co). May 20, 1971, Knight. A Gunfight. T363

ROSHER, CHARLES (c). n. d., ASC. T421

ROSS, HERBERT (d). May 17, 1972, Knight. Play It Again Sam. T469

ROSSEN, ROBERT (d). Oct. 19, 1961, Knight. T94

ROSSON, HAROLD (d-p). n. d., ASC. T412/3

ROSTEN, LEO (journalist). Dec. 12, 1963, Knight. T139

RUBIN, EDWARD. Nov. 27, 1967, Lesser. T229

RUBIN, EDWARD. Feb. 26, 1968, Lesser. T256

RUBIN, EDWARD. Nov. 9, 1970, Lesser. T325

RUBIN   INTERVIEWS ON TAPE

RUBIN, EDWARD. Mar. 21, 1971, Lesser. T349

RUBIN, RONALD (p). Feb. 26, 1970, Knight. T306

RUBIN, STANLEY (p). Feb. 1, 1968, Knight. The President's Analyst.
  T243

RUDDY, ALBERT S. (p). Oct. 24, 1970, Knight. Little Fauss and Big
  Halsey. T322

RUSSELL, ROSALIND (a). Mar. 23, 1969, Helen Keller Dinner. T388

RUTTENBERG, JOSEPH (c). n. d., ASC. T422

RYDELL, MARK (d). Fall, 1972, Knight. The Cowboys. T441

SAID, FOUAD (c-p). Apr. 6, 1972, Panel. The Technology of Survival.
  (Film conf). C-2

SANDERS, DENIS. Nov. 30, 1961, Panel. Cinema Symposium. T95

SCHARF, WALTER (co). Mar. 20, 1969, Knight. Funny Girl. T288

SCHLESINGER, JOHN (ex). Oct. 27, 1967. T456

SCHULBERG, BUDD (w-p). Dec. 9, 1965, Knight. On the Waterfront.
  T191

SCODINAK, CURT (w). Jan. 5, 1971, Knight. Writing in the 30's.
  T331

SEATON, GEORGE (w-d). n. d., MacCann. T59

SEITZ, JOHN (c). n. d., ASC. T411

SHAGAN, STEVE (w). May 14, 1964, Knight. From Russia With Love.
  T156

SHARP, HENRY (c). n. d., ASC. T423

SHARP, HENRY (c). n. d., ASC. T424

SHARTIN, ARNOLD. Mar. 11, 1968, Lesser. T267

SHAVELSON, MELVILLE (w-d). Mar. 5, 1964, Knight. T144

SHAVELSON, MELVILLE (w-d). May 20, 1972, Knight. War Between Men
  and Women. T464

SHAVELSON, MELVILLE (w-d). 1967, Knight. <u>Cast a Giant Shadow</u>. T245

SHAVELSON, MELVILLE (w-d). Apr. 6, 1972, Lecture. The Technology of Survival (Film Conf). C-2

SHAVELSON, MELVILLE (w-d). Mar. 28, 1968, Knight. <u>Yours, Mine, and Ours</u>. T246

SHAVELSON, MELVILLE (w-d). Mar. 18, 1971, Panel. Film and Finance (Film Conf). T445-1

SHEDLO, RONALD (p). Oct. 26, 1968, Knight. <u>Whisperers</u>. T272

SHOLEM, LEE (d). Nov. 6, 1967, Lesser. T226

SHOLEM, LEE (d). Nov. 16, 1970, Lesser. T326

SHOLEM, LEE (d). Mar. 8, 1971, Lesser. T339

SHURLOCK, GEOFFREY. May 11, 1959, MacCann. Censorship. T64

SHURLOCK, GEOFFREY. May 28, 1966, Knight. Censorship. T200

SIEGEL, DON (d). Jan. 7, 1971, Knight. <u>The Beguiled</u>. T332

SILLIPHANT, STERLING (w-p). Mar. 23, 1968, Knight. <u>Charly</u>. T249

SILVERSTEIN, ELLIOT (d). Feb. 16, 1967, Knight. <u>The Happening</u>. T270

SIMES, JOHN (publicist). Oct. 26, 1970, Lesser. T321

SINATRA, FRANK (a). Feb. 12, 1967, Cole Porter Dinner. T275

SINGER, ALEXANDER (p). Nov. 4, 1966, Knight. T218

SMITH, ROGER (p). Sept. 24, 1970, Knight. <u>C.C. and Co</u>. T312

SOLOW, SYD (p). Feb. 1972, DKA Banquet honoring him. T438

SOLOW, SYD (p). Apr. 6, 1972, Panel. The Technology of Survival (Film Conf). C-2

SPIGELGASS, LEONARD (w). Dec. 1, 1970. T330

STEIGER, ROD (a). Mar. 17, 1968, Vivien Leigh Dinner. T386

STERN   INTERVIEWS ON TAPE

STERN, EZRA E. (law). Mar. 11, 1968, Lesser. T267

STERN, STEWART (w). Oct. 3, 1963, Knight. Teresa. T132

STEVENS, GEORGE (p-d). Sept. 21, 1961, Knight. Giant. T84

STEVENS, LEITH (co). Apr. 3, 1970, Knight. Film music. T310

STEVENS, LESLIE (w-ex). Apr. 13, 1962, Knight. T103

STRUSS, KARL (c). n. d., ASC. T404

STUART, MALCOLM (p). Nov. 9, 1971, Knight. Mastermind. T370

STUART, MEL (d). May 7, 1971, Knight. Willie Wonka and the Choco-
    late Factory. T355

STUART, MEL (d). Apr. 13, 1972, Knight. One is a Lonely Number.
    T442

STULBERG, GORDON (ex). Oct. 31, 1968, Knight. T260

STULBERG, GORDON (ex). Apr. 7, 1972, Panel. The Economics of Sur-
    vival (Film Conf). C-3

STURGES, JOHN (d). May 9, 1963, Knight. The Great Escape. T127

SWERDLOFF, ART. Apr. 10, 1971, Lesser. T359

TANNURA, PHILLIP (c). n. d., ASC. T406

THOMAS, KEVIN (cr). Apr. 8, 1972. Panel. Critics and the Symbio-
    sis of Survival (Film Conference). C-5

THOMPSON, J. LEE (d). Mar. 9, 1962, Knight. Flame Over India.
    T100

THOMPSON, MARSHALL (a). Oct. 30, 1963, Knight. The Year of the
    Tiger. T136

THOROBY, WILLIAM. Oct. 26, 1962, Knight. Angel's Flight. T109

TIDYMAN, ERNEST (w). Mar. 16, 1972, Knight. French Connection.
    T439

TIDYMAN, ERNEST (w). Apr. 6, 1972, Panel. The Art of Survival
    (Film Conference). C-1

INTERVIEWS ON TAPE   WARRENTON

TIOMKIN, DMITRI (co). Feb. 14, 1961, Panel. Musical Comedy. T72

TIOMKIN, DMITRI (co). Mar. 18, 1965, Knight. T171

TOGAWA, NAOKI (cr). Oct. 4, 1966, Knight. T214

TROTTER, THOMAS. Apr. 28, 1966, Knight. Censorship. T200

TRUMBELL, DOUGLAS (d). Feb. 24, 1972, Knight. Silent Running.
    T437

TURMAN, LAWRENCE (p). Mar. 19, 1964, Knight. The Best Man. T146

TUSHER, WILLIAM. Feb. 1, 1961. Panel. Agents and Publicity. T43

VAN TREES, JAMES (c). n. d., ASC. T420

VARDA, AGNES (w-d). Dec. 5, 1967, Knight. T456

VARDA, AGNES (w-d). Feb. 27, 1968, Lippincott. T296

VIDOR, KING (d). May 5, 1957, MacCann. T61

VIDOR, KING (d). Feb. 28, 1968, Panel. Jean-Luc Godard. T297

VIDOR, KING (d). Feb. 9, 1962, Knight. The Big Parade. T99

VOGEL, JOSEPH (w-p-d). Sept. 24, 1968, Knight. The Numbers Man.
    T250

VOGEL, PAUL C. (c). n. d., ASC. T429

VORKAPICH, SLAVKO (e). Mar. 19, 1971, Panel. Film Education and
    the Audience (Film conf). T445-3

WALD, JERRY (w-p). Sept. 13, 1961, Knight. T83

WALKER, JOE (c). n. d., ASC. T426

WALLACH, ELI (a). Nov. 10, 1967. The Tiger Makes Out. T239

WALSH, DAVID (c). May 20, 1971, Knight. A Gunfight. T363

WALTER, JESSICA (a). Sept. 22, 1971, Knight. Play Misty For Me.
    T364

WARRENTON, GILBERT (c). n. d., ASC. T427

WEINGARTEN   INTERVIEWS ON TAPE

WEINGARTEN, LAWRENCE (p). Jan. 4, 1972, Knight. T373

WEISBART, DAVID (p). Oct. 27, 1966, Knight. T217

WEISSMAN, MURRAY. Jan. 7, 1971, Knight. The Beguiled. T332

WELLES, ORSON (a-p-d). May 12, 1971. T361

WENDKOS, PAUL (d). Apr. 23, 1964, Knight. Angel Baby. T153

WEST, MAE (a). Mar. 3, 1968, Knight. T244

WESTON, JAY (p). Fall, 1972, Knight. Lady Sings the Blues. T467

WESTON, SAM (p). Jan. 7, 1965, Knight. One Potato, Two Potato.
     T166

WEXLER, HASKELL (c). Apr. 16, 1964, Knight. A Face in the Rain.
     T151

WEXLER, HASKELL (c). Oct. 16, 1965, Knight. The Loved One. T187

WICKI, BERNHARD (d-a). Jun. 4, 1964, Knight. T158

WILDE, CORNELL (a-d). Mar. 10, 1967, Knight. The Naked Prey. T252

WILLINGHAM, CALDER (w). May 19, 1963. T19

WILSON, JOHN (p-w-d). Feb. 18, 1971, Knight. Shinbone Alley. T334

WILSON, RICHARD (p-d). Mar. 9, 1961, Knight. Citizen Kane. T74

WINCHELL, JOAN. Jan. 16, 1961. Panel. Hollywood Trade Papers.
     T41

WINKLER, IRWIN (p). Dec. 1, 1967. Point Blank. T242

WINTERS, SHELLEY (a). Apr. 29, 1965, Knight. A Place in the Sun.
     T181

WISE, ROBERT (p-d). Apr. 1971, The Andromeda Strain. T445-5

WISE, ROBERT (p-d). Feb. 1959, Mackey. MA thesis interview. T62

WISE, ROBERT (p-d). Music samples from Rio Conchos, Sound of Music,
     The Sand Pebbles. PAC 3

WISE, ROBERT (p-d). Sept. 26, 1963, Knight. The Haunting. T130

WISE, ROBERT (p-d). Sept. 24, 1964, Knight. T159

WISE, ROBERT (p-d). Mar. 4, 1971, Knight. The Andromeda Strain.
   T337

WYLER, WILLIAM (p-d). Jan. 25, 1962, Knight. The Children's Hour.
   T98

YATES, PETER (p-d). Oct. 3, 1968, Knight. Bullitt. T235

YORKIN, BUD (p-d). May 23, 1963, Knight. Come Blow Your Horn.
   T129

YOUNGSTEIN, MAX E. (ex). Nov. 28, 1972, Knight. T461

YOUNGSTEIN, MAX E. (ex). Mar. 18, 1971, Panel. Film and Finance
   (Film Conf). T445

YU, KIM (d). Nov. 14, 1963, Knight. T137

ZINNEMAN, FRED (d). Nov. 30, 1961, Panel. Cinema Symposium. T95

THE UNIVERSITY OF SOUTHERN CALIFORNIA FILM
CONFERENCE TAPES

The annual University of Southern California Film Conference began as the Aspen Film Conference in Aspen, Colorado. Economic fac-
tors and the relative convenience of holding the conference in Los
Angeles prompted its move to USC, where it has been held for the
past three years.

The purpose of the Conference is to encourage leading members of
the film industry to share their expertise or points of view on mat-
ters of general interest, both with their fellow panelists and with
the students, teachers and industry members who attend the event
each year.

Distinguished panelists have included Rouben Mamoulian, Jean
Renoir, King Vidor, Ray Bradbury, Arthur Mayer, and Charles Champlin, among many others. The general format for the panels features
a keynote speaker followed by input on the subject from each member
of the panel and a general discussion which later includes questions
from the audience.

Primary Cinema Resources: An Index

PRIMARY CINEMA RESOURCES: AN INDEX

1972 Film conference, April 6-8

C-1   "The Art of Survival"

   Keynote address: Rouben Mamoulian

   Panel: Peter Bogdanovich, Bruce Dern, Sydney Pollack, Ernest Tidyman, Bennett Tramer

C-2   "The Technology of Survival"
1/2

   Keynote address: Melville Shavelson

   Panel: John Alonzo, Wilton Holm, Monroe Price, Fouad Said, Syd Solow, Charles Woodward, Mort Zarkoff

C-3   "The Economics of Survival"
1/2

   Keynote address: Blake Edwards

   Panel: William O. Brown, Al Dorskind, Zane Lubin, Art Murphy, Gordon Stulberg, Aubrey Solomon

C-4   "Who Goes to the Movies, and Why?"

   Keynote address: Robert Radnitz

   Panel: Peter Bart, Dr. Allan Casebier, Bruce Corwin, Peter Guber, Doe Mayer

C-5   "Critics and the Symbiosis of Survival"
1/2

   Keynote address: Beverly Walker

   Panel: Charles Champlin, Roger Ebert, Manny Farber, Art Murphy, Kevin Thomas, Steve Greenberg

C-6   "The Young Film Maker and the Future"
1/2

   Keynote address: William Froug

   Panel: Tamara Assayev, Jonathan Axelrod, David Giler, John Milius, Rick Vaughnes

USC FILM CONFERENCE TAPES

1972 Film conference, April 6-8 (cont.)

C-7   "The Techniques of Survival"
 1/3
            Keynote address: Wilton Holm

            Arthur Knight moderates discussion with previous panel-
            ists.

SPECIAL COLLECTIONS

For the past several years, the University Library has been actively soliciting collections in the area of the Performing Arts. The response to these requests has been gratifying; at present, nearly one hundred collections have been acquired.

These contain a multiplicity of materials, but personal papers, memorabilia, scripts, and still photographs seem to be the most common elements. They vary greatly in size; some collections contain fewer than ten items, others have literally thousands. They are arranged and numbered in the order in which they were donated to the University.

At the present time, approximately one-fifth of the collections have been indexed and cataloged. This section contains a comprehensive list of all the collections, arranged alphabetically. There are detailed descriptions of the materials contained in forty-four collections. The other collections, which to date, have not been sufficiently inventoried, have briefer and more general descriptions. Space limits an exhaustive, item-by-item listing of the contents of each collection.

Many of the collections contain scripts. The descriptions list only the approximate number of scripts in a given collection. The specific titles may be found in either the Titles Index or the Screenwriters and Film Personality Index. The size of each collection is indicated as small (less than 50 items), medium (50-500 items), or large (more than 500 items).

Needless to say, these collections contain some of the most treasured materials in the Library. They may be used only in the Department of Special Collections, under the supervision of a librarian. Inquiries concerning the use of these materials should be directed to the Head, Department of Special Collections, Doheny Library, University of Southern California, Los Angeles, California 90007.

Primary Cinema Resources: An Index

SPECIAL COLLECTIONS

An alphabetical listing of the collections in this section.

Allen, Steve. No. 64
Anhalt, Edward. No. 27
Anthony, John J. No. 86
Astaire, Fred. No. 70
Backus, Jim and Henny. No. 26
Bakaleinikoff, Misha. No. 9
Bainter, Fay. No. 77
Biltmore Theater. No. 56
Brahm, John. No. 92
Brecher, Irving. No. 30
Burns, George and Allen, Gracie. No. 24
Burton, Jay. No. 28
Carlock, Marvin and Mary. No. 84
Chaplin, Saul. No. 15
Colt, Samuel. No. 18
Cooper, Gladys. No. 22
Cukor, George. No. 1
David, Mack. No. 37
Davis, Luther. No. 21
Defore, Don. No. 75
DeMille, Cecil B. No. 99
DeMille, William. No. 8
Devine, Andy. No. 80
Dieterle, William. No. 17
Doniger, Walter. No. 34
Dorr Historical. No. 13
Dunne, Philip. No. 41
Durante, Jimmy. No. 78
Duryea, Dan. No. 69
Eddy, Nelson. No. 55
Edens, Roger. No. 73
Eilers, Sally. No. 33
Farnum, William. No. 6
Fine, Morton. No. 23
Flicker, Theodore. No. 61
Fleischer, Richard. No. 31
Freed, Arthur. No. 62
Freeman, Y. Frank. No. 72
Freiberger, Fred. No. 40
Garnett, Tay. No. 65
Garrison, Greg. No. 48
Goodman, Hal and Klein, Larry. No. 35
Gosden, Freeman and Correll, Charles. No. 7
Grauman, Walter. No. 83
Haebel, Mrs. Otto. No. 71
Hamner, Robert. No. 42

SPECIAL COLLECTIONS

(Alphabetical - continued)
Harte, Betty. No. 47
Hopkins, George J. No. 4
Humphrey, Hal. No. 76
Imhoff, Roger. No. 57
Jacobs, Arthur P. No. 90
Jarre, Maurice. No. 20
Kaufman, Millard. No. 38
Knight, Arthur. No. 3
Kovacs, Ernie. No. 45
Laszlo, Ernest. No. 94
Lehman, Ernest. No. 19
Lesser, Sol. No. 68
Lewin, Albert. No. 44
Lewis, Jerry. No. 52
Littlefield, Constance. No. 14
Lord, Jack. No. 79
McHugh, Jimmy. No. 36
Mann, Abby. No. 60
Marion, Frances. No. 95
Newman, Alfred. No. 74
Oakie, Jack. No. 32
Olsen, Ole. No. 85
Pacific Pioneer Broadcasters. No. 16
Paramount Research Department.
Parker Advertising. No. 53
Parsons, Louella. No. 29
Pasternak, Joe. No. 81
Peters, Eleanor. No. 12
Powell, Eleanor. No. 67
Reynolds, Adeline deWalt. No. 96
Rivers, Johnny. No. 43
Roach, Hal. No. 10
Rodman, Howard. No. 58
Romero, Cesar. No. 93
Roos, Elizabeth Leslie. No. 2
Rubin, Benny. No. 88
Ruby, Harry. No. 39
Scheuer, Stanley K. No. 91
Schildkraut, Joseph. No. 46
Seltzer, Walter. No. 97
Shepard, Richmond. No. 89
Sisk, Robert. No. 66
Small, Edward. No. 82
Sothern, Ann. No. 87
Spigelgass, Leonard. No. 5
Stahl, John M. No. 11
Tiomkin, Dmitri. No. 51

SPECIAL COLLECTIONS

(Alphabetical - continued)
Twentieth Century-Fox Set-Stills
Vidor, King. No. 25
Wallace, Irving. No. 0
Weingarten, Lawrence. No. 59
Weisbart, David. No. 50
Windsor, Claire. No. 54
Wise, Robert. No. 49
Wray, Fay. No. 63
Wynn, Ed. No. 98

ALLEN, STEVE. No. 64. Scripts, manuscripts, scrapbooks, correspondence.

ANHALT, EDWARD. No. 27. Cataloged. Edward Anhalt (1914-   ) is a
well-known screenwriter who began writing in Hollywood in
the late 1940's. He received Academy Awards for Panic in
the Streets (1950) and Becket (1964).
    The Edward Anhalt Collection is large and would be of
particular value to a student of screenwriting. Naturally,
scripts and script drafts are its major strength:
    1. Scripts and other items relating to thirty films and
television programs (several unproduced). Many of the
scripts have personal comments written by Mr. Anhalt.
    2. Miscellaneous materials pertaining to the 1960 Writ-
er's Guild of America strike.
    3. Miscellaneous publicity clippings, 1952-1965.
    4. Biographical memoir written in 1965.

    The following materials are grouped according to indi-
vidual films: ·
    5. Becket. Script, clippings, approximately 100 con-
gratulatory letters and telegrams received after Mr. Anhalt
won an Oscar for his script.
    6. The Boston Strangler. Script draft, notes, step
outlines (2), structure outline, clippings, story board, research items, cast breakdown, correspondence, etc.
    7. Bugsy Siegel. Script drafts, script rejects, out-
line cards, notes, research reports.
    8. Hour of the Gun. Script, script roughs, notes,
treatment, point outline.
    9. The Madwoman of Chaillot. Script drafts, step out-
lines (2), notes, research clippings, copy of the play, correspondence, etc.
    10. The Passion of Mary Magdalene (unproduced). Script
drafts, outlines (2), treatment, notes, synopses (2), story
idea, correspondence, clippings, etc.
    11. Peter the Great (unproduced). Script drafts, con-
tinuity, notes, synopsis, correspondence, etc.
    12. Rachel Code. Script, synopsis, sequence breakdown,
notes, correspondence, clippings, photo, etc.
    13. The Salzburg Connection. Script drafts, synopsis,
notes, outline, script rejects, outline cards, research
photos, etc.
    14. The Sniper. Script, research clippings, publicity
clippings, correspondence.
    15. The Young Savages. Script drafts, novel, script
roughs, continuity outline, notes, etc.

ANTHONY, JOHN J. No. 86. Tapes, scripts, files, and radio transcriptions from the "advice" program of John J. Anthony.

ASTAIRE, FRED. No. 70. Uncataloged. Mr. Astaire (1899-   )
achieved fame as a dancer in a series of musicals which included Top Hat (1935) and Swing Time (1936). Toward the end
of his career, he converted to straight dramatic roles in On
the Beach, The Notorious Landlady and other films.
    At present, the Fred Astaire Collection contains only
the manuscript and galley proofs of his autobiography, Steps
in Time, published in 1960. The Library is hopeful that
other items will be added to this Collection in the future.

BACKUS, JIM AND HENNY. No. 26. Cataloged. Jim Backus (1913-   )
is a character actor who has appeared in a wide variety of
movies, television and radio programs. He is the voice of
the cartoon character, "Mr. Magoo." His wife, Henny, also
acted in radio shows and films.
    The Jim and Henny Backus Collection is medium-sized.
Scripts and recordings of radio programs are its main
strength:
    1. Scripts of nineteen movies in which Mr. or Mrs.
Backus acted.
    2. Scripts of fourteen segments of The Jim Backus Show
("Hot Off the Line"), a radio program.
    3. Script of the 1967 television version of Damn
Yankees.
    4. Approximately fifteen phonograph records of the
early 1940's War Department "Jubilee" radio programs. These
featured Bing Crosby, Bob Hope and Jack Benny as well as Jim
Backus.
    5. Three phonograph records of the Allan Young radio
show (1947).
    6. Phonograph records of approximately twenty-five
miscellaneous radio programs in which Jim or Henny Backus
participated.
    7. Miscellaneous items: original drawings of Mr. Magoo,
a bust of Jim Backus, program from It's a Mad, Mad, Mad, Mad
World, program from the 28th Academy Awards, scrapbook and
pictorial illustrations relating to Mr. Backus' book, What
Are You Doing After the Orgy?.

BAINTER, FAY. No. 77. Cataloged. Fay Bainter (1892-1968) acted in
many movies, as well as stage plays and television programs.
She received the Academy Award for Best Supporting Actress
in Jezebel (1938).

BAINTER, FAY. (cont.)
     The Fay Bainter Collection is large and contains a vari-
ety of materials:
     1. Stills and photographs from approximately fifteen
films.
     2. Scripts of fifteen stage plays.
     3. Stills and photographs from approximately twenty
stage plays.
     4. Clippings covering approximately twenty stage plays,
1912-1960.
     5. Ten stage play programs.
     6. Scripts of six television programs.
     7. Correspondence, 1917-1967. Most concerns dramatic
performances.
     8. Miscellaneous publicity clippings and magazine arti-
cles dating from 1906.
     9. Miscellaneous photographs--Miss Bainter's early
years in the theatre, publicity photos, photos of her family
and friends.
     10. Personal items and documents--U. S. Passport,
Screen Actor's Guild membership card, receipts, financial
statements and expenses, contracts, etc.
     11. Miscellaneous items pertaining to the Academy
Awards. A photograph of Miss Bainter receiving her Oscar in
1938 is included.

BAKALEINIKOFF, MISHA. No. 9. No information available.

BILTMORE THEATER. No. 56. Box office statements.

BRAHM, JOHN. No. 92. Uncataloged. John Brahm (1893-   ) arrived
     in Hollywood in 1936 after working as an actor and stage
     director in his native Germany. He directed many movies and
     television programs. The Lodger (1944) is probably his best
     known film.
          The John Brahm Collection is medium-sized. A variety of
     items are included:
          1. Two motion picture scripts.
          2. Two television scripts: "The Man from U.N.C.L.E."
     and "The Alfred Hitchcock Hour."
          3. Photo albums from three films: Broken Blossoms
     (1936), Special Delivery, and The Thief of Venice.
          4. Approximately forty musical transcription discs
     (12") from Brahm films.
          5. Miscellaneous items: clippings and publicity ma-
     terials, magazines with pertinent articles, theatre pro-
     grams, approximately 100 stills, director's copy of Romeo
     and Juliet in German with Brahm's notes, etc.

285

BRECHER, IRVING. No. 30. Materials relating to <u>The Life of Riley</u>.

BURNS, GEORGE and ALLEN, GRACIE. No. 24. Films and memorabilia.

BURTON, JAY. No. 28. Cataloged. Jay Burton is a writer who has
    worked on a number of television shows.
        The Jay Burton Collection consists entirely of scripts
    and sketches written for various television programs. The
    items are grouped according to the particular program for
    which they were written:
        1. "The Texaco Star Theatre" (1948-1953)--Approximately
    150 sketches and scripts.
        2. "The Buick-Berle Show" (1954-1955)--Thirty-six
    sketches and scripts.
        3. "The Perry Como Show" (1955-1959)--Seventy-six
    scripts.
        4. "The Julius LaRosa Show" (1957)--Four scripts.
        5. Eleven bound volumes of monologues, written mostly
    for Milton Berle.

CARLOCK, MARVIN and MARY. No. 84. 174 reels of 16mm film from the
    television series, <u>Fireside Theatre</u>.

CHAPLIN, SAUL. No. 15. Uncataloged. Saul Chaplin (1912-   ) is a
    songwriter, musical director and producer. He has worked on
    several famous musicals including <u>West Side Story</u> (1961) and
    <u>The Sound of Music</u> (1965).
        The Saul Chaplin Collection is quite small:
        1. Scripts of five feature films.
        2. A pre-production planning cross plot for <u>Can-Can</u>
    (Mr. Chaplin was associate producer of this film).

COLT, SAMUEL. No. 18. Books, letters.

COOPER, GLADYS. No. 22. Cataloged. Gladys Cooper (1888-1971), a
    distinguished British stage actress, began her Hollywood
    career in <u>Rebecca</u> (1940). Subsequently, she appeared in many
    films including <u>Now Voyager</u> (1942) and <u>My Fair Lady</u> (1964).
        The Gladys Cooper Collection is a huge assortment of
    theatrical and filmic materials:
        1. Items relating to approximately ninety plays which
    Miss Cooper optioned or appeared in--scripts, correspondence,
    memos, contracts, playbills, brochures, scrapbooks, clip-
    pings, etc.
        2. Items relating to approximately twenty-five films
    (1916-1960)--scripts, programs, clippings, correspondence,
    contracts, publicity, etc.

COOPER, GLADYS (cont.)
     3. Items relating to five radio programs--contracts, scripts, brochures, etc.
     4. Items relating to approximately thirty television shows (mainly "The Rogues" series, 1964-1965)--scripts, call sheets, shooting schedules, correspondence, contracts, clippings, etc.
     5. Papers relating to the management of the Playhouse Theatre, London, 1922-1934--correspondence, contracts, playbills, financial statements, memos, etc.
     6. Programs of forty-five benefit performances given between 1908 and 1956 for such organizations as "The Church of England Waifs and Strays Society" and "The Princess Beatrice Hospital."
     7. Materials relating to twelve plays and one film in which Philip Merivale appeared as a principal actor--programs, playbills, clippings, etc.
     8. Playbills for three plays in which Sally Cooper appeared.
     9. Materials relating to nine plays in which Joan Buckmaster appeared--playbills, programs, clippings, etc.
     10. Miscellaneous clippings, playbills, etc., from twenty-nine plays dating back to 1888.
     11. Approximately thirty unsolicited dramatic scripts.
     12. Approximately fifty magazines, and periodicals containing relevant articles (1934-1964).
     13. Fifty miscellaneous music scores.
     14. Approximately seventy-five photos and fourteen stills.

CUKOR, GEORGE. No. 1. Uncataloged. George Cukor (1899-   ) is one of America's most distinguished directors. Known particularly for his handling of sophisticated comedy, Mr. Cukor has been responsible for more than forty films since 1930. He won the Academy Award for My Fair Lady in 1964.
     The George Cukor Collection is, unfortunately, very small:
     1. Miscellaneous correspondence. Included is a letter from W. Somerset Maugham.
     2. Television script for the "This Is Your Life" program honoring Bessie Love, Sept. 24, 1963.
     3. Approximately fifteen stills showing Mr. Cukor at work with various "stars." Included: Marilyn Monroe, Jean Harlow, Greta Garbo.
     4. Miscellaneous photographs.

DAVID   SPECIAL COLLECTIONS

DAVID, MACK. No. 37. Cataloged. Mack David is an important com-
    poser and lyricist who has scored a number of films and
    television programs. Among the more famous films with music
    by Mr. David are To Kill A Mockingbird (1962), Hud (1963)
    and The Dirty Dozen (1967).
        The Mack David Collection is large and contains many
    items of interest to the student of film music:
        1. Sheet music dating from 1924. There are approxi-
    mately 550 items arranged chronologically.
        2. Approximately ten scripts of feature films.
        3. Miscellaneous items relating to several films: cor-
    respondence, budgets, advertising brochures, memos, con-
    tracts, etc.
        4. Fourteen reels of audio tape containing a wide vari-
    ety of music. A complete list of this music is contained in
    the catalog description. The tapes also contain interviews
    from radio and television programs.

DAVIS, LUTHER. No. 21. Teleplay materials from "Arsenic and Old
    Lace".

DEFORE, DON. No. 75. Cataloged. Don Defore (1917-   ) is an
    actor with movie, radio and television experience. His
    screen credits include My Friend Irma (1949) and Battle Hymn
    (1957), and he starred in the "Hazel" television series.
        The Don Defore Collection is large and contains a wide
    variety of materials:
        1. Scripts of thirty-one films in which Mr. Defore ap-
    peared.
        2. Ten films (mostly from television programs). In-
    cluded is the 1953 segment of "This is Your Life" which
    honored Mr. Defore.
        3. Sixteen phonograph records of late 1940's radio pro-
    grams. Most are from the "Lux Radio Theatre" and the "Fam-
    ily Theatre."
        4. Seventeen magazines ("Movie Life," "Screen Stars,"
    etc.) with pertinent articles.
        5. Miscellaneous publicity materials - press books,
    playbills, clippings, photos, over 250 stills.
        6. Contractual and other business papers.
        7. Personal items - biographical clippings and data,
    photos of 1966 Vietnam tour, wedding photo, family photos,
    Mr. Defore's high school yearbook.

DE MILLE, CECIL B. No. 99. Uncataloged. Cecil B. DeMille (1881–
1959) was one of America's most famous producer–directors.
Among the many "spectaculars" he brought to the screen were
King of Kings (1927) and The Ten Commandments (1956).

Cecil B. DeMille gave thousands of books to the University Library, but the cinema materials in his collection are,
unfortunately, rather scant:

1. Seventeen steroptican slides (views on both sides)
from the Cecil B. DeMille production Fool's Paradise (1921).

2. One bound volume entitled, "Mr. Cecil B. DeMille Ap-
praisal of Personal Property in his Study at Famous Players-
Lasky Studio." Date: December 8, 1920.

3. Three large scrapbooks containing foreign publicity
campaigns for two DeMille pictures, The Crusades and The
Greatest Show on Earth.

4. One large scrapbook containing still photographs of
DeMille's country estate.

DE MILLE, WILLIAM C. No. 8. Cataloged. William C. DeMille (1878–
1955) was active in the movie industry, primarily for Paramount Studios, from 1914 through the late 1930's. Although
overshadowed by his younger brother, Cecil B. DeMille, William distinguished himself as a director, writer and producer. In addition, Mr. DeMille worked in the Broadway
theatre, usually in association with David Belasco, during
the first decade of the twentieth century.

The William C. DeMille Collection consists primarily of
scripts and essays by Mr. DeMille and by his wife, Clara
Beranger. It is a large collection:

1. Approximately sixty film scripts. Some of these are
from the silent era, and many were written by the DeMilles.

2. Seventeen stage plays written between 1903–1940.
Most are by William C. DeMille.

3. Approximately thirty-five articles written by DeMille
between 1909–1940. Most of these deal with cinema or drama.

4. Biographical clippings covering Mr. DeMille's career
from 1920 to 1949.

5. More than 800 playbills from various theatres, 1900–
1953.

6. Miscellaneous materials: correspondence, treatments, outlines, clippings, etc.

7. Thirty-four albums containing photographs from silent films produced or directed by William DeMille.

DEVINE, ANDY. No. 80. Radio and TV scripts, phonograph records.

DIETERLE, WILLIAM. No. 17. Cataloged. William Dieterle (1893-) began as an actor in such German films as Paul Leni's Wax-works. He came to Hollywood in 1930 and soon established himself as a director of prestige movies. Among his more famous films: The Life of Emile Zola (1937), The Hunchback of Notre Dame (1939).

The William Dieterle Collection is large and may best be grouped according to individual films:

1. The Story of Louis Pasteur (1936)--eleven stills, memo.

2. The White Angel (1936)--research materials, biography of Florence Nightingale, synopsis, 140 stills.

3. The Life of Emile Zola (1937)--research materials, 160 stills.

4. Blockade (1938)--sixty stills (advertising and publicity).

5. Juarez (1938)--outlines, continuity, memos, research materials, research photos (approximately 300).

6. The Hunchback of Notre Dame (1939)--script, script drafts, research materials, synopses, outlines, memos, correspondence, clippings, publicity stills (more than 600).

7. Dr. Ehrlich's Magic Bullet (1940)--script, script drafts, research materials, treatment, memos, correspondence, twenty photos, sixty stills.

8. Dispatch from Reuters (1940)--script, correspondence, clippings, 200 stills.

9. All that Money Can Buy (1941)--120 publicity stills.

10. Tennessee Johnson (1942)--120 publicity stills.

11. Kismet (1944)--200 publicity stills.

12. September Affair (1950)--Twenty stills and a production book.

DONIGER, WALTER. No. 34. Scripts and set drawings from Peyton Place.

DORR HISTORICAL. No. 13. Records, sheet music, stills.

DUNNE, PHILIP. No. 41. Uncataloged. Philip Dunne (1908-) achieved fame as a screenwriter and writer-director. His credits include How Green Was My Valley (1942), The Robe (1953) and Ten North Frederick (1958).

The Philip Dunne Collection contains many valuable items. Scripts and other materials relating to writing are the major strength of this large collection:

1. Scripts of fifty feature films (some unproduced). Many of these contain stills and others (those directed by Dunne) are shooting scripts with notes and sketches.

DUNNE, PHILIP (cont.)

    2. Working copies of fifteen novels adapted by Mr. Dunne for the screen. Included: <u>Forever Amber</u>, <u>The Robe</u>, <u>How Green Was My Valley</u>, <u>The View from Pompey's Head</u>, etc.

    3. Manuscript of <u>Mr. Dooley Remembers: The Informal Memoirs of Finley Peter Dunne</u>, edited with an introduction and commentary by Philip Dunne. Also, clippings relating to this book.

    4. Miscellaneous production items pertaining to approximately thirty-five different films or projects: correspondence, treatments, memos, notes, estimates, budgets, research materials, synopses, etc.

    5. Five reels of taped self-interviews by Mr. Dunne. Among the topics discussed: "the function of the writer," "censorship," "on working with directors, producers, writers," "<u>The Robe</u>," "<u>The Agony and the Ecstacy</u>," etc.

    6. Publicity materials and clippings concerning Dunne and several of his films.

    7. Miscellaneous magazines (some containing articles or stories by Dunne).

    8. Miscellaneous items: speeches, story ideas, "Screen Writers Guild" data, "Screen Producers Guild" notices, congratulatory letters, etc.

DURANTE, JIMMY. No. 78. Scripts and transcriptions of Durante's radio shows, 1943-1947.

DURYEA, DAN. No. 69. Cataloged. Dan Duryea (1907-1968) was a prominent American actor. Often cast in the role of villain, he appeared in many movies and television programs.

    The Dan Duryea Collection is particularly strong in script materials. It is a large collection:

    1. Eight scrapbooks dealing with Mr. Duryea's life and career, 1924-1967.

    2. Scripts of approximately seventy films, 1941-1966.

    3. Scripts of approximately fifty episodes of the television series, "The Affairs of China Smith," 1952-1956.

    4. Scripts of approximately seventy-five miscellaneous television programs in which Mr. Duryea acted.

    5. Scripts and call sheets from approximately sixty episodes of the "Peyton Place" television show, 1967-1968.

    6. Scripts of six stage plays, 1952-1956.

    7. Miscellaneous items—correspondence, publicity booklets, articles, story treatments, call sheets for "The Affairs of China Smith," programs, notices, family Bible, etc.

EDDY, NELSON. No. 55. Cataloged. Nelson Eddy (1901-1967), an
actor-singer, made his film debut in 1933. His most famous
roles came in a series of 1930's musicals co-starring Jean-
ette MacDonald. These include <u>Naughty Marietta</u> (1935), <u>May-
time</u> (1937) and <u>The Girl of the Golden West</u> (1938).
   The Nelson Eddy Collection is particularly strong in
still photographs and phonograph records:
   1. Over 2200 publicity and personal stills. Included
are stills from approximately twenty-five movies.
   2. Approximately fifteen scrapbooks dealing with Mr.
Eddy's career, 1933-1967.
   3. Scripts of sixteen films and twenty-nine television
programs.
   4. Phonograph records of the "Nelson Eddy Radio Show,"
1944-1949. Approximately 118 different programs are represented; forty-one of these are from the "Kraft Music Hall,"
1947-1949.
   5. Booklets filled with concert programs, 1928-1950.
   6. Approximately 100 personal photographs.

EDENS, ROGER. No. 73. Books, musical manuscripts, sheet music,
scripts.

EILERS, SALLY. No. 33. Stills, scrapbooks, transcriptions.

FARNUM, WILLIAM. No. 6. Photos.

FINE, MORTON. No. 23. Cataloged. Morton Fine is a writer and producer whose major experience has been in television work.
He co-produced (with David Friedkin) the "I Spy" television
series (1964-68).
   The materials in the Morton Fine Collection are all related to "I Spy":
   1. Scripts of approximately forty different episodes of
the "I Spy" show. Some were co-written by Morton Fine.
   2. Miscellaneous production items from "I Spy": correspondence, staff and cast lists, call sheets, production reports, shooting schedules, memos, rough drafts, notes, revisions, etc.

FLICKER, THEODORE. No. 61. Interviews, scripts, financial records,
correspondence.

·FLEISCHER, RICHARD. No. 32. Cataloged. Richard Fleischer (1916-)
     has been a prolific motion picture director since 1946. His
     films include Twenty Thousand Leagues Under the Sea (1954),
     The Boston Strangler (1968) and Soylent Green (1973). He is
     the son of Max Fleischer, the cartoonist and producer who
     created "Betty Boop."
          The Richard Fleischer Collection is large and will un-
     doubtedly grow in size as Mr. Fleischer adds to it in coming
     years:
          1. Scripts of thirty-three feature films.
          2. Miscellaneous items (mostly clippings and sketches)
     relating to twenty-one films.
          3. General publicity items and contracts.

          The following materials are grouped according to indi-
     vidual films:
          4. Fantastic Voyage--script drafts, treatment, continu-
     ity, sketches, special effects data, call sheets, research
     photos, correspondence, etc.
          5. Dr. Dolittle--script, synopsis, correspondence, mu-
     sical data, budgets, publicity information, special effects
     data, sketches, casting information, notes, location slides,
     etc.
          6. The Seven Minutes--script drafts, story conference
     notes, casting suggestions, correspondence, publicity items,
     memos, etc.
          7. The Boston Strangler--script drafts, treatment, cor-
     respondence, production photographs, notes, shooting sched-
     ules, research material, story board sketches, budget, con-
     tinuity, publicity items, censorship notes, casting informa-
     tion, crew lists, expense accounts, notes, memos, preview
     photos, etc.
          8. Che!--script drafts, script revisions, publicity
     booklets in different languages, notes, sketches, reports,
     budgets, location photos, shooting schedules, publicity
     items, correspondence, memos, original map drawings, etc.
          9. Tora! Tora! Tora!--script drafts, budgets, call
     sheets, notes, photos, sketches, personnel list, reports,
     memos, correspondence, publicity clippings, etc.

FREED, ARTHUR. No. 62. Scripts, stills, correspondence, financial
     papers, phonograph records.

FREEMAN, Y. FRANK. No. 72. Awards, photos, clippings.

·FREIBERGER, FRED. No. 40. Cataloged. Fred Freiberger is a writer
     and producer. He was one of the producers of the highly ac-
     claimed "Star Trek" television series.

FREIBERGER, FRED (cont.)
        The Fred Freiberger Collection consists mainly of scripts
and production items relating to the "Star Trek" television
show:
        1. Scripts of seven feature films written (or co-
written) by Fred Freiberger. Some of these were never produced.
        2. Scripts from fifty-eight episodes of the "Ben Casey"
television program, 1961-63.
        3. Miscellaneous production items pertaining to approx-
imately twenty-five episodes of the "Star Trek" television
series: scripts, cast lists, memos, shooting schedules,
call sheets, production reports, outlines, articles, correspondence, etc.

GARNETT, TAY. No. 65. Cataloged. Tay Garnett (1898-   ) began
        his career as a director-writer in 1920. He directed some
        silents, many "talkies," and also worked in television.
        Perhaps his most famous film is the 1946 version of the
        James M. Cain novel, The Postman Always Rings Twice.
        The Tay Garnett Collection is medium-sized and consists
        almost entirely of scripts:
        1. Scripts of thirty-nine films. Some were written (or
        co-written) by Garnett, and most are shooting scripts, heav-
        ily annotated.
        2. Scripts for approximately twenty episodes of Three
        Sheets to the Wind, a half hour radio series created, pro-
        duced and directed by Mr. Garnett. It starred John Wayne.
        3. Two scrapbooks containing reviews, articles, post-
        ers, programs, etc. These relate to Tay Garnett's career
        from 1928 to 1937.

GARRISON, GREG. No. 48. Scripts, budgets, papers from Dean Martin
        television shows, 1966-69.

GOODMAN, HAL and KLEIN, LARRY. No. 35. Scripts.

GOSDEN, FREEMAN and CORRELL, CHARLES. No. 7. Materials relating to
        Amos 'n' Andy.

GRAUMAN, WALTER. No. 83. Scripts, treatments, photos, correspond-
        ence, memos, notes, 16mm prints of television programs.

HAEBEL, MRS. OTTO. No. 71. Uncataloged. The Mrs. Otto Haebel Col-
        lection is small and of limited usefulness. It consists of
        nine scrapbooks filled with programs from New York stage
        plays. The years covered are 1908-1944.

HAEBEL, MRS. OTTO (cont.)
        There are also some programs from opera, symphony,
    drama, and cinema presentations in the Los Angeles area.

HAMNER, ROBERT. No. 42. No information available.

HARTE, BETTY. No. 47. Stills, posters, scrapbooks.

HOPKINS, GEORGE J. No. 4. Scrapbooks of theatre programs, clip-
        pings, letters.

HUMPHREY, HAL. No. 76. Books, TV materials, papers, files, columns.

IMHOFF, ROGER. No. 57. Scrapbooks.

JACOBS, ARTHUR P. No. 90. Uncataloged. Arthur P. Jacobs (1922–
        1973), a producer, created the highly successful Planet of
    the Apes series.
            The Arthur P. Jacobs Collection is small. It contains
        budgets, script drafts, stills and photos, correspondence
        and publicity materials from the Arthur P. Jacobs' produc-
        tion, The Chairman (1969).

JARRE, MAURICE. No. 20. Original music scores.

KAUFMAN, MILLARD. No. 38. No information available.

KNIGHT, ARTHUR. No. 3. Uncataloged. Arthur Knight (1916–   ), a
        Professor in the USC Division of Cinema, is a distinguished
        film critic–historian. He is the author of a highly re-
        spected work on the history of the movies, The Liveliest
    Art.
            The Arthur Knight Collection contains the manuscript and
        illustration layouts of his book, The Liveliest Art. It is
        hoped that Mr. Knight will add to this collection in the
        future.

KOVACS, ERNIE. No. 45. Cataloged. Ernie Kovacs (1919–1962), a
        comedian whose cigar was his trademark, became an important
        television personality in the 1950's. Kovacs also appeared
        in several movies before his untimely death.
            The Ernie Kovacs Collection consists mainly of materials
        pertaining to his television career. It is a large collec-
        tion:
            1. Production materials relating to the "Kovacs Unlim-
        ited" television show, 1952–1953––scripts, rundowns, prop
        lists, sound effects lists, music credits, guest lists, etc.

KOVACS   SPECIAL COLLECTIONS

KOVACS, ERNIE (cont.)
     2. Production materials relating to "The Ernie Kovacs
Show," another television series, 1953-1957--approximately
400 scripts, rundowns, notes, treatments, cue sheets, etc.
     3. Production materials relating to several sessions of
"The Tonight Show" television program, 1955-1957--scripts,
rundowns, notes, treatments, cue sheets, etc.
     4. Eight scripts from miscellaneous television shows.
     5. Miscellaneous scripts, cue sheets, notes for uniden-
tified television programs.
     6. Script and publicity items for Operation Madball, a
movie Mr. Kovacs acted in.

LASZLO, ERNEST. No. 94. Uncataloged. Ernest Laszlo (1905-   ) is
an important American cinematographer. Among his many credits are Inherit the Wind (1960), Ship of Fools (1965), and
Star! (1968).
     The Ernest Laszlo Collection consists mainly of scripts.
It is medium-sized:
     1. Shooting scripts of approximately fifty films, sev-
eral unproduced.
     2. Two television scripts and two short subject scripts
of films made while Laszlo was in the Army.
     3. Miscellaneous items: stills, clippings, periodicals
relating to Mr. Laszlo's career.

LEHMAN, ERNEST. No. 19. Cataloged. Ernest Lehman (1920-   ) is
an important screenwriter who has also functioned as producer and director during his career. His films include
North by Northwest (1959), The Sound of Music (1965) and
Who's Afraid of Virginia Woolf? (1966).
     The Ernest Lehman Collection is large and especially
rich in scripts and script materials. Most of the scripts
are photostatic copies rather than originals:
     1. Approximately 130 miscellaneous scripts from Mr.
Lehman's personal film library.
     2. Approximately 120 synopses of potential properties.

     The following materials are grouped according to indi-
vidual films:
     3. The Prize--script drafts, revisions, script super-
visor's shooting script, out pages, writer's worksheets,
outlines, elaborative breakdown of the novel, changes, loop-
ing data, wardrobe breakdown, etc.
     4. The Sound of Music--script drafts, outlines, revi-
sions, rewrites, notes, screen tests, cast lists, crew lists,
rehearsal schedule, location information, shooting schedules, daily call sheets, music notes, music breakdown, German and Spanish translations of the screenplay, Lehman's

LEHMAN, ERNEST (cont.)
      notes to original director William Wyler, appendix to be
used by new director Robert Wise, continuity sheets of the
German film The Trapp Family, etc.
      5. Who's Afraid of Virginia Woolf?--script drafts, re-
visions, work pages, notes, location stills, casting data,
correspondence, memos, publicity material, sketches, progress
and production reports, budgets, contracts, breakdowns, published stage play (by Edward Albee), Broadway director Alan
Schneider's playscript, audio tapes: the original Broadway
cast recording of the play, the original rough dialogue
track, the composite (dialogue, music, and effects) sound
track of the film, etc.
      6. Hello, Dolly--script drafts, notes, outline, revi-
sions, research drawings, research photos, make-up tests,
wardrobe test stills, wardrobe research sketches, sheet
music, publicity, sketches, color transparencies and photos
of Barbra Streisand as Dolly, etc.

LESSER, SOL. No. 68. Cataloged. Sol Lesser (1890-   ) is one of
the pioneers of the film industry. He began as a film ex-
hibitor in silent days and later became a producer. Mr.
Lesser is an Adjunct Professor in the USC Division of Cinema.
      The Sol Lesser Collection is large and particularly
strong in items relating to the history of motion pictures:
      1. Early motion picture equipment: cameras, projectors,
etc. Also: glass plate and chromatrope slides.
      2. Scripts of thirty-five films produced 1933-1940.
      3. Scenarios of fourteen stage plays produced 1905-
1920.
      4. Miscellaneous production materials: correspondence,
contracts, scrapbooks, production books, clippings, etc.
      5. Approximately 230 stills from more than thirty
films. Many are "classic" films: Greed, Metropolis, The
Covered Wagon, etc.
      6. Approximately fifty items relating to the history of
motion pictures: pamphlets, booklets, magazines, clippings,
glass transparencies, correspondence, etc.
      7. Approximately 100 books. Most deal with show busi-
ness and movies.
      8. Thirty-six volumes of miscellaneous periodicals,
yearbooks, etc., dated 1903-1967.

LEWIN, ALBERT. No. 44. Papers, memorabilia.

LEWIS, JERRY. No. 52. No information available.

LITTLEFIELD   SPECIAL COLLECTIONS

LITTLEFIELD, CONSTANCE. No. 14. Uncataloged. Constance Littlefield
    is a writer of articles for various motion picture "fan"
    magazines. She uses the pseudonym, "Constance Palmer."
        The Constance Littlefield Collection consists of approx-
    imately seventy-five movie magazines (mostly from the
    1940's). Titles include "Movieland," "Screen Guide" and
    "Silver Screen." Each magazine contains an article by "Con-
    stance Palmer." There are also six spiral notebooks filled
    with her hand-written notes for the articles.

LORD, JACK. No. 79. Materials relating to the Hawaii Five-O tele-
    vision series.

MANN, ABBY. No. 60. No information available.

MARION, FRANCES. No. 95. No information available.

MC HUGH, JIMMY. No. 36. Original music scores.

NEWMAN, ALFRED. No. 74. Music, scripts, photographs, books.

OAKIE, JACK. No. 32. Books, theatre programs, photos, stills,
    transcriptions of "Jack Oakie College" radio programs.

OLSEN, OLE. No. 85. Books, scripts, theatre programs, sheet music.

PACIFIC PIONEER BROADCASTERS. No. 16. Scripts, disc transcriptions,
    commercials, radio spots.

PARAMOUNT RESEARCH DEPARTMENT. Paramount Studios donated a large
    portion of their Research Department to the University Li-
    brary. Included in this collection are a wide variety of
    stills, photographs, sketches and documents. Probably the
    most important use of these materials was in set and cos-
    tume design, but they were also valuable for location scout-
    ing and reference purposes.
        The items in this collection have not, as yet, been cat-
    aloged or arranged in any formal order. Thus, it is impos-
    sible to indicate all the films for which materials are in-
    cluded.
        Roughly, the years covered are 1937-1957. Many of the
    items were collected for pictures which never reached the
    screen. Some of the more famous films that were produced
    and are represented in the collection:
        The Hitler Gang (1944)
        The Lost Weekend (1945)
        Stalag 17 (1953)
        Rear Window (1954)

PARAMOUNT RESEARCH DEPARTMENT (cont.)
          The Bridges at Toko-Ri (1955)
          The Ten Commandments (1956)

PARKER ADVERTISING INCORPORATED. No. 53. Uncataloged. The Parker
          Advertising Incorporated Collection is a strange assemblage
          of materials. There are literally hundreds of short com-
          mercials done for television on 16mm and 35mm film. Most of
          these commercials are for Datsun automobiles. In addition,
          the Collection contains many radio commercials on audio tape
          and some slide materials.

PARSONS, LOUELLA. No. 29. 21 reels of tape.

PASTERNAK, JOE. No. 81. No information available.

PETERS, ELEANOR. No. 12. Photos of ballet dancers.

POWELL, ELEANOR. No. 67. Phonograph records.

REYNOLDS, ADELINE DE WALT. No. 96. No information available.

RIVERS, JOHNNY. No. 43. Autographed music scores, LP records.

ROACH, HAL. No. 10. No information available.

RODMAN, HOWARD. No. 58. Scripts.

ROMERO, CESAR. No. 93. Uncataloged. Cesar Romero (1907-   ), a
          handsome Latin actor, made his film debut in Metropolitan
          (1935). He has since appeared in many movies and television
          shows, often as a leading man.
              The Cesar Romero Collection is made up primarily of
          scrapbooks and assorted memorabilia:
              1. Thirty-one scrapbooks of assorted sizes documenting
          Mr. Romero's career.
              2. Twenty-one envelopes containing miscellaneous items:
          stills, clippings, letters, periodicals, programs, etc.
              3. Three boxes of 8x10 stills from Romero's films.

ROOS, ELIZABETH LESLIE. No. 2. No information available.

RUBIN, BENNY. No. 88. Photos, scripts, books, papers, clippings.

RUBY, HARRY. No. 39. Cataloged. Harry Ruby, a composer, wrote
          music for stage plays and movies including the Marx Brothers'
          production, Animal Crackers. For many years, he teamed with
          Bert Kalmar.

RUBY, HARRY (cont.)
        The Harry Ruby Collection is medium-sized and consists
entirely of sheet music and correspondence:
        1.   Sheet music for five songs composed by Ruby: "I
Want to Be Loved by You" (1928), "Nevertheless" (1931),
"Money Doesn't Grow on Trees" (1967), "Do All Your Living
Today" (1968), "I Love You But I Don't Like You" (1968).
        2.   Correspondence: approximately eighty-five pieces
dated 1929-1968.

SCHEURER, STANLEY K. No. 91. Undataloged. Stanley K. Scheurer
        worked as script supervisor on a number of famous films in-
        cluding West Side Story and Cleopatra.
        The Stanley K. Scheurer Collection is medium-sized and
consists of scripts and publicity materials:
        1.   Miscellaneous items pertaining to the film Cleopatra
(1962): scripts of Act I and Act II (it was originally to
be two films), two notebooks filled with Scheurer's notes on
the individual shots, a pressbook.
        2.   Shooting scripts (heavily annotated and containing
still photographs) from five other films.
        3.   Approximately sixty copies of "movie" magazines,
dated 1912-1932. Included: Photoplay, Screen, Motion Picture Magazine.
        4.   Publicity booklets for United Artists (1930-31) and
Fox Film Corporation (1930-31).
        5.   Scrapbook containing publicity clippings for many
old (mostly silent) films.
        6.   Miscellaneous movie-oriented clippings.

SCHILDKRAUT, JOSEPH. No. 46. Joseph Schildkraut (1895-1964), an
        Austrian actor, appeared in many American films between 1920
        and 1960. He won an Academy Award for his portrayal of
        Dreyfus in The Life of Emile Zola (1937).
        The Joseph Schildkraut Collection is relatively small.
It consists of approximately 100 still photographs of Mr.
Schildkraut. Most of these are from various screen per-
formances.

SELTZER, WALTER. No. 97. Uncataloged. Walter Seltzer (1914-   )
        began working in Hollywood in 1936. He produced One-Eyed
        Jacks (1959), The War Lord (1965) and Skyjacked (1972), among
        other films.
        The Walter Seltzer Collection is small and consists of
scripts and publicity materials.
        1.   Scripts of fifteen films produced by Walter Seltzer.
        2.   Five scrapbooks of publicity campaigns for Seltzer
films.

SHEPARD, RICHMOND. No. 89. Uncataloged. Richmond Shepard is an
    actor and director whose specialty is Mime. He has been
    seen on over 100 television shows and has directed plays,
    short films and one feature.
        The Richmond Shepard Collection is small:
        1. Manuscript of <u>Mime-The Technique of Silence</u>, a book
    by Richmond Shepard.
        2. Two lengthy articles by Shepard. One is about the
    "Living Theatre," the other on "Mime and Training for the
    Theatre."
        3. Program notes, clippings, stills and photos concern-
    ing the "Richmond Shepard Mime Theatre."
        4. Miscellaneous programs, stills, publicity materials,
    magazines with pertinent articles about Shepard.

SISK, ROBERT. No. 66. Cataloged. Robert Sisk produced feature
    films at RKO, Warner Brothers, and MGM in the 1930's and
    1940's. In the early 1950's, he left theatrical film pro-
    duction for television. He created the series "The Life and
    Legend of Wyatt Earp," starring Hugh O'Brien.
        The Robert Sisk Collection is a large assortment of ma-
    terials that spans the career of the producer from the early
    1920's to the early 1960's:
        1. Scripts of sixty feature films.
        2. Seventeen screen treatments.
        3. Scripts or synopses of five stage plays.
        4. Scripts of approximately 225 episodes of "The Life
    and Legend of Wyatt Earp" television series, 1955-1960.
        5. Miscellaneous materials related to the "Wyatt Earp"
    television show: production reports, cost reports, cast
    lists, credit sheets, sheet music, residual payment sched-
    ules, estimated negative costs, publicity materials, etc.,
    1955-1963.
        6. Scripts of approximately sixty episodes of "The
    Californians" television series, 1957-1959.
        7. Personal scrapbooks: 1920-1922, 1924-1926, 1927,
    1930-1931.
        8. Catalogues of unproduced properties: 1939 (Para-
    mount), 1942 (MGM), 1945 (MGM).
        9. Publicity photographs: 200 from thirteen motion pic-
    tures, thirty from "Wyatt Earp," twenty-five from various
    stage productions.
        10. Fifty-five group photos of Robert Sisk with show
    business personalities. Included: Louis B. Mayer, John
    Ford, Ginger Rogers, etc.
        11. Thirty-seven miscellaneous photographs. Most are
    of actors and actesses such as John Barrymore, Jr. and Lynn
    Fontaine.

SISK, ROBERT (cont.)

       12. Eleven plaques, medals, etc., won by Mr. Sisk and his productions.

       13. Programs of five stage plays produced 1924-1938.

       14. Souvenir booklets for one film (The Informer) and two stage plays.

       15. Miscellaneous personal correspondence and memos, dated 1924-1963. The catalogue description of these items is reasonably complete.

       16. Miscellaneous movie production papers: budget estimates, contracts, options, etc.

       17. Manuscripts of rejected feature film and television pilot outlines.

       18. Assorted papers relating to the Screen Producers' Guild: newsletters, membership roster, reports, arrangements for S. P. G. forums held at USC and UCLA.

       19. Sixteen miscellaneous magazines, 1928-1953. Included: Hollywood Spectator, The Screen Writer.

       20. Ninety books (mostly historical novels) owned by Sisk.

       21. Manuscripts of four books including Hollywood in Transition by Richard Dyer MacCann and Viva Gringo!, a novel by Borden Chase.

SMALL, EDWARD. No. 82. Scripts, letters, budgets, pressbooks, stills.

SOTHERN, ANN. No. 87. Films of Miss Sothern's television series.

SPIGELGASS, LEONARD. No. 5. Photos, theatre programs.

STAHL, JOHN M. No. 11. Uncataloged. John M. Stahl (1886-1950) began his career as a stage actor. He became a movie director during the silent era and made the transition to sound films. His credits include Magnificent Obsession (1935) and The Keys to the Kingdom (1944).

       The John M. Stahl Collection is medium-sized and consists largely of scripts and clippings:

       1. Scripts of twenty different films.

       2. Publicity clippings and reviews for many of Mr. Stahl's movies.

       3. Approximately twenty books (mostly novels).

       4. Miscellaneous correspondence.

       5. Miscellaneous synopses and treatments.

       6. Approximately fifty photos and stills (mostly of movie personalities).

SPECIAL COLLECTIONS   TWENTIETH CENTURY-FOX

STAHL, JOHN M. (cont.)
   7. Sketchbooks from <u>Immortal Sergeant</u> and <u>The Keys to</u>
<u>the Kingdom</u>, research book for <u>Parnell</u>, still album from
<u>Leave Her to Heaven</u>.

TIOMKIN, DMITRI. No. 51. Music scores, screenplays, scrapbooks,
  publicity notebooks, phonograph records.

TWENTIETH CENTURY-FOX SET-STILLS. It was the policy of Twentieth
  Century-Fox (and most motion picture studios) to have a
  photographer shoot stills of all the sets used in a particular movie. This provided "insurance" in case problems arose
  which necessitated re-shooting at a later date. If the
  original set or sets were no longer available, new sets
  could then be constructed from these still photographs.
   The set-stills donated by Fox cover the years 1932-1953.
  Approximately 220 films are represented; some of these were
  never produced. The contents are boxed in alphabetical
  order.
   The following movies, which were released, are included
  in this collection:
    American Guerilla (in the Philippines) - 1950
    Anna and the King of Siam - 1946
    Apartment for Peggy - 1948
    Arrow - 1950 (release title: Broken Arrow)
    The Beautiful Blonde from Bashful Bend - 1949
    Belles on their Toes - 1952
    Ben Blake - 1942 (release title: Son of Fury)
    Bloodhounds of Broadway - 1952
    Blueprint for Murder - 1953
    The Brasher Doubloon (see: The High Window)
    Broken Arrow (see: Arrow)
    Call Me Mister - 1951
    Captain from Castile - 1947
    Centennial Summer - 1946
    Chad Hanna - 1940
    Charley's Aunt - 1941
    Chicken Every Sunday - 1949
    Claudia and David - 1946
    Come to the Stable - 1949
    Confirm or Deny - 1941
    Daisy Kenyon - 1947
    Dangerous Crossing - 1953
    The Dark Corner - 1946
    The Day the Earth Stood Still - 1951
    Daytime Wife - 1939
    Deadline, U.S.A. - 1952
    Deep Waters - 1948

TWENTIETH CENTURY-FOX   SPECIAL COLLECTIONS

TWENTIETH CENTURY-FOX SET-STILLS (cont.)
        Diplomatic Courier - 1952
        Doll Face - 1946
        The Dolly Sisters - 1945
        Don't Bother to Knock - 1952
        Dragonwyck - 1946
        Dreamboat - 1952
        Elopement - 1951
        Escape - 1948
        Everybody Does It - 1949
        Fallen Angel - 1945
        The Fan - 1949
        The Farmer Takes a Wife - 1953
        Father Was a Fullback - 1949
        Fight Town - 1953
        Five Fingers - 1952
        Fixed Bayonets - 1951
        Follow the Sun - 1951
        For Heaven's Sake - 1949
        Forever Amber - 1947
        Fourteen Hours - 1951
        The Foxes of Harrow - 1947
        Fury at Furnace Creek - 1948
        Gentleman's Agreement - 1947
        The Girl Next Door - 1953
        Give My Regards to Broadway - 1948
        The Ghost and Mrs. Muir - 1947
        Golden Girl - 1951
        The Gorilla - 1939
        The Great American Broadcast - 1941
        Green Grass of Wyoming - 1948
        The Gunfighter - 1950
        Half Angel - 1936
        Halls of Montezuma - 1951
        He Married His Wife - 1940
        Hell and High Water - 1954
        Here I am a Stranger - 1939
        The High Window - 1947 (release title: The Brasher
            Doubloon)
        Hollywood Cavalcade - 1939
        The Homestretch - 1947
        Home Sweet Homicide - 1946
        Hot Spot -1941 (release title: I Wake Up Screaming)
        The House on 92nd Street - 1945
        I Can Get It for You Wholesale - 1951
        The I Don't Care Girl - 1953
        I Wake Up Screaming - (see: Hot Spot)
        I Was a Male War Bride - 1949

TWENTIETH CENTURY-FOX SET-STILLS (cont.)
           I Was an Adventuress - 1940
           I Wonder Who's Kissing Her Now - 1947
           I'd Climb the Highest Mountain - 1951
           I'll Get By - 1950
           Inferno - 1953
           The Iron Curtain - 1948
           It Happens Every Spring - 1949
           It Shouldn't Happen to a Dog - 1946
           The Jackpot - 1950
           Johnnie Apollo - 1940
           Junior Miss - 1945
           The Kid from Left Field - 1953
           Kiss of Death - 1947
           The Late George Apley - 1947
           Leave Her to Heaven - 1945
           A Letter to Three Wives - 1949
           The Magnificent Dope - 1942
           Man Hunt - 1941
           Margie - 1946
           Meet Me After the Show - 1951
           Miracle on 34th Street - 1947
           Monkey Business - 1952
           Moontide - 1942
           Moss Rose - 1947
           Mother is a Freshman - 1949
           Mother Wore Tights - 1947
           My Darling Clementine - 1946
           My Gal Sal - 1942
           My Wife's Best Friend - 1952
           Niagara - 1953
           Night Without Sleep - 1952
           Nightmare Alley - 1947
           No Way Out - 1950
           On the Riviera - 1951
           Orchestra Wives - 1942
           The Outcasts of Poker Flat - 1952
           Phone Call from a Stranger - 1952
           Pony Soldier - 1952
           Powder River - 1953
           The President's Lady - 1953
           The Pride of St. Louis - 1952
           Prince of Foxes - 1949
           Public Deb No. 1 - 1940
           Rawhide - 1951
           The Razor's Edge - 1946
           Red Skies of Montana - 1952
           Remember the Day - 1941

TWENTIETH–CENTURY–FOX   SPECIAL COLLECTIONS

TWENTIETH CENTURY–FOX SET–STILLS (cont.)
            Return of the Texan - 1952
            Rings on her Fingers - 1942
            Rise and Shine - 1941
            Road House - 1948
            Road to Rio - 1947
            Roxie Hart - 1942
            Sand - 1949
            The Scarlet Pen - 1951 (release title: The 13th Letter)
            Scudda–Hoo! Scudda–Hay! - 1948
            Secret of Convict Lake - 1951
            Sherlock Holmes - 1932
            Shock - 1946
            The Silver Whip - 1953
            Sitting Pretty - 1948
            Slattery's Hurricane - 1949
            Smoky - 1946
            The Snake Pit - 1948
            Something for the Birds - 1952
            Somewhere in the Night - 1946
            Son of Fury (see: Ben Blake)
            The Spider - 1945
            Star Dust - 1940
            Stars and Stripes Forever - 1952
            Stella - 1950
            Strange Triangle - 1946
            The Street With No Name - 1948
            Sun Valley (Serenade) - 1941
            Swamp Water - 1941
            Swanee River - 1939
            Take Care of My Little Girl - 1951
            Tales of Manhattan - 1942
            Tall, Dark, and Handsome - 1941
            Taxi - 1952
            That Lady in Ermine - 1948
            That Wonderful Urge - 1949
            13 Rue Madeleine - 1946
            The 13th Letter (see: The Scarlet Pen)
            Three Came Home - 1950
            Three Little Girls in Blue - 1946
            Thunder Birds - 1942
            To the Shores of Tripoli - 1942
            Tonight We Sing - 1953
            Twelve O'Clock High - 1949
            Unfaithfully Yours - 1948
            U.S.S. Teakettle - 1951 (release title: You're in the
                Navy Now)
            A Very Young Lady - 1941

TWENTIETH CENTURY-FOX SET-STILLS (cont.)
   Vicki - 1953
   Wake Up and Dream - 1946
   The Walls of Jericho - 1948
   Way of a Gaucho - 1952
   Weekend in Havana - 1941
   We're Not Married - 1952
   Western Union - 1941
   When My Baby Smiles at Me - 1948
   Where the Sidewalk Ends - 1950
   Whirlpool - 1950
   White Witch Doctor - 1953
   Within These Walls - 1945
   A Yank in the R.A.F. - 1941
   Yellow Sky - 1949
   You Were Meant for Me - 1948
   You're in the Navy Now (see: U.S.S. Teakettle)
   You're My Everything - 1949

VIDOR, KING. No. 25. Cataloged. One of America's most distinguished directors, King Vidor (1894-   ) began his work in
Hollywood in 1915. His many important films include The
Crowd (1928), Our Daily Bread (1933) and Duel in the Sun
(1946). Mr. Vidor is Artist in Residence in the USC Division
of Cinema.
  The King Vidor Collection is large and contains many
items of value:
  1. Scripts of fifteen films.
  2. General production correspondence. Items from David
O. Selznick, Samuel Goldwyn, Pare Lorentz, and other famous
individuals are included.
  3. Miscellaneous newspaper and magazine clippings and
reviews.
  4. Biographical data.

  The following materials are grouped according to individual films:
  5. An American Romance--script drafts, script revisions,
outline, notes, correspondence, assistant director's report
sheets, crew list, cast list, memos, daily film reports,
memos on music, sound department requisitions, publicity
clippings, etc.
  6. The Citadel--script revisions, story outline, correspondence, production notes, preview cards, etc.
  7. Duel in the Sun--script, script outline, settings
and props script, artist's sketches, correspondence, publicity photographs, research materials, publicity clippings,
etc.

VIDOR, KING (cont.)
     8. H. M. Pulham, Esq.--script copies (3), budget esti-
mate, notes on production techniques, correspondence, advertising, publicity release, clippings, etc.
     9. Northwest Passage--script, stills, correspondence.
     10. Our Daily Bread--script, dialogue continuity, cut-
ting continuity, assistant director's breakdown sheets, correspondence, budget, contracts, notes, shooting schedule,
artist's sketches, advertising, box office statements, financial statements, clippings, reviews, etc.
     11. So Red the Rose--correspondence, casting sugges-
tions, notes, information about music, preview cards, etc.
     12. Stella Dallas--script, script sequence breakdown,
script revisions and added sequences, shooting schedule, director's notes, editing notes, cast lists, correspondence,
research materials, clippings, etc.
     13. The Texas Rangers--script, advertising and publici-
ty ideas, budget, correspondence, notes on locations, sheet
music, outline of film's progress, etc.
     14. Witch in the Wilderness-script drafts, dialogue
continuity script, sequence outline, treatment, story outline, notes, correspondence, memos, research information.
     15. Miscellaneous items relating to: The Big Parade,
Broken Soil, The Champ, Comrade X, The Fountainhead, Hallelujah, National Velvet, The Patsy, Sam Houston, Solomon and
Sheba, These Crazy People, Three Wise Fools, The Wizard of
Oz.

WALLACE, IRVING. No. 0. Scripts, papers.

WEINGARTEN, LAWRENCE. No. 59. Uncataloged. Mr. Weingarten
     1893-1975), a producer, began working in the movie business
     around 1917. Among the multitude of films he produced were
     A Day at the Races (1937), Adam's Rib (1949) and Cat on a
     Hot Tin Roof (1958).
          The Lawrence Weingarten Collection consists primarily of
     scrapbooks and accolades. It is medium-sized.
          1. Thirteen scrapbooks mainly containing press clip-
     pings. Also included are stills, letters, advertisements,
     etc., relating to Mr. Weingarten's films. The scrapbooks
     cover the years 1929-1940, 1945-1949 and 1958-1964. Two are
     devoted to single films: The Unsinkable Molly Brown and
     Don't Go Near the Water.
          2. Approximately forty accolades, awards, or prizes won
     by Lawrence Weingarten and his productions. Included is a
     beautiful silver tray presented to Mr. Weingarten by the
     Allied States Association of Motion Picture Exhibitors as
     "Producer of the Year--1964."

WEINGARTEN, LAWRENCE (cont.)
   3. Daily production reports from four films produced in
1930. One of these is Buster Keaton's Forward March.
   4. Detailed budget estimates from eleven films includ-
ing the Marx Brothers' A Day at the Races.

WEISBART, DAVID. No. 50. Cataloged. David Weisbart (1915-1967)
   entered the motion picture business in 1935. After fifteen
   years as an editor, he began producing movies. His films
   include Rebel Without a Cause (1955) and Valley of the Dolls
   (1967).
   The David Weisbart Collection consists largely of materials pertaining to the films he produced. It is a large
collection:
   1. Miscellaneous materials (mostly scripts and treatments) relating to fifty-six films and television shows that
were never produced.
   2. Synopses of approximately thirty properties, 1950-
1960.
   3. Extensive materials (memos and correspondence) from
the story department at Twentieth-Century Fox, 1950-1959.

   The following materials are grouped according to individual films:
   4. Love Me Tender--script, publicity information, budgets, memos, correspondence, etc.
   5. Between Heaven and Hell-correspondence, memos, budget, publicity information, etc.
   6. The Way to the Gold--publicity information, correspondence, memos, score, treatment, synopsis, budget, shooting schedule, call sheets, etc.
   7. April Love--memos, correspondence, slides, music
data, etc.
   8. These Thousand Hills--memos, correspondence, budget,
shooting schedule, etc.
   9. A Private's Affair--memos, correspondence, budgets,
etc.
   10. Holiday for Lovers--script, correspondence, budgets, memos, scores, etc.
   11. Flaming Star--script, synopsis, memos, shooting
schedules, budget, correspondence, fifteen publicity stills,
etc.
   12. Goodbye Charlie--script, shooting schedule, correspondence, twenty-four stills, etc.
   13. Rio Conchos--scripts, shooting schedule, memo,
publicity items, correspondence, stills, photos, etc.
   14. The Pleasure Seekers--script, memos, advertising
brochures, eleven stills, three photographs, etc.

WEISBART, DAVID (cont.)
          15. Bandolero--script.
          16. Valley of the Dolls--script, correspondence, clip-
     pings, twenty-seven stills, etc.

WINDSOR, CLAIRE. No. 54. Photographs, photo albums.

WISE, ROBERT. No. 49. Uncataloged. Robert Wise (1914-   ) began
     his career as a film editor at RKO where he cut Citizen Kane
     and The Magnificent Ambersons. In 1943, he directed The
     Curse of the Cat People and has functioned as a director
     and, at times, director-producer ever since. Wise is per-
     haps best known for West Side Story and that financial
     blockbuster, The Sound of Music.
          The Robert Wise Collection is a gigantic potpourri of
     worthwhile material:
          1. Scripts of twenty-eight different films from The
     Curse of the Cat People (1943) to The Andromeda Strain
     (1971). Most are shooting scripts with copious annotations
     and some have appendices containing memos, budgets, sketches,
     etc.

          The following materials are grouped according to indi-
     vidual films:
          2. The Haunting - several drafts of the script, script
     revisions, research materials, notes, miscellaneous papers,
     etc.
          3. Two for the Seesaw - six drafts of the script, call
     sheets, casting information, location stills, correspondence,
     expenses, music, etc.
          4. West Side Story - story materials, casting inter-
     views, correspondence, musical score, publicity releases,
     memos, research materials, numerous stills, etc.
          5. The Sound of Music - hundreds of stills and contact
     sheets, schedules, music sheets, general production informa-
     tion, publicity materials, correspondence, memos, script ma-
     terials, notes on foreign dubbing, etc.
          6. The Sand Pebbles - job applications, research ma-
     terials, publicity, casting, story costs, several drafts of
     the script, expense accounts, budgets, press clippings,
     sketches, correspondence, many stills, photos, and contact
     sheets, etc.
          7. Battle! - a film that never came to fruition. It
     was to deal with the life of photographer Robert Capa.
     Several drafts of the script, research materials including
     books by Capa, tapes of Robert Capa's voice, many photos
     taken by Capa, correspondence, budgets, treatments, etc.
          8. Star! - research materials including the personal
     diaries of Gertrude Lawrence, hundreds of stills, records

WISE, ROBERT (cont.)
      (discs) of songs from the film, publicity items, correspond-
      ence, budgets, casting, legal matters, sketch books, script
      girl's script and notes, manuscript of Star! (a novel by
      Bob Thomas), etc.
          9. The Andromeda Strain - numerous drafts of the
      script, budget estimates, correspondence, publicity, re-
      search materials, shooting schedules, pre-production and
      post-production materials, sketch books, editing notes,
      memos, contract information, etc.
          10. Miscellaneous materials (mostly sketch books) re-
      lating to I Want to Live; Run Silent, Run Deep; Somebody Up
      There Likes Me; Tribute to a Bad Man; Two Flags West; Three
      Secrets; The Set-up; Odds Against Tomorrow; Executive Suite.

WRAY, FAY. No. 63. Uncataloged. Miss Wray (1907-   ) appeared in
      many films from the end of the silent era to the 1950's.
      Her most famous role came in the classic RKO feature King
      Kong, where she screamed her way to immortality. She was
      married to two important screenwriters. Her first husband,
      John Monk Saunders (1895-1940), was the author of Wings, a
      silent spectacular that won the first Oscar. Robert Riskin
      (1897-1955) wrote most of Frank Capra's famous films includ-
      ing It Happened One Night and Mr. Deeds Goes to Town.
          The Fay Wray Collection is not large but contains many
      items of interest. Included are materials from the careers
      of her husbands, as well as from her own career. The col-
      lection can be broken down into items relating to each of
      the three principals:
          FAY WRAY
          1. Ten large scrapbooks containing press clippings, re-
      views, pictures, programs, etc. These cover Miss Wray's
      career from approximately 1924-1939.
          2. Miscellaneous press clippings and magazines with
      pertinent articles.
          3. A large still collection including publicity photos,
      shots from individual films (such as King Kong and The
      Texan), and more recent photos.
          4. Miscellaneous items: copies of Miss Wray's early
      motion picture contracts, her high school yearbook, and a
      photo album from Erich Von Stroheim's The Wedding March,
      etc.
          ROBERT RISKIN
          1. Nineteen scripts written by Riskin. Mr. Deeds Goes
      to Town and You Can't Take It With You are autographed by
      members of the cast and crew.

WRAY, FAY (cont.)
>   2. Twelve short 16mm films produced by Riskin when he
worked for the Office of War Information during World War II.
>   3. A 16mm print of the Capra-Riskin movie, <u>Meet John
Doe</u>.
>   4. Three scrapbooks covering the years 1931-1945 (ap-
proximately). One of these deals exclusively with Riskin's
tenure at the Office of War Information.
>   5. Miscellaneous items: accolades, photographs, publi-
city papers, etc.
>   <u>JOHN MONK SAUNDERS</u>
>   1. One large scrapbook devoted to his career and one
scrapbook containing items dealing with the "team" of Wray
and Saunders.
>   2. Photographs of Saunders.

WYNN, ED. No. 98. No information available.